California
and the Dust Bowl
Migration

RECENT TITLES IN
CONTRIBUTIONS IN AMERICAN HISTORY

California
and the Dust Bowl
Migration

WALTER J. STEIN

Contributions in American History, Number 21

GREENWOOD PRESS, INC.
Westport, Connecticut • London, England

Library of Congress Cataloging in Publication Data

Stein, Walter J
    California and the Dust Bowl migration

    (Contributions in American history, no. 21)
    Originally presented as the author's thesis, University
of California, Berkeley.
    Bibliography: p.
    1. Agricultural laborers—California. 2. California—
Emigration and immigration. 3. Migration, Internal—
United States. I. Title.
HD1527.C2S76 1973   331.7'63'09794 70-175611
ISBN 0-8371-6267-X

Library of Congress Catalog Card Number: 70-175611

ISBN: 0-8371-6267-X
ISBN: 0-8371-7229-2 Paperback

First published in 1973
Second printing 1973
Paperback 1974

Greenwood Press, a division of Williamhouse-Regency Inc.
51 Riverside Avenue, Westport, Connecticut 06880
Manufactured in the United States of America

Contents

Preface

More than any other state in the union, California owes its prosperity and affluence to continuing streams of migrants. For a century, the state has viewed the entire United States as its eastern hinterland, from whence new arrivals bring fresh treasure and new blood. Only once has California lost its accustomed good temper with migrants and, in many ways, the anti-Okie hysteria of the depression years was paradoxical. Ironically, the phenomenon occurred during the decade in which migration was relatively smaller than at any other time in the state's history. The reaction of the 1930s was not directed at all migrants, but was focused upon the Okies, a group of newcomers from the South Central states (Oklahoma, Texas, Missouri, and Arkansas) who settled in the less populous, agricultural areas of the state, and who were white, old-stock Protestants not unlike those who had entered during the 1920s. Finally, although the migrant problem would not have arisen during prosperous times, it was not simply a direct outgrowth of the depression. Indeed, California's Okie crisis did not occur until 1938, a full three years after the migrant influx reached its peak. This study seeks to explain the brief period when California rejected migrant admirers such as those she had welcomed in the past.

From 1850 to 1930, interstate migration assumed an increasingly important role in California's development. Her birthrate remained low; had she been forced to rely upon native sons and the entry of foreigners, she would have remained insignificant among the states. California's growth through migration began almost with her entry into the Union.[1] The discovery of gold at Sutter's Fort in 1848 signaled the advance of the Forty-niners. By 1850, California had a population of 92,600, 70,000 of whom were American migrants.[2] The Gold Rush brought international recognition of California's abundant and diverse natural resources, and in the years following 1849, newcomers seeking not gold, but settlement, swelled the population. The Civil War, recurrent depressions in the 1870s and 1890s, droughts—nothing stopped the westward current of those who saw in the state an opportunity for economic improvement. By 1900, 1.5 million Americans lived in California, few of whom were native sons. Her population had increased fourteen times. Much of her empty land had been filled, and the state had taken an important place in the political and economic affairs of the nation.

California's development during the nineteenth century was impressive, but was eclipsed by her astonishing progress during the first third of the twentieth. Twenty-first in size in the 1900 census, she was eighth in the census of 1920. It was, writes the chronicler of this growth, "as if California acquired an entirely new population-and-a-half in that short span of time." The wholesale entry of midwesterners into the state between 1900 and 1920 "constitute[d] one of the most prodigous migrations in the annals of American Westering."[3] Henceforth, the pattern of California's growth was certain: her increasing population would be augmented by native American stock, and her prosperity would depend upon a continuing influx of migrants.

The Normalcy years accurately bore out this pattern.[4] Even the state's most vociferous boosters were surprised when the census of 1930 showed a 66 percent increase in the population. Nearly 2 million migrants had flocked to California, most of them to Los Angeles. At the close of the 1920s as depression fell across the nation, 5.5 million thriving Californians proudly faced eastward.

California's history was the history of migration—and the state's people knew it. During the eighty years of development from 1850 to

TABLE 1

CALIFORNIA POPULATION GROWTH

Decade	California Population at Beginning	California Population at Close	Total Increase for Decade	Total Migration for Decade	Per cent Gain*
1940 - 50	6.912 M	10.639M	3.726 M	2.687 M	39.6
1930 - 40	5.685	6.912	1.227	1.050	17.7
1920 - 30	3.432	5.685	2.252	1.882	33.2
1910 - 20	2.381	3.432	1.050	.880	25.6
1900 - 10	1.491	2.381	.890	.775	32.6
1890 - 1900	1.216	1.491	.273	.179	12.2
1880 - 90	.869	1.216	.348	.255	21.0
1870 - 80	.561	.869	.307	.172	19.4
1860 - 70	.361	.561	.180	.109	32.0

* Per cent gain by migration computed by dividing population at close of decade by total migration for decade.

Source: Warren S. Thompson, *Growth and Changes in California's Population* (Los Angeles, 1955), p. 25. Other volumes dealing with the statistics of California's population are: Commonwealth Club of California, *The Population of California* (San Francisco, 1946); and Frank L. Beach, "The Transformation of California" (Unpublished Ph.D. Thesis, University of California, 1963).

1930, California's politicians and businessmen had recognized fully the contribution of the migrants, and the state developed the habit of welcoming and encouraging newcomers. Beginning with the Gold Rush, increasing in volume through the 1920s, a chorus of promotional voices had beckoned, sirenlike, to Americans in other states, luring their savings and their talents west. Until 1930, private organizations had collaborated with the state government to ensure an ever-increasing supply of settlers. As early as 1869, Governor Henry H. Haight had announced to the legislature that "we need population—not of races inferior . . . but we need immigrants of kindred races who will consti- tute a congenial element and locate themselves and their families permanently upon the soil."[5] San Francisco's businessmen, Los Angeles' Board of Trade, the state Chamber of Commerce, the South- ern Pacific Railroad eager to dispose of its immense share of the public domain, and, finally, the state government itself—through its Division of Immigration and Housing—had echoed Haight's call until the Great Crash.

But even the onset of the Great Depression did not immediately disrupt the engrained pattern of friendship between "old" Californian and newcomer. The overloaded jalopies that carried the Okies to California had been crossing Route 66 by the thousands before they were even noticed. The great Okie migration began early in the 1930s and swelled to a flood in 1935; but not until 1938 was the state seized with migrant hysteria. The ensuing three years witnessed an outpouring of anxiety and a strident political conflict unparalleled elsewhere as Californians sought to stem the migrant tide or to obtain national aid in absorbing it.

Seen in the light of population statistics only, California's "migrant problem" seems inexplicable, for the influx of the 1930s was neither large, nor did it occur at a time of economic maturity in the state's growth, when she could no longer absorb new migrants because her industrial plant was complete. The migration of little over a million Americans to California during the depression was, in fact, far smaller, in absolute as well as proportional terms, than the increases in popula- tion in either of the decades that straddled the depression years, increases which were assimilated into the state with relative ease.

The antimigrant hysteria of the 1930s was not directed at all the newcomers of the depression years. The hundreds of alarmist articles, the restrictive legislation, the slashes in relief appropriations for "out-of-staters" were directed at only one-third of the migrants of the era. The Okies were the sole victims of the attack. California had reverberated with movements to exclude migrants before. Chinese, Japanese, Mexicans, and Hindus had been persona non grata and excluded from the state, abused by vigilance committees, and hampered by restrictive legislation; but the dust bowl migrants were white Protestant Americans, and never before had the state sought to impede the entry of such as these. Indeed, it had been heartland Americans from the Central Plains who had swelled the population in the 1920s and who, to the brooding Nathanael West, had personified the archetypal Californian. All their lives, they "had slaved at some kind of dull, heavy labor, behind desks and counters, in the fields and at tedious machines of all sorts, saving their pennies and dreaming of the leisure that would be theirs when they had enough. Finally that day came. They could draw a weekly income of ten or fifteen dollars. Where else should they go but to California, the land of sunshine and oranges?"[6]

For four years, as the rest of the nation watched war clouds gather in Europe, Californians were excited and frightened by something they had welcomed in the past: a relatively small and rather traditional migration of American citizens. The Okies were not the cause, but the focus, of a number of problems confronting the state, problems over which they had little or no control. They intruded upon an agricultural system that contravened every myth in the Jeffersonian pantheon, and they served as unwitting publicists for those who found California's agriculture and its social effects unsound. They aggravated social and economic dislocations evoked by the depression and became pawns in deadly conflicts that arose from hard times. Long-simmering tensions in California politics found vent against the Okie. A study of the Okie migration and its effects upon California illuminates the ambivalences and conflicts in the character of what has become the nation's largest—and, in many ways, zaniest—state.

Notes in Text

1. Demographers compute population growth as the product of three distinct factors: natural increase (the increase of births over deaths among the resident

population of the region); immigration (the entry of citizens of another country); and, finally, migration (movement within and across state lines).

2. Commonwealth Club of California, *The Population of California* (San Francisco, 1946), p. 21.

3. Frank L. Beach, "The Transformation of California (Ph.D. diss., University of California, Berkeley, 1963), pp. 9-17. By far the best single source on the subject of California's growth, 1900-1920. Especially provocative for its analysis of the social and political effects of migration, which, the author maintains, were "principally responsible" for the state's takeoff and transformation.

4. For a splendid account of California's growth in the 1920s, see Carey McWilliams, *Southern California Country* (New York, 1946), pp. 113-137.

5. Commonwealth Club, *Population of California*, p. 39.

6. Nathanael West, *The Day of the Locust* (Bantam ed., New York, 1959), p. 131.

Acknowledgments

This study began with a single, simple intention: to describe the impact of the great Okie migration upon California. But I soon found that this epic migration could not be understood without considering as well the general problem of migratory agricultural labor in the West. Nor could state politics, federal policies, labor unions in agriculture, and social relations in rural California safely be ignored, if the impact of the Okies was to be explained. To the amused impatience of friends, colleagues, and mentors, the manuscript inexorably grew in length, and my research entered areas that had been terra incognita when the study was first conceived. During these peripatetics, I received aid and comfort from many quarters.

The University of California, The University of Winnipeg, the John Randolph and Dora Haynes Foundation, and the Woodrow Wilson Foundation, supplied financial aid that made it possible to raise a family and nurture a manuscript simultaneously.

I am indebted to the staffs of the many manuscript libraries cited in my bibliography who gave invaluable assistance. The Bancroft Library was especially helpful: Dr. Tompkins and his staff tolerated my eccentric requests with a sincere desire to aid my research.

I would like to thank the Canadian Historical Association for permission to use material in chapters 5 and 6 that originally appeared in the association's *Historical Papers,* 1970.

Professors Lawrence Levine, Walton Bean, Michael Rogin, and Paul Taylor—all of the University of California—and several colleagues at the University of Winnipeg provided incisive criticism, friendly encouragement, and much good advice. Where I took their advice, the manuscript has undoubtedly been improved. For all errors, interpretations, and conclusions, I alone am responsible.

One disclaimer must be entered here. Several of my chapters are concerned with federal policy and New Deal activities as they affected California. I do not claim that any conclusions drawn in these chapters are necessarily representative of federal activities elsewhere in the nation during the Great Depression.

California
and the Dust Bowl
Migration

1

In Oklahoma I Busted—
In California I Trusted

The onset of the Great Depression weakened for the entire decade of the 1930s, the tendency of Americans to move easily from one place to another. In California and the rest of the nation, migration during the 1930s was exceeded by that of prior and succeeding decades.[1] During the early years of the depression (1930-1934), many of the nation's urban centers witnessed large increases in their transient populations. These transients were not migrants in the process of relocating their homes, but a curious collection of migratory workers, tramps, hoboes, and men and women out of work who wandered the country seeking work of any sort. The bonus army, composed of World War I veterans seeking early bonus payment and encamped at Anacostia Flats in Washington, D.C., was a reminder that the system did not always function beneficently for all. It was the most visible and best organized, but only one of many such transient populations. These wandering armies were an ever-present source of concern for metropolitan authorities, but, in the general context of the depression era, this aspect of migration was relatively insignificant. Far more significant migrations were beginning, and, as the depression wore on into the second half of the decade, major regional population shifts developed, only in part as

responses to the economic dislocation. The most important shift was
the exodus of Americans from the Great Plains to the Pacific states.[2] It
was from this population redistribution that California drew its Okies.

The migration from the Great Plains to the Pacific Coast was the
product of a powerful combination of pushes (reason for dissatisfaction
with the current location) and pulls (the attraction of a particular area
to the potential migrant). Myriad causes, some long-standing, some
ephemeral, produced sufficient dissatisfaction in the Great Plains during
the 1930s to push Americans from that unhappy region by the hundreds of thousands. The history of the Great Plains has been told many
times, and there is no need here for review in detail.[3] A number of
historical characteristics of the region nonetheless deserve mention, as
they contributed powerfully to the migration of the 1930s, influencing
reactions and shaping the habits of the California-bound.

The Great Plains tier of the United States embraces five states from
the Dakotas on the north to Texas on the south. Opened by the
transcontinental railroads to farmers in the latter third of the nineteenth century, the Plains rapidly filled with settlers moving west in
search of profits such as those achieved by commercial farming during
the bonanza days of the Civil War. The new settlers hailed principally
from the neighboring agricultural states directly east: Missouri, Iowa,
Illinois, Ohio, Kentucky, Tennessee, Arkansas, Mississippi, Alabama,
and Georgia.[4] By and large American-bred and American-trained
farmers, accustomed to medium-sized farms and traditional row-crop,
humid-climate cultivation, they were unprepared for the conditions
they would face. Ignoring the work of men like Major John Wesley
Powell, whose *Report on the Lands of the Arid Regions* warned in
1878 that the prairies were subject to recurrent drought,[5] these pioneers attempted to transplant into the arid Plains the too-small farms of
160-320 acres that had succeeded in their states of origin.

Great Plains farmers learned to live with the droughts, hail, floods,
grasshoppers, cold, heat, blizzards, and prairie fire visited upon them
like plagues. But the agricultural system that they developed was,
nevertheless, untenable. The farms remained too small, the droughts
were too frequent, and the one-crop system too subject to the vagaries
of an international market that cared little about the American standard of living.

With the intense cold of the winter of 1885-1886, there began in the Great Plains a boom-bust cycle that wore down even the strongest prairie sodbuster. In 1890-1891, the crops withered. Again in 1894-1896 the rains refused to come.[6] Unprepared to accept the fact that their agricultural system was wasteful, overcompetitive, and unsuited to the climate, Great Plains farmers continued to plant their wheat in the North, their cotton in the South. When the busts came, many chose to lay responsibility for the desperation of their lives on "Eastern money interests," railroads and speculators who were only partly to blame. Rather than leave the inhospitable Plains, they flocked instead, in greater numbers than elsewhere in the nation, to the Populist banner.[7]

When a boom cycle began in 1899, Plains farmers quit the Populists, cashed in their crops, and mocked those who had "trusted in God, busted in Kansas." In 1906, at the height of the Progressive era, a new wave of settlers inundated the then-prosperous Plains, this time pouring into Texas and Oklahoma. Drought followed them in 1913, but the seemingly providential return of rain in 1914, coupled with Europe's war, brought returned prosperity. Great Plains wheat and corn fed the Allies; Great Plains cotton clothed them. Peace came in 1918 and agricultural depression followed in 1919 and again in 1925, thus climaxing a chaotic half-century of agricultural life in the Great Plains.

Fifty years of life in a boom-bust agricultural economy produced in the Great Plains farmer a corresponding boom-bust psychology. Each boom had fostered an influx of migrants so great that, in the years from 1880 to 1920, the Dakotas, Kansas, Nebraska, and Oklahoma comprised the fastest growing region in the nation.[8] Each drought or depression, on the other hand, produced a countermigration out of the region, as disgruntled and broken settlers pulled up stakes and joined the exodus to California or the urban centers of the Midwest. The bust-induced outflow from the Plains was never as large as the boom-induced inflow; by 1920, as power farming and dry farming techniques were perfected, there were in the Great Plains too many farmers for too few farms.[9]

For those who remained in the region, a pattern of life was produced which would culminate in the mass migration of the 1930s. In spite of the profits of the various boom years, the economic fortunes of the average Great Plains farmer steadily declined between 1880 and

1930.[10] The tale has been told many times: quick profits in boom years required overcapitalization in land and machinery to produce bumper crops; the usual failure of expectations, arising from unforeseen drought or surpluses on the markets of the world, led in turn to increased debt, and still further overcapitalization, and still more wasteful use of the land. Throughout the 1920s, a steady decline in farm ownership continued. Owners fell to tenancy, tenants to farm labor. More and more wheat, corn, and cotton-belt farms fell into the hands of corporations cultivating the lands with machinery. The machines, breaking the land each year to produce one crop, wore out the soil and paved the way for the ravages of the dust storms of the 1930s.

By 1930, farm families that had lived upon the Plains for years had fallen victim to "an unwise distribution of population which took place in the absence of a national policy for soil conservation and population redistribution."[11] Unfortunately for its inhabitants, the population of the region was "in excess of that which [could] be satisfactorily supported under the existing pattern of ownership and land use."[12] Migration from Plains farms confirmed these conclusions. Even while the net population of the Great Plains increased, the farms of the region sustained a loss of some 2.5 million people.[13]

Neither the Great Depression nor the much-publicized dust storms of the mid-1930s initiated the migration, one stream of which, the Okies, ended in California. Both simply accelerated trends already evident in the 1920s.[14] Out migration continued to be greatest in states in which large exoduses had occurred during the Normalcy years. But migration from the Okie states was proportionately higher, compared to migration from the northern Great Plains, than it had been in the 1920s.[15] Finally, the exodus from the Great Plains followed traditional geographic patterns. Americans have tended to move west in parallel lines, and the 1930s marked no exception to this rule. The Pacific Northwest—Washington, Oregon, Idaho—tended to receive its migrants from the northern Plains; the people of the southern Plains moved to California, with Oklahomans leading the procession.[16]

Oklahoma's predominant position in the westward movement—she supplied approximately 100,000 new Californians, a tenth of the decade's total increase in the state—accounted for the tendency of Californians to call all migrants from Texas, Arkansas, Missouri, and Oklahoma,

"Okies." Conditions in the four Okie states were not identical. Nevertheless, despite minor variations in the pattern of pushes from these states, socioeconomic problems, as well as the socioeconomic backgrounds of the migrants themselves, were sufficiently similar that a close account of developments in one of the four supplies satisfactory explanation for the migration from all four states. Because Oklahoma supplied the largest share of migrants, that state will be used as a case study. Any generalizations drawn from the Oklahoma experience will apply to the largest number of migrants.

In 1940, Oklahoma Governor Leon C. Phillips appointed a committee "to make a study of the [interstate migration] problem" and report its findings to the House Committee on the Interstate Migration of Destitute Citizens (the Tolan Committee) when it held its forthcoming hearings in Oklahoma City. Reprinted in the committee's hearings, the governor's report presented an outline of conditions pushing people from the state. There could be "no question," it maintained, that most of the recent and excessive emigration of Oklahomans was attributable to one, or a combination of several, factors pinpointed by the investigators.[17]

The enumeration of causes began, not surprisingly, with a routine complaint of excessive and inequitable freight rates reminiscent of Populist rhetoric. Federal regulatory bodies had connived with common carriers in levying unfair freight rates upon Oklahoma-manufactured goods, thus preventing the citizens of the state from diversifying their economic activities. Coerced by railroads and the government "to depend upon the marketing of the raw products of the soil," Oklahomans had migrated to states less dependent upon agriculture.[18] With the ritual plaint delivered before a committee of the federal government, the brief moved to a more general appraisal of the state's problems.

As in other southern states, the governor's committee found, intensive mechanized cotton culture had made the tenant system irrelevant. The tenants had been driven off the land by tractors far more efficient than they. Farm laborers, too, had become unemployed when they were replaced by machines. Allied with farm mechanization, but listed as a separate cause, was the New Deal's policy of crop curtailment. Acreage restriction under the Agricultural Adjustment Acts and the cotton program had reduced cash-crop cultivation by a third, releasing to unemployment still more laborers and tenants.[19] Beneath these immediate results of crop restriction lay a deeper problem: despite the law, benefit payments had not been distributed to tenants; they had gone, instead, for the purchase of more tractors by landlords. The tractors, in turn, rendered large-scale farming more profitable and eliminated permanently the need for tenants.

Still another cause of rural dislocation leading to migration, the report continued, was drought, which had been intensified by a fifth cause—soil depletion. The two went hand-in-hand. Oklahoma's farmers had never been "soil conscious." They had tilled and retilled, planted and replanted, "until many of their best fields had been depleted of their fertility, some of them hopelessly."[20] Worn-out and unplanted, the land had lain naked awaiting the first winds.

Five specific causes of migration from Oklahoma—overreliance on agriculture, allegedly fostered by rate discrimination; farm mechanization; crop curtailment; drought; and soil depletion—culminated in a sixth general cause: low farm income, the committee's euphemism for rural poverty. In the final analysis, it was low farm income, fostered by the five enumerated causes, that had supplied the impulse to migrate. And rural poverty affected not only the farmer, but those dependent upon him: the farm laborers, the residents of the small towns who survived only on the farmers' purchases, the real-estate agents, the salesmen, and a host of others.

Significantly, the governor's committee never noted the depression as a cause of migration. Indeed, with the sole exception of AAA (the Agricultural Adjustment Administration), each of the problems mentioned had been present during the allegedly prosperous 1920s. "Old man depression," responsible for so many of the problems of the nation, had simply been the final straw, the last push, for Oklahoma's farm people.

In only one respect did Oklahoma's situation differ from those in central Texas, southwestern Missouri, and western Arkansas. Oklahomans always had a tendency to move in greater numbers than their neighbors, which accounted for the higher proportion of authentic Okies in the migrant stream. Oklahoma was by far the most youthful state of the four. Indian territory until the close of the nineteenth century, admitted to statehood in 1907, Oklahoma was fewer than thirty years old when the dust bowl migration began. Settled during recurrent booms in oil as well as land, the state produced migratory people, who "in the past . . . manifested and still exhibit a pronounced tendency to migrate." Oklahomans pulled up stakes easily, "they move about. An ordinary farmer in Oklahoma moves about every year or two." Thomas Benton recalled that "the early settlers coming to Oklahoma in trainload were too much under the influence of the moving itch . . . as tenants they exhibited the usual propensity to shift about from farm to farm."[21]

The great majority of migrants from the four Okie states agreed that the Oklahoma governor's committee had accurately pinpointed the economic ills that had led them to migrate. Arkansans and Texans, and to a lesser degree, Missourians, laid the blame for their uprooting upon a combination of natural and man-made agricultural conditions, all of which contributed to declining work opportunities within their home states. Most migrants told the same dreary tale of declining fortunes in agriculture or in rural towns. Some had hoped that the World War I boom would continue; they overcapitalized and went broke in the late 1920s. One farmer who had migrated to California on "Monday after Easter, 1938," explained: "I put mine in what I thought was the best investment—the good old earth—but we lost on that, too. The finance co. caught up with us. Managed to lose $12,000 in three years. My boys have no more future than I have, so far as I can see ahead."[22]

Others—the majority—had never seen anywhere near $12,000. Theirs was the more typical history of scrabbling for small profit on insufficient lands:

How well do I remember that good old Texas land,
Where I lingered on starvation until I was a man.

Then I started out to farm, in that plant [cotton] to prosper way
But when my crop was gathered my debts I could not pay.
. . . .
Don't let anyone fool you And lead you in to harm,
For you sure cant make a living on a forty acre farm
So when I see Old Texas one thing I truly hope.
It will be from California through a long range Teliscope [sic].[23]

A good example is Theodore, an Arkansas-born Oklahoman, who lost the family farm when his father died in debt in 1909. He worked on the railroad during the war, and decided in the mid-1920s to return to farming. But his 185-acre spread, purchased in 1927, was insufficient to provide a living. He supplemented his income with farm labor until 1931, when he lost the farm. "The only thing he had left was a 1926 Buick. He built a trailer—stuck it on behind his car and—the family hit the road." In 1937, after six years of peripatetic migratory labor in the crops of the Great Plains, he arrived with his family in California.[24]

For every farm owner in the migratory stream who had gone broke in the 1920s and 1930s, there were more migrants who had never owned a farm at all. They had been tenants or farm workers all their lives. But the conditions pushing them out of the Great Plains were not different from those affecting the Okies who had once been fortunate enough to own a spread. Declining income, unprofitable farm units, soil exhaustion meant no work and added up to desperate, grinding poverty. For many, it was a simple case of move or starve. Or, as one Okie put the case more colorfully:

> Seven cent cotton and forty cent meat
> How in the Hell can a poor man eat?
>
> Poor, gettin' poorer all around here,
> Kids coming reg'lar every year
>
> Fatten our hogs, take 'em to town,
> All you get is six cents a pound.
>
> Very next day you have to buy it back
> Forty cents a pound in a paper sack.[25]

Joe Kane's story, writ large, told the history of an entire region. A California pea picker, Joe felt that his ancestors had it better. "None of our folks—neither side—never lived like Gipsies." They farmed their own spreads. Tenants at first, Joe and his wife found migratory labor forced upon them.

> This here was sort of pushed on to me and Jenny Bell and the young ones. . . . We aint never owned nothin' much, but then we ain't had to

move every time a crop was laid by neither, lessen we was a mind to. Then back in 1930 things had got so doggone tough we sold off our furniture and radio and cows and chickens and all and pulled out of Texas for Missouri. . . . We thought for sure we was goin where things was better.

They weren't: opportunities for labor picking cotton in Texas and Missouri were scarce and the Kanes headed for California. "We might as well be Gipsies," Joe concluded, "and be done with it."[26]

"Went broke" and "couldn't find work" were unsophisticated but correct designations of conditions forcing the exodus from the southern Plains, especially the cotton belt. The migrants were unlettered, and only a few recognized themselves to be victims of a specific and complicated cycle in which three causative factors—drought, mechanization, and certain New Deal policies—each reinforced the other. Drought, after all, was not in itself destructive; its ravages were a result of the attempt to produce profitable crops on too-small farms. Mechanization had increased the size and the profitability of farms even in the arid regions, but then government had been forced to control the surpluses produced by the mechanized farms. To complete the cycle, government payments had increased the surplus-producing mechanization by purchasing tractors for those receiving the benefits.

A few migrants did analyze the manner in which this trio had affected them, however, as did "registration number W1" at the Federal Migrant Camp at Marysville, California, "Wife, husband, six children. Natives of Oklahoma. Do not like migrating . . . state they had a 200 acre ranch in Oklahoma. Raised cotton. Had nice home. Still have fine car. Were doing well and had money in the bank. Cotton acreage was cut to 30 by AAA[;] forced them into bankruptcy." "There's some mighty rich farm land in Arkansas," another migrant commented, "but a poor man can't touch it. It takes money to get started farming. . . . Rich men own the land now."[27]

By 1940, awareness was spreading among the migrants that they were casualties of farm technology. In 1935 and 1937, noted a witness before a Senate Committee on Unemployment Relief, California's migrants had commonly explained their plight as "went broke" or "burned out, blowed out, eat out [sic]."[28] By 1940, "tractored out" was entering the list of causes.[29]

The majority of migrants preferred to believe, however, that drought, or simple unemployment, rather than mechanization or crop-restriction, had played the primary role in their dislocation. One questionnaire distributed among the migrants, for example, resulted in the following replies to the question "Why did you leave?"[30]

Lack of work	2,173	48 percent
Drought	1,572	35 percent
Replaced by Machine	104	2 percent

In another survey, only 2 out of the 344 migrant heads-of-household coming to California from Oklahoma's richest cotton county, in which tractors had increased by a third during the depression years, reported "replaced by machine" as their reason for leaving Oklahoma. Nearly half of them reported, contrary to the fact that cotton production was flourishing in the region, that drought had forced them out.[31]

Man resents being replaced by the machine, and small farmers pushed out by technology preferred to avoid the reality of their situation. So too, did the New Deal administration refuse to face the fact that the Agricultural Adjustment Administration and the cotton control program gave rise to considerable migration from the southern Plains. By paying benefits directly to the landlord, the New Deal allowed tenants to be displaced by tractors or farm laborers. As the AAA's most recent student has found, its "tenant policies not only gave the landlords a motive for evictions but offered the tenants little protection against them."[32] Many of the displaced tenants chose to migrate rather than enter the ranks of farm labor which, in areas of the South, was called "nigger work."[33] One Oklahoma landlord was frankly aware of the relationship between AAA and migration:

> I let 'em all go. In '34 I had I reckon four renters and I didn't make anything. I bought tractors on the money the government give me and got shet [rid] o' my renters. You'll find it everywhere all over the country that way. I did everything the government said—except keep my renters. The renters have been having it this way ever since the government come in. They've got their choice—California or WPA.[34]

New Deal agencies denied throughout the depression that crop curtailment and benefit payments were responsible in part for the migration. The Department of Labor, for example, ignored the entire issue in its report, *Migration of Workers*, and boldly begged the question when it asserted that "recent drought" had forced the migration of "drought refugees." Ironically, one of the report's footnotes let the cat out of the bag when it noted that "the breakdown of tenancy, as well as drought, may be responsible for part of the heavy migration from Oklahoma. . . . A large number of the interstate migrants appear to have come from the cotton-raising portion of the State which was least affected by the drought." While the Labor Department was unintentionally admitting AAA's culpability in the problem, the latter was firmly maintaining that, far from hastening migration, it was preventing the exodus of drought refugees by "boosting farm income through parity payments."[35]

The migrants' refusal to admit that machines had displaced them, coupled with the Roosevelt administration's attempt to deny its role in the breakdown of tenancy in the southern Plains, accounted for the most persistent myth of the Okie migration. A national tendency existed to overemphasize the role of the dust-bowl area in the 1935-1940 migration.[36] When Californians sought names other than "Okies" for the migrants, they called them "dustbowlers," and popular writers invariably began their accounts of the migration with a paragraph or two of overblown prose describing the dust storms.

And, to be sure, the dust storms were dramatic. In April 1935, those who had sown the Plains soil with cotton and wheat and corn quite literally reaped the whirlwind of their wasteful and dangerous cultivation of marginal land. Overplowed, overworked, the topsoil lay in wait for prolonged drought. In the mid-1930s, the dry times came and the soil turned to dust. With the first winds, the dust rose and blew across the eastern half of the continent, some of it settling only when it reached the Atlantic Ocean. On many days during the great dust storms, the sky was black at midday; housewives removed half an inch of soil from their kitchen floors, and not even blankets stuffed beneath the doors and into the cracks around the windows prevented the inexorable advance of the dust. The storms were a menace to health and a dual catastrophe for agriculture. When the topsoil lifted, it destroyed millions of acres of marginal land; when it fell, it suffocated crops on well-tended acres.

Agronomists, and state and federal officialdom, recognized even in the dust storms a man-made catastrophe, the result of years of improper land use. The American people, including the migrants, found beneath these more rational explanations a kind of unconscious comfort in viewing the storms as a judgment from the Almighty. Here, at least, in these trying depression days, was one catastrophe wrought by God, not man. It was far more comforting, in a way, to be driven from the land by an "act of God" than to be harried off by an International Harvester. Throughout the 1930s, popular folklore persisted in so viewing the meaning of the dust storms. Woody Guthrie, himself an Okie and the most important American folk singer of his day, helped foster the popular conception of the dust storms as judgment in his "Dust Storm Disaster:"

> On the 14th day of April
> Of 1935, there struck
> The worst of dust storms
> That ever filled the sky
> . . . .
> From Oklahoma City
> To the Arizona line
> Dakota and Nebraska
> To the lazy Rio Grande
>
> It fell across our city
> Like a curtain of black rolled down
> We thought it was our judgment
> We thought it was our doom.
>
> The radio reported
> We listened with alarm
> The wild and windy actions
> Of this great mysterious storm.[37]

Or, hailing "so long, its been good to know you," Guthrie's migrants:

> . . . talked of the end
> of the world and then
> . . . would sing a song
> And then sing it again,

while the preacher said:

> . . . Kind Friends,
> This may be the end.
> You've got your last chance
> At salvation of sin.[38]

"It seems," one migrant told a reporter, "like God has forsaken us back there in Arkansas," and Guthrie, like an Okie Abraham, wrestled with a God upon whom he blamed the dust: "That old dust storm killed my baby, But it can't kill me, Lord, it can't kill me."[39]

By a process of extension, the dramatic and theatrical dust storms crowded the more prosaic droughts and tractors out of the public consciousness. Americans came to see "dust bowl" as synonymous with "drought region," which it was not. The actual dust bowl was but a part of the drought region and most of the Okies came neither from the dust bowl nor from the areas of worst distress in the drought region.[40] That Okies did come from the dust bowl was true; that the average Okie in California was a dust-bowl refugee was false. The dust bowl did witness large migrations during the depression years, but these were movements proportionately smaller than those of other, earlier, dust storms.[41] In part, this phenomenon was the result of an ironic twist in federal policy, because drought relief was distributed in direct proportion to the intensity of the drought, on a county-by-county basis. The most federal relief funds were spent, therefore, to protect the most worn lands in the nation, while farmers on less eroded lands received less aid and, therefore, could not save their farms.[42]

In response, then, to a continuing series of conditions that produced an unsatisfactory economic situation in the southern Great Plains states, farmers who had clung to the land on a bare subsistence level picked up their few belongings and left. For many, this was simple enough: "moving day," an old one-liner in the Deep South goes, "consists of calling the dog and spitting on the fire." The exodus of farmers and farm laborers took with it a large number of nonagricultural rural people who had relied upon the farmers for their livelihood—tradesmen, mechanics, townspeople of all sorts thrown out of work by depopulation of neighboring farm areas. A few city people, too, joined the Okie migration: oil workers, unskilled laborers, even (though rarely) a professional man or two from the few urban centers of the region. In all, over a half million people fled the Okie states during the depression years. Of these, over 300,000 ended their inter-state meanderings in California.[43]

California's Okies were attracted to the state by a combination of pulls as complex as the mélange of forces that had driven them from their home states. On the simplest level, of course, it may be said that all, with the exception of those few who came for reasons of health to bask in the yet smog-free climate, were pulled to California in the hope of improving their economic condition. Merely to assert this general rule, was, however, insufficient and unsatisfactory. It was precisely the specific manner in which they sought to broaden their opportunities that determined their reception in the state and their impact upon it. The question of why the Okies went to California excited as much controversy as any other question raised by the migrant influx.

Throughout the period, Californians strove to determine the reasons for the influx. In the anxiety aroused by the coming of the migrants, they hoped by discovering the cause to find a method by which to end the migration, or, if possible, to alleviate its worst effects. In many cases, they confused pushes with pulls. To say, for example, as many Californians did, "they came to California because of drought in their native states" was to obliterate this important distinction.[44] The state-ment really meant "they left their native states because of drought" and was of little use for California whose state government could, after all, do nothing to end the drought, or, for that matter, farm mechaniza-tion or depression in, say, Oklahoma. In practical terms, it was far more important that California determine accurately, and in detail, why migrants had chosen California as their destination. In this attempt they were unable to arrive at a consensus. Various groups in California, their perceptions colored by their varying relationship with the migrants, arrived at strikingly different conclusions.

The migrant influx added tension to deep divisions already tearing at the political and social fabric of the state. Farmers' organizations, particularly those representing the state's large ranches, found it expedi-ent to argue that the Okies had entered the state seeking a "soft touch" from overly generous state and federal New Dealers. In this, they were joined by their allies in county governments, and by business and citizens' groups eager to discredit the liberal side of California's political spectrum. Liberal and radical groups, on the other hand, insisted that a conspiracy of growers' interests had lured the migrants to the state in order to build a local labor surplus, thereby depressing already substandard agricultural labor wages. Both arguments contained just sufficient substance to acquire plausibility, and both have entered California's folklore. Neither, however, explained more than a trivial portion of the Okie migration.

Few Okies chose California in order to receive its allegedly munificent relief payments. Undoubtedly, some had been attracted for this reason, but, in the context of the total migration, their numbers were minimal. Although direct evidence for this conclusion is necessarily difficult to discover, since questionnaires never included "high relief payments" in their "Why did you come to California?" sections, there are various implicit arguments against this thesis.

First, it was incorrect to assert, as those who attacked the Okies as chiselers did, that California's relief structure supplied luxurious payments, sometimes six or seven times higher than Oklahoma's. During the depression years, "relief" was an omnibus appellation for a wide variety of benefits, comprising state emergency and unemployment relief, pension plans, WPA payments, and farm support payments in the drought region, along with a host of smaller, less significant programs for the blind, the indigent sick, and other specific groups. California's state unemployment relief payments were higher than those in the drought states, but the combined total of all payments that an Okie might expect to receive in California was not significantly larger than his check would have been at home. WPA payments and drought relief in the southern Plains narrowed the relief differentials, and the California average payment in 1940 ($42.99) was but 19 percent higher than the average in the drought states ($36.20).[45] Further, California's 12 percent higher cost of living minimized still more the advantages that migrants seeking the soft life would receive in California. Nor was state relief that easy to obtain: one year's residence was required and, although after 1938 the federal government extended grant-aid to the nonresident, the prospect of living high was dim.

In spite of the occasional story uncovered by those who insisted that relief had brought the Okies to California—tales of letters home proudly annoucing that an Okie family had bought a new car on California's relief payments, tales of an "underground railway" bringing whole clans to the San Joaquin Valley and swelling the relief rolls—there was scant evidence that relief had weighed heavily, if at all, in the decision of Okie families to migrate. This was the conclusion of the Tolan Committee instituted to investigate migration during the late 1930s, and this conclusion was borne out by movements in the depression years to states other than California.[46] Washington's state relief payments were *lower* than North Dakota's; yet the former received a large stream of migrants from the latter.[47] The migrants themselves denied that relief had drawn them to California, and, occasionally, they proved that they preferred starvation to the dole. When, for example, the Farm Security Administration instituted relief for nonresidents in early 1938, it stockpiled food supplies in warehouses located near the migrant camps. Since most of the Okie families did not seek aid until they were "entirely destitute and hungry," they were unable to wait for delivery of their checks.[48]

To counteract the prevalent "soft touch" argument, groups and individuals who opposed the state's growers on nearly every front argued that the migrants had been the victims of a conspiracy designed to lure them into the state. Advertisements had been placed in Great Plains newspapers promising agricultural work at high pay in California's fields, as part of a cynical plot to attract an ever-larger surplus of labor to the state. These charges, like those blaming the influx on relief payments, appeared plausible on the surface. They were, however, as incorrect; California would have attracted the Okies whether such a conspiracy had existed or not.

In 1939, Dorothy Ray, a field-workers' union organizer and close associate of California's radicals, charged that the grower-oriented Associated Farmers of California and the California Farm Placement Bureau had "deliberately spread advertisement and propaganda to draw migrants to the state for the purpose of creating a plentiful supply of cheap labor."[49] CIO and radical Californians were not alone in this belief. George Meany echoed the charge for the AFL when he asserted that the growers had brought the Okies in to serve as strikebreakers and to depress the already "pitiful" wages in the fields.[50] Ham 'N' Eggs, the inflationist old-age scheme that succeeded Dr. Townsend's movement in California, insisted that in the Okie migration could be discerned "the hand of the state's large financial interest and 'farmer' bankers."[51]

Finally, the major American novel to emerge from the depression's ferment enshrined forever in the American mind the myth of a growers' conspiracy. Of *The Grapes of Wrath*, more will be said later. For the moment, however, it should be pointed out that, had Pa Joad never seen a handbill announcing "Pea Pickers Wanted in California. Good Wages all Season. 800 Pickers Wanted," that magnificent Okie family might never have made the westward trek. Leaving little to the reader's imagination, Steinbeck went on to explain, through the agency of a disillusioned migrant returning to Oklahoma, that the growers "send out han'bills all over hell. They need three thousan' an' they get six thousan'. They get them men for what they wanta pay. If ya don't wanta take what they pay, goddamn it, they's a thousan' men waitin' for your job."[52]

Many of the Okies themselves claimed to have chosen California in response to advertisements, in which "the various Chambers of Commerce were advising agricultural laborers of the dust bowl areas that California was in need of thousands of cotton pickers. Any man that could pick cotton could make four dollars a day."[53] Or, as another Okie put it:

> The Arkies and Okies in nineteen thirty six,
> Cranked up their flivers and came west Sixty-six.
> . . . .
> Then the Chamber of Commerce sent an add back
> East for help and here came ten thousand more.[54]

"The reason," yet another Okie wrote, "is just like thousands of other folks—circulars all over the county, crying for help in the beautiful state of California."[55]

Three additional ingredients lent plausibility to the conspiracy theory. First, during the early 1930s, a few California growers had feared a labor shortage and had sought in the Great Plains a labor supply to compensate for an anticipated loss of Mexican labor.[56] Second, even after the onset of the 1935-1940 migration, isolated cases of such inducements continued to arise; for example, one labor contractor advertised for pea-pickers, promising a good crop at good wages when "the contrary was the case." Another time, ironically, one of the migrants bought an auto camp in the San Joaquin Valley, and, seeking to maximize his profits, advertised back home that "golden employment opportunities" existed in the vicinity of his camp.[57] Finally, and most important, the conspiracy thesis did apply—not to California's growers but, rather, to their eastern neighbors producing bumper cotton crops in Arizona.

Arizona cotton growers had early discovered what one *New York Times* reporter covering the migrant problem had dubbed the "neatest get rich quick scheme of the century." Arizona's cotton, grown in the lush, irrigated regions of Pinal County south of Phoenix, matured earlier than California cotton. This quirk of nature allowed Arizona growers to advertise for labor in the Great Plains and, once the cotton crop was laid by, to persuade the migrants to move west across the border into California. Since state relief payments were virtually impossible to obtain during the off-season—Arizona had raised her residence requirement for relief to three years in 1937—such persuasion was generally quite effective.[58] Thus, a steady stream of Okies lured to Arizona by the promise of work landed, finally, in California.

California's growers and their opponents both held Arizona culpable for a portion of the migrant influx. A "migrant committee" of the California State Chamber of Commerce, constituted, in part, by members of the Associated Farmers, accused Arizona growers of "carry[ing] on through their Farm Labor Service an active and elaborate system of labor recruiting, throughout the states of Texas, Oklahoma, and Arkansas, using handbills, newspaper advertisements, publicity stories, letters, travelling agents, and similar means of attracting pickers" and then pushing the migrants into California.[59] Carey McWilliams, a vociferous opponent of the state's large growers, confirmed the Associated Farmers' position upon this issue. "It looks to me," he wrote confidentially to a member of the FSA's staff in 1939, "as though the placement service is endeavoring to recruit a surplus of labor in Arizona with the thought in mind of pushing them along into the San Joaquin Valley later in October."[60]

If a conspiracy by California's growers existed, scant evidence to substantiate the charge could be found. When the La Follette Committee launched its full-scale investigation into California's agricultural system, it subpoenaed and seized the files of the Associated Farmers. These confidential records proved a bonanza: they betrayed a dismal story of labor-baiting, private strikebreaking armies and arsenals, collusion with local officials in exploiting labor, and violation of workers' civil liberties. The files supplied, however, little comfort for those who accused the group of conspiring to lure labor into the state. When the La Follette Committee reported to Congress, it was able to find the Associated Farmers guilty only of a sin of omission: they had not, La Follette charged, attempted to "stop an influx of workers before the growers secured all the labor they feel they need."[61] As for McWilliams, he backhandedly admitted that the migrant influx, unlike prior migrations of agricultural workers to the West coast, "was not altogether solicited" and that the Okies had come "without expense to the growers."[62]

It was not surprising that, in their public statements, the state's large growers were eager to allay California's anxiety that the specific needs of agriculture had been responsible for a problem afflicting the entire state. Associated Farmers propaganda consistently maintained that few advertisements were being distributed in the drought region; and, further, that those responsible for them were being ferreted out and reprimanded.[63] What was surprising was that in this, as in few other issues in which they were involved, their private comments were consonant with their broadcast propaganda. In correspondence with concerned chambers of commerce, for example, Associated Farmer Roy Pike stoutly denied that large growers had advertised in any area outside California.[64] Pike even investigated reports that the Los Angeles Chamber of Commerce was "boosting the state" in the southern Plains, receiving for his efforts an emphatic disclaimer from Dr. George Clements, manager of the chamber's agricultural committee.[65] And, finally, to the disappointment of the La Follette Committee, its subpoena had turned up a large file of correspondence in which the Associated Farmers demanded that the state's Farm Placement Service investigate reports of farm labor advertisements placed in midwestern newspapers, probably, Vice President Philip Bancroft of the Associated Farmers noted, by "people hostile to us and to the best interests of our California farmers."[66]

The absence of an Associated Farmers or chamber of commerce conspiracy was evidence neither of altruism nor public conscience on the part of California's agricultural interests. There was simply no need to advertise for Okies; they came without being lured to the state and, by 1938 and 1939, their numbers were too large even for the growers to view the influx with equanimity.

Although some migrants had chosen California because of advertisements, these were the exceptional cases. In the San Joaquin Valley, center of large-scale farms and focal point of the Okie migration, fewer than 4 percent of the migrants had come in response to advertisements.[67] Some, like Tom Small, an Arkansas migrant, had been told that such advertisements existed but, he added, "I never saw one myself."[68] Nevertheless, in a sense, it can be said that the migrant influx was the result of an advertising campaign: for fifty years, California had been boosted in the nation's press as a golden dream for Americans residing in the East. The migration was a legacy of this publicity.

Those who advertised California most to the Okies were the Okies themselves. More than any other single agent, reports from friends and relatives drew new migrants to California. With striking similarity, investigators in the state's agricultural counties discovered that two related factors had diverted the migrant stream to California: the desire to join friends and relatives who had settled in the region a year or two before, and reports from other migrants that work in the fields was easier to obtain and more remunerative than the same work in the southern Plains states. In Kern, Stanislaus, and Monterey counties, the overwhelming majority of Okies gave the same answer to the same question: "Why did you come to California?" They were here, they announced, to participate in the field labor reported to them by friends and relatives already in the state.[69]

In moving to California, the Okies were conforming to a familiar American pattern. For Great Plains farm people, the West had always seemed a land of economic opportunity.[70] Were droughts dessicating the land, drying out the soul? California had all the water it needed, all the time. Did last year's blizzard, tornado, or flood destroy property, profit, and, worst of all, tear at the sanity? California had sun, warmth, fresh air all year round. Did the treeless Texas landscape deaden the sense of beauty, limit fuel and building supplies? California was lush and green—pick your own trees, palms, redwoods. Were labor contractors in Oklahoma paying starvation wages, and for "nigger work" at that? California's growers paid well.

The promise of California, as the Okies saw it, contained just sufficient truth to provide "a basis for action" in migration.[71] The terrible irony was that each facet of the dream contained a hidden loophole. The richest lands in the state, for example, had been deserts for centuries. It had taken millions of dollars to irrigate them, and only then had they become the agricultural Edens known as the San Joaquin and Imperial valleys. Work in the fields did pay better, as the Okies believed; but the swelling stream of migrants crowded one another out of work. Pay was good, when one could get it, but the harvest season was short, and unemployment was the rule for most of the year. And, finally, as for the never-articulated, but always subconscious dream of owning, perhaps, one's own forty-acre spread—such was the fluff of mythology. California's agricultural system offered nothing to the small farmer. In short, the Okies came to a state whose southern half was too dry, whose northern half was too wet, and whose farms were sustained by expensive technology. "Tractored out" by the early stages of mechanization in the Plains, they moved to a state where agriculture was, quite literally, a modern industry.

But the Okies could not have known of these conditions and even if they had, the grip of the boom-bust psychology continued to influence their perceptions once in California. In the bad years, they had tightened their belts and waited for better times. When they came to California they ignored this week's unemployment: next week's job would pay well. Just as boom times had elated them back home in Oklahoma, so in California did two-dollars-a-day seem providential. Back in Texas, fifty cents was a good day's pay.[72]

The Okies themselves confirmed that a grapevine of rumor, fostered by letters sent "bak hum" and by word-of-mouth contacts along Route 66 and in the eastern states, was persuading migrants that California provided splendid opportunities. Steinbeck's Joads may have been warned by disappointed returnees to go back to Oklahoma, but most of the real Joads heard quite the opposite. Hurdle Jones "received word from my friends in Kern County that it was easy picking in Bakers-

field," and "took the first side door Pullman [freight car] and now am
a full fledged citizen of Kern County"; Will Davis who "blowed in from
Blanchard, Oklahoma," heard that work was plentiful in sunny California from a friend who "was out here last year, went back to Oklahoma
telling folks he hadn't had any trouble in getting work at higher pay";
Pink Allen and his family left for California with an uncle who told
them how good things were there.[73] When Oklahomans were told by
their state employment service that there was no work in California,
many replied "the Hell they ain't" and, the service's director noted, this
psychology spread rapidly throughout the state.[74]

The dust-bowl migrants came to California in search of work. They
sought work that they were already familiar with—agricultural work.
When the migrant stream was but a trickle, some of the Okies discovered that work in California agriculture was better than work in the
southern Great Plains. They told their friends back home. The friends
and relatives, struggling in Oklahoma or Texas with little hope of
improvement, decided to join those already in California . . . and the
migrant stream became first a river and then a flood.

The Okies had good reason to believe that California agriculture,
separated from their home states by 1,500 miles, would not be alien to
them. One specific characteristic of California's rural landscape served
as a magnet for Okies in search of work. They came in quest of a
particular sort of work in a particular crop, a crop which had virtually
determined the history of the South for 150 years: cotton.

Little white Bolls, acres of them, speckled in rows
                                                    . . . KING COTTON
Hope and despair, warmth and gold, rich and poor and poorer saluting
the inevitable. Planting, chopping, picking, ginning . . .
                                                    . . . KING COTTON
White and fleecy and clean, all the blood washed out
Shanties, fried mush and corn pone . . .
Migration . . .
                                                    . . . KING COTTON[75]

The consequences of the South's century-and-a-half flirtation with
cotton have been a major source of study for American historians, who
have emphasized the cotton culture and economy before the Civil War

and, of course, during the New South and Populist eras. Cotton's twentieth-century history, less dramatic but as consequential, has been, by and large, left to the agronomists. Almost totally unrecognized has been the spread of cotton culture beyond the American South. Without the movement of cotton into Colorado, New Mexico, Arizona, and, of course, California, there might have been no Okie migration; had the migration materialized anyway, its consequences would certainly have been far different.

In the decade following World War I, California's agriculture witnessed still another revolutionary change in its oft-changing history. "As suddenly as the coming of the 'gold diggers,' " cotton came to the Great Central Valley. In 1921, only 1,500 California acres had been planted in cotton. Experimenters soon discovered that an acre of California land would produce 370 pounds of the crop, a three-fold increase over the national average of 116 pounds.[76] Potentially a source of great wealth, cotton production increased fantastically: in 1926, 170,000 acres and 130,000 bales. By 1937, 600,000 acres of cotton made it the state's fourth largest crop.

Of sugar beets, artichokes, oranges, and grapes, the Okies knew little. Of cotton, they knew all. The crop required skill, especially in the picking season, when the novice could earn little more than fingers torn to raw flesh by the tenacious fibers, and the people of the southern Plains were professionals where cotton was concerned. News of California's bumper cotton crops spread into the migrants' home states during the 1920s and early 1930. It had been brought east by cotton pickers who had answered advertisements placed in local papers by California cotton growers who needed trained workers desperately for their new bonanza crop.[77]

It was not at all strange then, that when, around 1935, masses of Oklahomans, Texans, Arkansans, and Missourians decided once and for all to eschew life on the Plains for work elsewhere, many chose California. When asked why he had come west, the migrant would usually answer, "to find work." Asked "what kind of work?" he would nearly invariably reply: "What'd we come fer? To pick cotton. To find a new place—things were all finished back home."[78] "I started looking this way, and when I found cotton, that's where I stopped . . . you can pick and read about where they have got good cotton in Arizona and

California and about what it produces to the acre; and I come this way because I couldn't get any place else, and I got to the point where I couldn't support my family."[79]

A direct relationship existed between California cotton and the migrations; indeed, a vicious cycle arose in which migrants trained in cotton moved to California and, to utilize them, Californians planted more cotton, thus bringing in more migrants.[80] "The rains," one FSA camp manager wrote to a friend, "have come now, and there is hardly a cabin in the camp that is not surrounded by a thick stand of green fuzz. The cotton, too, has come, and with it a new influx of migrants, who are rapidly filling up a few remaining empty [tent] platforms."[81]

California's dust-bowl migration was the product of two forces, both impersonal, both relentless. Drought, depression, mechanization—the results of years of untenable agricultural life on the southern Plains—pushed the migrants into their first decision: "We've got to get out of this place." California's years of self-praise, its agricultural abundance, and its newly discovered cotton bounty pulled the Okies west on Highway 66.

For the migrants, the move was a wrenching, bitter, but necessary, relocation. Steinbeck told their story magnificently. For some it was unendurable. They collapsed and died along the way. For those who could endure, however, the crossing on Route 66 from Arizona into California was not the end, but the beginning, of greater woe. Forced into squalid ditch-bank camps to await the picking of crops they had not sown, pawns in struggles building before their arrival, despised by Californians who had arrived in the state only a decade earlier, the Okies found their California dream transformed into a nightmare.

For California, too, the migration was unsettling. It was not large in comparison with migrations before and after the depression. Nor was it much different in composition from other movements of Americans to the West. But Californians did not think—indeed could not have known—of statistics that might allay their anxiety. The problem was now, on the ditch banks, in the fields, in the bloody agricultural strikes and the divisive political conflicts.

For Americans, the story of the Okies would become a symbolic repository for the fears and deprivations of a nation attempting to cope with a major economic dislocation. Too, by coming to California, the

Okies would expose to the nation how far agriculture had deviated from Jefferson's vision. And, finally, for the New Dealers, the Okies would supply an opportunity for a doomed experiment in rural rehabilitation.

Notes in Text

1. Donald J. Bogue et al. *Subregional Migration in the United States,* Scripps Foundation Studies in Population Redistribution, No. 6 (Miami, Ohio, 1953), p. 11.

2. Ibid.

3. Scores of works cover the subject of the Great Plains. Among the better are: Henry David et al., eds., *The Economic History of the United States* (New York, 1945), vol. 5; Fred Shannon, *The Farmer's Last Frontier;* Carl Frederick Kraenzel, *The Great Plains in Transition* (Norman, Okla., 1955); Walter Prescott Webb, *The Great Plains* (New York, 1931).

4. Conrad Taeuber and Carl C. Taylor, *The People of the Drought States*, WPA Research Bulletin, Series V, No. 6 (Washington, 1937), p. 21.

5. John Wesley Powell, *Report on the Lands of the Arid Region of the United States, with a More Detailed Account of the Lands of Utah* (2d ed., Washington, 1879).

6. Kraenzel, *The Great Plains in Transition*, p. 144.

7. Richard Hofstadter, *The Age of Reform* (New York, 1955), pp. 22-130 passim.

8. Seymour Janow, "Migration Westward, Summary of a Decade," *Land Policy Review* 4 (October 1941): 12.

9. U.S., Department of Labor, *Migration of Workers* (Washington: GPO, 1938), I: 67.

10. John D. Hicks and Theodore Saloutos, *Twentieth Century Populism* (Lincoln, Nebraska, 1951), passim; Kraenzel, *The Great Plains in Transition*, pp. 137-164.

11. Janow, "Migration Westward," 12.

12. U.S., Congress, House, Select Committee to Investigate the Interstate Migration of Destitute Citizens, *Hearings*, 76th Cong., 3d sess., 1938, V: 1,763 (hereafter referred to as Tolan Committee).

13. Davis McEntire and Tyr V. Johnson, "Migration and Resettlement Problems in Pacific Coast States," n.d., Paul S. Taylor Collection, Bancroft Library, University of California, Berkeley, Carton 18. The figure of 2.5 million is probably inflated and somewhat deceiving. The authors are referring solely to farm population, and, therefore, farmers moving to cities within the state constitute a net loss in population. Further, the figure is based upon a computation of the increase in population that should have occurred—using 1910s birth rate figures—but didn't.

14. C. E. Lively and Conrad Taeuber, *Rural Migration in the United States* (Washington, 1939), pp. 30-31: "it appears that drought and economic depression accentuated previously existing trends without radically altering the direction of movement which had prevailed during the 1920's."

15. John N. Webb and Malcolm Brown, *Migrant Families* (Washington, 1938), p. xxiii.

16. P. E. Ryan, *Migration and Social Welfare* (New York, 1940), p. 23; John Blanchard, *Caravans to the Northwest* (Boston, 1940), p. 9; Department of Labor, *Migration of Workers,* p. 65; Willard W. Troxell and W. Paul O'Day, "Migration to the Pacific Northwest, 1930-1938," *Land Policy Review* 3 (January-February 1940): 34.

17. Tolan Committee, *Hearings,* Part 5, pp. 2,028-2,037.

18. Ibid.

19. Ibid., pp. 2,034-2,035; see also Arthur Raper, *Preface to Peasantry* (Chapel Hill, 1936).

20. Tolan Committee, *Hearings,* Part 5, p. 2,034.

21. See Otis D. Duncan, *The Significance of the Migrations of Oklahoma Farm Populations* (Stillwater, Okla., 1939), p. 1; Jonathan Garst to Isador Lubin, "Conference Called to Discuss Problems of Transients and Migratory Agricultural Labor," transcript, San Francisco, December 14, 1936, p. 8, Simon J. Lubin Papers, Bancroft Library, University of California, Berkeley, Carton 13; Paul Taylor *An American Exodus* (New York, 1939), p. 67.

22. Taylor, *An American Exodus,* p. 167.

23. *Tow Sack Tatler,* December 8, 1939.

24. "Case #33," Farm Security Administration Collection, Bancroft Library, University of California, Berkeley, Carton 2, Folder 60.

25. *Happy Valley Weekly,* December 3, 1938.

26. Lucretia Penny, "Pea Picker's Child," *Survey Graphic* 24 (July 1935): 352.

27. Marysville Camp Reports, September 7, 1935, Harry E. Drobisch Papers, Bancroft Library, University of California, Berkeley; "California's Greatest Problem," n.d., Lubin Papers, Carton 4.

28. U.S., Congress, Senate, *Hearings on a Resolution Creating a Special Committee to Investigate Unemployment and Relief,* 75th Cong., 1st sess., p. 1,163.

29. Paul Taylor, "Power Farming and Labor Displacement in the Cotton Belt," *Monthly Labor Review* 46 (March, April 1938), passim. See also Anna Louise Strong, *My Native Land* (New York, 1940), pp. 95-96, for a rather humorous communist account of the tractor problem. Contrary to "peasants" in the United States, Miss Strong insists, those in the U.S.S.R. "hung their tractors with garlands."

30. U.S., Department of Agriculture, Farm Security Administration, *A Study of 6,655 Migrant Households in California* (San Francisco, 1939), p. 31, Table 2.

31. Ibid., p. 35.

32. David Eugene Conrad, *The Forgotten Farmers* (Urbana, 1965), p. 208 passim. Many Californians blamed the influx upon the AAA. See, for example, an editorial in the *Bakersfield Californian,* December 9, 1940. Friends of the New Deal in Bakersfield agreed that AAA was responsible, but attempted to put the best face upon the matter. *Kern County Union Labor Journal,* August 12, 1938.

33. Nels Anderson, *Men on the Move* (Chicago, 1940), p. 214.

34. Taylor, *An American Exodus,* p. 80.

35. Department of Labor, *Migration of Workers,* pp. 57, 76n. 3; United States, Department of Agriculture, Farm Security Administration, *Migratory Labor* (Washington, 1940), passim. See also: U.S., Congress, Senate, Committee on

Education and Labor, Subcommittee of the Committee on Education and Labor to Investigate Violations of the Right of Free Speech and Assembly and Interference with the Right of Labor to Organize and Bargain Collectively, Pursuant to S. Res. 266, *Hearings*, 74th Cong., 1940, Supplement I, pp. 4-7 (hereafter referred to as La Follette Committee).

36. See, for example, Thomas Stokes, *Chip Off My Shoulder* (Princeton, 1940), pp. 395-96.

37. Woody Guthrie, "Talking Dust Bowl," Folkways Records, 1950, FA-2011.

38. Ibid.

39. Paul Taylor, "Again the Covered Wagon," *Survey Graphic* 24 (July 1935): 349; Guthrie, "Talking Dust Bowl."

40. Department of Agriculture, *A Study of 6,655 Migrant Households*, pp. 34-35.

41. Fred Floydd, "A History of the Dust Bowl" (Ph.D. diss., University of Oklahoma, 1950), p. 192.

42. Francis D. Cronin and Howard D. Beers, *Area of Intense Drought Distress*, WPA Division of Social Research, Series V, No. 1 (Washington, 1937), passim.

43. The figure on migration *from* the Okie states is drawn from Rupert B. Vance, *All These People* (Chapel Hill, 1945), p. 126, Table 31. The figure "over 300,000" on migration to California is, quite necessarily, an informed guess. In compiling its census on migration for the 1940 enumeration, the bureau chose to ask "In what place did this person live on April 1, 1935?" rather than, "In what place did this person live on December 31, 1929?" It is, therefore, impossible to get figures on net migration for the entire decade of the 1930s. According to the census, California gained 251,989 persons from the four Okie states during the period from April 1, 1935, to the close of 1940. (Commonwealth Club, *Population of California*, p. 113, Table 41). Considering the fact that the period 1930-1933 was characterized by low indices of migration, I have estimated that the total decennial migration was between 300,000 and 400,000, probably closer to the former, smaller, figure.

44. T. J. Woofter, "Travel Also Broadens Social Issues," *Nation's Business* 29 (April 1941): 22. See also Lee Alexander Stone, *Migratory Labor and Labor Camps* (Madera, 1937), p. 1.

45. Virgil Cazel to Walter Chambers, May 13, 1940, California State Relief Administration interoffice memorandum, Lubin Papers, Carton 13.

46. *San Francisco News*, October 8, 1940; Philip E. Ryan, *Migration and Social Welfare* (New York, 1940), p. 53: "Most studies of the migrant problem show that persons move regardless of the availability of relief in the places to which they come."

47. La Follette Committee, *Hearings*, Part 47, p. 13, 272; *Voice of the Agricultural Worker*, December 29, 1929 (hereafter *VOTAW*); interview with Mrs. Eleanor Engstrand, Berkeley, California, September 7, 1965.

48. Testimony of Mr. Mills, La Follette Committee, *Hearings*, Part 59, p. 21,930.

49. *People's World*, February 7, 1939; *Western Worker*, June 2, 1935.

50. George Meany, "Peonage in California," *American Federationist* (May 1941): 31; *East Bay Labor Journal*, May 3, 1940; La Follette Committee, *Hearings*, Part 60, p. 22,069.

51. *National Ham and Eggs*, March 4, 1939; *Tent City News*, October 21, 1939.

52. John Steinbeck, *The Grapes of Wrath* (Bantam Books ed., New York, 1955), pp. 130, 218.

53. "Case History-Louis," Farm Security Administration Collection, Carton 2, Folder 60.

54. *Tent City News*, January 19, 1940; *Happy Valley Weekly*, March 9, 1940.

55. *VOTAW*, July 9, 1940.

56. La Follette Committee, *Hearings*, Part 59, p. 21,888.

57. *Stockton Record*, May 11, 1938.

58. Malcolm Brown and Orin Cassmore, *Migratory Cotton Pickers in Arizona*, WPA Division of Social Research (Washington, 1939), p. xi.

59. Subcommittee of the Statewide Agricultural Committee of the California State Chamber of Commerce, *Problems of Interstate Migration in California, Preliminary Draft for Consideration of Migrant Committee* (n.p., n.d.,); see also, La Follette Committee, *Hearings*, Part 59, p. 21,863.

50. Carey McWilliams to Paul Taylor, October 11, 1939, Carey McWilliams Collection, University of California, Los Angeles.

61. La Follette Committee, *Reports*, 77th Cong., 2d sess., No. 1150, p. 322.

62. Carey McWilliams, *Factories in the Field* (Boston, 1939), pp. 306,308.

63. La Follette Committee, *Hearings*, Part 59, p. 21,863.

64. Roy M. Pike to Riverside Chamber of Commerce, August 22, 1939, George P. Clements Collection, University of California, Los Angeles.

65. George P. Clements to Roy M. Pike, August 25, 1939, Clements Collection, University of California, Los Angeles.

66. La Follette Committee, *Hearings*, Part 72, pp. 26,578-26,580. See also H. A. Miller to editor, *Christian Science Monitor*, "not for publication," September 12, 1939, Clements Collection, University of California, Los Angeles.

67. Walter R. Goldschmidt, *As You Sow* (Glencoe, 1947), p. 151.

68. *San Francisco News*, February 14, 1938; Tolan Committee, *Hearings*, Part 6, p. 2,210.

69. For Kern: Goldschmidt, *As You Sow*, p. 151; for Monterey: Walter Evans Hoadley, "A Study of One Hundred Seventy Self-Resettled Agricultural Families, Monterey, California, 1939" (Master's thesis, University of California, Berkeley, 1938), p. 58; For Stanislaus: Lillian Creisler, "Little Oklahoma, or, The Airport Community" (Master's thesis, University of California, Berkeley, 1939), p. 11.

70. Paul Landis, "Social Aspects of Farm Labor in the Pacific States," *Rural Sociology* 3 (December 1938): 422.

71. Ibid.

72. "Minutes of Farm Bureau Federation," La Follette Committee, *Hearings*, Part 73, p. 26,833.

73. *Bakersfield Californian*, December 16, 1935; *Happy Valley Weekly*, March 4, 1939; Testimony of Pink Allen, Tolan Committee, *Hearings*, Part 5, pp. 2,137-2,144.

74. "Notes from a conversation with Frank Kerr, October 16, 1940," McWilliams Collection.

75. *Covered Wagon News*, September 29, 1939.

76. McWilliams, *Factories in the Field*, pp. 193-198.

77. George Reed, "world's champion cotton picker" (he had picked 910

pounds in 9 hours in Decatur, Texas, in 1925), had been making annual treks to California's fields for years. "California cotton," he averred, "is easier to pick than Eastern cotton." Even Reed, however, could not have used his prowess to achieve wealth. His average "good pick," 500-600 pounds a day, would have brought wages of $3.75-$6.00. *Bakersfield Californian*, September 19, 1934; McWilliams, *Factories in the Field*, pp. 194-195.

78. *San Francisco Chronicle*, February 23, 1938.

79. Testimony of Mr. Derryberry, Tolan Committee, *Hearings*, Part 6, p. 2,210.

80. Khyber Forrester, "Trek to California Cotton Fields," *Nation's Business* 26 (May 1938): 48; La Follette Committee, *Hearings*, Part 51, p. 18,600; Carey McWilliams, "The Joads on Strike," *Nation*, 149 (November 4, 1939): 488-489; *San Francisco Chronicle*, February 23, 1938; "Material on Migrants, March 9, 1940," memorandum, Farm Security Administration Collection, Carton 2, Folder 72.

81. Fred Ross to Henderson, September 28, 1939, United States Department of Agriculture, Agriculture Stabilization and Conservation Commission Papers, Record Group 145, Federal Records Center, San Francisco, 36,880 (hereafter referred to as USDA ASCC Collection).

2

The Okie Impact

"Every where I go I hear nothing but the migrant problem," a concerned Californian wrote in 1940.[1] But, in one sense, there was no migrant problem; there were, rather, California problems made visible by the coming of the Okies. By displacing the Mexican labor force on California's farms, the Okies exposed an agricultural system that had existed for three-quarters of a century, but had lain hidden because its victims were alien, nonwhite, and thus unseen. The migrant problem rose and fell, not only because the Okies dislocated the economy, but because, for a brief few years, they provided a superb foil for political conflicts tearing at the state.

California's industrialized agriculture, born in the years immediately following the Civil War, was, for its time, both anomalous and a foretaste of things to come for American agriculture. From the beginning, no family-sized farms worked by an extra hand or two at harvest time dominated California's agricultural landscape. Nor were California's farms fashioned after the Southern postbellum model; they were not plantations broken into cropper units or worked by resident laborers. They were, rather, factories in the fields,[2] cultivated by migratory laborers who miraculously turned up for the harvest and disappeared once the crops were laid by. This agricultural pattern was produced by a combination of land monopolization, the necessity for expensive irrigation, and the availability of a floating supply of cheap migratory labor.

When the United States took possession of California in 1846, its decision to respect previously existing land grants determined the future of land tenure in the state. The Spaniards had been niggardly, issuing only thirty grants in the region; but the Mexican authorities, during the months just prior to transfer to the United States, connived with American speculators in a fantastic land boondoggle, issuing many fraudulent grants. The critical aspect of this fraud was "not that settlers were swindled and huge profits made, but that the grants were not broken up."[3] Intensive crops, cultivated and irrigated upon the immense ranches which evolved from these grants, became the model for the state's growing agricultural regions.

Three lush and fertile inland valleys dominate California's agriculture. Virtually two-thirds of the state's interior, from Chico in the north to Bakersfield in the south, comprises the great Central Valley, divided into the valleys of the Sacramento and the San Joaquin. The Sacramento Valley is humid and can sustain crops naturally; the San Joaquin Valley, however, requires expensive irrigation—a good deal of it supplied at public expense—for cultivating its year-round crops. Even the San Joaquin's fertility pales before that of the state's southernmost tip, the Imperial Valley, one huge garden, reclaimed from desert by water imported from other states, so hot that even its residents shun it most of the year. Turn off the Imperial's water supply, and her crops would die overnight. So long as the canals flow, she supplies harvests unparalleled elsewhere. These three valleys, and smaller growing regions—east and north of Los Angeles, around Monterey-Salinas, the tiny Napa and Livermore valleys famed for their wines—have yielded rich profits since the Civil War. In the wheat bonanzas of the 1870s (one wheat farm consisted of 57,000 acres), then in fruit, followed at the turn of the century by sugar beets and finally, beginning in the 1920s, in cotton, the state flourished. By 1930, over 180 different farm products grew in California, maturing throughout the year in the state's croplands.

There had been small family homestead farms in California for nearly a hundred years but they could not, and never did, dominate the state's agriculture. Corporate farms drew the bulk of profit and wielded the political and economic power inherent in the state's major industry. The costs of irrigation, coupled with the preexistent pattern of land tenure, demanded large-scale corporation farming. And—what concerns us here—intensive crops cultivated upon corporation farms required armies of migratory labor.

In the 1870s, wheat, the first of California's bonanza crops, collapsed in the wake of drought and depression. Growers sought and found a new, more profitable cash crop in fruit orchards. Fruit, however, could not be harvested by a few men operating machinery. The crop must be handpicked quickly, before it falls from the trees or dies on the vine, individually packed, and shipped. Without a plentiful supply of labor to perform these tasks, fruit, and later vegetables, would not be feasible crops. The conversion from wheat to fruit was a critical moment in California's agricultural history, begetting a pattern of labor relations that persists today. Except during harvest or thinning-time, the crops require little labor, and the agricultural regions seem deserted; an occasional outcropping of farm buildings is visible along the rural roads but the familiar American agricultural landscape of frequent homes, fences, and rusting machinery is nonexistent in, say, the San Joaquin Valley. But during harvests, the fields come alive with the thousands of migrants who pick the crops and then move on. Indeed, chroniclers of California's agricultural history have suggested that the continuation of the pattern of land tenure in the state has been "a direct response to the volume and the supply of agricultural labor."[4] Further, they maintain, intensive agriculture, coupled with irrigation and requiring large numbers of hand laborers, has been responsible for the growth in California of a "semi-industrialized rural Proletariat."[5]

Hundreds of volumes have explored the history of the urban industrial worker from 1870 to 1930. Few, however, have investigated the history of agricultural labor during the same epoch. Yet the system of migratory labor that developed in California harbored for these sixty years nearly every problem to which urban labor was subject, with the sole qualification that work and housing conditions, market instability, and exploitation of labor were even worse in California's fields than in many of the nation's cities.

Even more than in urban mass-production industries, intensive agriculture found in wages a flexible cost which, in hard times, could be manipulated to insure continued profit. Irrigation, land, and machinery costs, on the other hand, were relatively inflexible. Squeezed, like other American farmers, by the competitive advantages of industry during the postbellum years, California's growers kept agricultural wages low. Were wages occasionally to rise, surpluses of field labor nonetheless kept annual earnings of farm migrants below subsistence. Demand requirements for perishable crops can fluctuate on a day-to-day basis. A favorable market for California lettuce meant high lettuce-picking wages. It also meant, however, that growers must immediately harvest the crop with every available laborer. Growers, therefore, preferred that a large number of unemployed migrants be concentrated in the agricultural regions during harvest periods. The total cost of picking the crop was divided among the workers, and wages fluctuated inversely with the size of the total labor force. Low wages and labor surpluses in California were the rule, and the ethnic composition of the labor force enhanced the ability of growers to continue the exploitation of agricultural migrants.

The immigrants who supplied cheap labor surpluses in America's cities were not, to be sure, Anglo-Saxon Protestant stock. But they were mostly white and European. From the beginning, California's farm labor force was neither white nor European nor "American." Until the 1930s, two streams of migratory agricultural labor comprised California's harvest force. On the one hand was a sprinkling of single men, white American professional agricultural labor known as tramps and noted in the 1870s by Henry George and in the 1890s by Frank Norris. These were men who, after 1906, would help swell the ranks of the IWW, following the crops via freight, their red cards supplying free rides. Of far greater numerical importance than these bindle stiffs, however, were the nonwhite battalions who had picked California's lush harvests since the 1870s.

Had a plentiful supply of labor not been available, growers could not have converted their wheat fields into fruit orchards and vegetable gardens in the 1870s. Fortuitously for them, such a supply was ready and willing in the Chinese, who, by pouring into the rural regions, began a fifty-year flirtation between California's growers and aliens.

The docile Chinese in the fields were cherished by growers; they were all one could ask of agricultural migrant labor. But not all Californians had the same attitude. Years of anti-Chinese agitation in the state ended in 1893 and 1894 when violence and social pressures from rioting urban workers forced growers to end their reliance upon "John Chinaman." With the coming of beet sugar during the same decade, however, Japanese laborers obviated the need for their Chinese predecessors and, by 1909, 300,000 of them were cultivating California's beet sugar crops.[6] The Japanese were accepted by the Californians because, unlike the Chinese, they did not immediately settle in large aggregations and were less visible than the latter. But the Japanese desired, and soon obtained, land of their own and in turn became prey to a new wave of anti-Oriental hysteria.

In the 1910s, hoping to replace the now-hated Japanese, growers experimented with Hindus and with European immigrants, notably Portuguese and Italian. Their numbers were minimal, however, and, in the 1920s, as cotton was developing into a major crop, Mexican labor, augmented by gangs of Filipinos, became the mainstay of the state's agricultural army. At least 150,000 Mexicans—the Okies' immediate predecessors in the fields—were following California's crops in the Normalcy years.[7]

Growers found in the Mexicans a splendid labor supply. The *bracero*, whether Mexican or Mexican-American, knew the state's diverse crops, and handled cotton, fruit, sugar beets, and vegetables with great skill. While the Midwest's farmers suffered a depression in the grain market, California's reaped profit from the changing eating habits of the American people. Fruits, vegetables, and other perishables picked by Mexicans and shipped east brought profit to the growers and revenue to the state. Required only during harvest time, the Mexicans during off-season slipped away to Mexican towns on the outskirts of major cities like Fresno, Bakersfield, and especially Los Angeles, and went on relief.[8] During the 1920s, Los Angeles' Mexicans were studied, analyzed, and "Americanized" by social workers as few other groups in the state's history, and agriculturists favorable to Mexican labor became concerned over the "habit" of relief and what some noted as an unfamiliar "surliness" developing among them.[9] But the Mexicans were, for all that, bringing wealth to the state, and, for the prosperity decade, that was sufficient justification for retaining the Mexican-dominated agricultural labor system.

The onset of depression intervened and rapidly transformed the situation. In tight economic times, California's cities could not tolerate the relief-harvest labor-relief cycle that developed in prosperous times among the Mexicans. In 1930, urban relief authorities, especially in Los Angeles, embarked upon a program of voluntary repatriation for Mexicans and Mexican-Americans who chose to accept a free ride to Mexico City. At $14.70 per capita, repatriation was a bargain for the state. For the Mexicans, spurred by rumors of agrarian reforms by Mexico's perennial revolution, a free ride home seemed a welcome respite from hard times. From February 1931 to early 1933, the repatriation of Mexicans removed between 50,000 and 75,000 of the now-unwelcome group. By 1937, an estimated 150,000 Mexicans had returned home.[10] Simultaneously, the depression restricted the flow of new Mexican migrants into the United States: the first half of 1930 saw only one-fifteenth the normal annual Mexico–United States immigration of the 1920s.[11]

Neither the decline of Mexican immigration nor the repatriation decimated California's Mexican population; the majority remained. But for California's growers, the decline in total numbers brought concern. No sooner had the repatriation begun than agricultural journals noted "anxiety in numerous sections of the state. . . . It is reported that Mexican laborers are returning to Mexico at the rate of 10,000 per month, one of the greatest migrations ever witnessed. . . . It is feared that severe labor shortages will prevail in the cotton, fruit, and field crop districts this summer." Anticipated labor shortages did not develop in 1930 and 1931: there remained in the state many more Mexican laborers than growers required even at peak harvest times.[12] By mid-1933 and early 1934, however, both production in the fields and the supply of labor were diminishing. From a peak in 1933 of 186 workers for every 100 available agricultural jobs the harvest labor force declined by a quarter in 1934 to 142 men per 100 jobs, many of whom preferred to remain on relief rather than pick the 1934 crop at low wages.[13] These combined effects of repatriation and depression wage cuts persuaded the farmer that he was faced with an actual under-supply.[14]

Coming as it did, at precisely the moment when Mexican field workers had organized themselves into unions and gone on strike in the fields, bringing great anxiety to the growers, this contraction of the labor force might have had far-reaching results for California agriculture. As even a committee of the state chamber of commerce admitted, the increased planting of cotton during the 1930s, in view of a declining labor supply, might have accorded the migrant workers a "substantial increase in their annual earnings."[15] Or California's growers, conversely, might have turned more rapidly to mechanization in crops requiring less intensive manual labor, thus ending by quick, if unintentional surgery, the desperate social problem of migratory labor. These alternatives were cut short by the migration of the Okies, which so affected the labor market that liberal writers were, at first, hostile to the new migrants. "The growers were in desperate straits," one wrote, "until drought and depression intervened to turn the tide in their favor by started [sic] the great trek of the Dust Bowlers."[16] The migration foreclosed the possibility of higher wages suggested by the chamber of commerce. It was in agriculture, therefore, that, by preventing potential change, the Okies wrought their first major effect upon the state.

The Okies left their home states and followed Route 66 through New Mexico and into Arizona, where they often stopped for a short season in the cotton fields. Then they drove on into California, armed only with the name of one of a hundred valley towns—Delano, Shafter, Wasco, Arvin—where friends or relatives had already "lit." Sometimes they lacked even a destination other than the "cotton fields." For these, the highway pointed the route. From its desert entry into the state, Route 66 climbed northwest into the southern half of the San Joaquin Valley, where the cotton grew, and there the new arrivals stopped, swelling the population of earlier migrants already camped on ditch banks or on vacant lots outside the towns, in grower-owned shacks or, after 1936, in the federal migratory camps. Settled for the moment, they sought out the local growers' employment service or showed up early at the fields for anticipated work. The cotton picked, they drove their jalopies north to the Sacramento Valley or south to the Imperial, learning along the way how to pick the unfamiliar citrus, peach, grape, potato, or sugar beet crops. In this manner, they quickly supplanted the Mexican agricultural workers.

Wherever the Okies went within the state, their increasing dominance in the agricultural labor force was quickly noted. In late 1935, for example, the San Joaquin Valley bore the main brunt of the Okies. "North of the Tehachapi," Paul Taylor testified at the time, "I have never seen so many whites in California agriculture in my life as this year from Kern County up."[17] Not only the San Joaquin, but also the Sacramento Valley to the north received a flood of migrants so great that one of the first two federal migrant camps would be built near Marysville—Yuba City, the hub of that growing region. Even in the Imperial Valley, where whites were always considered unsuitable for "squat labor as in general they are too tall . . . clumsier and do much damage," the Okies moved in, supplanting Mexican and Filipino vegetable workers.[18]

Almost from the beginning, California's growers knew that major changes were taking place in their labor force. They were, after all, the group that first came into contact with the migrants. A Modesto farmer, for example, who had used only local labor in past years noted a sudden change: "about one hundred workers are employed on our farm. . . . However, recently the population has changed—new-comers from the Midwest and South constitute most of our labor supply." [19] Asked in 1937 to describe the "most significant factors affecting the quantity and quality of the agricultural labor supply," 75 percent of growers in the San Joaquin Valley, 70 percent in the Sacramento, and 52 percent in southern California placed "migration from other states" at the head of the list.[20]

Of immediate significance for growers was the question whether the Okies would meet the needs for an adequate labor supply: would they enter the fields in sufficiently large numbers to keep agricultural wages low? And, as importantly, could they be relied upon, like the Mexicans, to turn up when required and then disappear? Officials of the FSA found strong fears among Imperial Valley growers that the new migratory workers were "agricultural workers in the sense that they are only trying to work their way westward."[21] Bemused, FSA sought advice from State Senator John Phillips from the Imperial Valley. Phillips' response merely echoed the growers' concern: "When you speak of the changing migratory labor, that is changing from Mexican to white ... much of the labor ... is not what we could call genuine labor. It is merely a transitory group coming in from the east into the state which would seem destined to become the poorhouse of America."[22]

Nonetheless, from 1935 to 1937, the Okie labor supply exceeded the hopes and calmed the fears of California agriculture. Slowly recovering from production lows in 1933 and 1934, crops increased in value and volume. The available labor supply rose, however, at a far more rapid rate, each year exceeding the demand for labor by a larger proportion.[23] Growers admitted only backhandedly that the Okies were supplying their labor needs, while simultaneously denying that the influx of migrants was creating an oversupply. Prior to the 1937 cotton harvest, when a Los Angeles relief official warned that 70,000 destitute Okies were camped in the San Joaquin, the manager of the grower-controlled San Joaquin Valley Agricultural Labor Bureau scoffed at the claim and announced that "there will be little surplus labor when cotton and grapes are in full swing."[24] Despite such assertions, especially during the 1935 harvest when growers claimed there had been an actual labor shortage, the ever-increasing migrant stream clearly satisfied the growers, especially in the San Joaquin. In their yearly reports, the San Joaquin Valley Agricultural Labor Bureau's directors gave clear indication that the Okies were indeed fulfilling the state's requirements. In 1935, for example, they claimed that "local labor" (i.e., Mexicans) was inadequate and only "outside labor," brought in from other portions of the state, ended the undersupply. The harvests of 1936, 1937, and 1938, however, saw "adequate" supplies. In 1936 "it was extremely difficult to expedite local labor from labor centers and the labor that came voluntarily from the drought area came at the opportune time." In 1937 "we were ... especially fortunate in having sufficient for all our agricultural operations exception [sic] during the peak of the cotton harvest. . . . However, a large influx of cotton pickers from the drought area in Oklahoma and Arkansas, helped the situation at the opportune time." And, in 1938, when—as will be seen—an immense oversupply of migrants brought misery to the Okies and national attention to the problem, the bureau was still alleging local shortages, but grudgingly admitted the value of the Okie to California agriculture:

"Acute shortages of labor have been experienced up to within the last two years, however, there appears now to have been *some reversal* [my italics] of the situation due to the migration of the white laborer from the Southern Great Plains."[25]

In claiming labor shortages despite the Okie influx, the bureau and farmers who echoed its sentiments were not wholly disingenuous. Agriculture had become so accustomed to the "fluid Mexican workers who miraculously appeared on harvest day" that an efficient method of recruiting and transporting labor to the exact point where and when it was needed had never developed.[26] The San Joaquin Valley Agricultural Labor Bureau had, in fact, consistently maintained that such a system was desperately needed and long overdue. In each of its annual reports, the bureau's manager recommended that "proper steps be taken to prepare a program of labor reports for different crops where seasonal labor will be employed, so that when demands for labor are made, it may be possible to supply our growers without loss of time."[27]

In another way, however, users of harvest labor were being disingenuous. In justifying their use of Okie labor when local labor was unavailable, they blamed relief distributed to the locals, Mexican or white, for keeping them from the fields.[28] What they neglected to admit was the critical role the Okie influx played in keeping wages so low that local residents actually lost money if they went off relief in order to pick the crops. Had there been no Okie influx, wages in California agriculture likely would have risen. As events turned out, the size of the Okie influx allowed growers to hold farm wages down. Kern County's Health Department frankly admitted, for example, that 1937's Okie influx had provided "only enough surplus labor to maintain prevailing wage structure."[29]

A widespread assumption that Okies would not accept "Mexican wages" was but a strand in the fabric of California's unconscious racism. As one angry Democrat had written to Philip Bancroft, grower and Republican senatorial candidate in 1938: "The only reason you do not want farm labor organized is that you will probably have to pay WHITE AMERICAN CITIZENS decent wages, instead of hiring Orientals. SHAME."[30] This assumption was incorrect. The Okies did accept lower wages—wages that Mexicans, in fact, had refused. The new arrivals, disoriented, penniless, and unable to receive state relief for a year, accepted any wage in the cotton fields. In early 1936, when Mexicans in the upper San Joaquin Valley were threatening a strike for wages higher than the twenty-five cents an hour being paid there, migrants in the federal camp at Arvin were satisfied with the prevailing wage and, only a "few groups" would have refused twenty cents an hour.[31] In the same year, Oklahomans and Texans "anxious to work" replaced Mexicans in San Bernardino County who "after a taste of relief . . . were neither so efficient nor so anxious to work."[32] A rumor spread that the Hoover Ranch (owned by the family of the ex-President) had corralled on its property a group of new migrants from the southern Great Plains who, the informant feared, would work for anything.[33] In 1938, when the Okie oversupply of labor had brought concern to the state and the nation, growers used low agricultural wages as evidence of their desire for public service. In that year wages were cut from thirty cents to twenty cents per hour on the grounds that there were too many migratory workers from the Midwest and South who must be discouraged by forcing them to work at poor wages.

It was not wholly true that the Okies would "work for anything." The irony of their situation was that California's pittance seemed munificent in contrast with wages or tenant shares in their home states. The Associated Farmers continually emphasized this theme in their publications, as in the following, drawn from an anti-union pamphlet: "Once inside her Cabin, she whispered to me: 'Us folks don't dare talk. We were afraid of what might happen to us. We're glad to get eighty cents a hundred. Cotton picking here ain't like it was down in Texas. You can pick a sackful of California cotton in half the time it takes back home.' " Neutral sources reported similar comments, as did *The New York Times* correspondent who asked an Okie if he intended returning home. "Ahm agoin back to Oklahomy? I should say not mistah. Why this yere country is the promised land . . . we've made more money in the spud season than we made in three years back home. . . . Believe it or not, last yeah I made $240 cash money."[34] Another Oklahoman, Mr. Higgenbottom, told the Tolan Committee that he was glad he'd come to California. "You see, probably the cheaper wages there drives people out. . . .You see, the wages in Oklahoma—they are so scarce and there is so little, you know."[35]

Even the argument that California's wages were higher was not unimpeachable. Unquestionably, hourly or piece-rate wages were higher in California than in Texas or Oklahoma, and it was to this fact that the Okies honestly—and the growers sometimes guilefully—testified. But wages had to be amortized over the year, and California supplied fewer day's work for each Okie. The cost of living was higher, and transportation from job to job took still another bite from the paycheck.[36] Finally, growers well understood that the swollen labor supply furnished considerable room for maneuver in the area of wages. When the manager of the immense DiGiorgio farms refused to pay the prevailing wage of thirty cents an hour in the Arvin area of Kern County, he utilized popular fears of a grower conspiracy to strengthen his point. He "reminded his hearers that an advertising campaign in the Oklahoma and Arkansas press would bring out, on short notice, hundreds and probably thousands of workers from those states and that these workers would be very willing and quite happy to work for the 25 cents per hour scale."[37]

For the depression decade from 1929 to 1939, the migrant influx retarded the recovery of wage levels that should have accompanied the reviving farm income of the same period. California's agricultural income had suffered considerably during the initial stages of the depression. In 1932, the index of agricultural income, using 1924-1929 averages as a base figure of 100, stood at 60.[38] Beginning in 1933, however, farm income slowly began to increase. In 1937, a high-yield year, the index was 112, and by 1939, in spite of the 1937 recession and its effects, the index was 94.4. Farm wages did not, however, keep pace with farm income. In the bumper year 1937, for example, farm wages, using the same base period, were only 65 percent of what they had been in the years 1924-1929; and in 1939, they declined to 59 percent. Even making allowance for a 25 percent increase in productivity per worker that developed during the decade, it is clear that in relation to his employer, the agricultural laborer was earning far less in the late 1930s than in the late 1920s. His employer's income, on the other hand, was usually near, and sometimes above, that of the Normalcy years. In effect, California's growers recovered at the expense of the Okie migrants who picked the increasingly profitable crops.

As the above figures indicate, productivity per worker had increased during the decade, even while the Okies were supplying a growing excess of labor. Each year, more disinherited southern Great Plains migrants showed up in rural California to fill a declining number of paid jobs. Growers were satisfied with the labor oversupply and took advantage of it. In late 1936, for example, the Associated Farmers officially replied to charges that they had "met" the Okies "with hatred." The organization countered with an assertion that farmers "liked" the new "citizenry" from Oklahoma: "They have come here hopefully. They have brought their families. They want work. They will prove to be good citizens."[39] The seemingly beneficient influx of Okies nonetheless contained a hidden liability that, in 1938, would undermine the growers' satisfaction with this new wave of migrants, forcing them to take a leading role in political and social action to stem the influx from the Great Plains.

In order to understand fully California's migrant problem, one must realize that this was really two overlapping problems. On the one hand, the migrant problem was the response of California to the agricultural labor system that had developed, unnoticed save by a few, during the sixty years since 1870. There was, however, another migrant problem attendant upon the Okies' influx. The Okies were not bindle stiffs or single men. They were families, and they wanted to relocate permanently in California. They had never intended to become migratory agricultural laborers, carrying their few belongings from place to place, incessantly following the crops in a never-ending cycle of grinding harvest labor. Drawn by the promise of a new start in California's fertile valleys, they settled in the state's farming areas. As their numbers increased, they threatened to become a serious social and political dislocation in counties that could not possibly absorb a new population of such magnitude within sufficient time to avoid misery for the newcomers and expense for the older residents.

Unlike the Mexicans or the Filipinos, they did not disappear after harvest; they stayed. Unlike the Mexicans, they were not swarthy, not unseen; their poverty in the shacktown or ditch-bank settlements could not be ignored. By 1937, the Okies had become a local embarrassment, by 1938 a state concern, and by 1939, with the publication of *The Grapes of Wrath*, a national scandal. This was California's other migrant problem. Had the Okie been simply an agricultural laborer, his coming would not have convulsed the state as it did. That he was both agricultural laborer *and* new, poverty-stricken resident of the rural regions was the cause of the panic that gripped the "older" Californians, and threatened to drive a wedge between the growers and the valley towns that had, heretofore, coexisted in a tight symbiosis.

It has been demonstrated that the Okie influx, in absolute numerical terms, was not extraordinary. The net increase of some 300,000 or 400,000 erstwhile southern Great Plains people over the course of a decade was not, in itself, cause for alarm. Had they been distributed proportionally throughout the state's urban centers, even during the depression's dislocation, their coming would probably have gone unnoticed. Indeed, some Okies did move into Los Angeles and the Bay Area, and these metropolitan centers absorbed them in silence.[40] Even if inflated border counts of "persons entering the state in need of manual employment," or the fearful guesses of some that the influx was approaching 500,000 or 600,000 had been more accurate than the census returns, the total migration would still have fallen far short of the easily absorbed population increases of the 1920s and 1940s. One could conclude, therefore, that the Okie influx was unworthy of note; that it was a chimera, a myth fostered by radicals to discredit the growers or, conversely, by growers to discredit the Olson or Roosevelt administrations. Growers, the argument might continue, blamed the influx of Okies upon high relief payments, and radicals saw grower conspiracies to advertise for cheap labor, both for purely political reasons.

Such a conclusion would be incorrect. The Okies did not distribute themselves proportionally within the state, nor was their trek spread evenly across the decade. The majority of the refugees came to California between 1935 and 1937. This three-year period accounted for nearly half the entire influx for the decade and, consequently, the migration seemed larger than it actually was.[41] Further, since they had come to pick cotton, or to get a farm of their own, the great majority of them descended upon the state's agricultural counties, bringing with them poverty, and political and social habits different from those of the residents.

The Okies who left the Great Plains during the depression and who resided in California in 1940 were but a third of the total number of migrants to California during the decade.[42] One hundred eighty thousand of them, however, had taken up residence in agricultural regions of the state, and most of these, in turn, in the San Joaquin Valley. Small in absolute terms, the number was nonetheless large in relative terms, and herein lay the basis for the San Joaquin's, and to a lesser extent, the Sacramento Valley's anxiety. As Table 2 indicates, the agricultural counties received relative population increases far larger than the more diverse urban regions. During the 1920s, the cities, notably Los Angeles, had been the fastest growing areas in the state. The Okie migration reversed that trend. From 1935 to 1940, only one San Joaquin Valley county—Fresno—received smaller proportional population gains than Los Angeles; and Yuba County in the Sacramento Valley, and heart of the north's growing regions, gained fully half again

TABLE 2

POPULATION INCREASES, SELECTED COUNTIES, 1935-1940

County	Population change	Per cent Increase
Kern (SJV)	52,554	63.6
Yuba (Sacto V)	5,703	50.3
Madera (SJV)	6,150	35.8
Kings (SJV)	9,783	38.5
Tulare (SJV)	29,710	38.4
San Diego	79,689	38.0
Monterey	19,327	36.0
Stanislas (SJV)	18,225	32.2
San Joaquin (SJV)	31.267	30.4
Merced (SJV)	10,240	27.9
Los Angeles	577,151	26.1
Fresno (SJV)	34,186	23.7
San Bernardino	27,208	20.3
Sacramento	28,334	20.0
Santa Barbara	5,388	8.3
Alameda	38,128	8.0
San Francisco	142	0.8

Source: Commonwealth Club of California, *The Population of California* (San Francisco, 1946), pp. 19-20.

the population it had in 1930. In all, the Okie migration demanded that the San Joaquin and the Sacramento valleys absorb, during the depression years, twice as many migrants as had settled in them during the prior decade.[43]

For a variety of reasons the figures above, compiled from the Census of 1940, were probably conservative. For one, the defense boom had already begun in the major urban centers of the state, and Okies who had swollen the agricultural labor supply in 1937 or 1938 were beginning the trek that would assimilate them into the cities in the war years. Further, it was not inconceivable that census takers might have missed large numbers of Okies camped in squalor on the ditch banks in the more remote sections of the agricultural valleys. In any case, other estimates, taken earlier than 1940, supplied even larger rates of population growth, especially for the five upper (southern) counties of the San Joaquin Valley, which were the center of cotton cultivation in California. One compilation presented to the La Follette Committee estimated that Tulare, Madera, and Kern counties had each experienced 50 percent population increases; another survey added Kings to the counties undergoing 50 percent increases and estimated a 70 percent growth for Kern.[44] It was, in all, virtually impossible to assess accurately the migrants' numbers. A local census taken at the height of harvest season could, for example, count authentic migratory workers, as well as resident Okies, and come up with horrendous statistics, as when one writer terrified Madera's population with the following: "In 1930 the population of Madera County was 17,164; today it is around 35,000. Most of this increase has come since 1935 and most of the new residents are migrants. In other words Madera now has a footloose population approximately equal to its resident population."[45]

It would have been difficult for the state's undiversified agricultural counties to accommodate population increases of this magnitude even had the migrants been financially solvent. Their poverty, however, forced the migrants to settle temporarily under conditions inferior even to those they had left in Oklahoma or Arkansas. For those migrants who were fortunate enough to find work in the fields quickly, grower-maintained living quarters, squalid as most were, provided a measure of shelter at least during the working season. Some of the others found decent, if plain, housing in the federal government's rapidly expanding migratory labor camps. But the great majority of the newcomers found shelter where they could. These migrants pitched their tents along the irrigation ditches, in empty fields near the large ranches, and in private trailer camps. As the migration reached its peak in 1936 and 1937, the ditch bank settlements grew in size, number, and squalor, and finally became a menace to the Okies themselves and to the resident populations nearby.

The ditch bank settlements are not easily described. Journalists visiting them sought adjectives commensurate with the misery, ultimately falling back upon the photographs of Dorothea Lange whose camera captured with documentary ruthlessness the poverty sprouting in California's fertile valleys.[46] A journalist traveling through the state in 1937, for example, discovered "the haven of the fruit tramps in California's 'peach bowl' [in] the willow and cottonwood groves along the Yuba and Feather Rivers near the twin cities of Marysville and Yuba City." Disturbed by the poverty he had witnessed in the Sacramento Valley, he moved south to the San Joaquin and found that the northern region's camps were "clean and respectable" compared to conditions in Kern County. "There," he continued, "in the dry Kern Lake bottom, Tuckerton, Buttonwillow and Buena Park—migrants live in almost unimagineable [sic] filth—festering sores of miserable humanity."[47]

Journalists, growers and their opponents, liberals and conservatives, all who visited the ditch banks agreed at least that living conditions were loathsome. "Hungry 'Dust Bowl' refugees . . . are reportedly living in the fields and woods 'like animals,' " reported the *Berkeley Gazette* in 1937. Actress Helen Gahagan, later to be elected congresswoman from California, told relief investigators after visiting the Sacramento Valley camps: "I went around in a sick daze for hours after witnessing unimaginable suffering.[48]

Filth and squalor among the Okies was upsetting, for some even nauseating, but for the farmers who struck in anger at those who laid the blame for these conditions upon them, it was explainable. "The conditions," Lee A. Stone, Madera's controversial health director affirmed, "are not to be blamed on the growers, but on the people themselves."[49] The Okies had lived in squalor for generations, he continued, and were a degraded American stock. One of John Steinbeck's critics admitted that the Okie children in the camps were "probably hungry" and frequently developed high fever and dysentery. But, after all, these were simply the results of eating fresh fruit among people whose traditional fare was beans and fried dough. When visiting these camps, he continued, one should "keep his feet on the ground and remain clear in the brainpan," or he might "go off raving mad, write another 'Grapes of Wrath,' and thus falsely indict the whole California system of Agriculture."[50]

These explanations, even had they been accurate, did not remove the problem. In any event, the camps menaced the Californians as well as the migrants. Typhoid was not uncommon along the ditch banks where pure water was unavailable and the barest sanitary facilities nonexistent. Smallpox epidemics broke out in camps in Madera, Tulare, and Imperial; tuberculosis, malaria, and pneumonia were endemic.[51] None of these diseases asked of their victims whether they were Okies or "old Californians," and the possibility that contagion would spread from the ditch banks into the towns and cities brought prompt action by county health departments. As early as 1934, local officials had recognized the potential health hazard inherent in the ditch bank settlement, and had begun a systematic campaign of evicting migrants and destroying their camps.[52] Kern County's medical officials led the state in programs for eliminating the unsanitary camps, and Madera's Lee Stone, armed with a violent prejudice against the Okies, followed suit. By 1937, both counties had vacated large numbers of Okies from unsanitary camps.[53] Well-intentioned as these programs were, they could not solve the problem. Evicted Okies with no funds simply moved down the road, or into another, less concerned county, where they pitched new camps. And, of course, the constant influx of new migrants in 1936 and 1937 made a Hydra of the ditch banks: "Old" Okies, evicted, might move into the towns; newcomer Okies would take their place. The efforts of harried public health officials prevented the outbreak of serious epidemics. The final solution to the ditch bank camp problem was, however, supplied by the Okies themselves.

The ditch banks were dramatic evidence of the Okies' distress, but they were not the most significant form of settlement among the migrants. They were, rather, way stations along the Okies' road to permanent residence in the agricultural regions, especially in the San Joaquin Valley. The single, fundamental, irreducible fact about the

Okies was that they successfully resisted the inherent tendency of California's agricultural system to force them into permanent intrastate wandering, following the state's crops. Back in the southern Great Plains, the Okies had been permanent residents of agricultural counties. Even those who were agricultural laborers had a place to "light," and they retained that pattern in California. The dual meaning of the word "migrant"—it can mean "endlessly wandering agricultural laborer" or "person relocating from one state to another"—confused California for a time when it confronted the migrant Okies. The Okies were persons moving from one state to another; they were also agricultural laborers. For the most part, however, they were not "*migratory* agricultural laborers" in the traditional sense of the word. They did follow crops, they toured the length and breadth of the great Central Valley during harvest seasons. But—and here lies the key to California's "other migrant problem"—they retained a permanent residence in one of the towns in the agricultural regions. "Few have joined the ranks of the 'fruit tramp' and toted their family broods in rattletrap cars," noted one reporter, and Kern's health department explained the novelty of the Okies quite clearly when it reported to the county's board of supervisors: "Growers have lost their fluid Mexican workers who miraculously appeared on harvest day and silently slipped away after their work was done . . . the large family of the Southwesterner harvests the cotton of the Kern Valley; when the cotton harvest is over, the family hangs on."[54]

Because the Okies came permanently to relocate in California, they came in families; and, because they came in families, it was inevitable that they would ultimately establish residence in or near the rural cities. The breadwinner might migrate during the harvest season, returning home weeks or months later, but a residential base for these forays was necessary. Wives, after all, became pregnant; there were children to tend; and, even more important, the children went to school.

The Okies resented being called "migratory workers" even when they did migrate within the valleys during harvests.[55] When John Steinbeck, before writing *The Grapes of Wrath*, produced a series of articles about the new migrants, the *San Francisco News* published the reports under the title "California's Harvest Gypsies." At the Farm Security camp in Arvin, the camp manager was forced to obliterate the title when he distributed the articles to the campers, so furious were they at the implication that they were bindle stiffs no better than the Mexicans or Filipinos.[56] "Plunking down" at first where they could, the Okies soon reasserted their traditional desire to retain a permanent place to live by converting those squatters' camps that were located just outside towns into permanent suburban slums. No longer simply ditch bank collections of tents or lean-tos, the Little Oklahomas that dotted the rural landscapes of the San Joaquin Valley and, to a lesser extent, the Sacramento Valley, were themselves towns, their populations steadily increasing as Okies moved to them from the less-permanent ditch bank settlements farther from town, or from the Farm Security or privately owned agricultural labor camps.

By July 1939, Kern County could announce the total elimination of squatters' camps, but only in part was this the result of a two-year campaign by the county's health officers. A more important reason for the disappearance of the camps was the fact that the "Southwesterner [was] by instinct a home lover and poor fluid laborer."[57] The Okie had not departed Kern. The county had not lost undesirable squatters; it had gained new citizens. The squatters' camps had been replaced by permanent settlements populated almost entirely by recent migrants from the southern Great Plains. Southeast of Bakersfield, two virtually brand-new towns—Lamont and Weedpatch—supplied the DiGiorgio farms with labor. Older cities found new settlements on their outskirts. Delano, Wasco, McFarland, Shafter, Arvin, and the county's metropolis, Bakersfield, each had its Little Oklahoma.[58]

Nor was Kern the sole inheritor of such new settlements. Wherever the large farms attracted labor, there the Okies built new communities. To the north of Kern, Tulare County discovered that the small community of Earlimart had become an Okie town, and that Visalia and Farmersville were gaining new residents in direct proportion to the increase in cotton planting. Madera, Kings, and Fresno counties experienced similar growth in their towns. Outside Stanislaus County's major city, Modesto, an immense Little Oklahoma sprang up. What had been swampland encircling the town's airport now became a community of permanently settled farm laborers. Six miles north of Little Oklahoma, Salida's old residents found themselves far outnumbered by the new Okies.[59]

The development of Okie towns was not confined to the San Joaquin Valley. Other agricultural regions acquired similar but smaller suburban slums. Sacramento, capital of the state and the gateway to the rich northern valley, had given birth early in the depression to Hooverville, populated by unemployed single men. By 1939 Hooverville was well on its way to becoming an Okie town.[60] Marysville—Yuba City had two such Okie settlements, Bull Tract and Live Oak, the latter an entire Pentecostal community, which had migrated en masse from the Southwest.[61]

And, finally, the Okies established communities outside the two major valleys. Salinas had Hebron Heights, otherwise known as Little Oklahoma. Even the garden farms on the outskirts of Los Angeles attracted Okies, and migrant towns could be found at Sawtelle and Bell Gardens. Only in the Imperial Valley did the pattern fail to reproduce itself. There, the Mexican settlement, impermanent and unseen, remained the rule. But the Imperial, after all, had a climate so inhospitable that not even the grower lived there except when it was absolutely necessary, and Okies who had ended their California trek at Brawley generally moved north to settle in the San Joaquin after harvest.[62]

These Okie settlements, and uncounted others in the rural regions, all shared one characteristic with undeviating and almost uncanny similarity. With a rhythm produced by the ability of the migrants to find cash, the ditch banks became communities, integrated, poverty-ridden, and permanent. The journalist Ernie Pyle expressed in a singular manner what many other reporters and social scientists had observed in the Okie towns when he mused in mid-1941 about the question "whatever became of the Okies?"

> They say you can go into a big settlement . . . and you can judge by a man's place to the very month how long he has been here. . . . If he's living in a tent or trailer, he's been here less than six months. If a family is in a garage on the back of a lot, they've been here more than six months. If the garage now houses the car, and the family is in a two room shack in the front of the lot, they've been here more than a year. And if the house has expanded and living is fairly decent, they've been here more than two years.[63]

What Pyle described in 1941 was true of earlier Okie settlements, with one difference: before the coming of the defense boom, Okies had less money and the transitions noted by Pyle took longer. Nonetheless, the conversion from ditch-bank impermanence to residential permanence was inevitable.

The development of the Okie settlements brought a major change in California's relationship to the migrants. "What was once the problem of squatters camps along ditchbanks has now become the problem of the growth of rural and suburban slums."[64] This was the simple manner in which one sociologist put the fact that, after sixty years of disregarding a transient mass of alien male laborers, California's valley cities discovered that profits in agriculture did not always compensate for the human and financial losses that attended the labor system.

There was, paradoxically, no room for the migrants in the immense valleys. The possibilities for small-scale farming were negligible; agriculture required immense expenditures for land and irrigation. Industrial employment opportunities were limited, confined for the most part to canning, processing, and packing the crops grown on the outlying ranches. Depression conditions multiplied the difficulty of assimilating newcomers. What made the problem most pressing, however, was the fact that the Okies were not a typical group of California migrants: they were broke and they were chronically unemployed.[65] It cost public money to provide for them and their contribution to the state's taxable income was, by virtue of the low wages they could earn in the fields, very small. These new settlements affected the older towns in three ways, each of which increased the hostility and the concern of local residents toward the newcomers who now resided on the outskirts of town. The Okies required health services; they sent their children to school, thus increasing taxes required for educational services; and they collected relief.

Frequent raids upon the ditch bank settlements in the San Joaquin Valley counties had eliminated the dangers of epidemics. Communicable disease, however, was but a small part of the migrants' medical problems, and the removal of the ditch banks did little to end malnutrition or to limit costs of medical care for healthy migrants. Public health officers frequently despaired at the inherited dietary habits of the Okies, habits bred of generations of rural poverty in their home states. At the Brawley FSA camp, for example, a twenty-eight-year-old man died of pellagra while government nurses endeavored with little effect to persuade migrant mothers that a steady diet of soda pop was less valuable than milk for their children.[66] Poverty, as well as habit, prevented the migrants from eating meals adequate to provide resistance against minor illness, and the only recourse for sick migrants was to seek aid at county-supported public hospitals.

Illness was not the only physical condition that took Okies to the county hospital. Although they were not more prolific than the resident population, and, indeed, had fewer children per family than the national average, pregnant migrant women had little money for private physicians. In Kern County, in June 1937, 42 percent of the infants born had fathers from the four Okie states. In 1939, Kern's health directors pronounced the migrant use of county medical service "amazing." During the latter year, 75 percent of Okie newborns were delivered, at county expense, at the Kern General Hospital.[67]

Kern had the most enlightened county health department in California's agricultural regions, supplying medical care to anyone in need of prompt treatment, resident and nonresident alike; therefore, it was the most affected in the area of public health. Other counties, too, felt the influx. Madera, whose health director, Lee Stone, spent considerable time complaining about Okie degenerates, took its public-health problems as seriously as did Kern. Because these two counties supplied more inclusive health services to residents as well as Okies than any other county, their health and sanitation budgets doubled from 1935 to 1940. Tulare County's part-time medical staff did creditable work within its limitations. Each of the other San Joaquin Valley counties increased their public health budgets during this five-year period between 30 percent and 50 percent, as did Yuba County in the Sacramento.[68]

Increased public-health costs was not the most burdensome of the problems raised by the coming of the Okies. Of far greater significance, both in terms of county finances and friction between migrants and local populations, was the manner in which the migration affected educational systems in the rural counties. The Okies maintained smaller families than the national average. But, the migration also attracted a higher proportion of young people than the national population contained. Put another way, it might be said that while the Okies had fewer children in each family, there were many more families with children of school age than might be found in a more typical area of the country.

Therefore, the Okie impact upon educational facilities was proportionately larger than their impact upon other public services such as hospitals and prisons.

The migrant problem in the schools was exacerbated by the condition of the Okie children, who could not, for a variety of reasons, appear well-scrubbed, apple-in-hand, and smiling with anticipation in traditional Becky Thatcher fashion on the first day of school. The Okie family tended to settle down in one place, but not without some delay and considerable hardship. Their last months in the Great Plains and their first year in California were unsettled, transient, and characterized by restless scrambling for sufficient funds. Child labor, a matter of necessity rather than habit, was common during this initial stage of resettlement, and California's child-labor laws did not prevent it completely. Observers frequently saw small children dragging cotton sacks through the rows, their average ninety-eight-cents-a-day income contributing "substantially to family earnings." The desperation of the Okie migrants was probably nowhere more evident than in the fact that child labor in some cases "undoubtedly meant the difference between a living wage and relief status."[69] Some Okies reportedly left California to return to Arizona because county authorities in the former were "too strict," keeping children from the fields during the harvest season.[70]

Once settled, the Okies doggedly sought education for their offspring. Their move to California was designed to better their conditions, and schooling for the children was part of that design. Parents in Modesto's Little Oklahoma were "extremely apprehensive lest their children suffer from the same limitations of education that hampered them" and intended to use California's "splendid" educational system.[71] Okie parents at the FSA camps occasionally left their children in the government's care while themselves migrating in search of ripe crops so that the children could attend school. "My mother and father has gone to Idaho to pick spuds" one Okie child wrote to a camp newspaper. "I did not cry the morning they left," she added, and a friend explained, "I will be glad when school starts again. . . . I like to go to school."[72]

From 1935 to 1940, Okie children swelled the school populations in each of the agricultural counties to which their parents had migrated. They brought with them the necessity for increases in county disbursements for education, and, because of their deprivation during the first year or two of migration, they tended to be scholastically retarded by at least one full year. By nearly all measurements, the Okie children were not inferior to California children except that their absence from school had impeded their education; but their greater age at any grade level, coupled with the patterns of prejudice developing against the migrants, led a number of counties to attempt to segregate the Okie children in separate classrooms or in mobile schools, either of which increased still further the costs of education.[73]

County school district supervisors felt themselves harassed, overburdened, and encroached upon by the Okie influx. The case of Porterville's high school was typical. This Tulare County school had boasted for years of its high rating with the state's college system, and many of its students had received scholarships at Stanford and the University of California. "But," the district noted in late 1939, "the situation is rapidly changing. In the school year 1937-38, there were 88 Oklahoma-born students in the high school." The next year, 128 Oklahomans, 48 Arkansans, and 42 Texans swelled the school's Okie population to over 200. Further increases were predicted for the coming year. Teachers were "frantic, trying to teach these incoming migrant children," while simultaneously attempting to retain the earlier standards. Many of the Okie students, they discovered, required extracurricular tutoring. The Porterville school was "always in trouble with its budget." Nonetheless, local folk counted themselves lucky. Porterville was in the county's citrus belt, where fewer Okies settled. They recognized that schools in the neighboring cotton belt were faring worse.[74]

Amid a chorus of complaints from local school trustees, state legislators, and, finally, from the state superintendant of public instruction who dubbed the Okie influx a "calamity" for education in many districts, school taxes rose at a more rapid rate than population in the five counties of the upper San Joaquin. Fresno County's tax bill for schools increased 134 percent; Kings', 282 percent; Madera, Kern, and Tulare counties' school expenses varied between these two extremes. [75] Expense alone did not account for the anxiety raised by the coming of the Okies to the valley's schools. Local residents recognized that the migrants desired to send their children to the schools and feared that improved facilities would attract more migrants to their districts. Since, however, local residents also wanted *their* own children to benefit from superior educational facilities, they were confronted with a dilemma.[76] This dilemma, in turn, increased the irritation that communities in the rural regions experienced when the Okies arrived.

The higher tax rates that greeted rural Californians each year in the San Joaquin and Sacramento valleys were blamed almost totally upon the migrant influx. The state chamber of commerce asserted that "not all of the increases [in school costs, social welfare aids, hospitals, health, and sanitation] can be attributed to migrants, but most of them were caused by migration," and the valley's inhabitants accepted the argument.[77] Despite frequent complaints about the relationship between the migrants and increasing tax assessments, there existed considerable evidence that the migrants' effect upon local taxes was overemphasized in the public mind. One obvious explanation, neglected by valley residents, linked rising tax rates to returning prosperity during the years of slow recovery from depression lows. Tax rolls, assessments, and revenues all reached a nadir in 1933. By 1938 and 1939, however, county residents were capable of bearing higher assessments, and improved services purchased with taxes were now available to residents. These accounted for a great deal of the increased tax load. More subtle arguments demonstrated that, in one sense, the coming of the distressed migrants proved a bargain, possibly an asset, to allegedly harassed agricultural counties. Property taxes, for example, did not rise in proportion to increased expenditures: state and federal relief grants and subventions migrated to these counties with the Okies. Each dollar of federal or state relief entering the rural regions was a redistribution in their favor. Further, relief funds spent by the migrants on food or lodging contributed to business recovery in the valleys.[78]

Finally, while it was undoubtedly the case that local school requirements expanded to mammoth proportions in direct relation to the Okie influx, even here the issue was more complex than it appeared on the surface. The state assumed a large measure of education costs financed through the sales tax, and the PWA supplied many new school buildings at the nation's expense. In short, older residents in California's agricultural communities, faced with the demand for expansion of public facilities, made two errors: they overlooked the more favorable aspects of the Okie migration, and, rather than searching for more basic causes of increased taxation, they refused to go beyond the visible and convenient scapegoat supplied by the migrants.[79]   Ex post facto and rational arguments proving the Okies an asset allayed few fears. The presence of masses of dust bowlers along the approaches to the inland towns was upsetting and frightening. Taxpayers in Bakersfield, Tulare, Yuba City, and other towns could not avoid viewing with alarm the steadily increasing property taxes to which, they believed, the migrants had subjected them. In testimony before Senator La Follette, the president of the State Chamber of Commerce accurately assessed the frustration of rural Californians: "In the California counties of Fresno, Kern, Kings, Madera, and Tulare particularly, a strong feeling of injustice exists. People do not bear others' burdens if they feel those burdens are alien and unfair."[80] This phase of the migrant problem was certainly difficult for local people who became hysterical and for Okies who found it hard to accept with calm stoicism the life on the ditch bank, the low wages, and the sick children in the tent or shack. [81] Mutual hostility of local for migrant, migrant for local, led to prejudice from the residents and segregation and humiliation for the migrants.

The migrant problem in the inland valleys was not confined to the physical dislocation wrought by the Okie influx. Beneath the rational, conscious anxieties voiced by residents facing the "migrant hordes" lay a deeper, irrational pattern of prejudice and hatred directed at the migrant. This darker side of the California migrant problem colored, confused, and complicated an already serious situation and rendered attempts to solve the problem even more difficult.

The anti-Okie prejudice grew from the fertile soil of social stratification that had developed in response to the needs of industrialized agriculture.[82]   The half century from 1870 to 1930, which saw the growth of California's factories in the fields, also witnessed the evolution of a distinctive social structure in the inland towns dependent upon the great farms. In many respects, rural communities in California resembled those in the cotton belt of the deep South. Both contained classes and castes defined by race and employment.

California's valley towns were not like the rural communities in the Midwest or East where slavery had never supplied an agricultural labor force. Farming in the Midwest had produced a relatively fluid social structure in which white farmhands achieved status simply by purchasing or renting a farm, marrying the boss' daughter, or opening a store. No racial prejudice was directed at field hands, nor was their occupation considered an inferior one, unfit for white Americans.

Until the coming of the Okies, race had differentiated California's Mexican, Filipino, or Oriental field hand from the white populations of the inland towns. In the value systems of the white population, race combined with field work to produce a pattern of caste relationships between the racial minorities and the "Californians." Contacts between the two groups were stylized by racial prejudice and confined to employer-employee, vendor-consumer roles. In all other respects, minority races were separate from the dominant white community. Social advancement of a Negro, Mexican, Filipino, or Oriental was only "within his own group; he did not enter the social sphere of the white community."[83]

In the 1930s, the intricate system of social relationships that had developed around race and field labor was forced to attempt to accommodate itself to conditions changed by the coming of the Okies. The migrant population camped on the outskirts of town or ensconced within the FSA camps was rapidly becoming the mainstay of the harvest army. The Okies posed a problem that the social system had to resolve: they were white, old-stock Americans, but they were also field labor. California's towns faced the choice of responding to the Okies in racial or economic terms. The future unfolding of the migrant problem hinged upon whether the Okie's whiteness or his role as field worker took priority in the perception of the Californians.

The coming of an individual stranger, or of a small group of them, into a complex and highly organized social structure presents no great difficulty either for the stranger or for the resident. The "number of categories in which the stranger may be placed is large, and the personal characteristics of the individual are more fully evaluated" than they would be in a primitive society. "Personality . . . counts for more and the distinctions are finer."[84] If a few Okie families had migrated to each of California's small towns, their presence as Okies probably would have been totally unnoticed. Many of the towns' residents were transplanted midwesterners themselves, and the new migrants would have found status in the community upon the basis of their individual characteristics.

The Okies, however, did not come singly or in small groups. They came in droves, and their numbers precluded the possibility that the Californians in the affected areas would respond to them as individuals. Where large groups of strangers enter a community, residents strive to discover characteristics common to the intruders in order to relate to them more easily. In the search for an accommodation to the strange group, "the tendency [is] to follow lines suggested by the nature of the relationships which comprise the existing social order."[85] Despite their whiteness, the Okies rapidly became identified in the minds of rural Californians as field workers. Field workers had always been viewed as racial inferiors in the social order. In spite of their white skins, the Okies inherited the racial prejudice that Californians had hitherto applied to the minority groups.

Californians found in "Okie," "Arkie," and "Texie" convenient derogatory epithets by which to identify the newcomers. As one sociologist observed during the height of the influx: "The new migration elicits reactions of a somewhat ethnocentric nature, which attribute distinct physical and moral characteristics to the new native whites. These formerly were made to apply only to races. 'Okies,' 'Arkies' and 'Texies' have taken the place of 'Chinks,' and 'Dagos' in rural terminology."[86]

The content of anti-Okie prejudice was a composite of the most negative characteristics attributed by rural Californians to Negroes, Filipinos, Mexicans, and Orientals. The malnourished physique of the migrants, the deplorable settlements along the ditch banks, even the slightly nasal drawl which had come with them from the southern Plains were the touchstones for a stereotype of the Okie as a naturally slovenly, degraded, primitive subspecies of white American. Lee A. Stone, Madera's health director, maintained an almost Darwinian view of the Okie as a racial type, and many Californians echoed his analysis. In an instructional pamphlet directed to California farmers interested in improving the living accommodations for their field workers, Stone cautioned "sob sisters" against building cabins with more than one room. The Okies, he warned, would tear down the partitions:

> It is recognized that such a condition is not ideal and far from being what it should be, but on the other hand . . . one has to deal with a people whose cultural and environmental background is so bad that for a period of more than three hundred years no advances have been made in living conditions among them and ethically they are as far removed

from a desire to attain the privileges which present day culture and environment offers, than they were in the days before the revolutionary war. To many this indictment may seem too severe, but to me it is not severe enough. The poor white of the United States has lived in close proximity to an advancing civilization and culture for several hundred years and yet outwardly has made little or no advance.[87]

Stone's comments were public and official. Compared with private sentiments expressed by many Californians, they were also extremely mild. At taverns in the Sacramento Valley, one journalist encountered less analysis and more vituperation among the old-timers at the bar: "Damned Okies. No damned good. Don't do a damned thing for the town. Damned shiftless nogoods. Damned Okies. Damned bums clutter up the roadside."[88] FSA officials contemplating new camp locations were forced frequently to deal with virulent anti-Okie prejudice. One private letter, painfully handwritten to President Roosevelt and relayed by his staff to the FSA offices, summed up in microcosm the tendency of rural Californians to generalize from specifics when viewing the Okie:

> A Federal migratory camp is being established adjacent to my property at Porterville, Tulare County, California.
> Knowing the character of migrants from my experience in dealing with them, I object to these hordes of degenerates being located at my very door.
>
> These "share croppers" are not a noble people looking for a home and seeking an education for their children. They are unprincipled degenerates looking for something for nothing.
> The fact that they are leaving their native land unfit for human habitation is not surprising. Their ignorance and maliciousness in caring for trees, crops, vines, and the land is such that California will be ruined if farming is left to them.
>
> Please do not put these vile people at my door to depreciate my property and to loot my ranch.[89]

In addition to the charge that they were a degraded people, the Okies were indicted for other, often contradictory, offensive characteristics. On the one hand, they were accused of moral degeneracy, of incest, of "loose morals," and of "oversexedness." On the other hand, organizers attempting to lure the migrants into unions, as well as ministers of valley churches, found in the Okie a distasteful holier-than-thou rigidity. The Okie was simultaneously accused of "shiftlessness" and lack of ambition and of "stealing jobs" from native Californians.[90]

It is difficult to measure accurately the extent to which anti-Okie prejudice developed naturally, since a good deal of it was artificially induced by a propaganda campaign launched against the migrants in 1938. Whatever its origins, it penetrated deeply into the popular consciousness. In 1939, Lillian Creisler, a graduate student in economics at the University of California, investigated Modesto's attitude to the "Little Oklahoma" that had sprung up near the airport on the outskirts of town. Miss Creisler asked students at the city's junior college to write short essays about the migrants. The results indicated that the students either hated or were "tolerant to" the migrants in roughly equal proportions.[91] Both groups, nonetheless, shared common anti-Okie attitudes. Even students who sympathized with the plight of the migrants considered them inferior and degraded. They sympathized principally because they felt that California had attracted the migrants and must assume the responsibility for their poverty. Modesto's response to the Okies was typical of California's inland cities. Sociologists, economists, and journalists in other valley towns found similar anti-Okie sentiments to be widespread.[92]

One outgrowth of California's reliance upon minority racial groups to harvest its crops was the segregation of Mexican migrant workers into "Jim towns."[93] Since rural California had displaced onto the Okie the prejudices that had been applied to the Mexicans, it was natural that the migrants would be subjected to segregation and other external signs of their supposed inferiority. The most obvious manifestation of this phenomenon was the Little Oklahomas, the ghettos in which the migrants congregated. In part, these segregated settlements were the natural result of the migrants' poverty and, of course, their numbers; the valley towns had no place to put the new migrants, so the migrants built their own communities. The resident communities accepted the Little Oklahomas as normal for it was proper that migrant workers should be separate from the dominant white community.

The segregation of Okies into separate residential areas was not fostered by the Californians. It developed naturally. In other areas of community life that necessitated contact between the resident and the migrant, segregation and/or exclusion of the Okie was conscious community policy. Even when migrant children were not segregated in the classroom, their relations with the young Californians were strained by the prevailing anti-Okie attitudes. Friendliness might develop between Okie and Californian in the classrooms, but deep friendships were discouraged by the Californian's parents "as they feel it would cut down their social prestige."[94] Teachers, frustrated by the educational backwardness of their Okie pupils, spoke slightingly of them, and sometimes commented upon their alleged willingness to accept charity in the form of free school lunches.[95] Migrant parents could do little to undo the stigmatizing of their school-age offspring. The parents were Okies, too, and rarely made the mistake of attending Parents-Teachers Association meetings more than once. A couple of Okie mothers from Arvin once "came and sat near the edge [of a PTA meeting] but these two recognized that they were out of place and they never came again . . . they were dressed very sloppily and looked very shabbily and did not mingle with the others."[96]

Although the migrants were an intensely religious group, they were no more welcome at the local churches than their children were at the schools. Pastors of the established community churches avoided contact with the migrants, and missionary groups were shocked that ministers "utterly neglected" the FSA camps.[97] The migrants, in turn, avoided the resident congregations. As with the PTA, so with the churches: "The migrants don't come into our churches because they don't feel comfortable . . . they don't have the clothes. . . . They are more at home in the Church of Christ and the Nazarenes. These churches are more like their homes. They can live in a tent and feel comfortable there."[98]

Okies were excluded from clubs and service organizations in many valley towns and were thus deprived of any voice in these organizations. Migrants seeking to extricate themselves from the harvest labor market by entering the nonagricultural job market sometimes found that prospective employers were initially courteous. When the applicant's Oklahoma or Texas origin came up, courtesy became: "Sorry, but we cannot do a thing for you now."[99] Finally, in the summer of 1939, an event reported from the San Joaquin Valley summed up with ruthless precision the social role that Okies were expected to play: a sign appeared in the foyer of a local theater that read "Negroes and Okies upstairs."[100]

The migrants were aware of the manner in which they were viewed

by the Californians and resented it. Many had expected hospitality
"such as they knew in their homes to prevail in California," and were
"cruelly shocked, very shortly, by the rude hospitality of the employers
and country folk in California."[101]   Some, frustrated, went home to
Texas, Oklahoma, Arkansas. "We're going back to 'Big D'... where the
gen'ral sto' keeper treats yo' all lak humans, and where hospitality
reigns," one family announced when it left the Marysville FSA camp
"A fellow don't appreciate home until he comes to California."[102]
Most migrants, however, knew that "home" had been blown into the
Atlantic Ocean, been leveled by tractors, or been padlocked by banks.
They were determined to stick it out in California, and they lashed out
in bitter humor or anger at the prejudice directed against them.[103]   The
joke columns in the camp newspapers, the songs of Woody Guthrie, the
fugitive comments of migrants interviewed by "big city repor-
ters"—these were a catalog of the social tensions developing in the
Golden State's valleys:

> ... when they came over the mountains in 1849, they were called
> "pioneers," now when we come over the same mountains, in 1939, we
> are called migrants. Where in Hell did they get that word "Mi-
> grant"?[104]

> A tourist and his small son were traveling in California through the
> cotton belt. The son upon seeing a cotton picker stand up asked his
> father what it was. His father replied, "That's a cotton picker, son."
> The son boy after some thought said, "Daddy, them things look almost
> like people when they stand on their hind legs, don't they?"[105]

> Kaint see how cum folks kinda hate us migrants. The Good Book says
> as how Jesus went from place to place when he wuz on erf. Aint it so
> Jesus wuz a migrant?[106]

> Rather drink muddy water
> An sleep in a hollow log

> Rather drink muddy water
> An sleep in a hollow log

> Than to be in California
> Treated like a dirty dog.[107]

Notes in Text

1. *Bakersfield Californian*, April 2, 1940.
2. The term is Carey McWilliams'. Since 1940, however, the phrase has passed into general use. McWilliams' remains the best treatment of the rise of California's industrialized agriculture, and is relied upon heavily in this study for historical perspective. Carey McWilliams, *Factories in the Field* (Boston, 1939), passim.
3. Ibid., p. 15. See also, La Follette Committee *Reports*, 77th Cong., 2d sess., No. 1150, pp. 220-232 passim.
4. Lloyd Fisher, *The Harvest Labor Market in California* (Cambridge, 1953), p. 4. See also Varden Fuller, "The Supply of Agricultural Labor as a Factor in the Evolution of Farm Organization in California" (Ph.D. diss., University of California, Berkeley, 1940).
5. Paul S. Taylor and Tom Vasey, *California Farm Labor*, Social Security Board, Bureau of Research and Statistics, Reprint Series No. 2 (n.p., 1937), p. 2.
6. McWilliams, *Factories in the Fields*, pp. 79-106.
7. Ibid., p. 125. The precise number of Mexican workers is uncertain. Migrants, by virtue of their occupation, do not "stay put" long enough to be counted. Other estimates run to a figure as low as 80,000 workers, plus their families. See William T. Cross and Dorothy Cross, *Newcomers and Nomads in California* (Palo Alto, California, 1937), pp. 50-51.
8. A good résumé of the subject is Carey McWilliams, "Getting Rid of the Mexican," *American Mercury* 28 (March 1933): 322-324.
9. Dr. George P. Clements, Los Angeles' prime authority on Mexican labor during the era, predicted trouble as early as 1926. "The Mexican on relief is being unionized and used to foment strikes among the still few loyal Mexican workers. The Mexican casual labor is lost to the California farmer unless immediate action is taken to get him off relief." La Follette Committee, *Hearings*, Part 53, Exhibit 8743, pp. 19,673-19,675. "A Brief History of California's Agricultural Labor" originally published by the Los Angeles Chamber of Commerce.
10. *San Francisco News*, February 14, 1938. McWilliams, "Getting Rid of the Mexican," 323; Cross and Cross, *Newcomers and Nomads*, pp. 50-51.
11. *San Francisco Examiner*, August 5, 1930. Average annual rate, 1925-1929: 56,747; January-June 1930: 3,674 or (doubled) 7,348 for the entire year.
12. *Pacific Rural Press*, April 25, 1931; Cross and Cross, *Newcomers and Nomads*, pp. 50-51. In 1928, growers insisted that they required 80,000 field workers for peak periods in September.
13. California State Relief Administration, "Migratory Labor in California," mimeographed (San Francisco, 1936), p. 48.
14. W. V. Allen and A. J. Norton, "Agriculture and Its Employment Problems in California," mimeographed, n.d., Paul S. Taylor Collection, Bancroft Library, University of California, Berkeley, Carton 2.
15. Subcommittee of Factfinding to the Statewide Migrant Committee of the California Chamber of Commerce, *Report*, April 9, 1940, George P. Clements Papers, University of California, Los Angeles.
16. George H. Britton, "Parade of Races," manuscript, p. 1, Federal Writers Project Collection, Bancroft Library, University of California, Berkeley, Folder 709.

17. "Conference on Housing of Migratory Agricultural Laborers, Marysville, October 12, 1935." La Follette Committee, *Hearings*, Part 62, p. 22,599. See also Lillian Creisler, "Little Oklahoma, or, the Airport Community" (Master's thesis, University of California, Berkeley, 1939), p. 67.

18. "Miss Brace, January 25 [no year]," typed interview, Taylor Collection, Carton 2; author's interview with Mrs. Eleanor Engstrand, September 7, 1965, Berkeley, California; James Rorty, "Lettuce—With American Dressing," *Nation* 140 (May 15, 1935): 575; Carey McWilliams, "Memorandum on Housing Conditions Among Migratory Workers in California," California State Division of Immigration and Housing, March 20, 1939, pp. 3-4, Taylor Collection, Carton 2.

19. Creisler, "Little Oklahoma," p. 67.

20. California State Relief Administration, *Agricultural Laborers in the San Joaquin Valley, July, August 1937*, reprinted in La Follette Committee, *Hearings*, Part 62, p. 22,660.

21. Jonathan Garst to John Phillips, February 12, 1937, in Brawley Camp Reports, Simon J. Lubin Papers, Bancroft Library, University of California, Berkeley, Carton 13.

22. John Phillips to Jonathan Garst, February 19, 1937, U.S. Department of Agriculture, Agricultural Stabilization and Conservation Commission Papers, Federal Records Center, San Francisco, 36,881.

23. National Resources Planning Board, Field Office, Region VIII, *Some Effects of Recent Migration on California's Population and Economy, June 25, 1940*, p. 8, copy in Farm Security Administration Papers, Bancroft Library, University of California, Berkeley.

24. *Berkeley Gazette*, July 27, 1937.

25. Agricultural Labor Bureau of the San Joaquin Valley, *Annual Report*, 1936, 1937, 1938, 1939, in La Follette Committee, *Hearings*, Part 72, pp. 26,536-26,538.

26. Kern County, Department of Public Health, Sanitary Division, "Survey of Kern County Migratory Labor Problems, Supplementary Report as of July 1, 1939," mimeographed, n.p. copy in Carey McWilliams Collection, University of California, Los Angeles. See also Emily Huntington, *Doors to Jobs* (Berkeley, 1942), pp. 203-204.

27. Agricultural Labor Bureau of the San Joaquin Valley, *Annual Reports*, 1937, 1938, 1939, pp. 26,536-26,538.

28. Roy Pike to Commonwealth Club, in "California Farm Labor Problems," *Commonwealth Club Transactions* 30 (April 7, 1936): passim; Lewis Kuplan, "The Problems of Relief and Agriculture in California," manuscript, December 1937, McWilliams Collection; Commonwealth Club, Minutes of Section on Agriculture, April 14, 1936, copy in Harry Drobish Papers, Bancroft Library, University of California, Berkeley.

29. Kern County Health Department, Sanitary Division, "Survey of Kern County Migratory Labor Problem," Supplementary Report as of July 1, 1938, mimeographed, p. 6, copy in vertical file, Public Health Library, University of California, Berkeley.

30. Torn title page of *California Commonwealth* with handwritten notation, n.d., Philip Bancroft Collection, Bancroft Library, University of California, Berkeley.

31. Arvin Camp Reports, May 2, 1936, USDA ASCC Collection, 36,879.

32. Commonwealth Club, *Minutes of Section on Agriculture*, n.p.

33. Arvin Camp Reports, August 15, 1936, USDA ASCC Collection, 36,879.

34. Sue Sanders, *The Real Causes of Our Migrant Problem* (n.p., 1940): *New York Times*, July 18, 1937.

35. Tolan Committee, *Hearings*, Part 7, p. 2,823.

36. For an extended discussion of wages and costs for California migrant workers, see the following: La Follette Committee, *Hearings*, Part 62, pp. 22,529-22,530; *Wage Rates and Expenditures for Labor, California Agriculture, 1909-1935*, copy in Giannini Foundation Library, University of California, Berkeley.

37. Arvin Camp Reports, July 11, 1936. USDA ASCC Collection, 36,879.

38. These figures and the following statistical data are drawn from La Follette Committee, *Reports*, 77th Cong., 2d sess., No. 1150, pp. 384-385.

39. *San Francisco News*, October 23, 1936.

40. During the course of research for this study, I have turned up no studies viewing the coming of Okies to the major coastal cities with alarm, nor viewing them as a specific group.

41. Seymour Janow and William Gilmartin, "Labor and Agricultural Migration to California, 1935-40," *Monthly Labor Review* 53 (July 1941): 21.

42. Commonwealth Club of California, *The Population of California* (San Francisco, 1946), p. 19.

43. Commonwealth Club, *Population of California*, p. 57.

44. Testimony of James Musatti, La Follette Committee, *Hearings*, Part 59, pp. 21,864, 21,866-21,870.

45. Ben Hibbs, "Footloose Army," *Country Gentleman* 110 (February 1940): 7.

46. A large collection of Miss Lange's photographs of migrant Okies may be found in the Bancroft Library, University of California, Berkeley.

47. *San Francisco Chronicle*, March 8, 1937.

48. *National Ham and Eggs*, August 26, 1939. Berkeley Gazette, July 10, 1937.

49. Lee Alexander Stone, "What Is the Solution to California's Transient Labor Problem?" mimeographed (June 22, 1938), p. 6, copy in vertical file, Public Health Library, University of California, Berkeley.

50. George Thomas Miron, *The Truth About John Steinbeck and the Migrants* (Los Angeles, 1939), p. 20.

51. Stone, "What Is the Solution?" p. 2; Testimony of Lawrence Hewes, U.S., Congress, House, Select Committee of House Committee on Agriculture to Investigate the Activities of the Farm Security Administration, *Hearings*, 78th Cong., 1st sess., 1943, Part 2, pp. 624-625 (hereafter *Cooley Committee*); *Oakland Tribune*, February 1, 1938.

52. *Bakersfield Californian*, November 26, 1934, April 8, 1937.

53. Kern County, Health Department, *Supplementary Report as of July 1, 1938*, passim; Stone, "What Is the Solution?" passim; *Madera Express*, June 30, 1938; Testimony of Walter M. Dickie, La Follette Committee, *Hearings*, Part 62, p. 22,730.

54. *San Francisco News*, February 15, 1938; Kern County, Health Department, *Supplementary Report as of July 1, 1939*, p. 1.

55. Creisler, "Little Oklahoma," p. 35.

56. Arvin Camp Reports, October 10, 1936, USDA ASCC Collection, 36,879.

57. Kern County, Health Department, *Supplementary Report as of July 1, 1939*, p. 2.

58. Mary Helen Williamson, "Unemployment Relief Administration in Kern County, 1935-1940" (Master's thesis, University of California, Berkeley, 1941), pp. 25-26; testimony of Carey McWilliams, La Follette Committee, *Hearings*, Part 59, p. 21,891; Kern County, Health Department, *Supplementary Report as of July 1, 1939*, p. 7; Walter R. Goldschmidt, *As You Sow* (Glencoe, 1947), passim; "Interview with Mr. Thayer, Arvin," Bureau Agricultural Economics Collection, Federal Records Center, San Francisco, 306,068.

59. California State Relief Administration, "A Social Survey of Housing Conditions Among Tulare County Relief Clients," mimeographed (Visalia, 1939), p. 23; testimony of George Gleason, Tolan Committee, *Hearings*, Part 7, p. 3,005; Work Projects Administration, Division of Social Research and California State Relief Administration, *The Economic Problem of Rural Relief in California with Special Reference to Selected Counties*, Bulletin No. 7, Madera County (September 1936), pp. 10-11; Creisler, "Little Oklahoma," passim; *San Francisco Chronicle*, February 12, 1940.

60. Testimony of Carey McWilliams, La Follette Committee, *Hearings*, Part 59, p. 21,892.

61. Stuart M. Jamieson, "A Settlement of Rural Migrant Families in the Sacramento Valley," *Rural Sociology*, 7 (March 1942): 51, 57.

62. Federal Writers Project, "A Report on the Background and Problems Affecting Farm Labor in California," manuscript, Oakland, California, n.d., Bancroft Library, University of California, Berkeley, Testimony of George Gleason, p. 2,997.

63. *San Francisco News*, May 13, 1941.

64. Williamson, "Unemployment Relief in Kern County," pp. 25-26.

65. See, for example, the analysis in Davis McEntire et al, "Migration and Resettlement Problems in Pacific Coast States," p. 16, June 20, 1938, Taylor Collection, Carton 18.

66. Engstrand interview; Stone, "What Is the Solution?" pp. 1-6; S. F. Farnsworth, "Health of the Migratory Worker," address before the Health Officers' Section, League of California Municipalities, San Jose, September 15, 1937, in Taylor Collection, Carton 18.

67. U.S., Department of Agriculture, Farm Security Administration, *A Study of 6,655 Migrant Households in California* (San Francisco, 1939), pp. 48-51; Kern County, Health Department, "Relation of the Migratory Problem to Health and Hospitalization in Kern County," mimeographed (July 1, 1937), p. 2; testimony of Gleason, p. 3,003.

68. *San Francisco News*, February 15, 1938; La Follette Committee, *Hearings*, Part 59, pp. 21,866-21,870; Tyr V. Johnson and Frederick Arpke, *Interstate Migration and County Finance in California* (n.d., n.p.), passim.

69. James E. Sidel, *Pick for Your Supper* (National Guild Labor Committee, June 1939), pp. 3-5.

70. La Follette Committee, *Hearings*, Part 62, p. 22,743.

71. Creisler, "Little Oklahoma," p. 51.

72. *Voice of the Agricultural Worker* (hereafter *VOTAW*), September 10, 1940.

73. California State Relief Administration, *Agricultural Laborers in the San*

Joaquin Valley, p. 22,650: Two-thirds of migrant children were scholastically retarded at least one year; 40 percent, at least two years; 20 percent, at least three years; 10 percent, at least four years; Testimony of Gleason, p. 2,999; Theodore T. Dawe, *A Study of the Migratory Children in Kern County for the School Year, 1936-1937* (n.d., n.p.), copy in Federal Writers' Project Collection, Carton 703; La Follette Committee, *Hearings*, Part 62, pp. 22,742-22,744, *Bakersfield Californian*, September 11, 1937; *People's World*, February 21, 1940; *San Francisco News*, February 16, 1938.

74. *Pacific Rural Press*, December 30, 1939.

75. *Bakersfield Californian*, August 27, 1938; La Follette Committee, *Hearings*, Part 59, pp. 21,866-21,870.

76. *Los Angeles Times*, July 26, 1937; California League of Women Voters, Educational Facilities for the Children of Migratory Workers ("Penny Sheet No. 4," September 1939), p. 1, copy in Giannini Foundation Library, University of California, Berkeley.

77. California State Chamber of Commerce, *Migrants: A National Problem* (1940), p. 12.

78. Arpke and Johnson, *Interstate Migration and County Finance*, passim.

79. Ibid., pp. 3, 25-27.

80. Testimony of Harrison S. Robinson, La Follette Committee, *Hearings*, Part 59, pp. 21,737-21,738.

81. Testimony of Helen G. Douglas, Tolan Committee, *Hearings*, Part 6, p. 2,404.

82. I am indebted, except where otherwise noted, for material regarding the rural community in California, to Goldschmidt, *As You Sow*.

83. Ibid., p. 67; see also Davis McEntire, Tyr V. Johnson, and W. W. Troxell, "Migration and Resettlement Problems in Pacific Coast States," manuscript, June 20, 1938, Taylor Collection.

84. Margaret Mary Wood, *The Stranger* (New York, 1934), p. 283.

85. Ibid., p. 34.

86. Stuart M. Jamieson, "A Settlement of Rural Migrant Families in the Sacramento Valley," *Rural Sociology* 7 (March 1942): 50n. See also Goldschmidt, *As You Sow*, p. 47.

87. Stone, "What Is the Solution?" pp. 6-7.

88. *San Francisco Chronicle*, March 11, 1937.

89. Mrs. Effie Ball Magurn to FDR, April 17, 1940, USDA ASCC Collection, 36890.

90. John Steinbeck in *The American Guardian*, April 29, 1938, copy in Federal Writers' Project Collection, Carton 2; *Camp Herald*, December 19, 1941; Interview with Mrs. Caroline Decker Gladstein, San Francisco, October 5, 1965; "Interview with Pastor Dwight Brown," USDA BAE Collection, 306,068; Goldschmidt, *As You Sow*, p. 84; Creisler, "Little Oklahoma," p. 63, "Migratory Labor: A Social Problem," *Fortune* 19 (April 1939): 116; Douglas W. Churchill, "Exiles from the Dust Bowl," *The New York Times Magazine* (March 13, 1938): 20.

91. Creisler, "Little Oklahoma," p. 68.

92. Goldschmidt, *As You Sow*, passim; Gladstein interview; Jamieson, "A Settlement of Rural Migrant Families," passim; California State Relief Administration, "Agricultural Laborers in the San Joaquin Valley, July, August, 1937," in La Follette Committee, *Hearings*, Part 62, pp. 22,642-22,666.

93. Testimony of McWilliams, Part 59, p. 21,777.

94. *VOTAW*, April 30, 1940.

95. Shafter Camp Reports, October 20, 1939, USDA ASCC Collection, 36,886.

96. *Camp Herald*, November 14, 1941; Interviews with "Pederson" and Frank Stockton, USDA BAE Collection, 306,068.

97. Lloyd B. Thomas, "The Argonauts of Agriculture," *The Witness* 21 (July 22, 1937).

98. Goldschmidt, *As You Sow*, pp. 135-136; Interviews with Rev. John Woolett and Rev. Friesen, USDA BAE Collection, 306,068; Jamieson, "A Settlement of Rural Migrant Families," 58.

99. *Fresno Bee*, April 8, 1940.

100. Carey McWilliams, "California Pastoral," *Antioch Review* 2 (March 1921): 116.

101. Unsigned, untitled, undated manuscript, Drobisch Papers, Bancroft Library, University of California, Berkeley.

102. *VOTAW*, January 26, 1940. Also see *Covered Wagon News*, February 4, 1940: *Tow Sack Tatler*, November 11, 1939.

103. Creisler, "Little Oklahoma," p. 63.

104. *VOTAW*, January 26, 1940.

105. Ibid., December 8, 1939.

106. Arvin Camp Reports, February 22, 1936, USDA ASCC Collection, 36,879.

107. Margaret Valiant, *Migrant Camp Recordings* (n.p., n.d.), record no. 5059, "California Blues," copy in Giannini Foundation Library, University of California, Berkeley.

3

The Rise
of the Migrant Problem

With concern steadily increasing in the San Joaquin Valley over the rising migrant population, county authorities concluded that harassed localities must seek aid from outside quarters. In the slack season of 1937, Kern's board of supervisors sent a telegram to President Roosevelt, justifying the move on the ground that since the migrants were not Californians, the problem was a federal one. Within three days, representatives of the seven other San Joaquin Valley counties joined Kern's campaign. Again in July, Kern led the San Joaquin Valley Supervisors Association in requesting aid from the federal government, directing telegrams this time to Harry Hopkins and to the governors of all other states.[1]

These telegrams were less significant for what they said than for what they neglected to say. In 1938, local and state authorities would demand that migrants be returned to the states from which they originated and that federal authorities cease distributing relief to Okies in California. These telegrams, on the other hand, asked only that the federal government increase aid to migrants in the San Joaquin Valley so that "work opportunities be made available for the transients to improve the conditions" under which they lived.[2] In any event, the telegram campaign received no response. Accompanied by cries of "Will You Act, Mr. Merriam?" this initial attempt to extend the search for solutions to the migrant problem to the state and federal levels quickly subsided.[3]

The fate of Kern's attempt to interest the rest of the state in the migrant problem demonstrated the general indifference to the migrant influx that prevailed throughout California until 1938. In urban areas of the state, Okies were relatively rare, and they were hidden within the far larger populations of the cities. In any case, the cities had problems of their own, especially in the recession of 1937. It is, therefore, impossible to account for the sudden hysterical alarm with which California awakened in 1938 and 1939 to the fact that it had a migrant problem on its hands, simply by pointing to increased school and health costs in selected rural counties. In order to account for the furor over *The Grapes of Wrath*, the petitions, the attack upon the Farm Security Administration—in short, to explain California's migrant hysteria— deeper causes must be found.

The Okie migration was not a single cataclysmic event, but a process spread over five years. During the first years, the Okies displaced other migrant workers and their arrival was, therefore, partially obscured by the loss of the Mexicans. In order for the migrants to be viewed as a problem for the state and the nation, rather than simply for selected counties, two conditions were required. First, some event, dramatic in itself, would have to bring the attention of the state to the Okies. Second, a powerful publicity campaign polarizing attitudes to the migrants would have to be launched. Both these conditions were present in 1938.

Before 1938, the growing population of Okies in California had concerned only selected groups on a statewide basis. Health officials had spent years chasing the migrants from ditch bank to ditch bank, warning of severe epidemics if nothing were done to alter their condition. Labor unions, especially those in the newly organized CIO, viewed the migrant problem in its agricultural labor aspect and set off on a drive to unionize the new migrants. Farmers had been forced by the influx to consider the Okies' effect upon the labor supply. At times, too, local conditions of misery elicited interest for a day or two. Only once during the three years of greatest Okie migration (1935-1937) did

California engage in a discussion of the problem of depression migration, and then only in response to an event that involved the Los
Angeles mentality more than it did the Okies.

Before 1938, Californians generally viewed depression newcomers as
transients, not migrants, reflecting the fact that early in the depression
years, before the Okies had begun their move en masse to the West, a
steady stream of unemployed men had come to California seeking work
in industry or agriculture. Only occasionally had this influx of "bums"
been swelled by Okie families.

In August 1935, the federal government announced that it would
discontinue aid to transients by shutting down the Federal Transient
Service in September. Californians were subjected to a steadily mount-
ing series of alarms that the state would soon become the nation's
dumping ground for transient indigents.[4] Immediately following the
demise of the Federal Transient Service, a "Committee on Indigent
Alien Transients" recommended that "male, unattached, adult, indigent, alien, employable, transients" be fingerprinted, and arrested under
vagrant and pauper laws, where necessary. The report suggested, too,
that "Peace Officer Stations" be situated "at points of state ingress to
arrest persons of various violations" and to prevent tramps from using
the rails for ingress to the state as well.[5] In effect, the report recommended a selective blockade intended to intimidate and frighten away
those seeking work in California. State agencies took little notice of the
report.

In Los Angeles, however, the report received considerable interest.
Here the transient influx had irritated many of the city's oldtimers,
many of whom had lived there for as many as five or even ten years.
Transient pressure had "become so intense that the whole political field
[was] involved" and "hysteria virtually ruled."[6] The ebullient Hugh
Johnson had noted, for example, that Los Angeles was a "lesson in
looseness and aloofness." Her relief officials behaved in a manner as
hospitable as would an "Oklahoma rotary."[7] On February 4, 1936,
Police Chief Davis of Los Angeles, using the report's recommendations
as justifications, converted the Los Angeles police force into a frontier
legion and stationed 150 of his officers at the state's points of entry in
a "bum blockade." For a few weeks, small patrols of Los Angeles
policemen stood guard at the state's borders, rousting, searching, and

evicting across the borders nonresident hitchhikers, using their spare time to practice marksmanship and irritating local residents who viewed the deputies as Greeks did Turks. At Crescent City, for example, locals so insulted the border guards that, like occupying troops, they chose not to spend their off-hours in town.[8]

Los Angeles' bum blockade titillated the state and the nation, supplying Westbrook Pegler, for one, with an opportunity not to be missed. "Los Angeles," he commented, has once again proved that it is not a "state but a condition—and a clear one at that." Nevada residents took up a collection and erected a large sign reading "Stop! Los Angeles City Limits!" on the approaches to Reno. Quickly, the bum blockade took on many of the aspects of a Balkan cold war as headlines announced: "LA POLICE TIGHTENING BLOCKADE! RETALIA-TION BY ARIZONA, OREGON, IS THREATENED!" One "war" correspondent returned from the front to report:

> There are two armies assembled down there on the Blythe Bridge! One on the California side and one on the Arizona side. They include state patrol officers, constables, deputy sherriffs and I don't know what. . . .
> The California group had advanced to the middle of the bridge because if any of the itinerants headed this way once get on to California soil, the Arizona crowd won't let them return. So the middle of the bridge is guarded.[9]

For all its comic-opera aspects, the Los Angeles bum blockade raised a serious question which even Pegler had noted while poking fun at the city. It was, critics argued, "a conspicuous outrage against ordinary liberty in the United States," because it interfered with constitutional guarantees of freedom of movement. It was upon this issue that the ill-conceived blockade foundered. The state's highway patrol challenged its legality, and the state's attorney general privately notified Los Angeles of the unconstitutionality of the blockade. Ultimately, the Civil Liberties Union took the issue to federal court. Chief Davis retreated, announcing that the purpose of the bum blockade was to investigate criminals rather than to prevent impecunious transients from entering the state.[10] The bum blockade ended in disarray, and local authorities never seriously attempted again any similar action.

Even during the high point of the blockade, agricultural regions recognized the problem that migration across state borders might soon pose. Rural newspapers uniformly attacked the blockade, amusing their readers at Los Angeles' expense, but noted, nonetheless, that the transients posed "a real problem."[11] Even the unpredictable Scripps-Howard journals, later to become the chief protector of the Okie migrants, felt that a case could be made for Los Angeles' action.[12] How, the question was frequently asked in all these papers, could "richer" states protect themselves from immigrants from "poorer" states during periods of economic dislocation?

Nonetheless, from 1935 to 1938 the migrant problem merely simmered in California, boiling sporadically into public view for a moment or two, then cooling. Counties shouting for aid from the state could not persuade the populace that this major change in the agricultural labor supply was significant.[13] For the most part, the average Californian's pre-1938 attitude toward the migrants and their problems was indifference. The intense public concern that convulsed California and reached its peak in 1939 began only in January and February 1938, when nature and the New Deal conspired to produce the first statewide public reaction to the coming of the Okies.

In January 1938, California sunshine descended from the San Joaquin's skies for weeks, and massive floods inundated large portions of the upper valley, washing out the ditch banks and leaving the Okies hungry, sick, cold, and wet. Newspapermen flocked to the scene of the natural disaster and discovered everywhere a human disaster in hordes of migrants huddled for shelter under the few trees laboriously hand-planted years before in the once-desert regions. The Okies had become an immediate visible problem, and the state's newspapers, urban and rural, hammered the migrant's misery into the public consciousness.[14] Agents of charities touring the San Joaquin Valley to raise funds for the migrants in the days immediately following the floods found that residents had not known of the "conditions they have in the 'back yards.'" Even the San Joaquin Valley's ministers had not been aware that a critical situation existed in the wake of the floods. "We need," one minister wrote, "to be stirred up concerning our neglect."[15]

Stirred up they were, as the rains and the floods that came in their wake brought the problem more insistently to the public's attention than could thousands of social workers' reports. By March and April

1938, the Okies were headline news: "MIGRANT HORDE INVADES KERN!", "alarming reports of hunger and starvation"; "crisis . . . in the rich San Joaquin."[16] The Okies had become feature story material. Reporters by the score moved into the valleys, and, in their columns, often relied upon the bathos usually reserved for the Christmas-season "hundred neediest":

> God had done one of his most gorgeous jobs with the California landscape.
> The people who had stopped their cars looked and breathed deeply and spoke of the wonder of it. And, as their eyes drew back from the rolling fields and hills, they saw a clutter of migrant workers' hovels in a little depression near the road.
> And the boy in the back seat spoke, with shock in his voice: "Daddy—do people REALLY live there?"[17]

Under the friendly aegis of the Simon J. Lubin Society, which for two years had been seeking to interest Californians in the conditions of agricultural workers, charitable organizations and unions responded with a drive to aid the Okie migrants. An Emergency Flood Relief Committee collected blankets, clothing, cash, tobacco, and candy for the destitute migrants. Church groups, notably the Council of Women for Home Missions, engaged in similar immediate meliorative activities.[18] But charitable relief activities were, unfortunately, no answer to the social problem of agricultural labor. The floods had merely increased temporarily the permanent misery of sporadically employed, unhoused, migrants. Alert action by private and county groups had saved the day; but as the floods receded, political events in the nation's capital threatened far more severe dislocation in the months to come. In late February, Congress had passed the second Agricultural Adjustment Act.

From 1933 to 1935, the first AAA had permitted cotton growers in the southern Great Plains to evict their tenants, thrusting many Okies into the migrant stream. Now, the second AAA was about to exacerbate the travails of the first AAA's victims. California's cotton acreage was to be reduced from 618,000 to just under 400,000 in 1938. The cut in acreage would mean, in turn, a contraction of the demand for agricultural labor. To make matters still worse, the floods had ruined crops other than cotton that might have aided in taking up the potential labor surplus.[19] The predicted oversupply materialized in May

when "there [were] three to ten men for each agricultural job" in the
San Joaquin Valley. As one Okie described the chaos in the fields, "the
only way to get work out of there now is to sit at the end of the row
and when someone drops out just rush into the field and take his
place." From the San Joaquin, the surplus spread north into the
Sacramento, where there were "ten pickers to every pea in the pod,"
then elsewhere in the state. Public alarm spread with the Okies.[20]

By mid-1938, the Okies were continuous front-page news. Urban
areas, especially in the Bay region, were now alert to the existence of
the situation and feared that "the problem of the dust bowl migrants
[was] now washing up almost to San Francisco's doorstep with the
advent of the fruit season in the Santa Clara Valley." Ditch bank
settlements were springing up in San Mateo County.[21] Hastily organized caravans traveled the valleys, this time composed of social workers
seeking Okies, not Okies seeking work, and what had been local misery
came to statewide attention. Congressman J. F. T. O'Connor, for
example, received a severe shock on one such caravan, and confided his
emotions to his diary:

> After lunch we went to Arvin where we saw some very poor people—
> one tent a mother and her four children 5 to 14 all living in one small
> tent. . . . Here 14 yrs. recd 2 checks in 14 months from gvt. . . . Visited
> several other places and talked to people. Most came from Olk [sic] —
> driven out by drought. They were all fine citizens—just up against hard
> luck. All want work and a place. Arrived home 7 P.M. and went directly
> to hotel. This was a sad day to see fellow Californians in such need.[22]

The floods and the AAA had accomplished, with the Okies' aid, what
no amount of agitation on behalf of the Mexicans in preceding years
had been able to achieve.

In the midst of the massive Okie oversupply—even while the Agricultural Labor Bureau of the San Joaquin Valley was still complaining
about local labor shortages—the first whisper of resentment began to
threaten the relationship between growers and local towns. In February
1938, as events rapidly brought the migrant problem to a turning point,
an editorial in the *Bakersfield Californian*, long a powerful supporter of
California's corporate agriculture, hinted that the state's growers were

playing a dangerous game in their wholesale acceptance of migrant labor oversupplies. Entitled "Does it Pay?" the editorial clearly indicated the resentment that was beginning to germinate. The communities, with all their difficulties attending the Okie migration, seemed forced forever to play second fiddle to the alleged needs of the large farms:

> A dispatch from Merced noted that there are 5,000 migratory workers in Merced county alone destined, for the lack of shelter elsewhere, to remain here during the winter. Only 3,000 indigents are receiving direct cash relief, and note the language of the despatch. [sic] "Hundreds in Cotton Camps Throughout the County are Near Starvation, One camp of Forty Having Lived the Past Week on a Rice Diet." "Camp Owners in the Cotton Centers," says the same article, "are in desperation and threaten to turn away the dust bowl migrants."

To this point, the *Bakersfield Californian*'s editorial had simply expressed serious concern over a human interest problem, as it had for the past two years. The article, however, did not stop at that point:

> Every Californian must be concerned over a situation which creates an army of migrant laborers who are left without employment. A humane government cannot permit them to lack for food. Unquestionably they are at a less advantageous position than they were in the states from which they came, and obviously the situation as it now exists will become even more complex in the course of years. Thoughtful people will wonder, then, if it is advisable to continue an industry which attracts so many thousands of wage earners for this state—for what necessarily must be temporary employment. In the absence of some means of earning a livelihood later public authority must rescue them from starvation through taxation levied upon the public as a whole, and the amount needed even now is in excess of any profit that comes to the state through the growing of cotton. So it would appear that if the grower is directly advantaged, indirectly he and all the other permanent residents of the state are disadvantaged.[23]

Other journals had in the past linked the farmer's profits with the misery of the agricultural workers and tax monies of the local residents. The *San Francisco News* had for years inveighed against the harvest labor system and the large farms.[24] The *News* was, however, an urban liberal newspaper and growers had no need to heed its complaints. As one Associated Farmer had remarked:

> We are not responsible for them being here. . . . And now everybody

seems to infer that it is an agricultural problem purely . . . because they
came to the rural areas.

  As far as we are concerned we would be very glad to see 350, four
hundred thousand unfortunate people divided equally between Los
Angeles and San Francisco. These [are the] people who seem to be
criticizing . . . us mostly.[25]

Now, however, such criticisms were emanating from the agricultural
regions. The *Californian*'s editorial had used exceedingly strong language for that newspaper, and most important, the *Californian* was
voicing a sentiment that was developing in other rural areas. From 1938
to 1940, rural Californians suggested at intervals that the best way to
keep "these undesirables . . . out of the state" was to "put a prohibitive
tax on cotton or potatoes [in Kern a major crop worked by Okies] or
both."[26] By 1940 officials of church groups were suggesting that
"excessive taxes" be levied on large holdings, with the revenue used to
purchase small acreage tracts upon which the Okies might be resettled.[27] Business groups, as well as individuals and charitable organizations, frequently equated the Okie migration with the large, corporate
farms. The president of the State Chamber of Commerce observed that
"it may be fairly said that the people of California by their agricultural
activities created the problem."[28] This developing assault upon the
larger farms for complicity in producing the migrant problem should
not be overemphasized. It was but a minor wave in a sea of antagonism
directed ultimately not at the growers, but at the Okies. It was,
nonetheless, a foretaste of what could develop should the Okie migration continue without a simultaneous return of prosperity which would
divert the migrants into the cities or into other employment. As the
State Chamber of Commerce had pointed out, the Chinese, Japanese, or
Filipino could be sent back home when he became "too great a
problem." The growers simply could not treat the Okies with like
indifference for very long without reaping a reaction.[29] For the time
being, however, no united outraged rural citizenry was demanding the
destruction or subdivision of the large farms.

  The floods of 1938, then, coupled with the AAA, had satisfied only
one of the two conditions required to produce the migrant problem; a
cataclysmic series of events had brought the attention of the state to
the Okie influx. Valley residents, forced to endure the arduous consequences of an overflow from the fields, had begun to grumble, and

urban dwellers responded with concern for the plight of the migrants. There, however, the situation might have rested. The migrant problem would likely have returned to the quiescence of back pages in social welfare journals, had a new ingredient not entered the scene at precisely the same time as the floods and the AAA. Political events in California produced a strong possibility that the coalition of large growers and local businessmen that had dominated relief, labor, and social welfare policy in California was on the verge of losing that control. This major change in the state's politics transformed the attitude of the state's large farmers and their allies to the Okies who, hitherto, they had accepted with little complaint. The background for this complex, and somewhat paradoxical phenomenon may be traced to the 1934 EPIC campaigns, when the dust-bowl migration was yet a trickle.

The story of Upton Sinclair's capture of California's Democratic party in the 1934 election has been told elsewhere,[30] but one aspect of the EPIC campaign had a direct impact upon California's later migrant problem and requires discussion here. A utopian thinker and socialist novelist, Sinclair lacked the ability, requisite in successful politicians, to speak much and say little, all the while keeping himself out of political trouble. On several occasions during the 1934 gubernatorial campaign he had put his political foot into his mouth, and never with such suicidal effect as when he commented, "playfully," he later avowed: "If I am elected, about half the unemployed in the whole country will climb aboard freight trains and head for California."[31] A predominantly hostile press spread the story, frightening the voter with editorials threatening that if Sinclair were elected, bums would flock to the state, attracted to high relief and production-for-use programs. Hollywood's anti-Sinclair forces filmed "newsreels" depicting tramps on the march to California, and bogus handbills flooded the state:

> ATTENTION CITIZENS! OUR FRIEND AND COMRADE, UPTON SINCLAIR, WILL BE ELECTED GOVERNOR NOVEMBER 6. THIRTY DAYS THEREAFTER, THE POPULATION WILL BE DOUBLED—OUR SHARE OF THE UNEMPLOYED NOW ON ITS WAY TO CALIFORNIA WILL BE OVER 1,500,000 PERSONS—MEN, WOMEN AND CHILDREN. . . .
> IT WILL TAKE COMRADE SINCLAIR AT LEAST SIX MONTHS TO PROVIDE NECESSARY HOUSING AND WORK FOR OUR OVER 1,500,000 NEW FRIENDS.[32]

Such propaganda, absurd as it was, gained plausibility from the fact that the dust-bowl migrants—though not yet identified as such—were already beginning the long trek to California. In the San Joaquin Valley, automobiles from Arkansas, Texas, Oklahoma, and Missouri passed through Fresno carrying "Sinclair" signs, one reading, "Sinclair here we come, where's the job."[33] Reports spread that midwesterners were following the EPIC campaign with greater interest than Californians. Sinclair, of course, lost the election. But the fatuous comment he had made, coupled with the intense propaganda campaign it generated, fastened upon the state a fear that high relief payments would attract a host of indigents to bountiful California.[34]

Since the Okie migration did not begin in earnest until 1935, well after Sinclair's defeat, any attempt to blame one upon the other was doomed to fail. Nonetheless, California was unsettled politically throughout the 1930s, and maverick movements among the victims of depression cropped up time and again in the wake of the EPIC campaign. Dr. Townsend's movement was centered in the state, and Ham 'N' Eggs, an offshoot from the Old Age Revolving Pension Plan, Limited, was peculiarly Californian. These new utopian movements were designed to promote recovery and old-age security through large monthly doles to the elderly. They revived the fears that Sinclair had sown with his 1934 statement, and commentators frequently blamed the Okie influx upon them in later years. In late 1935, the *Oakland Tribune* noted the beginning of the dust-bowl influx and directly connected it with politics: "The penniless army of invaders mostly think they are arriving in Utopia. Some of the refugees . . . had heard that Dr. Townsend's plan was already in operation . . . others had heard that Sinclair was running the state and abolishing poverty. Others thought that Huey Long had started his share-the-wealth scheme, as an experiment, in California, and was starting the divvy on the fourth of July."[35]

The notion that millions of impoverished Americans would soon flock to California for the "divvy" frightened Californians of every political persuasion and economic status. California's farmers and their organizations, however, had a special, and quite rational, interest in the relief issue. Wages in California agriculture were directly dependent upon relief payments. The higher the relief, the less likely that its recipients would leave the welfare rolls to accept lower-paying work in the fields. As the historian of California's farm organizations has shown, there was yet a further reason for deep interest in relief policy on the growers' part. The members of the Associated Farmers and the Farm Bureau Federation were the state's wealthier farmers. As taxpayers, they had a personal stake in keeping relief payments low among all the unemployed as well as agricultural workers. Therefore, even though growers were actually subsidized by relief paid to their workers during the slack agricultural seasons, their policy against relief payments was "consistent and natural." There was, finally, a third facet to the growers' position on relief. California's larger farmers occupied a political spectrum ranging from conservative to far right.[36] The relief issue could be used to discredit the New Deal, either at the state or federal levels, and, after 1938, it would be used in such manner with considerable effect.

With the defeat of Sinclair's gubernatorial bid, and the inauguration of Republican Governor Frank Merriam, California's farmers found little utility in propagandizing the relief issue. The Merriam administration generally followed the recommendations of the farmers' organizations. In late 1935, the Federal Emergency Relief Administration (FERA) returned control of relief to the states, and California's new State Relief Administration (SRA) functioned carefully, efficiently, and, above all, conservatively.[37] Under Director Harold Pomeroy, the SRA established policies in perfect harmony with those of the Associated Farmers. The Pomeroy policy recognized that relief rates determined wage levels, and kept them low in order to protect prevailing wages in the fields. When it happened that the recipients preferred the smaller pittance of the dole to the slightly larger pittance paid for agricultural work, they were to be forced off the relief rolls when the demand for labor arose. This policy was euphemistically termed "first preference" for workers on relief.[38]

Federal relief agencies in California were not immune to criticism that they connived with growers and the SRA in maintaining low agricultural wages. By 1935, the state offices of the WPA seemed to some to have fallen under the influence of the agricultural interests and their employment agencies.[39] In mid-1936, state WPA Director Frank Y. McLaughlin lent credence to the charge in announcing that "able bodied men on the rolls of the WPA will have to accept work in the state's agricultural districts or be dropped from the relief rolls." [40] Within two weeks of McLaughlin's announcement, however, it became clear that although WPA—in its role as a depression work-making agency—could not compete with private employment, growers could not use WPA as an accomplice in maintaining low wages. The state administrator demanded assurances that "a reasonable wage" be paid before agricultural workers were dropped from the rolls, and a district director took back onto WPA employment pea-pickers who had refused work at egregiously low wages. "We do not intend," he declared, "to force these workers to become peons or slaves."[41] Despite these assurances, critics were never certain just how the agency defined "slaves." It remained unclear until 1938 whether WPA supported or alleviated low wages in the agricultural regions.

Despite the grower-oriented attitudes of state and federal relief agencies, the relief load mounted steadily during the Merriam years. The SRA became the most disorganized, and the most expensive, California bureaucracy.[42] The Okies contributed to the growth of the relief load, despite the fact that they had not come to California seeking relief. Once settled in the state, they found that without relief they could not survive. Their wages were too small to provide savings adequate for the slack seasons. Settled in undiversified interior counties, and with depression limiting work opportunities, the Okies established state residence and drew unemployment relief.

For many Okies, the necessity of accepting relief was the most irksome consequence of their move, but most recognized that they had no other recourse: "If it had a-been for the relief load in California, the people would a-starved to death for there are ten men to every job. At the present time there ain't enough work to employ half the people." Or, as another put it, "I'd be a bad man to set around and let my family starve, wouldn't I?"[43] There was scant difference between the attitudes of Okies towards relief and the response of Americans in general to the need for government aid during depression conditions. Forced by the agricultural system into substandard employment and poverty, Okies nonetheless voiced sentiments regarding the dole not unlike those of Herbert Hoover. "Relief takes that independent American citizen feelings away from a man"; "it makes bums out of them"; and at one FSA camp, the resident Okies exerted considerable pressure upon any of their number applying for relief when work was available anywhere. It would, they feared, "reflect on the whole camp" should one of them be thought a malingerer.[44]

During the years of the dust-bowl migration, 300,000 people, who had been in the state only one year, received aid, and the relief load rose at a higher rate in agricultural counties than in urban regions. The harvest labor-relief cycle into which the Okies were forced was evident from the violent monthly swings in caseloads in rural regions. In the dead time late in February each year, relief was four times higher than it was during the peak picking times in the fall.[45]

This rising case load brought some grumbling in the rural regions during the Merriam years, but nothing to compare with the outcry that would develop during the administration of Culbert Olson. Unemployment relief did not tax the counties to which the migrants came in the same way as did education and health expenses, since relief was a state obligation distributed on a county-by-county basis, and supported by tax-paying citizens equally throughout the state. Growers found little in state relief policies worthy of complaint. Relief maintained the Okies during slack seasons, furnishing a subsidy which was cut off during harvest times, forcing workers to the fields.

One other facet of the relief issue added further complexity to the attitudes of influential growers and processors towards the Okies. As long as the influx of impoverished rural families continued, the harvest labor supply would be safe, regardless of the policies of the state administration. Even should a Sinclair, or—after 1938—a Culbert Olson, become governor, American federalism would ensure a fluid harvest labor supply. Since relief was distributed only to migrants who had been in the state more than a year, Okies would have to work in the fields in order to survive.[46]

The floods of 1938 changed all this. Hitherto, some of the newcomers had sheltered themselves from low wages by taking up residence at the FSA camps where, even should they be penniless, they would not starve, and could work for their keep at such tasks as gardening and maintenance. But the camp program could not accommodate more than a fraction of the newcomers, and the others were left to their own devices. When the San Joaquin ditch banks were washed out in February, FSA recognized the inequity of this arrangement. More camps would take time to build, however, and the Okies were already in distress. Therefore, a grant-in-aid program was instituted specifically because "floods coupled with shortage of crops and an increased flow to California . . . brought about a condition of poverty and suffering, [and] it was the obligation of the FSA to take care of such people as did not qualify for county and state aid."[47] During the eight months between the floods of February and the harvesting of the decreased cotton crop in October 1938, the federal government supported 50,000 Okies through the grant-in-aid program, most of them in the San Joaquin Valley.[48] Originally a temporary arrangement, the grant-in-aid program became permanent. By 1940, ten grant offices were scattered throughout the agricultural regions of the state, one in each of the upper San Joaquin counties.[49] The grants-in-aid were supplied only to families, in which one member had worked at agriculture in the year prior to migration. That subsumed most of the Okies. For those not eligible for FSA grants, San Joaquin Valley WPA provided additional work relief, increasing its membership rolls in direct response to the 1938 influx into the cotton region.[50]

California state officials recognized the implications of both the grant-in-aid program and the use of WPA as relief agency. Early in the program it was clear the Governor Merriam and SRA Administrator Pomeroy were unfriendly to a system that kept Okies on federal, protected relief for a year, only to thrust them onto state rolls after they had established residence. FSA was prepared to make relief grants, but had no administrative system through which to distribute the funds. It therefore called on the SRA to perform the function of certifying needy migrants for grant aid. Pomeroy balked, and FSA turned instead, during the early stages of the flood relief program, to the public-health officials, who did cooperate.[51] Later, in April, the former California adminstrator of the FERA charged that Merriam had sent Pomeroy to Washington in an attempt to curtail the grants program and "hamstring" the FSA through a "superabundance of red tape." Finally, in July, the communist press reported that FSA and WPA programs had precipitated an open quarrel between Merriam and the federal administration. Pomeroy, the *People's World* reported, had refused to certify nonresident migratory families for WPA jobs or grant aid, and was giving relief to the incoming Okies only on condition that they use the funds to finance a trip home.[52] FSA, unintimidated, continued its program alone, constructing along the way the bureaucracy needed to administer the system through its own offices.

Thus, by a relatively simple, possibly unintentional stroke, agencies of the New Deal in California had removed the cushion of a continuous influx of Okies from under the large corporation farms. And the value of a steady supply of new migrants had lessened further because of other developments not directly related to FSA or the floods. For one, the AAA restrictions meant that fewer workers would be needed in the foreseeable future. Since there were already sufficient Okies to pick the crops and to supply the surplus required to keep wages low, growers, ginners, and their allies could now revert to their roles as taxpayers sincerely concerned with the effect on taxes of a new flood of unemployed; and, since FSA had gone into the relief business, a political attack upon the New Deal could be launched through that agency. Further, just when public attention was riveted upon the misery of the Okies, labor unions announced that they would launch an organizational drive among the migrants. This chapter in California's labor history, and its effect upon the migrant situation, will be discussed later. For the moment, it is sufficient to observe that the growers had no means of discovering whether the unionization drive would succeed. The mere mention of unions, however, had made of the Okies a far less satisfactory labor force than they had been in previous years.

Over these issues, the migrants had little control. They were foci, not institutors, of the relief, union, and crop-control programs in California. Nevertheless, the migrants themselves helped bring on the storm of legislation and publicity directed at them by following a traditional American pattern. By settling in the valley cities, they established residence, and by establishing residence, they achieved the franchise. They used the vote, and the way they used it affected California politics for years to come. Herein lay the second cause of the change in growers' attitudes to the Okies. The Okies entered a state undergoing major political transformation and they accelerated changes that might otherwise have taken years longer to occur.[53]

Until the election of 1938, California had been a one-party state whose key political battles had been waged between progressives and conservatives. Firmly in Republican hands, California had not had a Democratic administration since the 1890s. It makes little sense, however, to describe California's politics during the first third of the twentieth century in terms of party labels alone. Two factors in the state's political situation permitted considerable crossover between parties. First, the cross-filing system allowed politicians of either party to run in the primaries of both, and it favored the incumbent Republicans. Thus, for example, the perennially popular Hiram Johnson was a California Democratic nominee nearly as frequently as he was a Republican, and he often stood unopposed on both tickets. Another factor that complicated the state's political system was that, even more than in the national parties, Democratic or Republican affiliation was no certain key to political attitude or ideology. California's Democratic state and federal congressmen and senators occupied the ideological spectrum from far right to far left, and, to a lesser degree, the same was true of the Republicans. Hiram Johnson, for example, changed his political ideology only slightly during the thirty years of his senatorial career; but in the context of the changing times, he moved from progressive, to moderate, to reactionary, always, however, winning.

California's political parties were weak in maintaining discipline, in part because of the anti-boss legislation of the progressive era. In the absence of tight party regularity, pressure groups came to play a larger role than parties in the state's politics. Because farming constituted for years the largest industry in the state, California's farmers exercised political power far beyond their numbers.

California's large farmers, through the Farm Bureau Federation and, after 1934, the Associated Farmers, exercised political power in two ways. Formally nonpartisan, they controlled elections in the rural counties. This dominance was enhanced by the state constitutional amendment of 1926, which conferred representation in the Senate on a county, rather than population, basis. Second, in concert with important urban industrial and commercial groups—the State Chamber of Commerce and its local affiliates, the oil industry, canners and processors, merchant shipping, Miller and Lux, the Kern County Land Company, and A. P. Giannini's Bank of America (Bank of Italy)—they were a major portion of the state's conservative, anti–New Deal, economy lobby. The economy bloc represented itself as an effective hindrance to radicalism, socialism, criminal syndicalism, labor racketeering and excessive spending, all of which, they claimed, emanated from the cities.

During the depression years, this argument contained considerable truth, although not in the terms in which the lobby presented it. Wherever large, corporate farms dominated the agriculture of a county, its representatives in the state legislature, whether Republican or Democrat, tended to be members of the economy bloc, preventing social welfare legislation where possible, sponsoring referendums and initiatives where necessary.[54] Moreover, they were the major force in determining administrative policies, especially where relief impinged upon the agricultural labor system.

Alongside its conservative power bloc, California spawned some of the zaniest radical groups of the Depression decade. Dr. Townsend, Ham 'N' Eggs, Technocracy, EPIC, and a powerful Communist party were the alter ego of California's right wing.[55] These extreme groups on the California political spectrum exerted considerable pressure throughout the 1930s on center groups. The 1934 EPIC campaign had been the result of a polarization in the Democratic party with radical forces gaining the ascendant. Merriam's victory had been the result, not of Sinclair's ill-conceived public statements, but rather of the counter-movement of conservative and middle-of-the-road Democrats into the Republican electorate.

According to Robert E. Burke, Merriam's victory was the last gasp of the state's Republican party in the mid-depression years. Democratic registrations had begun to outstrip Republican, and the Democrats, aided by the "Hoover depression," were gradually building support in both houses of the legislature. This was indeed a significant change. In itself, however, it tells little. Since party affiliation was not always an indicator of political persuasion, an increasingly large Democratic vote might not necessarily mean that the state's electorate was now liberal or pro-New Deal. Some California Democrats stood in the same relation to the New Dealers in the state as "Cotton Ed" Smith stood to Franklin Roosevelt on the national level. Further, it is axiomatic in California politics that if an area has only a slight Democratic edge, it is safe Republican country. Fewer Democrats than Republicans in California tend to vote; safe Democratic areas are generally those with upwards of

58 or 60 percent Democratic registrations.[56] The coming of the Okies helped tip California's political balance in favor of the Democrats. The migrants were Democrats; they were pro–New Deal; they supported the radical wing of the party; their political power was concentrated in precisely the counties where the economy bloc held sway.

The Okies came from traditionally Democratic states and from the very groups within the South's Democratic parties that C. Vann Woodward had called the "the left-forkers."[57] Nominally Democrats, these small farmers, tenants, and agricultural workers accepted the racial biases of southern politics, but never accepted the economic positions of the New South Democrats who had taken control of the state parties. From this class of agricultural people the Alliances, the Populists, and, in 1912, the Socialist party, drew large portions of their membership. Tenants and agricultural laborers in precisely the areas of Oklahoma that fifteen years later supplied many of the migrants, had engaged in radical action during the 1917 Greencorn Rebellion.[58]

It is possible that a correlation existed between political ideology and the decision to migrate or not to migrate. Conceivably, conservative Okies may have decided to migrate in higher proportion than radical ones; the radicals could have chosen to remain at home and join the Southern Tenant Farmers Union. Or, conversely, the situation may have been reversed. Perhaps a higher proportion of radical Democrats entered the migrant stream than remained in the southwestern population. Oscar Ameringer, for many years a perceptive observer of Oklahoma politics and society, believed that there existed a definite correlation between radicalism and migration. "They fought then" he told Carey McWilliams, "and now they migrate."[59] Neither thesis can be proved. It is more likely that economic, rather than political, variables influenced the decision to migrate and that the migrants represented the political spectrum in roughly the same proportion as did the entire populations of the regions from which they came.

Whatever the selective migration of radical and conservative Okies may have been, it is certain that a great majority of them were Democrats. Those who worked most closely with the migrants saw them as the "original Grandfather Democrats . . . simply because they come from that section of the country where the Democratic party has been dominant for generations."[60] In addition to their nominal party affiliations, the Okies who came to California tended to be New Deal Democrats, not primarily for ideological reasons, but because they believed that the Roosevelt administration had done its best for them. Very few Okies recognized that AAA had been an accomplice in their uprooting. Even these migrants believed that the New Deal was beneficial and that the Farm Security Administration and the federal grant-in-aid program would not have been possible under the Hoover administration.[61] When the migrants did express their political attitudes, as in the FSA camp newspapers, the dominant themes in their support of the New Deal were tradition and self-interest. They always had been Democrats and saw no reason to change their vote now, asking "what have the Republicans done for us?" One Okie, for example, had pitched hay on the Hoover ranch close to Bakersfield. Returning to the federal camp, he expressed a sentiment common to many migrants when he wrote to the camp newspaper that "what we can't understand is how a man can take such interest in people six thousand miles away [the Finns, relief for Europe after World War I] and pay little attention to his own people."[62] Anti-Republican humor was common in the camp newspapers. A frequent joke told of the little girl whose three kittens were Republicans until, a week after their birth, their eyes opened up and they became Democrats.[63]

The Okies differed little in their political attitudes from the bulk of farm people who during the 1930s became members of what Samuel Lubell has called the Roosevelt coalition.[64] Theirs was an emotional support of the President not unlike that of the worker who believed that "Franklin Roosevelt is the only man who knows that my boss is a bastard." As one Okie mother put the case for voting for Roosevelt:

> The people all wonder why we hobo,
> If they would think they would surely know
> Old Hoover gave us this blow,
> Roosevelt being a friend, To Children, women and men,
> He would show them they wouldn't die from need,
> For all of them he could clothe and feed.[65]

An incident at the Marysville FSA camp in late 1939 demonstrated how firmly the Okies were attached to the Roosevelt administration and the personal figure of the President. A disgruntled Okie, signing

himself "Rejected," submitted to the camp newspaper an anti-Roosevelt letter that accused the administration of overtaxing the people,
conniving toward war, and killing little pigs. The campers were incensed
and replied in the next week's issue. "What I'm really worried about,"
one woman told "Rejected," "Is that we will not get a man as kind and
considerate in the next four years as President Roosevelt has been in
the last eight years." Another camper, answering "Rejected's" charges
that AAA had driven him west, noted that "the president might have
taken farms and collected taxes, but I don't know how in the (h-ll) we
would eat it if wasn't for him." One Okie chose to ignore discourse:
"Come on out, rat, if you're not ashamed." The paper's editor announced that he would henceforth refuse to print anti-Roosevelt letters:
"We, the migrant people, are dependent upon this administration so we
should all praise our president instead of slander him."[66]

The attitudes that kept the Okies firmly within the Roosevelt
coalition extended also to California state politics. The migrants disliked the Merriam administration and found in the progressive wing of
the state's Democratic party a friendly political haven. The victory of
Culbert Olson in 1938 brought from the Okies a strong, favorable
response to the new liberal governor. Attacks in the press upon the
Olson administration brought angry responses from the camp newspapers. When the *Kern Herald* attacked both Olson and the Okies, one
of the local FSA campers replied to the paper's editor:

> Can you blaim us this is the best state I was ever in and I have bin in
> several and your governor is the best as far as I can see and to prove this
> just look at the bunch that is fiteing him. Us Okies have to chip in to
> read a paper and I am sick and my nerves is bad and I caint stand the
> stuff printed like this so after the 17th please discontinue my paper.[67]

The best indicator of the Okies' political sentiments appeared in the
1939 special election on the Ham 'N' Eggs plan. This outgrowth of the
Townsend movement, an exceedingly complex proposal to give thirty
dollars every Thursday to citizens over fifty, was "by all odds, the most
fantastic, incredible, and dangerous" of the utopian plans born during
California's depression years. The plan was supported enthusiastically in
southern California during the 1938 election and endorsed by victor-
ious senatorial candidate Sheridan Downey, a veteran of the EPIC
campaign. Olson's position as nominee was equivocal, and the defeat of

the plan in the 1938 election saved him from taking a position upon its implementation as governor. By 1939, Ham 'N' Eggs promoters had gained sufficient strength to force Olson to call a special election on the plan. Olson himself had by then come to object to the program and after its defeat for the second time in the special election, the plan's promoters launched a recall petition against the governor.[68] But the plan and the recall petition slowly dropped from public interest and gradually died as prosperity returned.

The Okies experienced no conflict between their general support of Olson and their fervor for Ham 'N' Eggs. More than any other issue, save possibly the 1940 national election, the plan captured the attention of the migrants. For the Okies, the idea made excellent sense. Like other Californians who supported the scheme, they resisted the arguments of economists who prophesied that the plan would bankrupt the state and build a dictatorial bureaucracy required to administer it. For the Okies, Ham 'N' Eggs was "good" because its detractors were "bad":

> [On] this ham and eggs business, just look around and see whos agin it you havent heard the bankers say they were voting for it have you nor the businessmen not the big businessmen not the big lawyers they didn't vote for Roosevelt either did they. There is just two sides to those things, theres the working mans side and then theres the bankers, standard oil and the businessmen's side.[69]

Such an attitude was not confined to Okies in the FSA camps. Little Oklahoma's residents in Modesto were almost unanimous in favor of the Townsend and Ham 'N' Eggs schemes.[70]

Unless they could be converted into votes, the Okies' political attitudes were of little use to either party. As the migrants settled into the valleys, however, they did register to vote, in part because inclusion on the voter rolls was acceptable proof of residence when applying for relief grants or WPA employment. The selective impact of the migrants upon voter registration was indicated by the increases in various counties. By mid-1938, as the parties shifted into high gear for the coming primary and gubernatorial elections, voter registration in the state had increased by over 200,000.[71] A substantial amount of this increase had occurred in the rural regions, especially those which had received the largest dust-bowl influx. San Francisco's voter rolls had increased between 1936 and 1938 a scant 1 percent; Los Angeles' 4.67 percent. But in Madera County, the increase had been 35 percent; in Merced County 24 percent; and in Kern County 22 percent.[72] This increase in registration in the agricultural counties was due largely to the Okies. This conclusion is not simply the result of comparing increases in population with increases in the voter rolls. One must demonstrate that the increase was a direct result of the Okies' registering as voters. Such was the case. Studies of Okie communities demonstrated that in the shack towns, as well as in the FSA camps, 65 percent of the migrants were entering the voter rolls.[73]

Olson announced his candidacy in September 1937, and, in early 1938, his forces launched a powerful voter registration drive among the Okies in the San Joaquin and Sacramento valleys. In part financed from Mrs. Robert McWilliams' trust fund, the voter enrollment campaign had the support of the FSA. Democratic party organizers were given jobs with the Agricultural Workers Health and Medical Association, a FSA-sponsored cooperative medical system for the migrants. From this base, they were expected to enlist the Okies under the Olson banner. It was "absolutely essential," Mrs. McWilliams wrote to one of the organizers, "that work start at once. If we do not build up the Democratic Party this year we will be all under the Fascists next year." Other New Deal agencies were involved as well. Early in the campaign, Hiram Johnson wrote home to inquire about rumors he had heard in Washington of the use of WPA as a vote-getting device. Meanwhile, the Merriam forces, blaming Communists, noted that "Defeat Merriam!" literature was being heavily distributed among the Okies in the San Joaquin and Sacramento valleys.[74]

Olson swept the San Joaquin Valley. He received his highest percentage of votes in Kern, Madera, and Fresno counties and was more successful in the upper San Joaquin Valley than in his home county of Los Angeles.[75] The Democrats would have carried California handily without the Okies. Olson's margin over Merriam was over 200,000 votes and the Okies could not have accounted for more than half of those, even had all of them voted Democratic. What was significant about the 1938 campaign and election was that valley counties, hitherto the base of political support for the economy bloc and the organizations of the large growers, had turned Democrat and, more importantly, liberal Democrat.

The Okies had not wrought this political conversion unaided. The Democratic vote had been growing in the valley even before the migrant invasion, and the Progressive Raymond Haight had run his best race during the 1934 election in Fresno and Stanislaus counties.[76] To conservatives seeking convenient explanations for Merriam's defeat, however, the Okies' presence supplied a convenient single focus. And Democratic victory cries in 1938 strengthened the fear that a permanent Okie population in the San Joaquin boded ill for the economy bloc. In Kern, for example, Olson had carried the county by 9,000 votes. The local Olson organizer claimed that he alone had delivered 6,000 of those votes—and "a lot of them were so-called migrants." As one Okie put it, "Well, as almost everyone in California has gone Democrat, we are sure to get a square deal . . . Oklahoma, and Arkansas has seemed to change the politics a bit."[77]

Well before the election of 1938, conservative elements in the valley had not been unaware of the threat to their political future in the tendency of the new agricultural workers to settle down, acquire residence, and use the vote. Worry had arisen early within the Merriam camp that the state was falling into "alien control." The Merriam headquarters announced that California's primary vote "may be decided by the votes of migrant farm workers from the Mid-West drought area."[78] The tone of alarm that characterized these announcements made quite clear the fact that Republican forces were aware that the Okies were not their political allies. Republican post-mortems after Olson's victory demonstrated the degree of concern that the Okie influx had generated.

Philip Bancroft, northern region vice-president of the Associated Farmers until May 1938, had been badly defeated in his senatorial fight with Sheridan Downey. Bancroft could understand, he wrote to Hiram Johnson a week after his defeat, why he might not carry the urban regions, but, he continued, "the worst jolt the results have given me is not that of my personal defeat, but the realization that our former important farm vote is now pretty much a thing of the past. The representative farmers, large and small, from one end of the State to the other were well behind me; but their efforts were neutralized by the hundreds of thousands of unsuccessful farmers and farm laborers who would even vote for Ham and Eggs."[79] Friends warned Hiram Johnson that the Okie vote was as dangerous to him as it had been for Bancroft in 1938: "Keep in mind that all your work as Governor and Senator is unknown and unheard of by a vast population who have come into California from the southwest and are not voters and citizens of this state. They have been reared and trained as Democrats, coming as they do from Oklahoma, Texas and adjacent states."[80] For the remainder of the depression decade, Bancroft was certain that Olson and the national administration were deliberately encouraging migrants "to come into this state in order to pack it with Southern Democrats in the hope of keeping it safely Democratic for a long time to come."[81]

Bancroft was not alone in voicing this charge. So powerful did the Okie vote seem in the wake of 1938 that "many said publicly that this migration was encouraged" with such design in mind and that relief funds were being disbursed for political purposes in the valleys. "Looks to me" a valley businessman noted, "as if someone . . . was packing our relief rolls and voting lists with white trash. . . . Add two and two under those conditions and you don't get merely four—you get [the election of] 1940."[82]

Conservative local and state politicians resorted to various temporary maneuvers in an attempt to counter the political threat to them. In each of three elections held between 1938 and 1940 (the gubernatorial election of 1938, the special Ham 'N' Eggs election of 1939, the presidential election of 1940), sporadic efforts were made to prevent the Okies from voting. In the gubernatorial election of 1938, a number of county clerks had refused to register migrants whose residence in the state exceeded the required year, but who at the time were living in the federal migratory camps. The National Lawyers Guild entered a test case on behalf of a migrant denied eligibility, but the state supreme court, "composed of appointees of Republican Governor Frank F. Merriam" refused to hear the case since only four days remained until the close of the registration period.[83] During the 1939 special election campaign, a different tactic was used. The 1938 test case had affected only migrants in the federal camps, and had been reviewed after the election; migrants who resided at the federal camp, but had been in California for one year, were eligible to vote.[84] Now, however, a number of agricultural counties' boards of supervisors and district attorneys waged voter removal campaigns, carefully auditing federal camp and county records to determine whether newcomers were voting without first having established legitimate residence. On election day, Kern County polls were minutely scrutinized by "volunteer challengers" with the result that a number of residents of the Arvin and Shafter camps were indicted by the county grand jury for illegally registering as voters. In 1940, similar county attempts to prevent the migrants from voting occurred, but with less frequency.[85]

Such efforts could have little more than ephemeral value. The migrants were establishing residence legally, leaving the FSA camps for the Little Oklahomas. In time, volunteer challengers would discover few among the migrants whose vote had not been legally cast. And, by the 1940 election campaign, local Republicans sought to attract the migrant vote rather than remove it.[86] The state's northern Democrats for Willkie undertook a large-scale campaign to sell their candidate to the migrants, and Willkie's trip through the San Joaquin Valley was noted for a soft attack on FDR coupled with a frank admission from the Republican nominee that he wanted to be President and would do more for the Okies than FDR had.[87] Finally, two weeks before the election, the pro-Willkie *Californian* made county history with a front-page editorial conciliatory to the migrants. In a tone that must have shocked some valley residents, the *Californian* exhorted the Okies to vote for Willkie. Roosevelt's "TWO TERMS" the paper insisted, had offered them "NOTHING FOR THEIR FUTURE WELFARE." Willkie, on the other hand, would answer the migrants' problems.[88]

With public interest focused on the Okies, growers' organizations coalesced with the state's economy bloc to launch a major campaign against the migrants, and, through them, against the Olson and Roosevelt administrations. Their anti-migrant publicity, broadcast throughout the state, kept California's migrant problem burning in the public mind for two years. The major vehicle for this campaign was the California Citizens Association (CCA).

Shortly following FSA's institution of the grant-in-aid program, and in the midst of the pre-primary campaign for the 1938 state election, rumors began to spread that groups in Kern County were toying with the notion of organizing a committee "to protest giving aid to the out of state migrants." By late May these rumors were confirmed with the announcement that the Committee of Sixty had been formed for the purpose of removing a "peril to every working man and woman . . . in the migrant labor and relief problem of Kern county." The group planned an urgent appeal to the federal government to end the relief being administered to the nonresident migrants. Within two weeks, Kern's Committee of Sixty had become the statewide California Citizens Association.[89]

The newly formed association was something more than a group representing a cross section of concerned valley citizens. Its leadership comprised, among others: Arthur S. Crites, secretary of the Kern County Mutual Building and Loan Association, and chairman in 1934 of the Merriam gubernatorial committee; Alfred Harrell, publisher of the influential *Bakersfield Californian*; and A. Dimon, a vice-president of the Bank of America and manager of its Kern branches. Represented too, were the Anglo-California National Bank, and Kern's larger department stores and real-estate firms. One other member worthy of mention was Thomas McManus, owner of the McManus Insurance Company in Bakersfield, soon to become the secretary of the association and its most vocal spokesman during the following two years.

California's constitution, rewritten during the Progressive years, contained initiative and referendum provisions that favored the use of the citizens-committee device by pressure groups. The CCA was no exception to this tradition. A confidential list of contributors to the association compiled by the Lubin Society demonstrated clearly that the political and economic groups supporting the CCA were those who supported the Associated Farmers as well. Represented among them were twenty-seven oil companies in Los Angeles and the San Joaquin Valley; six banking and investment companies, led by the Bank of America; three of California's largest agricultural land companies (Miller and Lux, DiGiorgio Farms, and the Kern County Land Company); and, finally, various businesses, agricultural packinghouses, and public utilities.[90]

The significance of this group's composition cannot be overemphasized. Here, joined in one citizens' association, were three separate forces linked in coalition, each with its own reasons for seeking an end to the migration. Farmers' groups, including the Bank of America and the realty companies (since many of California's largest farms were in reality leased by these companies to tenants), desired, in the wake of the oversupply of 1938 and the removal of nonresident migrants from the unprotected labor pool, to force an end to the FSA grant-aid program. In addition, farmers' groups for two years had been attacking the FSA for its role in agricultural labor disputes. A citizens' revolt against the organization would supply needed aid in this campaign. Finally, groups supporting the Associated Farmers would support the CCA to demonstrate a sincere interest in removing the now unneeded surplus of Okies, in order to allay the resentment slowly developing against the labor system that characterized California's agriculture.

The dominant position of oil companies among CCA's backers had political overtones. While state senator, Olson had repeatedly introduced bills designed to control the exploitation of tidelands oil and had charged that the Merriam-Hatfield administration was "absolutely . . . under the domination and control of the Standard Oil Company . . . and its affiliated interests. A major campaign against the migrants would serve a number of purposes. Olson seemed to be a winner even early in 1938, and he could be discredited by discrediting the New Deal.[91] The charge that a New Deal agency was "bankrupting the state" by supporting the Okies until they could establish residence would agitate the voters, helping to divert them away from Olson's attack upon the oil interests.

The third force represented by the CCA's support was ideological. Oil companies, banks, larger growers and realty interests were among the most important conservative, anti–New Deal blocs in the state. Just as oil companies sought to discredit Olson for specific purposes, so too the entire group would seek to discredit the New Deal and Olson for more general ideological reasons. The California Citizens Association was, as one Farm Security Administration investigator notified his superior after visiting with the group, "plenty organized and have plenty of money . . . I honestly believe that this outfit has enough resources not to be taken lightly."[92] With its large financial resources, the CCA embarked upon a two-pronged assault upon California's migrants and their supporters in the state and federal governments.

A petition was the most public of the CCA's activities. Couched in terms designed to raise the specter of a migrant menace undercutting wages and bankrupting the state, the petition actually demanded only two courses of action from the federal government: first, that it cease distributing relief to the migrants within California; second, that it "aid and encourage the return of the idle thousands" to their home states.[93] Throughout the first two weeks of June, the petition was circulated in a thoroughly homespun manner. Teams of children from schools and YMCA groups were sent out to collect names. The petitioners competed for individual and team high-scores each day and week. By January 1939, when the petition was presented to Congress by Senator Johnson, it had 100,000 names and, more important, several hundred group endorsements. Like the contributors to the CCA's war chest, the endorsing groups represented a cross section of anti–New Deal forces within the state. Most prominent were the local chambers of commerce. Well represented among the endorsees were the American Legion, the county farm bureaus, realty and insurance agents' associations, fraternal organizations, and home-owners' protective associations. In short, despite the CCA's claim to represent "persons in every walk of life," it was an agent for the coalition against which Culbert Olson would strive during his four futile years as governor of California.[94]

The CCA petition was a propaganda device more than it was an effort to gain leverage with the federal government. Furthermore, the CCA cooperated with farmers' groups in a publicity campaign not directly related to the petition wending its way through the counties. Secretary McManus barnstormed the state, speaking before state and congressional committees and on radio broadcasts. In these appearances and in his pamphlets, he presented an image of the migrant which could have no other effect than to increase the scorn with which Californians viewed the newcomers. "No greater invasion by the destitute has ever been recorded in the history of mankind," he averred; they "will soon control the political destiny of California." What made the Okies so dangerous, in McManus' view, was that they represented a group alien to California: "They come from the impoverished submarginal stratum of the east Texas cotton belt and from southeast Missouri and Northeast Arkansas. . . . They represent the lowest economic group in their home states." He continued by claiming that they accepted relief with no qualms and tended to vote for schemes like Ham 'N' Eggs. By 1940, McManus was a well-known figure and could be seen taunting Okies demonstrating in Olson's favor during the relief battle of 1940 with "Why don't you go back to Oklahoma?"[95]

Despite its intemperate tone, the CCA's attack upon the migrants generally took second place to its assault upon state and federal relief policies. McManus frequently avowed that the Okies would not be in California were state relief policies not carried out with "utter disregard of the taxpayers who must pay the bill. The barriers have been let down." Why, McManus asked rhetorically, were the barriers dropped; and answered his own question with more rhetorical ones:

Is this an attempt to coerce and intimidate our lawmakers?

Is it an attempt to create a more serious situation than exists in reality?

Is it an attempt to create for future use a great political power?

Is it an attempt to change the political and economic complexion of our state?[96]

One further accusation frequently appeared in the CCA's literature. If the administration was attempting to change the political and economic complexion of the state by encouraging Okies to migrate to California, so were the radicals and the Communists. The CCA was contemporary with a CIO attempt to unionize Okies employed in the fields. McManus echoed Associated Farmers arguments that the FSA was coddling CIO organizers and providing "rich soil for the growth and spread of subversive doctrines. . . . The Communists are quick to grasp every condition that can be cultivated . . . to bind these unfortunate persons together."[97]

Whatever the intrigues that McManus believed underlay the Okie migration, he threatened dire consequences for the state unless the influx were ended. "We might as well be candid with you. California is bankrupt." "Are we going to stand by and see our best efforts in building up a democratic social order utterly, devastatingly and irrevocably destroyed by a social and political economy that has for its purpose the subsidizing of human misery?"[98]

In order to avert the terrifying catastrophe on California's doorstep, the CCA proposed a disarmingly simple solution: cut the economic threads binding the migrants to California by increasing the residence requirement from one to three years and persuade Californians to exert sufficient pressure upon the FSA to force the federal government to return the excess Okies to their home states.[99]

The CCA was but one organization in the intense propaganda campaign launched in 1938 to achieve this dual aim. The State Chamber of Commerce and the growers' groups had shown interest in the new organization at its inception. The Farm Bureau Federation's position regarding the Okies echoed that of the CCA, while the Associated Farmers concentrated their barrage upon the FSA and the labor unions. From 1938 to 1940, the journals of these three organizations, in coordination with the *Pacific Rural Press*, printed and reprinted CCA-oriented articles and editorials.

One flank of this united attack joined the CCA in the attempt to persuade the public that the migrants had entered the state seeking its higher relief payments. Philip Bancroft led the attack for the Associated Farmers, noting that "the home states of the migrants have done practically nothing to keep out their citizens, except perhaps to encourage them to start migrating to California while our own state has endangered the relief of our deserving and needy citizens by throwing our doors wide open to the destitute of the other forty seven states and inviting them to enter." [100] Another Associated Farmer, Roy Pike, manager of the immense El Solyo ranch, inferred from personal experience that "this westward trek was largely stimulated because these migrants invariably found, when they arrived in California, that Federal relief payments were twice or thrice as much [as in the home states] ... these early comers wrote back to their relatives to join them for this reason." [101] One such alleged letter, produced in an article reprinted by the Associated Farmers, cropped up time and again after 1938:

> Dear Oddessa,
>   You and Coy must try and come to California this fall. We've got everything we want now. We get our relief checks for forty dollars every two weeks and we've bought a new car. We go into town every two weeks and get [free relief] commodities. That helps a heap on our grocery bill and the case worker comes out and gives the children clothes so that they can keep in school. You sure want to come out.
>   Your sister,
>   Bessie

From Bessie and Oddessa, the Associated Farmers broadened the attack to include all the California migrants, loosing the specter that Sinclair had unknowingly conjured in 1934. "Nowadays," the reprint continued, "the county seat is Mecca every two weeks when these wayfarers go for their relief. ... The street is crowded with good-looking cars, many of them new, and the mommas and poppas laugh and joke and stand in line for their handout."[102]

The migrant's morality came under scrutiny as well. *California*, the journal of the State Chamber of Commerce, joined the CCA in what was probably the single most scurrilous public attack upon the migrants during the entire period, an attack couched in terms designed for maximum effect upon its readership:

> "Tobacco Road has come to California," a dozen different men said to me up and down the valley. I thought the play, with all its poverty and filth, was a gross exaggeration—until the same kind of folks landed here on us. . . . And there is so much unmorality among them—not immorality; they just don't know any better. There was a father who was arrested for outraging his daughter. His whole family appeared in court to defend him, and when he was sent to jail his wife said, "They oughtn't to send paw to jail for that. She's his own property and he can do what he pleases with her."

The purpose behind this attack was unveiled when the article concluded with a warning to the terrified—and titillated—reader: "Before long the newcomers will be voters in this state—voters with perhaps a balance of power for even more relief than they can get today. That's something to think about." [103] It remained for the *Pacific Rural Press*, a month later, to suggest a course of action. The journal announced in its "Call to Californians" that a "citizens' revolt" was underway in Bakersfield. Why not write "Tom McManus," get copies of the petition, circulate them, and help save California from this unhealthy tide swept in by the Farm Security Administration?[104]

The steady stream of propaganda broadcast by the CCA and intensified in the state's business and farm journals exerted a powerful effect upon popular belief in the state. By January 1939, the CCA was able to declare favorable articles and editorials about its activities in nearly every newspaper in the state.[105] Its petition had been circulated, it avowed, in 457 cooperating towns and cities. These were not idle boasts. By 1939, newspaper editorials habitually identified the migrant problem with the relief problem, frequently naming the CCA as the source of information.[106] Meanwhile, the *Bakersfield Californian*, whose editor was a founding member of the CCA, poured a torrent of antimigrant, antirelief, anti-FSA invective into the southern half of the state.

When the Olson administration took office in January 1939, the CCA drive had borne considerable fruit. Writing to resign his membership from the Committee to Aid Agricultural Organization, the state's new director of immigration and housing warned that the campaign had "taken on very serious proportions throughout the state. . . . I think it highly advisable that your group assume the responsibility for organizing a counter campaign."[107] It was, by then, too late to organize such a campaign.

In February 1938, the problem of the migrants sprung to public attention when floods washed out the ditch banks. Within ten months, what could have become simply an exercise for California in absorbing one more wave of newcomers—albeit poorer than most—became instead the migrant problem and the Okies became a political football. By January 1939, the CCA and its allies had prepared the state for the next act in the scenario of California's politics. A new administration, led by a governor and staffed by men hostile to the groups that had built the CCA, would now be forced to attempt relief and welfare legislation in an atmosphere that equated any attempt to ease the problems of the unemployed and the poor with an invitation to degenerate, incestuous, Communist-vulnerable Okies to come to California and live off the fat of the land.

Notes in Text

1. *Bakersfield Californian*, March 9, 13, July 23, 1937; *Farmer-Labor News*, August 27, 1937.

2. *Bakersfield Californian*, July 23, 1937; *Marysville Appeal-Democrat*, August 9, 1937.

3. *San Francisco News*, July 23, 1937.

4. *Bakersfield Californian*, January 20, 1936; *Oakland Tribune*, August 24, 1935.

5. California State Relief Administration, "Transients in California," mimeographed (San Francisco, 1936), p. 245.

6. Dr. George Clements to Mrs. J. S. B. Clements, February 14, 1935, George P. Clements Paper, University of California, Berkeley.

7. Hugh Johnson column, *San Francisco News*, December 17, 1935.

8. California State Relief Administration, "Transients in California," pp. 245-249, 250.

9. *San Francisco News*, March 11, 1936; *Bakersfield Californian*, February 5, 14, 1936.

10. *San Francisco News*, March 11, 1936; *Open Forum*, February 22, March 14, 21, 1936; *San Francisco Examiner*, February 5, 1936.

11. *Marysville Appeal-Democrat*, February 6, 8, 1936; *Bakersfield Californian*, February 8, 1936.

12. *San Francisco News*, February 6, 1936.

13. See, for example: "California Farm Labor Problems," *Commonwealth Club Transactions* 30 (April 7, 1936): 153-196.

14. *San Francisco News, Bakersfield Californian, Marysville Appeal-Democrat*, January-February 1938, passim.

15. Constance Henderson to——, n.d., Federal Writers' Project Collection, Bancroft Library, University of California, Berkeley, Carton 10; The Rev. A. C. Mintz to Mrs. McWilliams, April 14, 1938, Federal Writers' Project Collection, Folder 852.

16. *Berkeley Gazette*, March 15, 1938; R. C. Timmons and C. J. Glacken, "Medicine Follows the Crops," *Survey* 75 (March 1939): 71; *Kern Herald*, April 22, 1938; *People's World*, March 22, 1938; *San Francisco News*, February 16, 1938.

17. *San Francisco News*, April 28, 1938.

18. *San Francisco News*, March 24, April 9, 1938; *San Francisco Chronicle*, March 11, 1938; *Fresno Bee*, August 7, 1938; *Labor Herald*, March 24, 1938; Mrs. McWilliams to Henry Schmidt (ILWU), March 16, 1938, Federal Writers' Project Collection, Carton 10.

19. *Fresno Bee*, July 26, 1938; *Bakersfield Californian*, July 26, 1938; D. E. Odom to Mrs. McWilliams, March 20, 1938, Federal Writers' Project Collection, Carton 852.

20. *San Francisco News*, May 5, 27, 28, 1938; Bob Hardie to Fred Soule, July 19, 1938, U.S. Department of Agriculture, Agricultural Stabilization and Conservation Papers, Federal Records Center, San Francisco; Lee Alexander Stone, "What Is the Solution to California's Transient Labor Problem?" June 22, 1938, p. 11, copy in vertical file, Public Health Library, University of California, Berkeley; *Fresno Bee*, July 26, 1938; *San Francisco Call Bulletin*, July 18, 1938.

21. *San Francisco News*, July 25, 27, 1938.

22. J. F. T. O'Connor diary, June 26, 1938, J. F. T. O'Connor Collection, Bancroft Library, University of California, Berkeley.

23. *Bakersfield Californian*, February 10, 1938.

24. See, for example, *San Francisco News*, July 16, 1937, February 24, 1938.

25. Testimony of Stuart Strathman, La Follette Committee, *Hearings*, Part 60, pp. 22,077-22,078.

26. "Letters," *Bakersfield Californian*, July 28, 1938; California State Relief Administration, *Agricultural Laborers in the San Joaquin Valley, July, August 1937*, reprinted in La Follette Committee, *Hearings*, Part 62, p. 22,663.

27. *Bakersfield Californian*, December 9, 1940.

28. Harrison S. Robinson, "Let's Tackle This Migrant Problem," *California* 30 (January 1940): 10; Kern County Health Department, Sanitary Division, "Survey of Kern County Migratory Labor Problem, Supplementary Report as of July 1, 1938," p. 1, copy in vertical file, Public Health Library, University of California, Berkeley.

29. Robinson, "Let's Tackle This Migrant Problem," p. 10.

30. See, for example, Arthur M. Schlesinger, Jr., *The Politics of Upheaval* (Cambridge, 1960), pp. 113-123.

31. *San Francisco Chronicle*, October 4, 1934.

32. "Attention Comrades!" handbill, California Ephemera Collection, University of California, Los Angeles.

33. Frank J. Palomares to F. A. Stewart, November 3, 1934, La Follette Committee, *Hearings*, Part 72, p. 26, 554.

34. Luther Whiteman and Samuel L. Lewis, *Glory Roads: The Psychological State of California* (New York, 1936), pp. 226-227, 241.

35. *Oakland Tribune*, August 2, 1935.

36. Clarke A. Chambers, *California Farm Organizations* (Berkeley, 1952), pp. 83, 202.

37. Ibid., p. 85.

38. *Bakersfield Californian*, April 10, 1936.

39. Carey McWilliams, *Factories in the Field* (Boston, 1939), pp. 286-287.

40. *San Francisco News*, April 30, 1936.

41. Paul Taylor, "From the Ground Up," *Survey Graphic* 25 (September 1936): 529.

42. Robert E. Burke, *Olson's New Deal for California* (Berkeley, 1953), pp. 78-79.

43. "Social Attitudes Expressed by Migrants," (n.d., manuscript), Carey McWilliams Collection, University of California, Los Angeles, folder entitled "relief."

44. Garst to Phillips, February 12, 1937, Simon J. Lubin Papers, Bancroft Library, University of California, Berkeley, Carton 13; *Covered Wagon News*, January 20, 1940.

45. California State Relief Administration, *The Problem of Interstate Migration as It Affects the California State Relief Administration* (September 28, 1940), p. 8.

46. Chambers, *California Farm Organizations*, p. 85.

47. La Follette Committee, *Hearings*, Part 59, pp. 21,929-21,930; Howard Hill, "Fifty Thousand on Federal Farm Relief in California," *Implement Record* 35 (June 1938), 48; *San Francisco Chronicle*, February 18, 1938.

48. United States, Department of Agriculture,. Farm Security Administration, *A Study of 6,655 Migrant Households* (San Francisco, 1939), p. 5.

49. Mary Gorringe Luck and Agnes B. Cummings, *Standards of Relief in California, 1940* (Berkeley, 1945), p. 57; locations were at county offices in Kern, Imperial, Madera, Riverside, Solano, Fresno, Yuba, Santa Clara, San Joaquin, Tulare counties.

50. *Bakersfield Californian*, February 23, 1938.

51. ———to A. L. Shafer, n.d., Federal Writers' Project Collection, Folder 709; *Bakersfield Californian, February 19, 1938; San Francisco News*, February 1, 1938; *People's World*, January 21, 1938.

52. *People's World*, April 28, July 25, 1938. 53. The following background discussion relies heavily, except where noted, upon Burke, *Olson's New Deal for California* passim, and Chambers, *California Farm Organizations*, chaps. 18, 19, 20.

53. The following background discussion relies heavily, except where noted, upon Burke, *Olson's New Deal for California,* passim, and Chambers, *California Farm Organizations,* chaps. 18, 19, 20.

54. Chambers, *California Farm Organizations*, p. 181, for a list of members of the economy bloc.

55. Exciting discussions of California's radicalisms during the Great Depression may be found in the following: Carey McWilliams, *Southern California Country* (New York, 1946), chaps. 12-14, and Luther Whiteman and Samuel L. Lewis, *Glory Roads: The Psychological State of California* (New York, 1936).

56. Author's interviews with various members of California Bay Area Democratic party during his numerous, if misguided, youthful attempts to help improve the character of American life through work within the established party organizations.

57. C. Vann Woodward's conception of the "twin forks" of southern Democracy is most usefully established in his *Origins of the New South* (New Orleans, 1951).

58. Works Projects Administration, Federal Writers' Project, *Labor History of Oklahoma* (Oklahoma City, 1939), pp. 40-42.

59. "Notes from A Conversation with Oscar Ameringer," McWilliams Collection, Oklahoma folder.

60. Gladstein interview.

61. "Social Attitudes Expressed by Migrants," *Happy Valley Weekly*, February 4, 1939.

62. *Voice of the Agricultural Worker*, December 22, 1939.

63. *Covered Wagon News*, February 18, 1939.

64. Samuel Lubell, *The Future of American Politics* (Garden City, 1951), passim.

65. *Happy Valley Weekly*, December 31, 1938.

66. *VOTAW*, December 22, 29, 1939; see also *Happy Valley Weekly*, May 20, 1939.

67. *Kern Herald*, January 25, 1940.

68. Carey McWilliams as quoted in Burke, *Olson's New Deal for California*, pp. 15, 109-112.

69. *Covered Wagon News*, October 28, 1939. See also *Tow Sack Tatler*, October 28, 1939; *Tent City News*, September 23, 1939; *Covered Wagon News*, September 29, 1939; November 11, 1939; California State Relief Administration, "Migratory Labor in California," p. 212.

70. Lillian Creisler, "Little Oklahoma, or, the Airport Community" (Master's thesis, University of California, Berkeley, 1939), p. 60.

71. *Marysville Appeal-Democrat*, August 16, 1938.

72. Other similar, if smaller, increases, were reported for: Kings, Tulare, Stanislaus counties, 15 percent; Mariposa County, 10 percent; Fresno County, 7.5 percent. *California* 28 (October 1938): 20.

73. Testimony of Miss Bauer, Tolan Committee, *Hearings*, Part 6, p. 2,578; F. W. Mortensen et al., "A Progress Study of 347 Families Occupying the Labor Homes and Cooperative Farms on 16 Projects of the F.S.A. in Region IX, 1940," manuscript, Farm Security Administration Collection, Carton 2.

74. Lillian Monroe to Mrs. McWilliams, April 10, 1938; Mrs. McWilliams to Monroe, May 10, 1938, Federal Writers' Project Collection, Folder 852. See *San Francisco Chronicle*, July 26, 1938; *Fresno Bee*, July 31, 1938.

75. Burke, *Olson's New Deal for California*, p. 33.

76. Ibid., p. 5.

77. *San Francisco Examiner*, March 6, 1939; *Tow Sack Tatler*, November 1, 1938.

78. *Marysville Appeal-Democrat*, August 16, 1938; *San Francisco Chronicle*, July 26, 1938; *Fresno Bee*, July 31, 1938.

79. Philip Bancroft to Hiram Johnson, November 11, 1938, Hiram Johnson Papers, Bancroft Library, University of California, Berkeley, Part III, Box 23.

80. Doherty to Hiram Johnson, December 1, 1939, Johnson Papers, Part III, Box 35.

81. Philip Bancroft to Hiram Johnson, April 9, 1940, Bancroft Collection; see also *San Francisco Examiner*, April 30, 1940.

82. Thomas W. McManus, "The Migrants Are Still Coming," KPMC, Bakersfield, radio broadcast, June 4, 1940, p. 5, Paul Taylor Collection, Bancroft Library, University of California, Berkeley, Carton 3; "Migrants Are Becoming Voters," 21; *Bakerfield Californian*, October 31, 1940; *Sacramento Union*, March 7, 1940; *Turlock Journal*, October 31, 1940.

83. *San Francisco Examiner*, September 24, 1938; *People's World*, September 28, 1938; *Berkeley Gazette*, September 25, 1938; *San Francisco Chronicle*, September 27, 1938; *Fresno Bee*, September 27, 1938; *San Francisco News*, September 27, 1938; *Oakland Tribune*, September 23, 1938.

84. *National Ham and Eggs*, September 16, 1939; R. W. Henderson to "Hughes" (Hewes), November 6, 1939; USDA ASCC Collection, 36,879.

85. Winters Camp Reports, August-September 1939, USDA ASCC Collection, 36,889; *Bakersfield Californian*, October 15-23, 1939; passim; *Delano Record*, September 29, 1939; *Fresno Bee*, October 19, 1939; *Bakersfield Californian*, November 4, 1939; R. W. Henderson to "Hughes" (Hewes), November 6, 1939, USDA ASCC Collection, 36,879; Indio Camp Reports, June 1940, USDA ASCC Collection, 36,884; Frank Doyle to Hollenberg, July 20, 1940, USDA ASCC Collection, 36,889.

86. Carey McWilliams, "Civil Rights in California," *New Republic* 102 (January 22, 1940): 110.

87. *San Francisco News*, September 21, 1940; *VOTAW*, October 15, 1940.

88. *Bakersfield Californian*, October 16, 18, 1938.

89. ——to A. L. Shafter, n.d., Federal Writers' Project Collection, Folder 709; *Los Angeles Times*, May 25, 1938; *Bakersfield Californian*, May 24, 1938; *Fresno Bee*, June 9, 1938.

90. "Contributors to California Citizens Association," typed list, Lubin Papers, Carton 12; *People's World*, Aug. 2, 1938.

91. Burke, *Olson's New Deal for California*, pp. 19, 6-22.

92. Charles Blout to Jack Henderson, May 28, 1938, Lubin Papers, Carton 12.

93. "Petition by the Citizens of California," Lubin Papers, Carton 13: "California is faced with economic chaos and financial ruin through the influx of tens of thousands of families, displaced in other states and pauperized by the depression, who are attempting to eke out an existence in agriculture and other labor here.

"California now is giving daily support to over 800,000 people in all forms of relief. We have four agricultural workers for every single available job.

"California does not have housing facilities for these people, and they are now living throughout the state, in tents and trailers, under conditions most menacing to the public health.

"These people are immediately given relief by the Farm Security Administration, under a supposition that there will be available work for them in agriculture. They cannot find that work unless they take jobs which now go to men and women who have established a legal residence here.

"To place these people upon Works Progress Administration projects would only aggravate this most serious situation.

"The influx of these people in such large numbers is destroying our wage structure, is periling industry, is laying a burden of confiscatory taxes upon our property, and is increasing unemployment and distress among our resident population.

"We request that all agencies of the Federal Government provide relief for these people in their home communities, and that information be disseminated at the source of the influx by the Federal Government that there will be no relief available for them if they migrate to California. That the Federal Government aid and encourage the return of the idle thousands now here to their respective homes, there to be given aid by the State and the Federal Government."

94. *Bakersfield Californian*, June 1-15, 1938; *San Francisco Chronicle*, January 10, 1939; *Los Angeles Times*, January 10, 1939; *Congressional Record*, 76th Cong., 1st sess., 1939, LXXXIV, Part 1, 63; Burke, *Olson's New Deal for California*, passim.

95. *San Francisco Chronicle*, February 17, 1940; California Citizens Association, "Statement to Assembly Unemployment Relief Committee" (Bakersfield, February 14, 1939), p. 5, Bureau of Public Administration Library, University of California, Berkeley; *San Francisco Chronicle* (Fresno edition), March 12, 1940.

96. California Citizens Association, "Statement to Assembly Committee," p. 2.

97. Thomas McManus, *Report to the California Citizens Association* (Bakersfield, October 1, 1938), p. 2, copy in Bureau of Public Administration Library, University of California, Berkeley.

98. Thomas W. McManus, "California Faces Bankruptcy," KPMC, Bakersfield, radio broadcast, April 2, 1940, copy in Taylor Papers, Carton 3; California Citizens Association, "Statement to Assembly Committee," p. 10.

99. *San Francisco News*, March 7, 1939.

100. Philip Bancroft in "What Should America Do for the Joads?" *Town Meeting* 5 (March 11, 1940): 2.

101. Roy M. Pike, an open letter to President R. G. Sproul, University of California, on Daily Californian article praising "Factories in the Field," October 7, 1939, Clements Papers, UCLA; see also testimony of James Musatti, La Follette Committe, *Hearings*, Part 59, p. 21,863.

102. See, for example, an undated letter from Mrs. Russell Richarson to———, John Randolph Haynes Foundation Manuscript Collection, Bureau of Government and Public Research Institute, University of California, Los Angeles; Alice Reichard, "California's Adult Children," *Country Gentleman* 110 (February 1940): 8.

103. Loring A. Schuler, "Dust Bowl Moves to California," *California* 28 (August 1938) passim, 8; see also "Migrants Are Becoming Voters," 20.

104. *Pacific Rural Press*, September 17, 1938.

105. *Congressional Record*, 76th Cong., 1st sess., 1939, LXXXIV, Part I, 62-63.

106. Some examples are: *Marysville Appeal-Democrat*, August 16, 1938; *Los Angeles Examiner*, February 27, 1939; *Sierra Sun* (Truckee), February 29, 1940; *San Francisco Chronicle*, February 26, 1940; *Chico Record*, March 1, 1940; *Lodi Times*, March 25, 1940.

107. Carey McWilliams to Committee to Aid Agricultural Organization, January 30, 1939, McWilliams Collection.

4

The Olson Administration and the Okies

"Every humane instinct, every impulse of intelligent self-interest, cries out against permitting the dust bowl refugees now huddled in California's valleys from being made the football of politics."[1] So had the *San Francisco Chronicle* warned in the midst of the gubernatorial campaign of 1938. Humanitarianism and self-interest notwithstanding, it was unavoidable that the migrant problem be drawn into the political maelstrom; it was too intimately connected to issues facing the state. Culbert Olson's attempt to bring a New Deal to California began late in the depression. For that reason alone, it had less chance of success than similar state reform movements that had begun earlier during the more crisis-oriented years. The tardiness of California's New Deal was not, however, fatal in itself. Olson's plan was beaten not by the slow recovery after the recession of 1937, but rather by powerful opposition in the state legislature. The Okie migration supplied one weapon in the battle against him. The Okies had helped elect Olson; now their presence and the anxieties it had produced helped destroy his effectiveness.

The Merriam administration had held office during the peak years of the Okie migration, but had done little about it, one way or the other. In matters involving agricultural labor, Merriam and his relief administrator, Harold Pomeroy, had adhered to the growers' positions. Insofar as the problems raised by interstate migration were concerned, however, Merriam had been for the most part inactive. He had attempted, at intervals, to interest the federal government in the problem, but even then, his was a passive role. In 1936, for example, the Colorado legislature had asked the federal government to look into the problem of "transient relief." Only after that state's resolution had been sent to California did Merriam announce that his "sentiments . . . were in accord" with Colorado's and he invited the governors of the eleven western states to join him in a demand for federal aid to transients.[2] By 1937, Merriam was being prodded by liberal as well as conservative journals to take some sort of action, but he did little. The Okies were, after all, supplying needed agricultural labor, and few outside the farm regions knew the magnitude of their deprivation. As late as 1937, the Okies were a joke in the state legislature: "you never saw [a jackrabbit] these days but a hungry Oklahoman was chasing it," one solon commented, and the Okie problem rested at that level of interest.[3] With the organization of the California Citizens Association (CCA), the Okies ceased to be a topic for humorous conversation, becoming instead a source of friction and fear for "older" Californians. By then, however, an election campaign was on, and the problem awaited the inauguration of the Olson administration.

In January 1939, the new administration entered Sacramento. Harold Pomeroy departed to become executive secretary of the Associated Farmers, an act symbolizing the fact that, on nearly every matter involving the Okies, the Olson administration was to install policies directly opposite those of the outgoing Merriam regime.[4] For Olson, the migrant problem impinged upon three separate and distinct issues. First, the coming of the Okies had raised the question of interstate migration and freedom of movement across state lines in response to the hope of broadened opportunity. Had the time come, in the face of the depression, to restrict this freedom? Second, the Okies played a role in the single most acrimonious issue facing the state, the "nightmare of relief."[5] Were the Okies responsible for the burden of relief? If so, should they be thrown from the relief rolls and persuaded to leave the state or, conversely, should they be accepted as new citizens, with attempts made to put them to "productive work"? Finally, by displacing the Mexicans in the fields, the Okies had exposed to public view the nature of California agriculture. What rights should state and federal government accord to agricultural labor and what, in the final analysis, should California do about the pattern of farming that had developed during the preceding half-century? To each of these questions Olson and his aides supplied answers that widened the ideological and political gulf separating them from the economy bloc, the Associated Farmers, and the California Citizens Association.

Olson did not share the popular view of the Okie as a degenerate, degraded loser in the American struggle for survival, and he would not countenance attempts to interfere with their movement across the continent into California. As early as 1935, when he was state senator, he had treated with scorn the fearful cries that Sinclairism and Townsendism would attract hordes of indigents to the state. In that year, California's assembly, still vibrating from the EPIC campaign, had passed the Redwine-Jones "indigent exclusion" act directed at "paupers, vagabonds, and indigents," subjecting them to imprisonment, fine, and deportation. Senator Olson treated the bill with a heavy dose of ridicule and sarcasm. He would support it, he announced, except that it was too narrow as it stood. He attempted to amend the bill to include among the excluded groups, "financial racketeers, stock and bond jobbers, industrial monopolists, watered stock manufacturers, corporation plunderers, despoilers of the savings of the poor, bank wreckers and defaulters, sweat shop owners and child labor exploiters, defrauders of widows and orphans, fraudulent promoters, family deserters, violators of private or public trusts, bribers of public officials, recipients of bribes, beneficiaries of fraudulent contracts secured through public agencies, millionaire wartime profiteers and promotors of war."[6] Olson had neglected to include lawyers and saloonkeepers among the groups excluded, but he had made his point. Despite *Los Angeles Times* assertions that "no piece of legislation . . . is of greater importance to the welfare of California," a mirthful Senate twice defeated the bill.[7]

As in 1935, so throughout his career as governor, Olson never fell victim to fear of the Okies. Speaking extemporaneously before a conference at Omaha, Nebraska, in 1940, Olson presented a sympathetic and positive vision of the migrants and their role in California's future:

> There are in California . . .your relatives and relatives of Arkansas and Kansas and Oklahoma, and all the Central and North Western states, as well as most of the others, people who have come to California for that salubrious climate. We have there all the wonders of nature which we are blessed with. We find not all of them coming out to spend any wealth they made here. It seems many of them have been defeated in life here and the Middle West. They have fought despair in this land of free enterprise and capital, and they have found themselves stricken with poverty. They have gone to California to see if they could get a foothold there and we have met them with outstretched hands.
> You are our American citizens and relatives and together we expect to work for the common welfare of all of us. While they are being acclimatized and assimilated on our soil so they can be placed at work we had to levy some taxes out there because we don't want them to starve—we want them to eat and be clothed. They are good, industrial [*sic*] American citizens like the rest of us out there and like our own native sons they believe that we should work and earn our living by the sweat of the brow, but it takes a little time. . . .
> We expect to go on building the West and welcoming those who come.[8]

Unlike the Republicans, Olson had little to fear from the migrants. They were his political allies, and this may account, in part, for his accepting with apparent equanimity what the Associated Farmers and the economy bloc could not tolerate. The theme of political self-interest should not, however, be overemphasized. Olson believed that California should accept and could assimilate the migrants, but he remained aware that hectic, unsystematic, rumor-induced migration was wasteful and, more important, unsettling for resident and migrant alike. Migration unguided, Olson insisted, was migration to trouble. "No single aspect of the dust-bowl migration to California," he told the Tolan Committee, "has been more deplorable than the absence of . . . guidance, planning, and direction . . . many migrant settlements have grown up in the State located in the most unlikely areas with respect to soil considerations, work opportunities, and future development."[9] Americans had the right, Olson believed, to move wherever they pleased. Governments, state and federal, had the responsibility to provide employment opportunity to migrants, or, better still, to improve opportunity in the home states in order that fewer Americans would be induced to migrate. Should a state receive a disproportionate share of migrants, the federal government must supply aid "not only to provide temporary relief and assistance, but to finance resettlement projects themselves, and also to guide and direct the flow of migration."[10]

On the night of his election, Olson was thinking about the interstate-migration facet of the migrant problem. Franklin Roosevelt had telephoned to congratulate him upon the victory, inviting Olson to the White House "to talk things over." Olson told reporters that he expected to accept the invitation, and that he would stress the problem of interstate migration: "I will try as far as possible to solve that problem with federal and state co-operation in order to get these people decent conditions in employment and care for their needs . . . the transient from another state I feel to be a federal problem to be met also by state cooperation."[11]

While governor, Olson never acquiesced in the popular tendency to equate the Okies with unemployment. Testifying before the Tolan Committee, he held in contempt those who blamed "rising relief loads" upon the migrants camped in California's rural areas. He attacked "special-interest pressure groups" who had "seized upon the migrant problem as a means of lowering all relief standards" in the state. Olson claimed in 1940, with a bitterness born of experience, that these groups launched "cleverly timed publicity campaigns," usually on the eve of a legislative session. The "migrant problem," Olson correctly understood, had "lent itself readily to unfair exploitation for partisan political purposes. Taxpayers naturally want to see their burdens lightened, and when they are made to believe that hordes of migrants are flooding the State, draining its resources and undermining its standards, they frequently react in a manner that works an injury not only to migrants but to long-time residents in this State." Interstate migration had actually been good for the state, Olson asserted. With a subtle sleight-of-hand, he went on to explain that California had "profited handsomely" from the $193 million spent by *tourists* and *travelers* in 1939. Olson's guile in identifying tourism with the Okie migration did not blind him to the danger that he might be convincing his listeners that the state did not require aid in absorbing the migrants. He concluded by noting that "under present conditions an enormous aggregate of new population in a particular area . . . does constitute an extraordinary problem for any settled community.''[12]

Olson's answers to two of the three distinct questions raised by the Okies were, then, consistent and relatively uncomplicated. The migrants, he asserted, were good Americans down on their luck. Their migration to California had been chaotic and a cause of immediate dislocation. Given time and a return of prosperity, however, the Okies would become an asset to the state. Of far greater complexity, and potentially far more controversial, was Olson's position on the Okies in their role as agricultural laborers. The governor believed that "of all the grave and serious problems which the present Olson administration has inherited from prior administrations, none is, perhaps, more acute than that of migratory farm labor in this state." Relief, Olson knew, was a problem that extended into this facet of the migrant problem as well. When the governor accused "special-interest pressure groups" of presenting misleading propaganda in an attempt to identify relief with the Okies, he was referring, at least in part, to the Associated Farmers, which had a clear and specific interest in keeping relief payments low. Speaking before Senator La Follette, he stated, "relief has a direct bearing upon the problem of migratory farm labor in this state." Olson noted that since 1933, California farm wage levels had approximated the level of relief payments and that the Merriam administration had connived with growers in a policy of "work or starve." Low relief payments meant low farm wage levels and these, in turn, meant degradation, penury, and dislocation for farm labor. Unwelcome in the community except during harvests, farm workers suffered legal disabilities as a result of their inability to remain in one place long enough to establish ties. They were unrepresented in Congress, unfairly treated in labor disputes, and unprotected in the exercise of their civil liberties.[13]

Olson, therefore, understood well the social effects of the agricultural system that had developed in California. He sympathized with the plight of California's harvest army, and had little regard for California's corporate farmers. The Associated Farmers he despised; the Farm Bureau Federation, which had generally been hostile to him, could expect few favors from the new governor. Nonetheless, Olson never seriously questioned the pattern of agriculture that had bred both the migrant worker and the Associated Farmers. During the latter stages of his election campaign, Olson had been given the opportunity to consider the implications and value of large-scale corporate agriculture vis-à-vis family farming. A policy committee had prepared a confidential brief outlining the "problems of coping with California [*sic*] situation," which dwelt at length upon the nature of California agriculture. The brief recognized the "import of the gigantic industry which California agriculture has become overnight," but refused to believe that this "startling fact" doomed the American image of yeomen farmers working quarter- or half-sections.[14] The report cautioned Olson to avoid the tendency "to predict that with increasing mechanization there will disappear all the advantages of country life as it has been known in the past." The agricultural problem, the report insisted, should not be subsumed to the "familiar battle between employer and employee which rages in urban industry." Rather, small farmers should be encouraged and aided by government in their attempt to become economically viable.

Olson was, however, no Jeffersonian, and he was unlikely to accept the report's conclusions. He did not object to industrial agriculture. He simply detested those who owned the factories in the fields and manipulated their bounty for personal profit and with little regard for the farm worker or for the residents of the adjoining towns. While candidate, Olson rarely excoriated large-scale farming; instead, he called for conservation and flood-control projects upon which to employ agricultural labor during the slack season.[15] In his testimony before both the Tolan and La Follette committees, Olson maintained a consistent theoretical position: accept the efficiency of industrialized agriculture but remove the disabilities that prevent agricultural laborers from sharing fairly in the system. To this end, he recommended excising the abuses that marred an otherwise acceptable pattern of agriculture. The La Follette Committee, he hoped, would suggest legislation that would defend migratory agricultural workers from the "illegal practices" adopted by powerful grower groups.[16] Before the Tolan Committee, Olson recommended the "advisability of including agricultural labor within the protection of most modern social legislation. By this I refer in particular to . . . wages and hours, social security, and the National Labor Relations Act."[17] Finally, throughout his gubernatorial career, Olson did not avoid what was potentially the

most controversial corollary of his position. Because the condition of
the farm workers was intolerable, migrant farm workers should be
encouraged to organize agricultural labor unions to protect themselves
from exploitation. No other single facet of his position regarding
agriculture brought Olson more criticism from his enemies. His activities concerning agricultural unions conformed with his ideas, and af-
fixed the state's large growers even more tightly to the anti-Olson
coalition in the state legislature.

   Olson's appointments to state agencies intimately connected with
the migrant problem served notice upon the growers and the economy
bloc that the halcyon days of the Merriam administration were over.
Dewey Anderson, Olson's relief administrator, infuriated the opposition
by reversing the Pomeroy policy in every particular. Under Pomeroy,
nonresident Okies requesting immediate emergency aid received grants
only upon condition they leave the state; under Anderson, the policy
was changed to include a consideration of "the family's plan for its
future well being" and "the conditions from which the family is
attempting to escape."[18] In a subtle way, Anderson's policies were
national in scope where Pomeroy's had been concerned only with
California. Anderson believed that it was not "to the economic advantage of this country to create stranded communities in non-productive
areas, i.e., Dust Bowl Area, solely for the reason they cannot secure
relief elsewhere."
   Anderson deviated furthest from policies to which the state's growers had become accustomed in regard to Okies who had established
residence, and especially those who had become agricultural workers.
The prevailing-wage policy of the Merriam years was replaced by a
fair-wage policy. Hitherto, unemployed agricultural workers were
thrown from relief rolls unless they accepted work in the fields at
prevailing wages. Now, the State Relief Administration determined a
fair wage for work in the fields. Should the growers offer less, the SRA
would supply a protective umbrella for the field workers by retaining
them on the relief rolls.[19] Twice during 1939, the Olson administration
attempted to set fair wages for field work. Its decision that a fair wage
for cotton-chopping or picking was 27½ cents per hour (the growers

had proffered 20 cents) helped initiate the immense cotton strike of 1939.[20]

Olson's relief policies brought powerful opposition from grower organizations.[21] His appointment of Carey McWilliams to head the State Division of Immigration and Housing infuriated them. The Division of Immigration and Housing had been founded by Governor Hiram Johnson in 1913 to ease the problems of foreign immigrants to California and, in the wake of the bloody Wheatland hop-fields riot of field workers in 1913, to report upon violations of various state acts relating to the housing of migratory agricultural workers. Under the leadership of Simon J. Lubin, a near-fanatic in his opposition to the state's large growers, the division had functioned effectively until the postwar reaction of the 1920s, when, his funds decimated and his inspectors handcuffed by lack of support, Lubin resigned in disgust and the division languished until 1939.[22]

McWilliams revived the moribund division, announcing that after September 1, 1939, his inspectors would check carefully for violations of the state's housing laws.[23] Although understaffed and subjected to considerable attack from growers, the division publicized the worst conditions in the privately owned labor camps. McWilliams even took to the radio, appealing to residents of agricultural regions to report violations of the housing acts.

McWilliams' role as commissioner of immigration and housing was not his most important function with the Olson administration. What earned for him from the large growers the title "the state's number one agricultural pest, outranking pear blight and boll weevil" was his position as the administration's conscience on agricultural matters.[24] McWilliams was a radical advocate of limiting private enterprise where it impinged upon the public welfare. Long before John Steinbeck began his investigations into the tribulations of the Joads, McWilliams had delivered a powerful blow at California's large growers in a series of muckraking articles, which had appeared first in 1935. Revised in 1939 and expanded into a book, *Factories in the Fields* described the accretion of the large farms by speculators and their subsequent exploitation of agricultural labor. In no sense was the book a detached narrative account of a peculiar phase of agriculture in America. It was a polemic and a plea for change. McWilliams, like Olson, did not object to large-scale farming. His solution to the problems inherent in industrial farming, however, laid him open to the charge of "red" from sources as diverse as Lee Stone, Madera's right-wing health director, and Paul Scharrenberg of the AFL.[25] The final solution, McWilliams insisted,

> will come only when the present wasteful, vicious, undemocratic and thoroughly antisocial system of agricultural ownership in California is abolished. The abolition of this system involves at most merely a change in ownership. The collective principle is there; large units of operation have been established, only they are being exploited by private interests for their own ends. California agriculture is a magnificent achievement; in its scope, efficiency, organization, and amazing abundance.... In the meantime, the dust-bowl refugees, unlike the pioneers of '49, have made the long trek West to find not gold but labor camps and improvised shantytowns. It is just possible that these latest recruits for the farm factories may be the last, and that out of their struggle for a decent life in California may issue a new type of agricultural economy for the West and for America.[26]

McWilliams' historical account of the growth of the industrial farms was controversial enough. His cry for collectivism was a crimson flag waved at the state's growers. The book had been published at precisely the time when McWilliams was an important member of the Olson administration, and he could not be ignored. He rapidly became the state's and the nation's resident authority on the problems of migrant labor, as well as of the Okie migrants. Olson's right-hand man on the subject of agriculture, he improvised caravans of social workers to tour the Okie settlements in the San Joaquin Valley, served as Olson's representative at statewide conferences on migrant labor in the valleys and, finally, slugged it out verbally with Philip Bancroft on the question "what should America do for the Joads?" on the nationwide "Town Meeting of the Air."[27] Despite persistent complaints from the conservative opposition, Olson retained McWilliams throughout the whole of his administration.[28]

Olson, McWilliams, Anderson, and others in the administration were determined to inaugurate fundamental changes. Olson's program included reforms as various as public ownership of private utilities, reorientation of the tax structure, repeal of infringements upon civil liberties (the Criminal Syndicalism Laws), production-for-use, and increased social welfare activities. Nestled within Olson's broad program lay an "ambitious program with respect to migratory labor." The new governor sought to augment the Farm Security Administration's labor camp program by committing the state to building thirty labor camps of its own. In addition, and probably as a result of McWilliams' prompting, Olson desired to create a permanent fair-wage standard board to determine wages for agricultural labor. Housing laws concerning migrant workers, Olson hoped, would be strengthened; labor contractors, responsible for so many of the travails of the Okies, would be regulated more strictly.[29] None of Olson's plans ever materialized. With the exception of one bill regulating labor contractors, his program for migratory labor collapsed in the face of determined opposition from the legislature.

The governor had entered office riding high upon the crest of a wave of Democratic sentiment and looking ahead to four years of reform. Within two weeks, his New Deal for California had become a shambles. He had found, as had reformers in other states during the latter years of the depression, that governors could only propose; legislatures, however, could and did dispose. The economy bloc marshaled its forces, enlisted Democrats sufficient to destroy Olson's majority in the legislature, and forced the governor into a retreat from which he never regained the initiative. Insofar as legislation affecting the Okies was concerned, Olson spent two years simply attempting to protect relief and labor policies inaugurated under his predecessors, and even here, he failed.

The early skirmishes of the 1939 legislative battle gave ample augury of what lay ahead for Olson. Worn out as a result of personal illness followed immediately by the death of his wife, the governor was in no condition to fight with full vigor the attack upon his budget and his legislative program that developed when the legislature returned from a recess in early March. The Republican minority, its ranks swollen by the defection of conservative Democrats, launched a full-scale attack upon the governor's budget, cutting to the bone Olson's suggestions for raising revenue in order to implement his social welfare programs.[30] A major portion of the budget covered appropriations for relief, and it was on this subject that Olson's troubles coincided with those of the Okies. Spurred by a steady stream of propaganda linking relief with the "chiseling hordes of indigents" from other states, the economy bloc severed the relief appropriation from the budget. By this action, Olson's opponents ensured that government housekeeping functions could continue while the relief issue was subjected to further scrutiny. The ensuing war between the governor and the legislature, described by one reporter as "the wildest legislative scramble . . . seen in the capital since 1923," included three battles over the migrants.[31]

First, members of the economy bloc, in a move that directly affected the Okies, sought to cut taxes by lowering the entire relief appropriation. This ensured that the State Relief Administration, despite its desire to protect agricultural workers from low wages, would find its operations considerably restricted by lack of adequate funds. That the Okies played a large role in the attempt to cut relief appropriations became clear when Senator Harry C. Westover (Democrat, Santa Ana), one of Olson's lieutenants, took to the radio in an attempt to marshal public opinion against the budget cuts. Westover called for an "equitable" solution to the relief issue and noted that "as long as California continues to offer a better place to live and a better place to earn a living, we can expect migration to this state."[32] The migrants would come with or without relief payments; when they arrived, however, they might require relief and, as Westover noted, "a hungry man is a dangerous man." Relief payments were, in effect, "an insurance against revolution." But arguments such as these carried little influence. When the relief appropriation was finally passed in July, it had been trimmed considerably.[33] Worse, Olson could not relax even with this straitened appropriation: the appropriation was for an interim period only, and he was required to return in early 1940 for a special session of the legislature which would vote funds to permit relief to continue until the next full-dress regular session.

The second battle in the 1939 relief war involved Olson's proposal for farm wage determination boards, which, by establishing a fair wage, would supply guidelines to the SRA for the release of migrants from the relief rolls. The economy bloc had already seen the Olson administration in action in May, when an ad hoc board led by Carey McWilliams had established a fair wage for cotton chopping in the Madera region. Under the relief appropriation of June 1939, State Relief Administrator Dewey Anderson was required to file a letter with the legislature, stating that it was "not the desire nor the province of SRA to set agricultural wages."[34]

The relief cuts, coupled with Anderson's humiliation at the hands of the legislature, were a setback to Olson's ambitious plans for furnishing at least a modicum of social equity for the migrants. Obscured by this noisier conflict over the specific relief appropriation lay hidden a far more dangerous onslaught upon the governor's relief policies. The appropriations struggle had merely limited SRA's power. Meanwhile, a movement was developing to destroy the SRA and return the administration of relief to California's fifty-eight counties. In March 1939, several employees of SRA's Bakersfield office charged that they had been "ousted or transferred" by assistant relief administrator William J. Plunkert because they had failed to accept his "radical" political positions. Plunkert was charged, as well, with nepotism, as his wife was WPA research director in San Francisco. Pressure from legislative committees investigating the "relief mess" forced Olson to discharge Plunkert.[35] Nonetheless, March and April 1939 were full of rumors, threats, and alarms, many of them emanating from the CCA, which linked SRA with an attempt to bankrupt and revolutionize the state.

Just then, supervisors of eight counties met at Madera to demand a twofold attack upon the "monthly influx of thirty-five hundred to seven thousand migrants" which, they asserted, was "creating a crisis."[36] The supervisors demanded federal legislation to curb the influx and a general lowering of relief payments. They called, further, for the return of relief administration to the allegedly less radical, fiscally more responsible, counties. Five days later, the State Supervisors Association met at Sacramento in annual convention, and Olson warned the body that he would oppose strenuously any attempt to return relief to the counties.[37] Newspapers in the agricultural regions fastened upon the idea, nonetheless, and by April and May county administration of relief was a commonplace solution to the so-called relief mess. The *Marysville Appeal-Democrat,* for example, suggested that California might emulate Texas, an interesting idea since Texas was supplying many of California's Okies: "The state of Texas offers a striking example of successful operation of such a system. Local residents who need assistance are cared for by the counties. Migrants are taken care of entirely by the federal government on WPA, FSA and other alphabetical departments."[38] Both the Associated Farmers and the State Farm Bureau Federation entered the lists in favor of the proposal in 1939.[39] So powerful was the movement to return relief to counties that on the eve of the final vote on the relief appropriation, Olson was

forced to threaten to veto any plan that envisaged county relief administration. Such a plan, he insisted, would replace one administration
with fifty-eight, create chaos out of an already complex situation, and
intensify the load upon areas receiving the bulk of the Okie influx.[40]
For the moment, Olson's tactic prevented the elimination of the State
Relief Administration. The relief appropriation passed, with the funds
to be administered by the state agency, not the counties.

Olson emerged from the relief battle bloodied but with modest
success. Relief was not, however, the sole concern of the 1939 legislature, and Olson had to cope with an additional attack upon the Okies,
not in their role as relief clients but in their role as interstate migrants.
Just before the 1939 legislature had taken its February recess, Assemblyman Frederick Houser (Republican, Los Angeles) introduced bill
1356, designated an "indigent exclusion act." Like the Redwine-Jones
bill of 1935, which Senator Olson had helped slay with ridicule in the
Senate, the Houser bill would have restricted the number of persons
entering the state by banning the entry of "paupers, vagabonds and
fugitives from justice."[41] When the legislature returned from its recess,
the Houser bill, backed by the chamber of commerce, had gained
considerable support. The number of legislators who favored it was
"surprisingly large, so strong [was] sentiment against the influx of
migrants from the dust bowl areas."[42] Olson invoked once again his
threat of the gubernatorial veto: "I'll veto this or similar bills," he
announced, adding with amusement, "if they promise not to recall
me."[43] Despite his light treatment of the Houser bill, Olson saw in it a
serious threat. Again he worked through Senator Westover to ensure its
defeat while simultaneously attempting to put before the public the
constitutional right of all Americans to settle wherever they chose.
Olson's efforts succeeded, and the Houser bill died in committee. On
balance, the 1939 legislature was a draw. Olson had scored a point for
the Okies in his defeat of the Houser bill. He had, however, lost a point
on a measure to provide migrant farm labor camps at state expense
when the Tenney bill for this purpose was defeated in the Senate.[44] On
the issue of relief, he had achieved a compromise, at best.

Olson's time of troubles in 1939 was nothing compared with the
battle looming upon the 1940 legislative horizon when he was required
to return early in the year for a special session to provide further funds

for the SRA. The atmosphere of late 1939 and early 1940 had been poisoned still further by the injection of two additional ingredients into the already acrimonious statewide debate on the Okies. *The Grapes of Wrath*, published in mid-1939, had polarized sentiments concerning the Okies around the terms of reference defined by John Steinbeck. As will be seen below, the reception of the novel in California's agricultural regions was quick, hostile, and violent. Embarrassed by the volume, and simultaneously furious at the image it presented of them to the nation, the state's agricultural pressure groups and their allies in the legislature emerged from their corner of the legislative ring spoiling for a fight.

The Grapes of Wrath was only half the weight of the total chip that the economy bloc and the farm groups carried on their shoulders for the 1940 struggle. In late 1939, the United States Senate's Committee to Investigate Violations of Free Speech and Rights of Labor (the La Follette Committee) had received additional appropriations for the purpose of inquiring into the California labor situation. It made clear from the start that the major portion of its California activities would be concerned with anti-labor practices of the Associated Farmers and, to a lesser extent, the Farm Bureau Federation. The La Follette Committee's investigators served the same purpose for liberals during the depression as did the Dies Committee's investigators for the conservatives. La Follette's men seized records, held biased hearings, and left the state's growers with a severe case of social paranoia, part of it induced by the fact that Olson and McWilliams played major roles in aiding the committee's California work. In the minds of the growers, the La Follette Committee hearings fused with the nationwide uproar over *The Grapes of Wrath*. As the columnist for the *San Francisco News* noted wryly in December 1939, it was a "secret" that Carey McWilliams had "whipped up" Olson's statement before the La Follette Committee. The growers, the column continued, "would about as soon the Governor had turned to John Steinbeck—whose book . . . should have been called the 'Sour Grapes of Wrath'—as to the author of 'Factories in the Field.' "[45]

The special legislative session was scheduled to convene on January 29. The preceding four weeks witnessed full-scale propaganda drives linking the migrant problem with the relief fight shaping up in the legislature. The Hearst press gave prominent place to a series of feature articles, which echoed the CCA's position. Of the Okies, the author charged, "give them a relief check and they'll head straight for a beauty shop and a movie." Of the State Relief Administration and the FSA: "All this help . . . all this gratuitous service—it's giving a few a real and well-deserved boost. But it's making bums of many more." The articles supplied a solution as well: "What can we do? Get busy. Decide once and for all whether we're mice or men. Stop being suckers . . . refuse to be taken for a ride. Throw every red out of office on any state or federal job."[46] Meanwhile, state legislators opposed to Olson issued frequent calls for a change in relief policy. Senator William Rich (Republican, Marysville), for example, announced on the eve of the legislative session that he would support all restrictions upon the Okies: "Stop setting migrants up in camps. If they come to this state, let them starve or stay away. I'm firmly against this idea of supporting people on state and federal funds—better than they've ever been supported before."[47]

The redoubled attack on the migrants and the SRA did not go unopposed by Olson and his lieutenants. Olson counterattacked with an assault upon the San Joaquin Valley "slum-lords" who, he insisted, were making money out of the deplorable conditions in the Little Oklahomas. The deeper purpose behind this statement was to assert that valley counties were no place to lodge the administration of protective programs for migrants. Rural counties, he noted, "have shown no indication that they realize the seriousness of the problem or that they accept the responsibility for doing anything about it."[48] Meanwhile, McWilliams used the month preceding the special session for a barrage at the Associated Farmers who, he asserted, were "making a concerted effort to have the administration of relief taken out of the hands of the Democratic state administration and returned to the Republican-controlled Boards of Supervisors in the counties."[49]

Olson was in political trouble even before the legislators resumed their seats. Although the session was called for a specific purpose, the Republican caucus, allied with Democratic members of the economy bloc, embarked immediately upon a campaign to replace the Olson-backed officers of the assembly with men of their own choice. In a move symbolic of tough sledding ahead for the Okies as well as for Olson, Seth Millington (Gridley), a Sacramento Valley Democrat of conservative hue, nominated Gordon Garland, San Joaquin Valley Democrat, for speaker of the assembly. Garland, "conservative to the core" and a leading member of the rump group of anti-Olson Democrats, represented Tulare and Kings, two of the five counties inundated by migrants in the upper San Joaquin Valley. Elected as speaker, Garland utilized his flair for the dramatic by tearing from the rostrum a telephone allegedly connected with Olson's office.[50]

The new speaker was a San Joaquin Valley farmer, a member of the Farm Bureau Federation and frequently addressed the Associated Farmers. Valley newspapers reported that Garland's election had been hailed by the Associated Farmers of Kings County as a "victory for California farmers" and "generally approved" elsewhere in the valley.[51]

While the assembly was handing Olson a defeat in electing its new speaker, the Senate became the focus of the campaign to destroy the SRA by returning relief to the counties. Bill 50, sponsored by Republican Senator John Phillips of Banning, and otherwise known as the "county relief bill," was passed by the Senate on February 3, to the outraged cries of the administration, especially since Olson had recently been given additional grounds for objecting to the destruction of the SRA inherent in the Phillips bill. One of Carey McWilliams' hastily organized caravans had toured the San Joaquin Valley and reported upon its return that county-administered relief would entail considerable deprivation and humiliation for Okies in the valley. There was "no comparison" the committee report observed, "between the treatment of the migratory families by the Federal relief camp authorities and county officials and private individuals." One of the unqualified recommendations of the group was that relief should remain firmly in the hands of the SRA.[52] The day before the Senate vote, Olson attempted to exert pressure upon boards of supervisors in the San Joaquin, notifying them by telegram that should the Phillips bill pass, county tax assessments would have to rise to a level commensurate with the Okie population.[53] The bill passed anyway. Observing that "the people of California" had not elected "an administration controlled by the State Chamber of Commerce or its subsidiary political organization known as the Associated Farmers Incorporated," Olson announced on the radio that should the assembly pass a similar bill, he would veto it.[54] The assembly took the dare and passed a similar bill sponsored by economy-bloc Democrat Jeannette Daley. The Daley bill received the assent of the Senate and was transmitted to the governor, who vetoed it. Since the original vote in the assembly on the Daley bill had been relatively close, no override of the veto was attempted.

By his veto of the Daley bill, Olson had saved the Okies from being thrown to the not-so-tender mercies of the county authorities in the agricultural regions for the second time in less than a year. His salvaging of the SRA was, however, his last political gasp insofar as protection for the migrants was concerned. Thereafter, his fortunes declined steadily. Requesting funds from the legislature for the continued operation of the still-breathing, but moribund, SRA until the next regular session, Olson was functioning in an atmosphere of near total hostility. Assembly committees, notably one led by Samuel Yorty, a recent convert to violent anticommunism, were investigating the SRA and reporting (on the basis of the testimony of "disgruntled" ex-employees) that radicals had taken full control of that unhappy agency.[55] Determined to retain a watchdog role in its relations with the SRA, the legislature voted only an interim appropriation good until June 1, 1940. The governor would have to run the relief gauntlet for more funds once again in May.

The outstanding feature of the Unemployment Relief Appropriation Act of 1940 was not its short-term appropriation. In the new law, the anti-Okie reaction found vent in major changes in the administration and eligibility requirements of the SRA. The relief measure changed drastically the residence requirement. Hitherto, one year's continued residence in the state had conferred eligibility for relief from the SRA. Now, a minimum of three years was substituted. For migrants entering the state after June 1, 1940, five years would be required. Further, the size of the maximum cash grant to any family, regardless of the number of dependents, was trimmed by 40 percent of its prior amount.[56]

When the specific bills embodying these several provisions were sent to Governor Olson, he vetoed them. But in a vote that was "only one of several signs of unrest among Olson's close followers," both houses overrode his veto, and the Emergency Relief Appropriation bill, with its new residence requirements, became law on February 23, 1940.[57]

The new relief law was accompanied by a chorus of exultation from most quarters and a few notes of gloom from within the dwindling

circle of administration supporters. Associated Farmers groups applaud-
ed the new legislation but continued to call for the return of county
relief.[58] Editorials in rural journals supported the Associated Farmers'
position. For example, *The Echo*, a newspaper in Gordon Garland's
home town, greeted the new regulations with an editorial headline
announcing "CHISELERS STARTING HOME!" and observed that the
new relief laws would hopefully "keep migrants from coming to the
state broke who wait around and sponge around on relief."[59] As might
have been expected, the CCA accepted much of the credit for the new
rules. After nearly two years of intensive lobbying, it could not avoid
gloating, and, in its victory literature, it continued to hammer at the
chiseling hordes:

> We had a case in Bakersfield where the wife of a relief recipient died of
> tuberculosis. The father was sent to Keene and the five children placed
> in the care of county welfare. Later the father made a very desperate
> plea to get the money to return to his home in Missouri. Finally the
> welfare agency yielded to his plea. Two months later, back he came to
> Bakersfield in an automobile with a new wife and four more children.
> That made nine children altogether, and this man said to the welfare
> agency: "Now all we want you to do is to give us $20 a month for each
> child, and the missus and I will get along just fine."[60]

There would be "no further opportunity," McManus announced stern-
ly, for that sort of thing.

The new relief rules hit hard at migrant families in the San Joaquin
Valley, especially since the slack agricultural season was underway
when the new regulations went into effect. Immediately following the
institution of the new relief rules and schedules, the SRA attempted to
survey families thrown off relief. One-third of the random sample of
migrant families selected for the survey had disappeared. Forced into
arrears on their rent and utility payments, they had moved, the investigators believed.[61] Among the two-thirds who had been found, severe
hardship and frantic migration had followed in the wake of the cutback. The return of these families into the migrant stream as a result of
the relief bill confirmed the opinion of anti-migrant groups that their
attack upon the Okie as a shiftless ne'er do well was valid. The
economy bloc issued two pamphlets congratulating itself for the fact
that "thousands of migrants who came here seeking support at the

expense of California taxpayers are planning to return to Oklahoma, Texas, Arkansas, and other States from which they came."[62] Meanwhile, legislative groups continuing their investigation of the relief problem declared that migrants were returning home for fear of being investigated and exposed.[63]

One other event, trivial in itself, served to demonstrate how firmly the anti-relief, anti-migrant psychology had fastened upon the state's opinion-making apparatus. Within a week of the passage of new relief laws, Carey McWilliams paid an emergency call upon federal relief officials in Washington, D.C. Aware that the relief cutback would result in considerable dislocation for the Okies, McWilliams hoped to persuade federal officials to take up the slack in relief administration left when the SRA increased its eligibility requirement and decreased its payments. The Washington administration, itself going out of the relief business in anticipation of returning prosperity and foreign concerns, held out "no hope whatever . . . of sufficient assistance." Furious, McWilliams told reporters that "Hell is going to start popping before long in California unless solutions of the relief and migratory labor problems are found." McWilliams dubbed the new rules "cockeyed," and charged that they were "forced upon the state by the same old reactionary 'gang' that has been running California for fifteen or twenty years . . . that 'gang' now is working through the Associated Farmers."[64]

McWilliams' intemperate "Hell will start popping" comment provoked a storm of rebukes from journals throughout the state. His prediction that the migrants would not take the new law "lying down" and would probably launch "serious demonstrations" if nothing worse, was denounced as rabble-rousing and an invitation to trouble.[65] Even the *San Francisco News*, the mercurial Scripps-Howard journal which had been unique among large-circulation journals in its support of the migrants, parted company from the administration. "KEEP YOUR SHIRT ON, CAREY!" the journal intoned, and its cartoonist depicted a wild-eyed McWilliams, clenched fist in air, blathering "disaster . . . woe . . . Hell will start popping."[66] Nor did the Associated Farmers miss the opportunity that McWilliams had presented. With editorial opinion united against the migrants as never before, John Watson, president of the organization, delivered a swipe at the commissioner of immigration and housing. If "Hell" were on the verge of "popping," Watson observed, it was simply because "such pests" as McWilliams were trying to protect a "rotten political machine building class hatreds."[67]

With the close of the first special session of 1940, both McWilliams and the SRA were surviving under a sentence of ultimate extinction. The days of both seemed clearly numbered. Olson still had to undergo interim appropriations battles, two more of which occurred in 1940, before the SRA was executed in 1941. The big battle, however, had been the one in February and March; SRA was now under relatively tight control by the legislature, and Olson's requests for appropriations slipped through both houses more easily in the later sessions. In part, this was because Olson had chosen a new relief director. Olson's first SRA administrator, Dewey Anderson, had resigned in August 1939, charging that Olson had allowed the body to become a political boondoggle for office-seekers. Olson replaced Anderson with Walter Chambers, a professional social worker, who had held subordinate positions within the SRA.[68] As administrator during the February battle, Chambers took blows from the right and from the left, the latter accusing him of secret membership in the Associated Farmers.[69] He finally resigned in June. Olson's choice of Sidney G. Rubinow, his third administrator, was interpreted as a "gesture of appeasement" to the "tories."[70] Rubinow fired SRA workers by the score and won applause from the economy bloc. With Rubinow's apparently strong hand at SRA's helm, there materialized between legislature and governor a short honeymoon, which permitted Olson's interim relief requests, straitened though they were, to pass review easily. In December, angered by the administrator's too-friendly relations with legislators opposing the governor's relief policies, Olson peremptorily fired Rubinow, thus unintentionally facilitating SRA's destruction at the 1941 legislative session.[71]

California's migrant problem affected politics in diverse and often peculiar ways. In addition to the relief battles of that year, 1940 also witnessed a county attack upon the migrants that found its way into the United States Supreme Court. The state legislative battles had involved the Okies in their role as relief clients, not specifically in their alter-role as interstate migrants. Olson maintained that the "right to migrate" was fundamental and unalienable, and few, even among the economy bloc, had questioned that right. It remained for the San Joaquin and Sacramento valleys' county governments to attempt to overturn the traditional constitutional right of American citizens to cross state borders without hindrance.

In the fearful early years of the depression, before "Okie" or even "New Deal" or "EPIC" were familiar American terms, twenty-eight states quietly passed laws making the intentional transportation of indigents across state lines a criminal offense.[72] During the Hoover-Roosevelt interregnum, when state and private charitable funds ran out, hard-pressed legislatures sought to protect themselves in this manner from feared invasions by tramps. These acts were not directed at indigents, but at those who knowingly brought them across the border into the state. California's indigent act had been passed in May 1933, and incorporated into the statute books as Section 2615 of the California Welfare and Institutions code.[73] During the seven years prior to the intense anti-Okie sentiment of late 1939 and early 1940, the law had been a dead letter. In December 1939, however, attorneys-general in Tulare and Kings County began invoking the old statute. At Visalia, several Okies were given suspended "road camp" sentences for violating Section 2615 on the condition they return with their families or friends to their states of origin. Tulare County convicted twenty-two Okies under the statute. From Tulare, the movement spread to Kings County, and then into the Sacramento Valley. At Marysville, in Yuba County, the Okie lay reverend Fred Edwards was arrested and charged with driving his indigent brother-in-law Frank Duncan, from Spur, Texas, to Marysville, California. Edwards was convicted and received a six-month suspended sentence. The American Civil Liberties Union, convinced of the unconstitutionality of Section 2615, immediately offered, in the FSA camp newspapers and elsewhere, to defend any migrant arrested under the statute.[74] Early in April the ACLU filed a brief of *amicus curiae* and supplied the Okie preacher with a lawyer.

In February, the diminutive deportation campaign ended abruptly, having captured, at most, a few dozen offenders of the indigent exclusion law. The ACLU took credit for the cessation, confident that its publicity had frightened county authorities.[75] More likely, the passage of the new relief measures by the state legislature persuaded county prosecutors that the deportation of Okies had become an inefficient solution to a problem now in the hands of the economy bloc at Sacramento. In any event, the Edwards case and a similar one at Tulare (the case of Richard Ochoa) had begun the slow judicial process that guided California's migrant problem to the Supreme Court. In April 1940, the Madera Superior Court took the cases under submission and in December, the Supreme Court of the United States agreed to review the Edwards case.

Nearly a year later, the Supreme Court ruled the California law, and by extension similar laws in twenty-seven other states, unconstitutional. Speaking for the five justices in the majority, Justice Byrnes held that Edwards' conviction and Section 2615 itself were undue interferences with the commerce clause. It had been "settled beyond question that the transportation of persons is 'commerce,' within the meaning of that provision," Byrnes observed.[76] Citing a decision from Cardozo, he argued that the several states "must sink or swim together" and the attempt to interfere with the free movement of persons within the stream of commerce was, therefore, unconstitutional. The majority decision in the Edwards case was a victory for the Okies and for Olson's position regarding interstate migration. The decision was, nonetheless, a tortuous and convoluted climb along what appeared to others as a relatively straight path. By resting its decision upon the commerce clause, the Court, in a sense, had seen Okies as Justice Taney eighty years before had seen the slave Dred Scott. The Okies were indeed persons, the majority had noted, but the decision also seemed to imply that the issue concerned the interstate transportation of a commodity: indigent depression migrants.

For Justices Jackson, Douglas, Black, and Murphy, the California law was unconstitutional, but the four refused to follow the majority's analytical trail. The concurring opinions, written by Jackson and Douglas, spoke to the citizenship clauses of the Fourteenth Amendment. Jackson's brief went onto the farthest juridical limb. For seventy-five years, he noted, the Supreme Court had hesitated to define the specific "privileges and immunities" of citizens under the Fourteenth Amendment which states might not infringe. "This Court should . . . hold squarely that it is a privilege of citizenship of the United States . . . to enter any state of the Union, either for temporary sojourn or for the establishment of permanent residence therein and for gaining resultant citizenship thereof. If national citizenship means less than this, it means nothing."[77] It was true that states retained the right to establish residence requirements, but those applied without reference to a citizen's financial position.

Broadening still further the terms of his decision, Jackson argued that indigence could not limit an American's rights. "Does 'indigence' . . . constitute a basis for restricting the freedom of a citizen, as crime or contagion warrants its restriction?" Nothing could be more dangerous than to make the possession of property a basis for unequal or exclusive civil rights. Jackson concluded his brief with an unjudicious swipe at California's attempt to restrict Okie migration. Speaking of Edwards' indigent brother-in-law, he observed that "California had no right to make the condition of Duncan's purse . . . the basis of excluding him or of punishing one who extended him aid." And, finally, "Unless this Court is willing to say that citizenship of the United States means at least this much to the citizen [the right freely to migrate], then our heritage of constitutional privileges and immunities is only a promise to the ear to be broken to the hope, a teasing illusion like a munificent bequest in a pauper's will."

A minor inflammation erupting out of California's temporary migrant infection, the Edwards case occupies an important place in constitutional interpretation. The minority, and Douglas especially, laid bare the implied departure from established attitudes towards citizenship and movement in the California anti-Okie reaction. Migration in search of broader economic opportunity was a privilege vouchsafed all Americans. The poor, however, were more likely to use that privilege than the rich. If each state erected its own Chinese wall either through border blockades, indigent exclusion laws, or, the decision also implied, unreasonable residence requirements, an important safety-valve in American life would disappear. The decision was, moreover, a step along the road to defining the rights that had devolved upon the freedman in the Fourteenth Amendment. Edwards and his brother-in-law had been denied by a state the rights they held as citizens of the United States. In spelling out a specific immunity and privilege of state citizenship under the Fourteenth Amendment, Douglas and his three colleagues had opened a small door in the search for equal rights.[78]

As with so many other events in the tangled history of California's migrant problem, the political battles and judicial decisions of 1940 and 1941 were essentially irrelevant. The relief cuts, the attempt to return relief to the counties, the changed residence rules, even the Edwards affair—for all its significance as a precedent—were shadow-boxing with reality. The migrant problem had arisen contemporaneously with the Munich agreement during the last year of the long truce that separated the First and Second World Wars. The special session of 1940 had rewritten California's relief laws only two weeks before the European blitzkrieg erupted. In May 1940, Roosevelt's program of preparedness had gone into full swing, and prosperity began its rapid return. The war-induced prosperity brought surcease for California and its Okies. A sharp drop in relief loads that materialized in 1940 was only partly a result of the new residence requirements. Summer and fall were peak employment periods and many of those on relief hard hit by the new regulations soon found work in the fields. When the next slack period developed in the winter of 1940 and 1941, however, the relief rolls did not rise as they had during the preceding five years. The defense boom was gaining momentum, carrying many of the Okies out of the rural regions into the cities upon a wave of defense contracts awarded to California's shipyards and aircraft plants. Henceforth, rural California would reverberate with a new crisis—underemployment in the fields—as the competitive advantage of defense work diminished the supply of migrants.[79] Ironically, it was at precisely this moment in California's history that her greatest single migration began: a new wave of Americans, many of them Okies, was crossing the continent to participate in the boom. Now, however, there were sufficient jobs for them, and the migrant problem disappeared with the depression.

The migrant and relief problems were virtually extinct when Olson's second legislature convened in early 1941. Nonetheless, the economy bloc was even more powerful in 1941 than it had been previously, and it delivered two gratuitous blows to the surviving apparatus for protection of the unemployed and the Okies. One of these attacks, founded upon the continuing desire to destroy the SRA, succeeded by default.

Conservatives in both parties were furious at Olson's peremptory dismissal of Sidney Rubinow, the only relief administrator they believed they could trust. Rubinow toured the state advocating the return of relief to the counties, and Senator Phillips again embodied the proposal in a bill. Passed by both houses, the Phillips bill was killed by Olson's veto in May. In angry response, the economy bloc refused to appropriate funds for the continued operation of the still-extant SRA and, in mid-June, the legislature adjourned. SRA was still alive, but had no funds with which to function. In the absence of a viable SRA, the burden of relief fell upon the counties, and the long struggle for the return of county relief was over. SRA survived in suspended animation until the legislature delivered the coup de grace in 1943.[80] The actual demise of the agency in 1941 brought little hardship either for the counties or for the migrants.

Returning prosperity had not, however, ended the necessity for protecting migratory agricultural workers. Despite the cries at the county, state, and federal level over the condition of field workers, little had been done to ensure for them a standard of living or a degree of equity commensurate with that of their urban counterparts. By revitalizing the Division of Immigration and Housing, Carey McWilliams had begun this formidable task. But the economy bloc was determined to extend agricultural "pest control" to include McWilliams who still apparently outranked pear blight and boll weevil in the catalog of farmers' woes. In February 1941, bills to abolish the division were introduced in both houses of the legislature. Senator Phillips and Assemblyman Earl Desmond (Democrat, Sacramento) sponsored bills to transfer the division's records and responsibilities to the State Department of Public Health, which would have converted McWilliams' organization into a weak and relatively minor administrative office.[81]

Charging that the Associated Farmers, the Chamber of Commerce, and the Southern Pacific Railroad had issued orders to their "cow county" stooges to "get McWilliams' scalp," the radical press fought to build a counterlobby for the purpose of protecting the division from extermination.[82] To an extent, the attempt succeeded. Between February and May, the movement to "save the Division" gained momentum as labor unions, social workers' organizations, and "prominent judges and lawyers" from Los Angeles issued statements of praise for McWilliams and his work.[83] But the sense of anxiety that had characterized California's response to the migrant problem was evaporating as war in Europe crowded the Okies off the front pages of the newspapers.

The movement never achieved broad public support. Consequently, the legislature was unhampered in its drive to destroy McWilliams, except for the possibility of Olson's veto.

Allegedly for the purpose of "streamlining" executive organization, bills to abolish the division were referred to committees on governmental efficiency in May. In the meantime, funds for the continued operation of the division were removed from the budget by the ways and means committees. McWilliams fought back, canceling speaking engagements in order that he might be present to save his division from the assault. At hearings upon the bills, McWilliams was repeatedly called a Communist (a charge which he strenuously denied), and members of the economy bloc admitted, with a good deal of candor, that the bill was a direct attack upon McWilliams and his philosophy. "McWilliams is in a position to pass on certain philosophy to aliens," Assemblyman Poulson (Republican, Los Angeles) averred, "think of the power he has!"[84]

Passing easily through the committees, the bills were sent to the legislature where similar charges punctuated the debate. The division was accused of "undermining agriculture in California," and its director was diagnosed as having a "diseased mind . . . policies and philosophy [that] are foreign to this government."[85] The final votes on the bills showed how deeply legislative sentiment ran against the author of *Factories in the Field*. In the assembly, the vote was 48 for, 17 against; in the Senate, 23 for, 9 against. [86] Fortunately for McWilliams, the bills had wasted considerable time passing through various committees. They reached the floor late in the legislative term, enabling Olson to kill them with a pocket-veto. Had the governor been forced to return the bills to the legislature, there is little room for doubt that the necessary two-thirds to override would have been easily mustered. In all but the final result, the bills were a victory for the economy bloc. Good fortune alone had saved the division. It limped on, discredited and shorn of funds.

With McWilliams' humiliation, California's legislative battles over the Okies ended. In 1942, a new Republican candidate defeated Olson's attempt to remain governor. Earl Warren's administrations adjourned internal conflict and concentrated upon winning the war and protecting

California's oversized piece of the war industries pie. For every Okie who had made the trek from 1935 to 1940, two Okies came during the wartime boom. For every migrant that California gained from 1930 to 1940, she gained three in the following decade. Many of the migrants of the war years were as penniless as the Okies who had displaced the Mexicans in California's fields during the depression years. The new Okies did not frighten Californians, however, for they rapidly found work. In any case, the state had found a new bogey in the Japanese.

As for Olson, the reasons for his long frustration and ultimate defeat have been assessed with considerable insight by Robert E. Burke, who notes that in part the fault lay in Olson himself: he could not administer nor had he entered office with a program flexible enough to prevent the consolidation of a multigroup coalition opposed to his policies.[87] The defeat of his little New Deal had not, however, been primarily his responsibility. His opponents *were* powerful and accustomed to techniques of control in which they had been schooled during twenty years of Republican administration. The people of California were mercurial in their political behavior and Olson could not rely upon the Democrats for support as could liberal politicians in other states. Finally, although Burke does not note the phenomenon, the Okies had supplied Olson's opposition with a superb political foil. They were an external enemy upon whom could be blamed the myriad travails of a state undergoing internal turmoil.

Olson's New Deal came too late to make use of the reform spirit that had swept the nation in the mid-thirties, and it achieved little. Insofar as the Okies were concerned, Olson and McWilliams could, at least, have pointed with pride to some impressive attempts. Both had avoided the natural and politically expedient tendency to fall victim to fear of an Okie menace. Both had understood that the Okies raised two problems: that of California agricultural labor and that of interstate migration. Both had sought to solve these problems by aiding, not attacking, the Great Plains people who were defenseless and disoriented, and whose poverty made a mockery of the American dream. Finally, despite their blunders and defeats, both had attempted to achieve a more equitable relationship between the people of California and their most precious asset—the fertile lands that had caused the Okies to look so enviously to the West for their salvation.

Notes in Text

1. *San Francisco Chronicle*, May 26, 1938.
2. Ibid., March 10, 1936.
3. *San Francisco News*, April 30, 1937.
4. Robert E. Burke, *Olson's New Deal for California* (Berkeley, 1953), p. 79.
5. The phrase is Robert E. Burke's. Ibid., p. 78.
6. *The Open Forum*, June 22, 1935.
7. *Oakland Tribune*, May 30, 1935.
8. "Extemporaneous Speech before Western Delegates, July 13, 1940, Omaha," Culbert Olson Papers, Bancroft Library, University of California, Berkeley, Carton 6.
9. Testimony of Culbert Olson, Tolan Committee, *Hearings*, Part 6, p. 2,242.
10. Ibid., p. 2,241; California, Governor's Commission of Reemployment, *Report* (Sacramento, 1939), p. 67.
11. *People's World*, November 11, 1938.
12. Testimony of Olson, Tolan Committee, *Hearings*, p. 2,240-2,241.
13. Culbert L. Olson, *Culbert L. Olson's Statement Before Senate Committee on Education and Labor* (San Francisco, 1939), pp. 1, 3-5, 10, 11, 18.
14. "Confidential Report to Governor Olson," October 23, 1938, manuscript, pp. 3-4, Farm Security Administration Collection, Bancroft Library, University of California, Berkeley, Carton 6.
15. *People's World*, July 1, 1938.
16. Olson, *Culbert Olson's Statement*, p. 3.
17. Testimony of Olson, Tolan Committee, *Hearings*, p. 2,243.
18. California State Relief Administration. *Preliminary Report, Transient Program* (Los Angeles, February 1939), p. 17.
19. Clarke A. Chambers, *California Farm Organizations* (Berkeley, 1952), p. 89.
20. See below, pp. 256-258.
21. Chambers, *California Farm Organizations*, passim.
22. For a complete account of the early activities of the division, see, Samuel E. Wood, "The California State Commission of Immigration and Housing" (Ph.D. diss., University of California, Berkeley, 1942).
23. Lee Alexander Stone, *Carey McWilliams Demands Labor Camps Be Put in Order* (Madera, 1939).
24. Carey McWilliams, "California Pastoral," *Antioch Review* 2 (March 1942): 103.
25. Stone, *McWilliams Demands*; Paul Scharrenberg, "Factories in the Field," *American Federationist* 47 (January, 1940), 62-63.
26. Carey McWilliams, *Factories in the Field* (Boston, 1939), p. 325.
27. *San Francisco News*, November 9, 1939; *Bakersfield Californian*, May 27, 1939; *Fresno Bee*, May 27, 1939; "What Should America Do for the Joads?" *Town Meeting* 5 (March 11, 1940).
28. Burke, *Olson's New Deal for California*, pp. 141-142.
29. Carey McWilliams, "What's Being Done About the Joads?" *New Republic* 100 (September 20, 1939): 178-179, 180.
30. General material on the legislative sessions has been drawn, except where otherwise noted, from Burke, *Olson's New Deal for California*.

31. Ibid., p. 67.

32. *Sacramento Bee*, March 18, 1939.

33. Burke, *Olson's New Deal for California*, p. 91.

34. Ibid.

35. Ibid., pp. 83-85.

36. *San Francisco News*, March 3, 1939.

37. *People's World*, March 9, 1939.

38. *Marysville Appeal-Democrat*, April 14, 1939.

39. Chambers, *California Farm Organizations*, p. 92.

40. Burke, *Olson's New Deal for California*, pp. 90-91.

41. *San Francisco Call-Bulletin*, January 24, 1939.

42. *San Francisco News*, March 10, 1939.

43. *Los Angeles Examiner*, March 11, 1939.

44. *People's World*, June 20, 1939.

45. *San Francisco News*, December 9, 1939.

46. *San Francisco Examiner*, January 7, 14, 1940.

47. *VOTAW*, February 9, 1940.

48. *Fresno Bee*, January 29, 1940.

49. Carey McWilliams, "Civil Rights in California," *New Republic* 102 (January 22, 1940): 108-109.

50. Burke, *Olson's New Deal for California*, p. 121.

51. *Dinuba Sentinel*, January 30, 1940.

52. Bay Area Committee to Aid Agricultural Workers, *Report to State Relief Administration re Migratory Workers* (n.p., n.d.), pp. 1-2.

53. *The Hub*, February 9, 1940.

54. Typed speech, n.d., Olson Collection, Carton 6.

55. Burke, *Olson's New Deal for California*, pp. 119-138.

56. Mary Gorringe Luck and Agnes B. Cummings, *Standards of Relief in California, 1940* (Berkeley, 1945), pp. 16-17; *San Francisco Examiner*, March 10, 1940; California State Relief Administration, *The Problem of Interstate Migration as It Affects the California State Relief Administration* (September 28, 1940), p. 4.

57. *Marysville Appeal-Democrat*, February 26, 1940.

58. Ibid., March 14, 1940.

59. *Woodlake Echo*, March 22, 1940. See also *Orange News*, March 1, 1940; *Los Angeles Independent Review*, February 29, 1940.

60. Thomas W. McManus, "Relief in California," *KPMC*, Bakersfield, Radio Broadcast, March 19, 1940, Paul Taylor Collection, Carton 3.

61. Oliver Carlson, *A Mirror for Californians* (Indianapolis, 1941), p. 169.

62. Herbert B. Scudder, *Economy or New Taxes . . . Which?* (n.p.; Citizens Economy Bloc of California, n.d.), pp. 6-7; Jerrold L. Seawall, *The Truth About Relief* (n.p.: Citizens Economy Bloc of California, n.d.), p. 4.

63. *Fresno Bee*, March 13, 1940.

64. *San Francisco News*, March 5, 1940.

65. *Oakland Tribune*, March 9, 1940; *Oroville Mercury-Register*, March 6, 1940; *Tulare Bee*, March 7, 1940.

66. *San Francisco News*, March 6, 1940.

67. *Oroville Mercury-Register*, March 6, 1940; *San Francisco News*, March 6, 1940.

68. Burke, *Olson's New Deal for California*, pp. 92-94, 119-138.

69. *People's World,* January 18, 1940.

70. "Tory Relief in California," *New Republic* 102 (June 17, 1940): 813.

71. Burke, *Olson's New Deal for California,* p. 137.

72. Broad discussions of the constitutional issues raised by interstate migration may be found in the following: "Depression Migrants and the States," *Harvard Law Review* 53 (1939-1940): 1,031-1,042; "Interstate Migration and Personal Liberty," *Columbia Law Review* 40 (1940): 1,032.

73. "Every person, firm or corporation, or officer or agent thereof that brings or assists in bringing into the State any indigent person who is not a resident of the state, knowing him to be an indigent person, is guilty of a misdemeanor." *American Civil Liberties Union News* (January 1940): 1-2.

74. *Fresno Bee,* December 18, 1939; *American Civil Liberties Union News,* February 1940; *Bakersfield Californian,* December 16, 1940; *Marysville Appeal-Democrat,* February 10, 1940; *Voice of the Agricultural Worker,* January 19, 1940.

75. *American Civil Liberties Union News* (February 1940).

76. Henry Steele Commager, *Documents of American History* (5th ed., New York, 1949), p. 648. The entire text of the decision may be found in: "Edwards vs. the State of California" (314 U.S. 160), *Supreme Court Reporter* 62 (October 1941): 165-172. Commager has been used for citations in light of its greater availability.

77. Commager, *Documents,* p. 649.

78. Comment on the Edwards case appears in the following: *Columbia Law Review* 42 (1942): 139-142; *Texas Law Review* 20 (1941-1942): 616-619; *University of Chicago Law Review* 40 (1941-1942): 711-733.

79. See the chart in Burke, *Olson's New Deal for California,* p. 165.

80. Ibid., pp. 162-167.

81. The specific legislation was: Senate Bill 1096 and Assembly Bills 2161-2163.

82. *People's World,* February 5, 1941.

83. Ibid., April 11, May 16, 22, 1941; *Kern County Union Labor Journal,* February 28, 1941.

84. *People's World,* April 11, 1941.

85. *San Francisco News,* May 10, 1941.

86. Burke, *Olson's New Deal for California,* p. 161.

87. Ibid., pp. 230-233.

5

The Migrant Problem
and the Federal Government: I

California's migrant problem was affected by federal activities that arose and subsided in two distinct waves. From 1933 to 1938, federal policies and agencies initiated in response to national, depression-induced situations provided Californians seeking a solution only with vague possibilities. The Federal Transient Service and the Resettlement and Farm Security Administrations, conceived at the federal level, did not speak directly to California's problem. These agencies, however, contained mandates and organizational structures sufficiently broad that their California offices were able subtly to reinterpret national policy to fit the state's needs. Not until 1939 did the specific problem of the Great Plains refugees in California receive serious interest from Congress or the President and then only after the publication of *The Grapes of Wrath* had made the condition of the Okies a blatant fact of American life.

Federal attempts to ease the problems of California's Okies were inevitably complicated by the migrants' dual role. The migrants were both interstate refugees and California's new agricultural laborers, some of them migratory, some settled. Each of their roles involved a separate problem and therefore implied a separate solution. Unless the interrelation of these roles was recognized, no attempted solution promised permanent, beneficial results. In fact, no solution came forth in the depression years. Instead, as with so many other severe problems in the American past, the coming of war ended the Okies' distress. This chapter will discuss the first phase of federal activities relating to the migrants, in which the Federal Transient Service attempted to ease the consequences of depression migration, and the Resettlement Administration developed programs designed to alleviate the plight of marginal farmers in the Great Plains and agricultural workers in California.

During the Hoover years, the nation had experienced a marked increase in the number of transient, unemployed wanderers, generally single men thrown from work in the first stages of the depression. Theirs was a nomadic life, encompassed by temporary jobs, skid roads, hobo jungles, and ceaseless attempts to avoid local police except when jail seemed the only possibility of a meal and a bed. Most were neither professional hoboes nor migratory laborers such as those who have followed the crops or the oil strikes throughout the nation's twentieth-century history. They differed from the rest of the nation's unemployed in one respect only: in moving from their states they lost their resident eligibility for relief. They were not, moreover, the most significant migrants of the depression years. Early in the New Deal years, their numbers dropped rapidly as they went home for work on WPA or in private business and industry. The people of the Great Plains were already packing their jalopies in preparation for the more important migrations to come, but the "bums" were more spectacular and more visible than the families crossing the nation in search of new homes. They therefore received the larger share of federal interest in the problem of interstate migration.[1]

In December 1931, the Seventy-second Congress wrote provisions for the nonresident transient unemployed into a number of relief bills.[2] At the time, the problem had received virtually no study, and these provisions were therefore quite vague. Their sole significance for later legislation was their recognition that disparate and conflicting state residence requirements often imposed legal liabilities on transients. For example, a man might lose residence in one state after six months continuous residence away from home; his new state of origin, however, might not accept him as citizen for three years; for two-and-one-half years, he would be a citizen of no state. Any comprehensive federal relief bill administered by the states would require protection for transients in this anomalous position.

A comprehensive relief bill was passed during the First Hundred Days, when the Roosevelt administration decided that the federal government should enter the business of direct relief. Section 4(c) of the Federal Emergency Relief Appropriations Act (FERA) entitled the new relief administration to "certify out of the funds made available . . . grants to states applying therefore to aid needy persons who have no legal settlement in any one State or Community."[3] Harry Hopkins immediately inaugurated a division of transient activities under the FERA, and invited the states to participate in the program and receive husky grants-in-aid for the purpose. Only Vermont remained aloof. By the close of 1933, the other forty-seven states had established transient programs under FERA. These transient programs shared one common characteristic in that all failed to consider seriously the interstate migrations of needy families. They concentrated instead upon the less significant but more obvious problem of transient single men. Federal Transient Service activities consisted principally of providing "congregate shelters in cities and camps outside the cities for unattached men."[4]

In spite of its failure to recognize transient families as a separate problem, the Federal Transient Service found that this group occupied an increasingly larger role in its activities. By 1935, over 200,000 migrating needy families received federal aid of one sort or another, and California rapidly became the state most dependent upon the agency's aegis.[5] Her monthly share of the grant-in-aid program varied between a quarter and a third of a million dollars, twice the amount any other state was receiving.[6] The families obtaining aid from the California arm of the Federal Transient Service were, in the main, the first harbingers of the Okie migration that would increase in momentum after 1935, and they became entangled almost immediately in the confusions growing out of their dual role. The FERA act had drawn a rigid distinction between "bonafide transients" and "seasonal migratory workers," with the latter excluded from Federal Transient Service aid on the grounds that relief distributed to migratory agricultural workers was really a subsidy furnished their employers.[7] However, the Okies were both "bonafide transients" *and* agricultural workers. They received aid from the Federal Transient Service, but only as interstate migrants.

The Federal Transient Service carried its peak load in California just when the state experienced its attack of jitters over a "tramp" invasion should Upton Sinclair capture the gubernatorial election. Functioning within the State Emergency Relief Administration, its relations with branches of the relief agency that distributed aid to residents were strained by the developing tendency in California to equate transients with chiselers. The service seriously considered reorganizing itself as a permanent body separate from the FERA, but New Deal policy obtruded upon the deliberations.[8] By mid-1935, the Roosevelt administration had determined that the federal government could well afford to remove itself from the business of direct relief. FERA was gradually phased out, and direct relief was replaced with public works and work relief programs.[9] But local budget planners, confident that the Federal Transient Service would continue to function during 1936, had not allocated sufficient funds for transient relief. In California, which contained 14 percent of the nation's homeless unemployed in April 1935, social workers feared that "tens of thousands of transients in need face[d] actual starvation" in the wake of the Federal Transient Service's death.[10] The federal government's sole attempt to aid interstate migrants ended. California's Okies camped on the ditch banks found agricultural jobs where they could and tried to survive for the year required to establish state residence.

The death of the Federal Transient Service marked a minor detour upon the road of expanded powers for the federal government. The New Deal years witnessed an immense growth of the federal bureaucracy and a closer relationship between the individual citizen and the national government than had existed ever before. Despite this growth of federal power and responsibility during a time of economic collapse and widespread poverty, the nation continued to define indigence as a state matter. The most migratory of people, Americans could safely remain poor so long as they stayed home. As residents, they were eligible for state relief and, if employable, for federal aid through PWA or WPA. Should they choose to move to another state they crossed an ill-defined border into a twilight zone where neither the state nor the central government would accept the responsibility for alleviating their poverty.

Although they comprised a major segment of the "one-third of a nation, ill-housed, ill-clothed, ill-fed" of whom FDR spoke frequently, the Okies and the larger group of farm people of which they were a part were excluded from the bulk of New Deal social welfare legislation.[11] During the 1930s, urban industrial labor finally achieved government recognition and aid: they were granted the right to bargain collectively, protected by state and federal minimum wage and maximum hour legislation, supported in their old age by social security, and bolstered during unemployed periods by government insurance. The largest single group of workers in the nation, however, received no such benefits. Instead, agricultural laborers were systematically exempted from NLRB, the Wages and Hours Bill, and the Social Security Act.[12]

Franklin Roosevelt was aware of the condition of the marginal farmer and the agricultural laborer, and it was neither cold-heartedness nor ignorance that led his administration to overlook them in major recovery and reform legislation. It was, rather, faint-heartedness. Attempts to include the rural poor in welfare bills were often blocked by the timidity of their friends and the vehemence of their enemies. In deliberations upon the Social Security Act, for example, the bill's friends had strenuously opposed the inclusion of agricultural labor for two reasons. First, it would be impossible to administer the plan were it forced to take cognizance of migratory seasonal workers. Second, the legislation's backers warned, the bill's opposition could not be vanquished if it included farm labor employers as well as industrial employers. FDR agreed that farm employers and their representatives in Congress were a formidable hostile bloc. In conversations with Norman Thomas, for example, he recommended patience and hinted that he and his aides were "frankly in fear of the powers of Southern Senators."[13]

Excluded from social welfare legislation, the poorer farm people also received short shrift in agricultural recovery legislation. The first AAA failed to install administrative machinery to insure that tenants and laborers, as well as owners, received the benefits of crop control. Tenants reaped the bitter harvest of crop restriction in lessened income, laborers in diminished employment. Many of the Okies among them simply left the Great Plains in the wake of AAA. In its second year, the first AAA attempted to protect tenants but owners had by then discovered numerous techniques for avoiding distributing funds to tenants.[14] The second AAA, by limiting cotton production, had simply increased the distress of Great Plains people who had already moved to California.

In short, the Okies were victims of a kind of social schizophrenia to which agriculture in America has always been prone. After 1900, successful farmers foreswore Jeffersonian mythology for pragmatic organization into cooperative marketing agreements and political lobbies.[15] The AAA marked the seduction of the movement for agricultural reform by the siren call of large-scale corporate farming. Lulled by the Farm Bureau Federation, the AAA adopted a vision of agriculture emcompassed by large, efficient, and prosperous farms, and was indifferent to the problems of less successful farmers working marginal lands.

To say only this of the New Deal agricultural policies, however, would be to ignore the complexities of the era. Despite its hard-nosed pragmatism, New Deal agricultural policy had another side. "Hardheaded, 'anti-utopian,' the New Dealers nonetheless had their Heavenly City," William E. Leuchtenberg has noted of the Greenbelt towns, and he could well have broadened the generalization to include the entire agency under which they functioned.[16] In the Resettlement Administration (RA), later the Farm Security Administration (FSA), some New Dealers recognized the distress of the rural poor and, in the face of determined opposition, sought to alleviate their hardships.

The Resettlement Administration and the Federal Transient Service both evolved from the relief program of the first New Deal. During the First Hundred Days, FDR and his advisers drew no distinction between urban and rural relief. Federal doles, distributed through the state offices of the FERA, were designed primarily to serve two purposes: to support the destitute in immediate distress and, hopefully, to promote recovery by infusing large amounts of cash into the economy. Relief under FERA, therefore, was distributed equally and without prejudice to destitute farmers as well as to the urban unemployed.[17]

FERA directors in agricultural areas soon discovered, however, that direct rural relief "did not help the farmers in any permanent way," and, moreover, that "work-relief projects were difficult to establish and maintain in rural areas with scattered populations." By mid-1934, many of the state Emergency Relief Administrations had organized subordinate branches designed specifically to aid the distressed populations of the rural regions. Known as Rural Rehabilitation divisions, these public corporations broadened their dole-granting activities to include loans and grants to farmers for the purchase of seed, feed, and machinery. In several states, the policy of loans for rehabilitation automatically evolved into a program for resettlement. Marginal farmers tended to work marginal land, and grants for the purpose of working worn-out land seemed a profligate waste of human and natural resources. State directors of rural rehabilitation reasoned that it was better to resettle marginal farmers on good lands, and then supply the loans and grants.[18] Unintentionally, FERA ranged far afield into rehabilitation and conservation. At no time were these rural rehabilitation programs in the several states granted congressional sanction. Instead, they operated under the congressional mandate that FERA distribute relief to the unemployed.

FERA was not the only agency concerned with problems of rehabilitation among the nation's worn-out farmers and worn-out lands. In the hectic days following FDR's inauguration, several alphabet agencies had entered upon projects touching marginal agriculture. AAA had a land policy section, which retired or resuscitated overworked land, the Department of Interior had a division of subsistence homesteads, and PWA had a land planning committee.[19] In less significant ways, even the Office of Indian Affairs and the National Park Service engaged in policy decisions affecting land and farming.

By 1934, a half-dozen disparate New Deal agencies attempted to help the marginal farmer. AAA, the administration supplying aid to the more prosperous, but depression-struck farmer, functioned under a single title and under congressional authority, but programs for the tenant, the cropper, the weaker farmer upon the agrarian landscape, aptly resembled Raymond Moley's characterization of the New Deal in general: "to look upon these policies as the result of a unified plan was to believe that the accumulation of stuffed snakes, baseball pictures, school flags, old tennis shoes, carpenter's tools, geometry books, and chemistry sets in a boy's bedroom could have been put there by an interior decorator."[20]

Franklin Roosevelt may have harbored more solicitude for the plight of the land than for the plight of the marginal farmer, but conservation required a simultaneous attack upon rural poverty. The marginal farmer must be resettled, rehabilitated, or moved to the city if the lands which yearly degenerated under his frantic attempts to harvest a profit were to be saved. The confusion under which disparate agencies functioned severely limited the possibility for effective action. In 1934, accordingly, Roosevelt requested Rexford Guy Tugwell to begin a comprehensive review with the ultimate purpose of coordinating land policy and rural rehabilitation agencies.[21] Tugwell's study culminated in April 1935, when Roosevelt ordered the formation of the Resettlement Administration and transferred to the new body the various land use and policy agencies which had developed under various titles during the two preceding years. Roosevelt appointed the most controversial of first New Dealers to head the new organization. "Rexford the Red," the "collectivist" feared above all others by those disenchanted with the New Deal, swept into the administrator's office determined to effect a fundamental reconstruction of America's agricultural ideology.[22]

RA began its short, stormy career under an emotional cloud. The new agency had no congressional sanction, and Tugwell's position supplied a convenient and powerful focus of antagonism for anti–New Deal forces, upon whom Tugwell later blamed the administration's failure.[23] Moreover, the RA contained several internal organizational problems. Its programs were diverse and often contradictory. Tugwell believed in a kind of agricultural collectivism similar to that of Carey McWilliams. In traditional New Nationalist fashion, both sought to apply the collective principle to achieve better use of land and people within a liberal capitalist economy. Tugwell, therefore, devoted his most strenuous activities to RA's smallest and most controversial activity: the resettlement projects and the retirement of submarginal lands.[24] Through these programs Tugwell intended to present a vision of America enhanced by suburban "communities" in the deepest sense of that word.

RA's larger and more costly activities left unsatisfied Tugwell's desire to weaken outmoded concepts of fee-simple ownership and

individual farms that had fastened upon most farmers when the westward movement began a century and a half before.[25] Despite Tugwell's
visionary plans, the bulk of RA's, and later FSA's, activities were not
devoted to making America over but simply to making loans. During
the program's life, both lent or granted outright nearly $1 billion to
marginal farmers under the rural rehabilitation program.[26] In effect,
the agency became a credit office for farmers unable to obtain rehabilitation loans from private sources. This phase of the program succeeded
in that it enabled many small farmers to overcome the ravages of
economic or natural disaster. Indeed, the loans program helped keep
many marginal farmers on lands in the Great Plains. Without the loans,
they might have migrated to California and swollen still further the
Okie population there.[27] Nevertheless, neither Tugwell nor the other
agricultural reformers in the RA responded to the loan program with
enthusiasm. They continued to pour their emotional energies into the
far smaller resettlement and community-planning activities.

RA's diverse and varied programs presented the marginal farmer with
options representing all sides in the continuing national debate over the
future of American agriculture. If he turned to the rural rehabilitation
offices for aid, he was lent sufficient cash at low interest to enable him
to hang on until the next boom or war, when he could recoup losses
sustained during the bust years. On the other hand, if he turned to the
resettlement program, he became a subject in experiments launched by
idealists who believed passionately that agriculture in the traditional
pattern was untenable, despite the huge profits that even marginal
farmers reaped during boom years. RA offices would retire his lands
from cultivation and relocate him onto one of the Greenbelt communities or cooperative farms. From 1935 to 1943, however, most farmers, suspicious of the cooperative projects, simply took the loans and
went home to the family-sized farm.[28]

RA's conflict of purpose was symptomatic of still another of its
peculiarities. In part because it housed so diverse a collection of
agricultural ideologies, the agency labored under an uncoordinated and
chaotic organizational structure. It claimed four missions and performed them through four major divisions. Twelve coordinate satellite
divisions revolved about the big four. Its geographical organization
increased the complexity of administering sixteen divisions. Because its
predecessors had been state-supervised FERA agencies, RA retained a

pattern of decentralization. RA's sixteen divisions were administered by eleven regional offices and smaller offices in each state and most counties.

In Region IX, comprising California, Utah, Nevada, and Arizona, RA's decentralized structure led it into experiments that bore little relation to the goals delineated by Tugwell, Roosevelt, or the other men who had planned the administration's program at the national level. Had it been forced to attempt in Region IX to fulfill the goals laid out in Washington, it would have been rather like an army moving across California's landscape in search of a battlefield, and, indeed, an enemy. What had loomed so large in the thinking of RA's founders in Washington, namely, the problem of a dispossessed tenantry attempting to eke a living out of worn-out lands, simply did not exist to any significant degree in California or Arizona. RA's goals were tailored to states like Oklahoma, Texas, or Arkansas where small, economically untenable units had dragged owners into tenantry, healthy Americans into sickness, good land into dust bowls, prosperity into poverty. California's lands were superbly cultivated, irrigated, and protected from nature's ravages by scientific farming; her farmers were healthy and prosperous; and, ironically, while many California farmers were tenants, they belonged to the tenant class in name only. No similarity existed between Joseph DiGiorgio, one of the state's biggest farmers, who worked lands leased from the Bank of America, and the South's tenant families described with such ruthless precision by James Agee and Walker Evans.[29]

But, if the deeper significance of the founding of RA meant that the federal government intended to bring some measure of support to the losers in agriculture's competitive struggle, it did apply to California's migratory agricultural workers. By extending RA's specific goals to the program's larger implied meaning, the directors of Region IX turned from the problems of tenantry and rural poverty to that of migratory labor in California. This was not a specific response to the coming of the Okies. They were as yet a small portion of California's harvest labor force. It was their sole stroke of good fortune that, when their trek increased in volume, it was directed toward a state where federal programs designed for migratory labor had advanced far beyond those in any other region.

The genesis of the migratory labor camp program in the western states lay in California's Rural Rehabilitation Division. Well before the formation of the RA, the scheme was conceived in the offices of Harry Drobisch, State Director of Rural Rehabilitation. At the time, Rural Rehabilitation was an arm of the conservative State Emergency Relief Administration and Drobisch's freedom was limited by the policy decisions of his superiors. With his advisers, he recognized the problem of California's migratory laborers who stood "at the foot of the socio-economic scale in our state" and who "constitute[d] numerically the major element among our rural relief clients."[30] It was one thing to feel concern for the migratory laborers, however, and quite another to attempt to convert sympathy into action. Drobisch's options were few and not solely because of the hostilities that action might produce among his superiors. There was, in fact, little that could be done by a relief agency to aid the migratory worker. Relief directors could not tamper with the system of agriculture, nor could they distribute cash to agricultural laborers who were excluded from unemployment relief legislation. In any event, agricultural laborers were poor when they worked, as well as when they were unemployed. To increase their income by government payments would provide a subsidy to the state's farmers.

Drobisch chose immediate palliative rather than long-range curative action. He formulated a project based upon the fact that a majority of the strikes in which agricultural workers had engaged during 1933 and 1934 had grown out of their demands for decent housing.[31] The state and federal governments could supply clean, decent living accommodations for agricultural laborers in the form of concentrations of tidy tents or cabins located in the central valleys where intensive agriculture predominated. But Drobisch's superiors did not view the project with solicitude, and the program was "held up for lack of diversion of funds."[32] Accordingly, Drobisch requested of FERA in Washington that the federal government directly supply Rural Rehabilitation Division with $100,000 for the "erection of camps for migratory laborers in California."[33] Drobisch enlisted State Senator Culbert Olson and Mrs. Robert McWilliams as agents for the program, and the pair managed to obtain a federal grant for the construction of two labor camps on land leased to the Rural Rehabilitation Division by the San Mateo County Board of Supervisors.[34]

At first, Rural Rehabilitation was uncertain of the purpose or the goals of its camp program. In a report issued by the division on the day Franklin Roosevelt inaugurated the Resettlement Administration, Drobisch and his staff observed that California's migrant camp program was a variation upon the national theme, an "adaptation . . . to take care of California conditions growing out of the preponderant element of landless wage laborers in the rural population, the army of migrant workers which moves en masse from place to place for one harvest after another along a 700 mile trek; and the flood of drought refugees from the stricken states of the Middlewest." Taken out of the larger context of the report, this justification for the program was sufficient. This was, after all, a relief measure. The report continued, however, by asserting that the migrant camp program had been drawn to "conform to the premises and procedures of the national program *for restoring distressed rural people to a condition of self-support and security.*" The report did not, indeed could not, explain how labor camps would transform migrant workers into yeomen farmers. Since RA's national goals did not clearly take migrant workers into account, the program could only be justified were it made to appear a step along the upward road to farm ownership for the migrants.[35]

The Rural Rehabilitation Division was transferred from the FERA-SERA to the newborn RA scarcely a month after the decision to begin the migrant camp program. In one sense, California's Rural Rehabilitation preferred its separation from SERA. RA's directorate showed a "more widespread interest in the problem" than had that of the SERA and promised that "impediments . . . encountered in the old Administration may not stand in [the] way in the future."[36] Nonetheless, RA's national officials balked at the camp project, not because it interfered with grower control over migratory workers, but rather because it seemed to lead nowhere, providing little for the migrant worker and a government subsidy for his employer.[37] Drobisch spent the remainder of 1935 attempting to persuade the RA's leadership in Washington, D.C., that the migratory camps were a legitimate program within the administration's mandate.

The key to the impasse was the attitude Tugwell would adopt toward the program. On a theoretical level, Tugwell's ideology probably left little room for the camp program. Like Carey McWilliams, he did not object to the system of farming that had evolved in California; it was efficient, modern, and productive. It was the mode of ownership, the exploitation of labor, and the absence of community in the factories in the fields to which the administrator would object. The migrant camps promised no alleviation of these unpleasant concomitants of California agriculture. In August 1935, Tugwell clarified his intentions regarding Region IX's role in RA. Out of a tentative budget of $91 million for the national program, he allocated $10 million to Region IX. The funds were to be applied to RA's goal of rehabilitating 300,000 "rural destitute" families, including "the moving of 50,000 more to fertile lands 'where they will have opportunities to achieve economic independence.' "[38] For RA to encourage migration to Region IX was the last thing California's RA administrators desired; worse, Tugwell had not even mentioned migrant laborers or migrant camps.

Fortunately for Region IX's administrators, Tugwell was due to inspect California's facilities in October. RA had already constructed two camps. The units planned for San Mateo County had failed to materialize, but land had been obtained and camps constructed at Arvin in Kern County and another at Marysville in Yuba County. Drobisch determined to make his case at the camps. When Tugwell arrived in California to inspect Resettlement Region IX, Drobisch's planned itinerary included visits with the migrants. At Marysville, Tugwell announced that he was "favorably impressed."[39] The chief's caravan then moved south into Kern County to visit the Arvin camp, and he was apparently as impressed with it.

The psychological impact upon Tugwell of his visit with the early arrivals in the Okie migration cannot be directly assessed. Like many other New Dealers, Tugwell's self-image was that of a man pragmatic, tough-minded, and hard-nosed in analyzing the ills of a nation. Beneath the pragmatism, however, lay a core of sympathy for the poor, a sympathy that provided the outrage in his "make America over" poetry. Where head conflicted with heart, Tugwell may have favored the heart. In any event, Tugwell did not comment publicly upon the camps or the condition of the Okies in them. Instead, he traveled to Los Angeles later that week where, speaking before the California Democratic Clubs, he delivered what his biographer has termed the "hardest-hitting" speech of his career.[40] "How deep," Tugwell asked his audience, "are the sources of your indignation?" He scolded the plutocracy for "poor sportsmanship": they had accepted under Hoover policies they attacked under FDR; they put private interest before public interest; they charged "communism!" at any program directed at aiding the less powerful groups in society; and, Tugwell concluded, in a sentence that more than any other during his career brought him the nickname "Rex the Red," they were courting revolution: "We have no right to expect that the disestablishment of our plutocracy will be pleasant. These historic changes never are."[41] How heavily the Okies weighed in Tugwell's violent attack cannot be determined. One thing, however, is certain: in spite of the fact that the labor camp program conflicted with his deeper philosophical positions, he approved plans for its expansion. A plan Drobisch had hatched in September to construct camps housing all California's 150,000 to 200,000 migrant workers was to be allowed to proceed.[42]

Before embarking upon its expanded program, the Region IX administration had to overcome deep internal divisions. It appeared during the early days of reorganization under RA that the agency might become a political boondoggle. Although Tugwell was opposed to "playing politics with RA jobs," some of his subordinates apparently were not. Drobisch had been notified early in July 1935 that "future appointments [to the RA] will have to have the endorsement of some Democratic politician," and was, he noted, "mighty sorry" ro receive this news."[43] But in the administration of the camps Drobisch and his successors were apparently able to impede the politicization of the agency.

Personal differences concerning the direction of the program were a more important source of division than patronage politics. In 1936, Californians were not yet aware of the extent of the Okie migration, and there were those within the RA who continued to see in the state a suitable, indeed perfect, area for the relocation of drought sufferers. Tugwell had held this view in August 1935 when he had allocated funds to resettle Great Plains farmers on the West Coast. Employees in the regional office who supported Tugwell's resettlement idea complained bitterly during 1936 that although Region IX employed over 200 people, it had "virtually . . . nothing to show on the credit side. . . . [After] one year's work, the RA in this state has not resettled one client."[44]

Finally, despite the fact that Tugwell had approved the program,

Drobisch's projects were once again jeopardized by his superiors. When Jonathan Garst, the new administrator for Region IX, arrived in California with his aide, Walter Packard, the two adamantly opposed Drobisch's plans for an expanded migratory labor camp program. Garst considered the camps "dangerous to the administration," and recommended that they be turned over to local authorities. Drobisch attempted to persuade Garst out of his opposition to the camps, while camp managers considered the new director's position "*idiotic*, and worse, . . . *criminal*." Garst apparently preferred resettling migratory workers on small homesteads to lodging them in migratory labor camps. The former option was more attuned to the national goals of the RA.[45]

By mid-1936, conflicting goals within Region IX's leadership confronted the agency with a choice between two distinctly different policies. On the one hand lay Drobisch's plan for an immense migratory labor camp program. On the other hand, administrators friendly to the resettlement concept sought to relocate "selected drought sufferers" in California and place them upon cooperative community projects. Drobisch's plan prevailed for two reasons.

For one, the Okies themselves rendered RA's plans for resettlement in California gratuitous. As the migration grew, RA's officials realized that AAA, mechanization, and drought were performing the task of relocation in a manner more ruthless and in far greater magnitude than RA could ever hope to accomplish. More importantly, however, the national debate over RA's more utopian policies played a major role in the metamorphosis of Region IX's program.

With the possible exception of the writers' and actors' projects of the WPA, no New Deal agency sustained more severe congressional criticism than RA-FSA.[46] In the view of Congressmen opposed to the agency, its activities fell into two categories. The larger share of funds was utilized for the rehabilitation of marginal farmers upon lands owned in fee-simple. Few found serious fault with this phase of the program. For conservative legislators, however, the less traditional activities of its predecessor RA brought the entire FSA into disrepute. Greenbelt towns, cooperative industrial and agricultural communities operating upon leased lands, plans for relocation of drought-stricken communities—these laid FSA open to charges that it was subverting the American yeoman into a collective farmer working on an FSA soviet.

Chairman Cooley of the committee that investigated FSA's activities in 1943 expressed this dichotomized view when he noted that efforts to "give a degree of aid and comfort to the *worthy* [my italics] tenants and sharecropper of America" were "very worthwhile." But, Cooley believed many of FSA's experiments should never have been undertaken, especially those functioning under the "pet policies of government ownership of land" which "cannot mean home ownership" for participating farmers.[47]

Hostile congressional attitudes were exacerbated by the character of RA's leader. As his biographer notes, it was probably true that Tugwell was the only man in the nation with the verve, the foresight, and the sheer bull-headedness to build an agency for the purpose of eliminating the desperate problem of rural poverty by attacking the very system of fee-simple individual ownership of lands. These personal qualities, however, led Tugwell into breaches with Congressmen who suspected his patriotism. "Rex the Red" was unable to take Senators like "Cotton Ed" Smith seriously and returned their disapproval with scorn. [48] Unfortunately for RA, only a consummate diplomat with a reputation for "conservative realism" *might* have been able to protect the more "utopian" projects by maintaining satisfactory relations with Congress.

So when Tugwell resigned in December 1936, his departure was widely unlamented. By 1937, RA had been rechristened Farm Security Administration and placed under the direct control of the Department of Agriculture. It received congressional sanction under the Jones-Bankhead Farm Tenant Act, but the act also forced FSA to restrict itself to more limited goals than those of its predecessor. FSA operated with tight budgets under severe congressional scrutiny. Nonetheless, it continued to be one of the most controversial of New Deal programs, the butt of congressional humor, and the focus of anti-Roosevelt antagonism.

Even before Tugwell's resignation, the cross-pressures upon RA coupled with the magnitude of the unplanned Okie migration to California to produce a major policy decision: in September 1936, Region IX's directors dropped plans to resettle Okies in California.[49] By 1937, the resettlement idea was dead, and Region IX spent the remainder of its life building camps for a mass of migrants and denying strenuously that it had encouraged their move to California.

Although Region IX was now committed to directing its activities toward the migrant camp program, Drobisch's project never developed to the magnitude he had originally intended. The camp program had been sanctioned by Tugwell and grudgingly accepted by Jonathan Garst, but it remained a stepchild, largely ignored by national FSA and Congress even after *The Grapes of Wrath* had publicized the situation in California. The Cooley Committee, for example, spent virtually no time investigating California's migrant camps, although it subjected both the loan and cooperative project programs of FSA to minute, almost microscopic, scrutiny. FSA did not allocate funds to the camp program in anywhere near the proportion in which it supported even the Greenbelt towns. In 1937, Greenbelt families earning between $1,000 and $2,000 per year received an average $16,000 each in aid from the federal government. The migratory camp program was not even provided the $1.5 million which had originally been allocated for Region IX. As the *San Francisco News* concluded, "if the green belt project is extravagant and impractical, then the California program is niggardly and a direct shirking of Resettlement's first duty, which is to take care of distress and dislocation among farm families."[50]

FSA's niggardliness and Congress' indifference to the activities in Region IX followed logically from the traditional American image of agriculture. Farmers were not placed in the same category with workers. Whether tenants, croppers, or owners, they were believed to occupy positions upon a social ladder ascending upward to yeomanry. "Worthy tenants and share-croppers" (Cooley's phrase) were entitled to financial aid from the government, provided that such aid was directed toward the ultimate goal of fee-simple ownership. California's harvest armies, however, were stratified rigidly as laborers, on farms if not factories, and were unlike the more typical farmhand of the Midwest. California agriculture could not support them as independent farmers. Their problems were not the kinds of agricultural problems for which traditional solutions could be suggested, and legislators, as well as FSA administrators, in Washington were unable to empathize with the agricultural migrant worker.

Weakened by congressional indifference to the plight of the migrant farm worker, Region IX was also subjected to hostility from legislators who saw in the migratory labor camps a cynical attempt to subsidize California's large farms. Senator Richard Russell expressed these sentiments during recurrent debates on FSA appropriations. He insisted that he had no objection to aiding the migratory laborers, but "it occurs to me that a comprehensive [camp] program carried on over a long period of years of this nature is going to be of as much a benefit to the big corporation farms by furnishing them cheap labor as it is going to be to the people whom we are trying to help."[51]

Throughout the period until Pearl Harbor, the camp program was prey to a combination of attitudes that slowed the program and forced it to abandon its broader goals for more limited ones. Drobisch had originally planned a string of camps sufficient to accommodate all of the state's harvest workers and to help solve the social problems of California agriculture. By 1936, however, RA officials were observing that the camps could "only serve as a series of demonstrations." "I doubt," Jonathan Garst observed, "if the Federal government will ever undertake construction of camps for all the migratory workers in California. The best to be said is that we will try to demonstrate the way in which the camp problem can be handled."[52]

Limited funds meant limited dreams, and Garst had set his sights a bit lower; a few model camps, he now hoped, would dot California's countryside, persuading growers by example to improve private accommodations for the migratory workers. Growers did not suddenly and unanimously take up the challenge. In any event, as the Okies poured into the state's valleys, conditions along the ditch banks and in private camps worsened in response to the sheer magnitude of the migration. RA found itself constricted between the Scylla of small budgets and demonstrational camps and the Charybdis of alarming increases in misery among the migrants. RA gradually expanded its program to meet the problem of rising numbers of migrants but never with sufficient speed to satisfy those who hoped that the camp scheme would bring a final solution to the migrant worker's plight. Garst was accused at intervals of delaying the program, and regularly responded that funds were being diverted from Region IX to the Great Plains for the purpose of anchoring in their home states Okies who would otherwise have migrated westward.[53]

Region IX's office scrambled for funds, built more camps, expanded subsidiary activities aiding the migrants, and all the while justified the ballooning program as demonstrational. By 1940, the string of "demon-

strations" running north from the Imperial to the Sacramento comprised sixty-nine distinct installations, ranging from grant-in-aid offices
to cooperative farms, and had become a major federal activity within
the state.[54] FSA continued to lay the greatest emphasis upon the
migratory labor camps: fifteen were completed or under construction
in 1940, and three mobile camps constituted a new departure in the
program. These were movable installations carried by trailer from one
lesser harvest area to another, following the movements of the Okies
from place to place. FSA was forced by circumstances to develop
additional programs peripheral to the camps. As long as the camps
could not accommodate every migrant Okie worker, FSA could not
condemn migrants not resident in the camps to the vagaries of a
worsening situation in California. Programs designed to aid Okies outside, as well as within, the camps grew slowly at first, and were given an
accelerative impetus by the great floods of January and February 1938.

After February 1938, Okies neither legally residents of California
nor residing in one of the FSA camps were entitled to receive federal
relief checks during periods of unemployment. The grant-in-aid program has been discussed above; it bore an intimate relation to the
political problem of relief and residency and helped bring on the
migrant crisis. Poverty among the Okies was not, however, the sole
concern of FSA's regional administrators. From the beginning of the
migration, the Okies had provided a two-edged public-health problem.
The ditch-bank settlements increased markedly the potential danger
from epidemics of typhoid, malaria, or tuberculosis which, once started, might spread from the Okies to the resident Californians. Public-
health authorities in the counties managed to prevent epidemics, but as
long as the ditch banks and shack towns with their unhygienic surroundings continued to exist, the valleys remained under the threat of
communicable disease.

A greater, if less spectacular, public-health problem that followed
the Okie influx was the inability of destitute migrants to provide
adequately for their own medical needs. Minor illnesses, contagious or
otherwise, went untreated; pregnant women bore their children on
damp tent floors; limbs cut during harvest work festered beneath
hastily improvised bandages torn from cotton tow sacks; and children
went without the kind of nutrition they required.[55] County and state

agencies responded to this aspect of the Okie medical problem with indifference. Migrants needing emergency care were treated at local tax-supported hospitals, but injury, chronic or minor illness, and malnutrition were not considered within that category. Federal officials were disturbed by a "noticeable trend . . . manifested by the action of numerous county boards of supervisors throughout California . . . curtailing the extension of medical aid to the nonresident sick."[56]

With the formation of the grant-aid program, FSA moved as well into the complex area of the migrant's medical needs. The result was an experiment in medicare limited to migrants engaged in agricultural work and ineligible for health service from the state. In early March 1938, Region IX organized the Agricultural Workers Health and Medical Association (AWHMA), incorporated under the laws of California and Arizona, and supported with an initial grant of $200,000 in federal funds. Adapting to California's needs a smaller program first begun by FSA in the Dakotas, the AWHMA issued membership cards to eligible Okies which entitled them to obtain medical aid from any physician who joined the organization's panel. The physician billed the association; the association, in turn, could bill the patient, should his economic status improve sufficiently to enable him to pay without hardship.[57]

The AWHMA evolved into one of the more successful of Region IX's activities. In addition to branch offices within the grant-in-aid stations, it had constructed by 1940 six offices of its own and twelve clinics at which Okies could receive medical care. It supplied medical care to nearly 40,000 of the state's nonresident migrants. Since not all members of the association required care, and, moreover, since only the Okie agricultural workers with less than one year in California were eligible, it is clear that the AWHMA managed to organize a large majority of its potential membership.[58]

New Deal agricultural policy contained several paradoxical elements. AAA harkened to the privately owned large farm. RA, on the other hand, had looked two ways at once; while it attempted to foster the collective principle upon extensive farms, it simultaneously looked back with nostalgia to the homestead concept. FSA's camps, grants-in-aid, and the AWHMA were designed to protect the workers in the factories in the fields. On a smaller scale, however, the RA began and the FSA completed programs attuned to both the collective principle and the homestead.

The collective principle was embodied in two full-time and several part-time cooperative farms. At Casa Grande, Arizona, and at Mineral King Farm, near Visalia in Tulare County, California, RA placed selected migrant families, most of them Okies, upon government-sponsored, cooperatively owned, large farms. Using the argument that "small farmers simply cannot compete today with large industrial ranchers," government advisers warned the Okie applicants that they "must be willing to give up their individual say-so and obey the orders of a manager, in return for security and a roof over their heads."[59] In the circumstances, most of the applicants were prepared to risk the cooperative venture, although all of them had originally told RA that they desired above all else small farms of their own. A total of sixty-six Okie families farmed the two experiments in full-time cooperative agriculture in Region IX. By 1943, though still prospering, both farms were in a state of disarray induced by the development of antagonisms among the cooperators and the refusal of the groups to adopt fully the collective principle. Both experiments died quietly in the latter years of World War II. They were sold, and their profits divided between the cooperators.[60]

The part-time cooperative farms were a compromise between Jefferson's yeoman and Tugwell's cooperator. Recognizing the strong tendency of many Okie families to remain settled in one place on a year-round basis, Region IX constructed seven hundred labor homes upon vacant lots adjoining the migrant camps. Clean but by no means luxurious, the three-room cabins were rented to the applicants for $8.20 a month. At twelve of the sixteen labor home projects, farms ranging in size from eighty to three hundred acres were placed at the disposal of the tenants to be utilized cooperatively. Produce from the part-time farms was intended, primarily, for the tenants' own use; surpluses were sold at local prevailing prices, and first choice of the cooperative farm's produce went to the migrants residing at the adjoining labor camps.[61]

Viewed theoretically, FSA's California activities provided a ladder by which destitute migrants could climb, step-by-step, to security. Incoming Okies might first receive cash grants and medical aid to tide them over the hardest initial moments of transplantation; then on to the migrant camps where, once employed upon the corporate farms, they might live in clean and secure homes; from the labor camps they might move to the labor homes where, having achieved a small amount of savings, they cooperated with their neighbors in farming for profit; and, finally, the Okies would leave the protective shield of FSA and, rehabilitated, each venture out upon his own. Despite some peculiarities, the scheme conformed to the traditional agricultural pattern of upward mobility from hired hand to tenant to owner. Unfortunately, the plan failed at the higher levels. Unquestionably, a high proportion of the Okies availed themselves of the grants and the medical plan. A smaller, but significant, number of them passed through the migrant camps. From that point on, however, movement upward became exceptional. The cooperative part-time and full-time farms could accommodate, at most, eight hundred families, and the final step to full farm security was so rare that it was virtually nonexistent. No rarer item resides in the full corpus of Region IX's records than a report emanating from the Shafter camp in May 1941. Raymond McFarland, one of the tenants at the labor homes, had "left . . . in rather a *unique fashion* [my italics] ." The McFarlands had owned a 320-acre ranch in Colorado before the depression. The family was now returning to the ranch, "after having benefited for two years by the low-rate modern facilities of the Shafter Garden Home Area. In this time, they have so rehabilitated themselves that they are in a position to take a Rural Rehabilitation loan on their ranch."[62]

Lack of funds was not the sole reason for FSA's failure, either in California, or, indeed, throughout the nation, to set a significant number of dispossessed farm families back upon the road from total deprivation to farm ownership. FSA's concept of rehabilitation was an attempt to keep pace with a rapidly receding past. The rise of corporate agriculture meant that the great majority of dispossessed farm families would emerge from the depression as workers in the agricultural fields or in the cities, and not as owners or tenants. The labor camps provided an unintended subsidy to the larger growers, a fact which disturbed many FSA officials. Nonetheless, the camps were the most realistic of FSA's activities among California's Okies. The camps were the most numerous, and most important, of Region IX's programs.

If the assessment of agriculture's future that underlay the camp program was realistic and pragmatic, it was also the case that, in its relations with the Okies, the program demonstrated many of the less pragmatic features of the New Deal. The organization, operation, and management of the migrant camps provides an opportunity to observe in micro the more idealistic face of the New Deal. In its internal workings, the program was an unsuccessful experiment in "planned democracy," the New Deal's term to connote "fraternal community." It was, moreover, a case study in frustration for the managers who were unable to convert the Okies from rugged individualism to cooperative citizenship. The refusal of the Okies to turn overnight from sows' ears to silk purses under the guiding hands of the camp managers provoked a coercive response from these young reformers who had set out with the notion that the conversion of the Okies was a simple matter of social engineering.

Notes in Text

1. See, for example, Ellery F. Reed, "The Federal Transient Program," manuscript, n.d., chap. V, passim, Federal Writers Project Collection, Bancroft Library, University of California, Berkeley, Carton 12.

2. John N. Webb, *The Transient Unemployed*, WPA Division of Social Research Monograph Number 3 (Washington, 1935), pp. 9-10.

3. Webb, *The Transient Unemployed*, pp. 9-10; Reed, "The Federal Transient Program," chap. IV, p. 3.

4. John N. Webb and Malcolm Brown, *Migrant Families*, WPA (Washington, 1938), p. xiii.

5. Ibid., p. xiv.

6. Reed, "The Federal Transient Program," chap. II, p. 9.

7. John N. Webb, *The Migratory-Casual Worker*, WPA Division of Social Research Monograph Number 7 (Washington, 1937), pp. ix-x.

8. Reed, "The Federal Transient Program," chap. IV, p. 3.

9. Samuel Rosenman, ed., *The Public Papers and Addresses of Franklin D. Roosevelt*, (New York, 1938), IV: 167-168.

10. California State Relief Administration, "Transients in California," mimeographed (San Francisco, 1936), p. 3.

11. See David Eugene Conrad, *The Forgotten Farmers* (Urbana, Illinois, 1965).

12. Harry Schwartz, *Seasonal Farm Labor in the United States* (New York, 1945), p. 26.

13. Arthur M. Schlesinger, Jr., *The Coming of the New Deal* (Boston, 1959), p. 378; M. S. Venkataramani, "Norman Thomas, Arkansas Sharecroppers, and the

Roosevelt Agricultural Policies," *Mississippi Valley Historical Review* 47 (September 1960): 225-246.

14. Conrad, *The Forgotten Farmers*, pp. 64-82.

15. Richard Hofstadter, *The Age of Reform* (New York, 1963), pp. 46-47.

16. William E. Leuchtenberg, *Franklin D. Roosevelt and the New Deal* (New York, 1963), p. 345.

17. Testimony of C. B. Baldwin, U.S., Congress, House, Select Committee of the Committee on Agriculture to Investigate the Activities of the Farm Security Administration, *Hearings*, 78th Cong., 1st sess., 1943, Vol. 1, pp. 8-9 (hereafter Cooley Committee).

18. Ibid.

19. Bernard Sternsher, *Rexford Guy Tugwell and the New Deal* (New Brunswick, 1964), pp. 263-265.

20. Raymond Moley, *After Seven Years* (New York, 1939), pp. 369-370.

21. Sternsher, *Tugwell and the New Deal*, pp. 263-264; Schlesinger, *The Coming of the New Deal*, p. 368.

22. Sternsher, *Tugwell and the New Deal*, p. 5; Sidney Baldwin, *Poverty and Politics* (Chapel Hill, 1968), is the definitive study of the Resettlement Administration—Farm Security Administration, and will be cited extensively throughout this chapter. Also valuable, especially for the more utopian aspects of FSA activity, is Paul Conkin, *Tomorrow a New World* (Ithaca, 1959).

23. Rexford Guy Tugwell, "The Resettlement Idea," *Agricultural History* 33 (October 1959): 159-164.

24. Sternsher, *Tugwell and the New Deal*, pp. 5, 268; Conkin, *Tomorrow a New World*, pp. 146-152.

25. Sternsher, *Tugwell and the New Deal*, pp. 268-269ff. for discussion of Tugwell's plans for the Resettlement Administration.

26. Ibid., p. 271; Baldwin, *Poverty and Politics*, pp. 193-201 passim.

27. Irene Link, *Relief and Rehabilitation in the Drought Area*, WPA Division of Social Research, Rural Research Section, Research Bulletin, June 1937 (Washington, 1937), p. 5.

28. Sternsher, *Tugwell and the New Deal*, pp. 270-273; Schlesinger, *The Coming of the New Deal*, pp. 370-373; Baldwin, *Poverty and Politics*, pp. 87, 203-208.

29. James Agee and Walker Evans, *Let Us Now Praise Famous Men* (Boston, 1941).

30. Harry Drobisch to FERA, March 15, 1935, Harry E. Drobisch Papers, Bancroft Library, University of California, Berkeley.

31. Drobisch to FERA, March 15, 1935, Hewes to Drobisch May 15, 1935, both in Drobisch Papers.

32. Mrs. R. McWilliams to Culbert Olson, March 19, 1935, Federal Writers Project Collection, Carton 10.

33. Drobisch to FERA, March 15, 1935, Drobisch Collection.

34. Mrs. R. McWilliams to Culbert Olson, March 19, 1935, Drobisch to Mrs. R. McWilliams, March 21, 1935, Mrs. R. McWilliams to Frances Perkins, March 24, 1935, all in Federal Writers Project Collection, Carton 10.

35. "Tentative Program of the Division of Rural Rehabilitation, California Emergency Relief Administration, April 30, 1935," typed manuscript, George Clements Papers, University of California, Los Angeles, Box 19. See also Paul S.

Taylor, "The R.A. and Migratory Agricultural Labor in California," *Plan Age 2* (June 1936): 26-29. During the resettlement phase of the administration the migrant labor camps program was a minor, "inherited" one. Not until the formation of FSA in 1937 was a "Migratory Farm Labor Section" created within the agency; and not until 1939 did Congress appropriate specific funds for migrant labor camps. See Baldwin, *Poverty and Politics,* pp. 93, 222-223.

36. Lowry Nelson to Paul Taylor, June 11, 1935, Paul S. Taylor Collection, Bancroft Library, University of California, Berkeley, Carton 3.

37. Hewes to Drobisch, May 15, June 18, 1935, Drobisch Papers; Lowry Nelson to Paul Taylor, June 11, 1935, Taylor Collection, Carton 3.

38. *Oakland Tribune,* August 9, 1935.

39. *Bakersfield Californian,* October 24, 1935.

40. Sternsher, *Tugwell and the New Deal,* p. 241.

41. Rexford Guy Tugwell, "The Progressive Task Today and Tomorrow," *Vital Speeches of the Day* 2 (December 2, 1935): 130-131.

42. *Bakersfield Californian*, September 13, 1935, for Drobisch vision of a chain of camps.

43. Sternsher, *Tugwell and the New Deal*, p. 290; Drobisch to Arthur and Larry, July 19, 1935, Drobisch Papers.

44. "Conference with Miss Geach, July 3, 1936," Drobisch Papers.

45. "Review of Steps Taken in the Development of the Program for Farm Laborers, October 21, 1936," memorandum, Drobisch Papers; "Confidential Memo on Migrant Camps, May 20, 1936," Taylor Collection, Carton 3.

46. Conkin, *Tomorrow a New World*, pp. 175-185; Baldwin, *Poverty and Politics,* pp. 113-125.

47. Cooley Committee, *Hearings,* Part 1, pp. 1-3.

48. Sternsher, *Tugwell and the New Deal,* pp. 281, 306; Conkin, *Tomorrow a New World*, pp. 146-154.

49. Clements to George Hecke, September 2, 1936, in Clements Collection.

50. *San Francisco News,* August 3, 1937. The figure $16,000 seems large, but is substantially correct. "Unit costs" at Greenbelt, Greendale, and Greenhills, the three garden city projects, were $15,395, $16,623, and $16,093, respectively. It should be pointed out that the average unit cost of all thirty-seven RA communities, which included farm communities, forest homesteads, and cooperative plantations and farms, was $10,834. See Conkin, *Tomorrow a New World*, pp. 336-337.

51. U.S., Congress, Senate, Committee on Appropriations, *Hearings*, 76th Cong., 1st sess., 1939, p. 192.

52. Taylor, "The R.A. and Migratory Agricultural Labor in California," 28; "Jonathan Garst Address at Stockton Conference," manuscript, Farm Security Administration Collection, Carton 9.

53. *San Francisco News,* August 8, 1936, July 28, August 24, 1937; *Labor Herald,* September 1, 1938.

54. La Follette Committee, *Hearings*, Part 59, p. 21,919.

55. "Agricultural Workers Health and Medical Association," in La Follette Committee, *Hearings*, Part 59, p. 21,937.

56. Testimony of Culbert Olson, Tolan Committee, *Hearings*, Part 6, p. 2,237.

57. "Agricultural Workers Health and Medical Association," mimeographed release, Farm Security Administration Collection, Carton 7.

58. La Follette Committee, *Hearings*, Part 59, map facing p. 21,919, 21,938.

59. Edward C. Banfield, *Government Project* (Glencoe, Illinois, 1951) is a study of Casa Grande Farms. See also Katherine Douglas, "Uncle Sam's Co-op for Individualists," *Coast Magazine* (June 1939), reprint copy in Bureau of Public Administration Library, University of California, Berkeley.

60. Testimony of Walter Packard, La Follette Committee, *Hearings*, Part 59, pp. 21,810-21,815 for résumé of cooperative farm system. See Banfield, *Government Project*, passim, for analysis of disruption of project during war years.

61. Testimony of Omer Mills, La Follette Committee, *Hearings*, Part 59, pp. 21,927, 21,938.

62. Shafter Monthly Report, May 1941, U.S. Department of Agriculture, Agricultural Stabilization and Conservation Commission Collection, 36,886 Federal Records Center, San Francisco.

6

The FSA Camps

FSA camps were the only places in California where migrants congregated under the direction of administrators with more than passing interest in their condition. Apart from their goal of providing sanitary housing for farm workers, the FSA camps were also an attempt to achieve a social end. At the camps, the Okies were to be exposed to managed, cooperative self-government. Under the direction of their camp managers, Okie "rugged individualists" would learn to subordinate private goals to the welfare of the group.

The key FSA personnel in the endeavor were the camp managers who lived at the camps and were in constant intimate contact with the campers. Tom Collins, organizer of Guam's public-school system, and later administrator of a private school for disturbed boys, was FSA's most important camp manager. Perfectly suited for the job, Collins was both trailblazer and trainer for the camp program. He prepared the psychological ground in new camps, served as their first manager, and then moved on, leaving the functioning units for managers he had trained. Collins' role in the camp program brought him considerable publicity, and it was to him that John Steinbeck dedicated *The Grapes of Wrath*.

Collins' fellow-managers comprised a group with various back-

grounds but relatively similar attitudes. At the inception of the program, it was decided to avoid hiring trained social workers as managers.
Region IX officials tended to mistrust them: "it would take the average
trained social worker so long," one wrote, "to fill out forms, write
histories, and do the usual intake routine to which she was accustomed,
that by the time she had determined eligibility the starvation would be
complete." Instead, the administrators "selected sympathetic but vigor-
ous young people with no tradition of case work technique."[1] Many of
the managers were graduate students from the University of California,
imbued with a strong sense of camaraderie, dedicated, idealistic, and
determined to nurture cooperative democracy within the camps. Some
mangers were socialists, most were liberals, and all approached their
jobs with a messianic zeal.[2] As one explained his commitment to the
program, it was his good fortune to have found the job: "we know our
administration as 'Resettlement.' To those with whom we work, the
migratory laborers, it is not 'Resettlement,' it is re-birth, re-living the
re-building of hope. . . . With their cooperation we are, most certainly,
helping them to help themselves. May nothing occur to cause a cessation of this program."[3]

More missionary than managerial in temper, these young men would
not have been content simply to perform administrative tasks at the
camps, and FSA policy reinforced their intention to remake the Okies
under their care. "In managing the camps," the regional directors were
instructed by their Washington offices, "the FSA accepts the responsibility for sponsoring recreational, cultural, health, home industry and
self-help programs for the enrichment of the life of the campers."
Further, directors were authorized to "redelegate to regularly appointed camp managers any or all of their authority" with the sole
qualification that managers function in accord with national FSA
policy.[4] So broad a mandate provided the local managers with considerable power, which they did not hesitate to exercise. Camp managers
generally interpreted their mission to enrich the life of the campers in
two ways. While they strove to break cultural habits they termed
"degraded," which had been engrained in the Southwest for generations, they also attempted to instill in their wards new patterns of social
and political behavior, which should convert them into model citizens
of a model community sculpted by committed young liberals.

Not all Okie characteristics were termed "degraded"; some were "quaint"—folklore, for example, which the managers sought to preserve. Okie songs were assiduously collected, dialects studied, peculiar names recorded. In 1941, the Woodville camp became the scene of America's "first festival of the folklore of the migratory agriculture workers from the Southwest" replete with fiddling, tall tales, and hog calling.[5] The more sentimental of the FSA's employees romanticized the campers. One nurse, for example, attempted to give her superiors at the head office "the feel of" working with the migrants:

> See? For one thing, you would see the most magnificent sunbonnets that ever baffled man. . . .
> Hear? Well, if you have an ear for language, you would be interested in following dialects, in identifying Old English songs and phrases which have survived generations.
> . . . if, like the writer, you should have the harmless hobby of collecting names, you would find some merry moments, even in dull files. Wouldn't Obed Goforth, or Pink See Boggs cheer any bleak day?[6]

Considering the fact that *Fortune*'s reporter had found "Five Foot Two" and "Twelfth Street Rag" among the most popular songs in the camp, these hyperbolic comments may have been more apropos of the tiny collections of mountain people huddled in the Ozarks than of the typical California migrant. In any case, the nurse's sentimentalization of the Okies did not prevent her from approaching them with a good deal more uplifting zeal than anthropological interest. We shall "pump into these people," she continued, "the medicines, the vitamins, the calories, the teaching . . . to rebuild their lives in a new and different environment."

Urban, secular, and educated, the managers were all the Okies were not. Many of FSA's managers believed that Okie cultural patterns that did not fit their concept of the quaint were matters for "rehabilitation" or, rather, reform. "In strange surroundings, without friends, their life-long rural economic and cultural pattern shattered, they were in need of social as well as economic rehabilitation," FSA policy announced.[7] The migrants' religion held a prominent position on the list of items to be rehabilitated.

Few areas in the United States during the 1930s remained either as fundamentalistic, or as emotional, in religion, as the Great Plains states that supplied the bulk of California's Okies. The average Okie migrant belonged to a small, highly sectarian church of the "hell-fire and damnation variety."[8] Basically eschatological in outlook, these churches may have provided for the Okie a compensatory psychological release from grinding rural poverty. Anthropologist Walter Goldschmidt, studying the Okies in the San Joaquin Valley, found that they consistently emphasized the values of the next world in lieu of the deprivations of this world. "The real blue bloods," one Okie told him in a comment typical of many, "are those who are saved." The saints, the migrants maintained, are persecuted on earth, but that did not matter, for they will be uplifted in heaven.[9] Insofar as many of FSA's employees were concerned, however, the Okie churches were neither sophisticated nor very fastidious. "We prays and shouts to git closer to Gawd," one migrant told FSA's consultant.

Some of the migrants were "holy rollers," and others, faith healers—and both varieties annoyed the managers.[10] One official feared that these religions were "productive of fanaticisms and irrationalities which can seriously disturb the general social equilibrium." The management of the camps would have been "heartily glad if it could keep out the churches, letting the people attend the ones of their choice in the town."[11] Despite their irritation with the Okie religious practices, however, the managers knew they could not interfere "with the individual's or group privilege of freedom of thought and worship."[12]

Unable to forbid the outright entry of the churches into the camps, several managers instead took steps to protect their campers from the more "irrational" aspects of their religions through various methods of indirect interference. The Marysville camp manager, for example, attempted to dissuade Pentecostal preachers from visiting the installation by refusing to permit them to take up collections.[13] Arvin's camp manager justified his open disapproval of a faith-healing sect on the grounds that their refusal to accept modern medicine might lead to the spread of communicable diseases among the campers. He developed a complex system of observation for the cautious group's clandestine services, notifying his superiors that when he heard sounds "very much like a dog on a distant hill baying a mournful ritual at the full moon," he knew that services were in progress for an ill Okie. He was never able to surprise the faith healers at work, and concluded that the congregation had lookouts stationed on the job. The secret war continued without let-up. A month later, he could report at least one minor victory in his campaign to secularize the "ultra-religious" campers, some of whom had forbidden their children the worldly pleasures of visiting the camp's amateur theater. He was "gradually breaking this condition," and some of the Okie mothers were accepting the fact that their children were taking part in rehearsals for a short play.[14]

Religion was the Okies' most important emotional prop, and managers usually found that the campers could not be detached from it. But more worldly patterns of behavior seemed accessible to reform, and managers attempted zealously to institute in their wards different attitudes regarding manners and morals. During the early days of the camp program, managers and other observers discovered that the Okies' recreations were simple, inexpensive, and generally solitary, the result of years of rural isolation. The Okies were accustomed to self-entertainment and disliked formal group activities. Back home, they had preferred possum and coon hunting to organized sport, and they retained those patterns in California when they could.[15]

Gradually, camp managers developed programs designed to foster a habit of organized group activity. A typical week's schedule of evening entertainment included meetings of the Young People's Clubs, a dance, a boxing match, an amateur night, movies, and a convocation of the camp council.[16] During the day, migrant women were taught prenatal care, initiated into the mysteries of sophisticated plumbing fixtures, and, most controversial of all, instructed in the FSA's birth-control program.[17] The latter intruded upon the Victorian sensibilities of the migrants who reacted with outraged modesty to the visits of Margaret Sanger's Birth Control League, as well as to films on prenatal care and female cancer prevention.[18] And managers found that social habits died as slowly as religious ones. Few attended the dances, and while many women had shown some interest in birth control not one, a manager complained somewhat hyperbolically, "ever did anything about it."[19]

In one area, no attempt was made to change the Okies' habits: racial segregation was maintained within the camps. The question of what to do with Negro, Mexican, or Filipino workers at the camps came to RA's attention in 1936 when Mrs. Bertha Rankin, upon whose land the Arvin unit had been built, reminded the regional office of the presence of nonwhite migrant workers in the San Joaquin Valley. "You know what we forgot," she asked rhetorically, "—a unit in the Kern county migrant camp for the colored folks." She had driven to the camp in search of accommodations for three Negro cotton pickers and had been told that "they couldn't put colored folks with the white people," which, she agreed, "of course is true."[20] When queried about the matter by his superior at the regional office, Collins replied that Mrs. Rankin had misunderstood the nature of racial relations at the camp. Negroes, Mexicans, and Filipinos were not excluded from the camps, and FSA "do[es] not discriminate—color—race or creed." Camp policy, he continued, was simply to recommend that black field workers be placed in one unit: "If a need arises . . . we . . . can easily solve it by suggesting to the Negro group that they occupy a certain section, and if necessary explain to them the advantage of having the colored group to itself." In light of the fact that California's Negroes were "very, very strongly opposed to segregation in tax supported camps or communities," however, FSA should not "officially go on records as having sections for the segregation of the Negro." FSA never did officially segregate the racial minorities from the Okies, but apparently the unofficial practice became policy, as was indicated by rare notations in the camp newspapers.[21]

FSA managers' attempts to reorient the religious practices and social mores of Okies were intermittent and not a major source of friction between the campers and the managers. A far more serious problem intruded upon relations when the managers attempted to redefine the meaning and implications of the democratic concept for the Okies. Throughout the life of the camp program, this issue more than any other brought anger and frustration to manager and camper alike.

The Okies may not have thought consciously of the manner in which they interpreted democracy. They were, nonetheless, firmly ensconced within the more individualistic, libertarian side of the democratic ideology. The Okie liked to think of himself as "beholden to no one," an individual making his way alone with neither aid from, nor gratitude to, the government or anyone else. Observers were unanimous in dubbing the Okies "rugged individualists," and the migrants' behavior lent validity to the sobriquet. It was their "rugged individualism" that caused the attempt to unionize them to founder and die; it was in their desire to own farms of their own that FSA's collective farm principle met its greatest obstacle. Their religion, their entertainments, their refusal to accept state relief with equanimity—all these testified to the fact that the Okies placed by far the greatest emphasis upon "liberty" to the detriment of "equality and fraternity."

Unaccustomed to the interdependent life made inevitable by industrialization and the rise of cities, the Okie was able to do as he pleased because he was white, isolated on his farm, and free from the restraints imposed upon dwellers in more populated areas. The Great Plains migrant was not anti-social, not a ruthless egocentric who preferred isolation to neighborliness. Indeed, the records of the migration are filled with moments of altruism and charity. Goldschmidt visited a Pentecostal meeting in the San Joaquin Valley, for example, during which the entire congregation prayed that two young penniless newcomers would find work with the aid of the Lord. John Steinbeck, living with the Okies during his research for *The Grapes of Wrath*, was obviously moved by the abiding sense of shared misery which drew them together into a community of the dispossessed.[22]

When the needs of the group conflicted with the desires of the individual migrant, however, the group invariably took second place. In this, the Okies were basically no different from other Americans, but their refusal to accept certain restraints was more obvious. The southern Great Plains migrant was unprepared to observe minor regulations that other Americans observed simply by force of habit. The Marysville camp manager saw in the migrants a hatred for the law and was shocked to find them idolizing Pretty Boy Floyd and other criminals. The migrants had an "outlaw psychology," he concluded.[23] Other managers frequently complained that the campers refused to observe traffic regulations upon the camp grounds and, worse, that they would not obey quarantines imposed by local public health authorities. "For some time," Shafter's manager reported, "we have had difficulty enforcing rules of isolation, people who were isolated would wander into camp. Last week I had a man and woman arrested for breaking isolation. . . . When the man was sentenced, he said, 'Sure are mighty strict here in California.' "[24] The best summation of the Okie psychology came from the Marysville camp where "experience" showed "that this group [was] very independent. 'Thou shalts,' or other phrases bearing on the 'must' bring resentment. Of course, this is typical of all independent groups.

[With most such groups] one gets immediate response through 'suggestions.' When such groups are from Oklahoma, Texas or Arkansas, it requires, at times, several personal contacts."[25]

From the local camp manager to Rexford Tugwell at the Washington office, FSA's officials envisioned their agency's social mission to be the obliteration of the more individualistic facets of the Great Plains migrants' personality. It was, after all, upon rugged individualism that Tugwell blamed the desperate condition of America's agricultural people and their lands. He proposed instead a collective principle which demanded that members of a community subordinate personal desire to group needs.

The device through which the sense of community was to be achieved at the Casa Grande and Mineral Kings cooperative farms was the farm manager. He assigned the tasks, determined the allocation of acreage, and set the prices at which produce would be sold. FSA hoped that the habit of group decision-making would gradually replace the manager's role at the farms.[26] No such cooperative enterprise united the migrants at the FSA camps, however, and the habit of group decision-making would have to emerge from a well-planned social and political environment. To achieve this end, Region IX officials drew up a constitution for the camps, under which the campers provided the legislative and judiciary, the manager provided the executive, and all worked together in ideal self-government.

The constitution that would transform the Okies from rugged individualists into cooperative citizens was printed on a mimeographed FSA form and became a standard text for all the camps. When a new camp was opened, the blank spaces were filled in, and an "instant republic" modeled on the American Constitution sprang to life:

> WE, THE PEOPLE OF THE   MIGRATORY LABOR
> CAMP, IN ORDER TO FORM A MORE PERFECT COMMUNITY,
> PROMOTE THE GENERAL WELFARE, AND INSURE DOMESTIC
> TRANQUILITY, DO HEREBY ESTABLISH THIS CONSTITUTION
> FOR THE   MIGRATORY LABOR CAMP.[27]

All legislative powers granted by the constitution were vested in the community council, a body composed of three members from each of the camp's subdivisions and elected by all campers over twenty-one. Its powers comprised the promotion of the general welfare, management of the community fund to which all campers contributed, and regulation of the camp's community property. Judicial powers were lodged in the community court, chosen by the council. Its duties included interpreting the camp constitution, adjudicating disputes between campers, and trying cases involving violations of the council's ordinances.

The powers of both the council and the court were necessarily limited. The camp was not an autonomous body, and its members were subject to the laws of the state of California. In a theoretical sense, however, the constitution conferred upon the court and the council powers like those exercised by their federal counterparts in Washington. In practice, the provisions governing the camp's executive made clear that this was to be a guided democracy, under which the campers had the power to make only decisions judged progressive by the manager. The executive power was lodged in the camp manager, who was neither elected nor subject to the desires of the camp council. He held absolute veto power over the community council in situations where he believed their decisions conflicted with government policy or with law. Similarly, decisions of the court were to be "rendered in the form of a recommendation to the camp manager," and were not binding.[28]

Despite the fact that managers held essentially dictatorial power at the camps, they chose to exercise it only rarely. In minor altercations with the council, they generally chose the road of gentle persuasion in preference to the veto power, which served as their ultimate deterrent. The migrants were a proud and easily offended group. For the successful manager, discretion was the key to acceptance by the campers.[29] When, for example, one of the camp councils determined to "blow the works" and lavish the camp funds on an "ice cream feed," the manager cautioned that this would afford "only momentary pleasure." His persuasive powers were successful in this case, and he exultantly notified his superiors that "we now have a brand new mimeograph machine and public address system," purchased with the ice cream money.[30]

Similar tactics prevailed when religious problems threatened to disrupt relations between manager and campers. As one manager told an observer: "Maybe Jehovah's witnesses want to give the camp a good working over. One of the saints comes to me and requests permission. I could tell him no and get rid of him in ten seconds, but that might make a martyr out of the guy. So I make a date for the guy with the Council," who, hopefully, "finally see the [Witnesses'] racket and unanimously tell him they don't allow peddlers in their camp" when he asks for contributions.[31]

Managers frequently executed the decisions of the council or the court in good faith. At various camps, councils passed strong ordinances regulating the use of liquor at the units, and a few banned alcohol entirely. When families at one camp violated these regulations, the camp court imposed sentences upon them. When the miscreants refused to abide by the decisions of the court, the manager called upon the local sheriff and had them forcibly evicted.[32] Under normal circumstances, warnings from the council and the manager, or in severe cases, a visit by the local sheriff, were sufficient to ensure that wayward campers fell back into line.

Migrants involved in crimes or disruptions were barred from residence in the camps, as were those who failed to conform to models established by camp managers. When, for example, the manager of Westley asked permission to evict two campers, he observed that the council had charged them with drunkenness. This was not, he continued, his major indictment against them: "Neither family has been accepted into the social gatherings of the camp, therefore I consider them unworthy for future residents of our government camps."[33] By 1940, FSA managers had established a blacklist. The Shafter camp manager reported to the head office that there were "perhaps two thousand families that are barred from this camp or other camps, because they are problem families. Please never lose sight of the fact that these families before coming here lived at a standard far below that which we must keep in our camps. Bringing them quite abruptly [sic] into a higher civilization, is a problem that one must experience to realize."[34]

Despite the managers' efforts, FSA's experiment with "temporary, cooperative communities" under the aegis of guided self-government steadily deteriorated. During the early days of the program, it had appeared that the program would succeed. All their rugged individualism notwithstanding, the migrants turned out in high percentages for camp council elections. At the Marysville camp's election in late 1936, 90 percent of the eligible migrants voted for camp council members. A few weeks later, a visitor from the Quartermaster Corps was impressed by the "democratic management by the residents of the camps. With about 85 per cent of the campers emanating from truly American villages and descendants of sturdy American stock," he observed, "they are eager to maintain the American tradition of government . . . the 'town hall' form of government decides the conduct of the camps."[35]

This early spurt of participatory democracy was more apparent than real. Indeed, it is difficult, in the light of events that followed, to account for it at all. It is possible that during the early days of the camp program, the migrants were so demoralized, so apathetic, that, told to *be* democratic, they *were* democratic. In any event, as the migrants settled into the camp program, they reverted to accustomed habit and largely ignored the cooperative democracy that FSA had conceived for them. By 1940, camp after camp had fallen into a pattern of petty gossip, political apathy, and constant exhortations from the managers that the campers be democratic.

The Marysville camp had been FSA's California showcase. In 1937, it was "a place where people worked, played and lived for one another instead of against one another." The camp of 1940, a long-time resident of the unit complained, "is just a place of bickering and fussing." [36] Democracy at the camp had collapsed: "The Chairman opens the meetings and the manager takes it over." These comments cannot be dismissed as the accusations of one disgruntled camper. Throughout the FSA camp system, manager and migrant alike were noting an increasing unwillingness of the residents to engage in the process of camp decision-making. At the Firebaugh camp in 1941, the manager complained that the remark most frequently heard among groups gathered around the common buildings was "To Hell with the Council." Campers charged that the council had ceased to function democratically: "We can go on open meeting night and discuss some rules that the campers don't want and next meeting night the one man council will pass it over the campers." Accused by the manager of "failing to take an active part in the government and operation of your community," the campers did nothing to retire the council which they had vocally consigned to perdition. Two months later, only 13 of the camp's 326 voters turned out to elect a new council.[37]

The identical pattern was repeated at the Indio and Gridley camps. At Indio, the camp newspaper's Independence Day issue began with a jeremiad from the manager: "This space was reserved for news of the election which supposedly was to be held on Thursday night at the Social Center. But what we want to know is what happened to the voters? . . . Democracy never will work by itself. Only the people by making their will known can make it work. You must vote to make the Community Council really YOUR COUNCIL."[38] Earlier, at the Gridley camp, the manager had been grieved at the absence of campers at the general meetings.[39] "Some of the remarks made at the camp," he complained, "wouldn't do justice to a child. If you don't like the rules made by past sensible campers you shouldn't force yourself to suffer any longer." Regaining his composure, he excused some campers' "lack of good judgment" and concluded: "After all I know that it is necessary to do a good deal of educational work around here."[40]

A number of factors conspired to produce the collapse of FSA's social experiment. First, the migrants were not different from other groups in their inability or unwillingness to cast off habit patterns that had taken years to produce. A mimeographed constitution, its blank spaces filled in by the campers, might provide the mechanisms for FSA's ideal democracy, but it could not turn the migrants into latter-day Madisons and Hamiltons. There were, nonetheless, deeper reasons for the failure of the plan, and these grew from the breezy, optimistic, often unrealistic manner in which reformers of the depression era approached social problems.

The migrants reached California in desperate social and economic dislocation. They were vulnerable, defenseless, and disoriented. American citizens, they were nonetheless rejected socially and exploited economically in California. Outside the camps, they were a class of pariahs, detested by the older Californians, the butt of political campaigns, the focus of an intense anti-migrant propaganda drive. The circumstances of their migration, the employment they accepted, and the fact that they were different and somewhat less sophisticated than the Californians all forced upon them the role of an inferior the instant they left the camp boundaries. FSA demanded of the migrants a dual, almost schizoid, role. In the midst of their rejection by California, they were asked by their camp managers to function within the camps as ideal citizens of an ideal republic. To maintain both roles was a near-impossible task.

If the migrants had somehow succeeded in playing their dual roles simultaneously, other forces would still have doomed the experiment. The maintenance of the camps was essentially a simple matter of housekeeping concealed by an apparently complex arrangement of subsidiary activities. An FSA camp was not a Puritan settlement on the American frontier in the 1650s; it was a housing unit located within a functioning county in a modern state. Friends of the FSA occasionally equated the camp councils with "town hall democracy," but the migrants understood that camp democracy was really a game. The constitutional issues with which the campers were asked to deal—ice cream feeds versus mimeograph machines, for one—were trivial problems compared with the deadly struggle for existence that they waged daily when they left the camp's boundaries. Adults engaged in attempting to make a new life in California, they had two choices when they confronted FSA's democracy: they could ignore it, or, by playing the game, they could engage in what must have seemed childlike pursuits.

Finally, the frequent appeals demanding that the campers be democratic did not conceal the fact that the managers held the coercive power should they choose to exercise it. The blacklists did exist; so did the occasional guidance from the managers. To these poor, proud, and independent Okies, the managers must, at times, have seemed insufferably patronizing. In a very real way, FSA differed little from institutions where authority actually resides elsewhere than in the subordinate groups upon whom a democratic veneer is overlaid. In mental hospitals, petty problems are resolved in the wards by councils of patients; doctors and orderlies exercise the real power. On college campuses student governments represent students in such matters of significance as the allocation of funds to the football team and the college daily, the time and location of campus events, or the construction of new offices for the student body president; power resides, however, in the administration, as those engaged in political action outside the campus quickly discover. It is not without significance that, during the 1960s, student activists dubbed student government with the adjective "sandbox" in recognition of the parental powers of administrators over student democracies. FSA's democracy was a sandbox democracy.

The migrants were more realistic than the managers in assessing FSA's role. The campers rejected FSA's attempt to transform them, but they appreciated deeply FSA's desire to aid them. They understood

that their condition made them objects of charity and wards of the
government, rather than independent farmers able to stand on their
own. The camps were oases at which dispossessed migrants received
some comfort and a good deal of support.

One migrant wrote to the Thornton Camp:

> We really do appreciate
> The town we call our home,
> The town in California,
> The town we always roam.
> It's called the city of Thornton
> The only place to be
> In the state of California,
> Is the place where we live free.[41]

Upon his return from a trip to the cotton fields in the South, another
observed that "no one really knows how to enjoy a good place to live"
until they have experienced the drunks, mud, stench, and foremen at
the private camps.[42] Much of the migrant's appreciation for the camps
was buttressed by solid common sense. They realized that their poverty
and their migration had diminished their independence and removed
their freedom to choose between alternatives. They were in no condition to save themselves, and some external agency would have to
extricate them from their predicament. To many Okies, the FSA camps
were a deliverance: "Let's be thankful," one observed, "that the good
Lord has saved us from being a tramp."[43] Another commented that
"only some of us Okies and a few of the Angels know" what the camp
had come to mean for migrants who had

> traveled the long road hoping for the best
> Hungry and tired and dirty
> Always a heading west.[44]

Finally, one woman evaluated the relationship between the Okies and
the camps with ruthless precision: "I believe in the old saying 'Beggars
can't be chosers.' I think we are getting wonderful help. . . .it is given to
us by a very generous government. They don't have to do it."[45]

In short, the Okies were not Americans who conformed easily with
the managers' image of managed self-government. Moreover, neither
California agriculture in the 1930s nor the FSA camps with their

limited role in the life of the migrant were adequate schoolrooms for initiating the migrants into the mysteries of cooperative democracy. Saddled with an unrealistic view of the simplicity of its task, Region IX failed to produce a new man out of the Okie. Nevertheless, the agency achieved some limited successes. Unquestionably, it provided the migrant with accommodations better than those available anywhere else in the state. It fed, clothed, and supported him during the labor over-supply and unemployment crisis of 1938. It protected him from county administrators and growers whose sole interest lay in removing the migrant from the region or profiting from his labor. Finally, FSA introduced the migrants to many of the physical trappings and social patterns of a life more modern than that in the southern Great Plains. In all, the best epitaph for the dying social experiment was the comment of one manager who had accepted a "sassing" with some grace and a good deal of patronization from a migrant woman who had refused to clean up her cabin:

> This woman, like a majority of the campers probably lived in Oklahoma, with a hard dirt floor, there was no lawn to cut, the slop was thrown on the ground out the kitchen window, after dark instead of going to the toilet they did the job of [sic] the back porch, if they ever did anything for the good of the neighborhood it was the result of force of some kind. They seldom voted for one reason or another, they lived easy going lives, no hurry no rush. . . . Taking citizens from such a back ground and putting them in a government camp, expecting to build a good temporary, cooperative community, is quite a job. I know in our talks to the public we do not paint such a picture of the people we work with, yet we in the field know that the picture is a true one of the majority of them, and the fact that we have done a fair job with them, is I think a miracle.[46]

In addition to its conscious transformation of FSA's national goals to fit California's specialized needs, and its attempt to instill a sense of cooperative democracy in its clients, Region IX's office played an important role in easing California's migrant problem. Without intending to perform the task, FSA and its camps served as way stations on the road to assimilation of the Okies into California society. The camps provided neutral territory at which the first natural contacts between migrant and old-timer could occur. In this lay the federal government's most significant contribution to the solution of California's migrant problem.

For specific and complex reasons, California's growers and their organizations detested the FSA camps. The camps were federal islands at which migrants could join labor unions and where organizers functioned openly and unmolested. FSA's grant-in-aid program exacerbated the antagonism of corporate agriculture to the federal agency. Because they collected federal relief during their first year in California, FSA's Okie clients were protected from the necessity of accepting field work at any wage in order to survive. Finally, the growers and their allies suspected FSA's personnel. California took part in the reaction that led to Tugwell's excoriation and resignation. In the view of many agriculturalists, the regional directorate supplied little Tugwells in abundance. It was Dr. George Clements' personal opinion, for example, that RA was part of an immense conspiracy to subvert the nation: "Dr. Tugwell and his administrative aides intend to form myriads of socialistic if not Communistic centers among the farmers of the United States: This is based on the general picture of Dr. Tugwell set up for the regimentation of farmers and some knowledge of the type of socialists and communists in the organization."[47]

Ideology as well as self-interest led growers to attack RA, even though it provided them with housing for their laborers at public expense. Growers boycotted many camps, sought their removal, and made FSA one focus of the propaganda campaign launched by CCA in 1938. The campaign against FSA could not have been launched if attitudes in the rural communities had not coincided with the growers' views. The steady increase in FSA installations did not go unnoticed by the valley residents. The decision to build a camp, a grant office, or an AWHMA clinic usually brought anger from nearby communities prone to the developing pattern of anti-Okie prejudice.

One underpinning of community antagonism against the FSA camps was the tendency of rural Californians to assume the value systems of the larger growers. FSA located its camps where migrants congregated; migrants congregated where harvest work was available; therefore, FSA would always be forced to function in areas potentially most hostile.

However, the tendency of rural towns to adopt the growers' values was not the sole, nor even the most important, reason for community hostility to the FSA camps. A deeper cause lay in social prejudice against the Okies. The Okies were needed by growers as cheap harvest labor but were unwanted by the communities who profited indirectly from their labor. To the valley towns, an FSA camp meant a permanent population of "undesirables," and townspeople reacted quickly and consistently to the threat.

Community opposition to the camp program ranked high among the agency's major problems. Nearly every camp planned prior to 1941 was built amid petitions, letters, resolutions and complaints, which kept FSA's troubleshooters constantly on the move. A rumor, an article in the local newspaper, or an offhand comment from an FSA official was sufficient to spark reaction from townspeople who resented the establishment of a camp in their area.

There were racial overtones in the prejudice directed at the Okies, and in the opposition to the establishment of federal camps there was much that is reminiscent of the reaction of white communities confronted with an influx of black strangers. The events that took place at Brawley were a typical case. The Imperial Valley had encountered fewer Okies than areas farther north, but word of the migrant hordes had preceded the migrant camps into the area. In mid-1936, the Imperial County Farm Labor Council, counterpart of the San Joaquin Valley's Agricultural Labor Bureau, notified RA by resolution that the rumored establishment of a camp at Brawley would attract a "disturbing element."[48] This was a standard protest from growers who feared that labor unions would follow the federal camp into the region.

When RA publicly announced in early 1937 that the rumored Brawley camp would be built, nonagricultural groups within the community joined the growers in protest. In January, the Rental Protective Association was formed. The influx of Okies, it argued, would lower property values and create a flood of "unlawful elements," which would require the town to increase its police force.[49] Brawley's city council warned RA that it would refuse to cooperate with the federal government and earnestly requested that the plan be dropped.[50] By mid-February, a citizens' petition had been sent to RA, and Brawley's residents attended meetings at which they "voiced resentment against the migrants as people." The Brawley petition's assertion that "at least ninety percent of the taxpayers and property owners of the City are opposed to the establishment of this camp" was probably only slightly exaggerated.[51] Finally, Tom Collins, dispatched to Brawley as a troubleshooter, found that local people had heard that the Arvin camp was a breeding ground for trachoma; that Okies were generally "not clean and . . . did not make use of sanitary facilities"; and that property values would plummet as a result of the camp.[52] Despite the opposition, FSA built the camp.

The Imperial Valley, where a near-feudal relationship existed between Mexican labor and the owners of the immense vegetable ranches, was not peculiar in its reaction to the FSA camps. Similar events occurred in the San Joaquin and Sacramento valleys. In 1940, FSA's plans for a new camp for Tulare County touched off panic that a "new influx of refugees from the Ozark plateau" would inundate the towns of Woodville, Porterville, and Farmersville. FSA was inundated in turn by a flood of complaints from the local Parent-Teacher Association, Grand Jury, chamber of commerce, and private citizens.[53] As usual, the community's complaints ran the gamut of fears from lessened property values to increased crime and disease, overcrowded schools, and hordes of undesirables. The Tulare protest contained one additional significant facet. Along with other groups opposed to the camp, the local Granges petitioned FSA to halt the program.[54] That the Granges, which opposed the Associated Farmers on nearly every issue relating to farm labor in the 1930s, joined the protest clearly indicates that negative reaction to the migrant camps was not confined to large growers who saw in the camps a threat to their interest.[55]

At Ceres, a tiny town south of Modesto, citizens ridiculed a combined migrant camp and labor home project as "one of the nuttiest" stunts yet tried by the New Deal. The town's commissioner of public health and safety warned Tugwell that it would be as difficult to make Ceres accept the units as it was "to make the citizens of Boston drink tea which they did not want." At mass meetings, Ceres' residents insisted that the migrants would "greatly lower" the "standard of our population" and expose the town's schoolchildren to "objectionable and subversive influences."[56] The Ceres protest was so vehement that FSA abandoned its decision: the camp was not built and only the labor homes forced Ceres into contact with the Okies.

Similar protests took place from 1935 through 1941 at Marysville, Sonoma, El Centro, Gridley, and Windsor.[57] One town even protested a camp that had never been contemplated by FSA. Senators Johnson and Downey received protest letters from citizens of Delano who claimed they had heard that a camp was to be established near the town. A puzzled Senator Downey investigated and found that FSA had never discussed Delano as a camp location.[58]

Apart from Ceres' successful protest, FSA did not allow community objections to deter the decision to build. The program was sometimes slowed by protests, especially those emanating from growers' organizations. Nevertheless, FSA continued to construct camps until it became one of the largest New Deal agencies in the state. When they took charge of their new units, camp managers found that they were unwelcome in the rural communities whose citizens felt that the Roosevelt administration had foisted upon them an unnecessary and dangerous concentration of migrants.[59]

When the initial resentment to the Okies and the camps eased, however, rural communities gradually developed tolerance, followed by a mildly positive sentiment, toward the migrants. The Okies at the camps did not conform to the stereotypes that had fostered the anti-Okie prejudice in the early days of the migration. Unlike the ditch banks and the Little Oklahomas, the camps were clean, organized, and generally quite law-abiding. Under FSA's care, the Okies discarded the physical characteristics that had made them visible on the ditch banks. Their accents, of course, remained, but the outward signs of poverty and desperation—the dirt, the skinny children, the ragged overalls— gradually disappeared. Since the Okies were white beneath the grime, the camps made it possible for them literally to scrub off the badge of their inferiority.

Other influences fostered the conversion of the towns' initial hostility into cordiality. The camps anchored a necessary labor supply to the area, but they did not require outlays of tax funds from the county. Moreover, the camps brought cash to the rural areas. At Brawley, retail merchants reaped an additional $16,000 in annual sales to the campers, and the town benefited from a $13,000 contribution from the FSA for the construction of the town's water supply.[60] Finally, the camps never developed into the hotbeds of radicalism that rural communities had feared. Instead, the Okies proved to be as hostile to the agricultural unions as were the old-timers.

With some surprise and a good deal of pleasure, FSA discovered that, within a year or two, each camp gained a measure of community goodwill. At Brawley, where 1937 had begun with protests inaugurating the birth of the camp, resident and migrant fraternized in 1939. The merchants were placing advertisements in the camp newspaper, and the manager reported that he had the support and cooperation of the local journals.[61] FSA found, with amusement, that the "same organizations and individuals who presented the most bitter of our California experience when the Brawley camp was being considered about three years ago" were requesting that FSA locate additional mobile camps in the area.[62]

Managers reported similar revolutions in sentiment at other locations where camps had been greeted at first with hostility. At Shafter, "just about all the bitter opposition to our program has evaporated in the locality"; at Winters, "farmers and townspeople . . . hold a most unusual friendliness toward this F.S.A. camp. . . . A far different feeling exists than did two years ago in this area"; at Thornton, "everyone is praising the government for what it is attempting to do" at the camp; at Marysville, "all who have followed the record of the . . . camp will agree . . . that the camp is a fine thing for labor and for the district in which it is located"; at neighboring Yuba City, local sentiment was "almost 100 per cent" for FSA.[63] And, finally, at Ceres, where citizens imagined themselves as beleaguered Bostonians asked to drink FSA tea in 1936, three years of contact with the labor homes project brought second thoughts. In 1939, the district supervisor of the town's high school requested that Ceres' representative in the state legislature investigate the current status of the old migratory camp plan. The town's residents, he explained, were "now favorable to the idea" and felt that the land, which was still available, would be "an ideal spot for a model village."[64]

Out of the tolerance that developed toward the camps grew the first slow gropings toward breaking the pattern of segregation that had characterized relations between camp and town. Small points of contact appeared that departed from the stylized and ritualized employer-employee relationship that hitherto had been the only communication between Okies and residents. High school classes toured the camps and "came home with a better feeling for the migrants." Yuba City provided a public library for its camp and did not request compensation from the FSA. At Shafter, the local Kiwanis sponsored a boy scout troop at the camp. The chamber of commerce in Hemet Valley learned to greet the migrants each year when FSA's mobile camp rolled into town.[65] The camps and their residents had begun the slow and often tedious process of assimilation into the community.

These small signs of change in the Californian's attitude to the Okies should not be exaggerated. They were necessarily limited to the immediate surroundings of a camp. Nonetheless, in the midst of the panic and prejudice that gripped the state, at the height of the anti-migrant campaign waged at the statehouse and in the press, FSA provided islands at which stereotyped patterns of behavior were shaken. But even if every migrant had lived under the wing of FSA, the camps alone could not have destroyed the anti-Okie prejudice. Equality for the Okie migrant awaited his move to the city and his departure from an economic and social position that automatically made him an inferior in the eyes of the Californians. World War II completed this transformation. Despite these qualifications, however, it is also true that, in its own tiny way, FSA demonstrated that folkways change when ritual patterns of contact are broken. Forced by FSA into communication with Okies who were not camped along the ditch banks, townsfolk quickly forgot that they had once strenuously opposed the FSA units.

The first phase of federal activity concerning California's Okies encompassed the Federal Transient Service and the Resettlement Administration-Farm Security Administration migratory labor program. These agencies were neither planned nor did they develop as specific responses to California's Okie crisis. FTS was a failure and is properly consigned to footnotes in studies of the New Deal. The FSA, on the other hand, was a complex, exciting, and highly significant program of the New Deal. Its California directorate subtly converted the agency's national goals into a program suited to the peculiarities of California agriculture, launched a social experiment in guided democracy, and aided the assimilation of the migrants into the state.

A second phase of federal activity began in 1938 and gained momentum with the publication of *The Grapes of Wrath* in 1939. At the executive and legislative levels, the federal government became aware that California had a special problem on its hands. It is to the national concern with California's Okie problem that this study now turns.

Notes in Text

1. R. C. Timmons, "Medicine Follows the Crops," manuscript, Farm Security Administration Collection, Carton 2.
2. Interview with Mrs. Eleanor Engstrand, Berkeley, California, September 7, 1965; Westley Camp Reports, July 4, 1939, United States Department of Agriculture, Agriculture Stabilization and Conservation Commission Papers, Federal Records Center, San Francisco, 36,889.
3. Arvin Camp Reports, May 23, 1936, Harry E. Drobisch Papers, Bancroft Papers, University of California, Berkeley.
4. FSA Instruction 550.3, in La Follette Committee, *Hearings*, Part 59, pp. 21,934-21,935.
5. See, for example, Margaret Valiant, *Migrant Camp Recordings*, Farm Security Administration (n.p., n.d.), Giannini Foundation Library, University of California, Berkeley; FSA News Release, September 1941, in FSA Collection, Carton 8.
6. Miss Mary Sears, "Agricultural Workers Health and Medical Association," typed report, Farm Security Administration Collection, Carton 2.
7. Farm Security Administration, "Community Activities and Education Among Western Farm Workers," mimeographed (San Francisco, April 1941), Farm Security Administration Collection, Carton 2.
8. Engstrand interview.
9. Walter R. Goldschmidt, *As You Sow* (Glencoe, Illinois, 1947), pp. 157-159.
10. Eric Thomsen, *Our Migrant Brother* (Council of Women for Home Missions, n.p., n.d.); Marysville Reports, September 7, 1935, USDA ASCC Collection, 36,891; Kern Reports, January 25, 1936, Drobisch Papers.
11. John Beecher, "The Migratory Labor Program in California," p. 11, typed report, Farm Security Administration Collection, Bancroft Library, University of California, Berkeley, Carton 9.
12. Kern Reports, January 25, 1936, Drobisch Papers.
13. Marysville Reports, September 7, 1935, USDA ASCC Collection, 36,891.
14. Arvin Reports, January 25, 1936, Drobisch Papers; Arvin Reports, February 22, 1936, Simon J. Lubin Papers, Bancroft Library, University of California, Berkeley, Carton 13.
15. Arvin Reports, November 14, 1936, Lubin Papers, Carton 13; Lillian Creisler, "Little Oklahoma, or, The Airport Community" (Master's thesis, University of California, Berkeley, 1939), p. 55; see Arvin Reports, November 14, 1936, Lubin Papers, Carton 13.
16. Tolan Committee, *Hearings*, Part 7, p. 3,002.
17. Mildred Delp, "Baby-Spacing Report on California and Arizona, March-August, 1940," mimeographed report, Farm Security Administration Collection, Carton 9; "Migratory Labor: A Social Problem," *Fortune* 19 (April 1939): 100; *Happy Valley Weekly*, January 14, 1939.
18. Warren Engstrand to Harvey Coverley, March 20, 1942, USDA ASCC Collection, 36,881; "Migratory Labor: A Social Problem," 100; *Happy Valley Weekly*, January 14, 1939.
19. "Migratory Labor: A Social Problem," 100; *Tent City News*, May 13, 1939.

20. Bertha M. Rankin to Irving Wood, October 6, 1936, USDA ASCC Collection, 36,879.

21. Eric Thomsen to Tom Collins, October 9, 1936, Collins to Thomsen, October 12, 1936, USDA ASCC Collection, 36,879. For example, "Unit Four" at the Indio camp was "opened up and cleaned for the colored people" in 1939, and the issue did not arise again. Happy Valley Weekly, November 11, 1939.

22. John Steinbeck, The Grapes of Wrath (New York, 1939), passim.

23. Marysville Camp Report, August 29, 1936, USDA ASCC Collection, 36,891.

24. Shafter Camp Reports, January 1940, USDA ASCC Collection, 36,886; Camp Herald, November 7, 14, 1941.

25. Marysville Camp Reports, August 24, 1935. Drobisch Papers.

26. Testimony of Walter Packard, La Follette Committee, Hearings, Part 59, pp. 21,818-21,819.

27. "Constitution," Farm Security Administration Collection, Carton 2.

28. Ibid.

29. Arvin Camp Reports, February 22, 1936, USDA ASCC Collection, 36,879.

30. "Narrative Report, Region IX, March, 1941," Farm Security Administration Collection, Carton 2.

31. Beecher, "The Migratory Labor Program in California," p. 4.

32. "Narrative Report, Region IX, March, 1941."

33. James Eastley to Mr. Hollenberg, July 15, 1940, USDA ASCC Collection, 36,889.

34. Shafter Camp Report, November 1940, USDA ASCC Collection, 36,886.

35. W. F. Baxter, "Migratory Labor Camps," Quartermaster Review (July-August 1937): 6.

36. Voice of the Agricultural Worker, May 7, 1940.

37. Camp Herald, October 10, 17, 24, December 17, 1941.

38. Happy Valley Weekly, July 4, 1941.

39. Tent City News, July 15, 1939.

40. Ibid., September 2, 1939.

41. New Hope News, May 10, 1941.

42. Marysville Camp News, January 8, 1938.

43. Covered Wagon News, April 21, 1940.

44. VOTAW, September 9, 1941.

45. Happy Valley Weekly, March 9, 1940; Covered Wagon News, October 13, 1939; VOTAW, March 15, 1940, December 8, 1939.

46. Ray Mork to R. W. Hollenberg, June 18, 1940, USDA ASCC Collection, 36,885.

47. "A Confidential Brief Concerning the Activities of the RA as Conducted by Dr. Rexford G. Tugwell, Administrator, February 9, 1936," memorandum, George P. Clements Papers, Special Collections Library, University of California, Los Angeles, Box 9.

48. "Resolution, Imperial County Farm Labor Council, May 12, 1936," Taylor Collection, Carton 3.

49. Farm Labor News, February 19, 1937.

50. Brawley City Council to RA, telegram, January 19, 1937, USDA ASCC Collection, 36,881.

51. "Petition to Hon. Frank Merriam," n.d., USDA ASCC Collection, 36,881; Garst to Phillips, February 12, 1937, Lubin Papers, Carton 13.

52. Tom Collins to Eric Thomsen, March 1, 1937, USDA ASCC Collection, 36,881.

53. *San Francisco Chronicle*, March 7, 1940; "Resolution, American Legion, 15th District, February 25, 1940," Chamber of Commerce to Alfred J. Elliott, February 20, 1940; "Grand Jury, Resolution, January 5, 1940; Elliott to Alexander, January 11, 1940; 21st District PTA to Hiram Johnson and Sheridan Downey, February 2, 1940. All USDA ASCC Collection, 36,890.

54. "Resolution, Tulare Grange No. 198, February 7, 1940," "Resolution, Poplar Grange No. 359, January 9, 1940," USDA ASCC Collection, 36,890.

55. Clarke A. Chambers, *California Farm Organizations* (Berkeley, 1952), pp. 196-202.

56. *Salida News*, July 24, 1936; John Speers to R. G. Tugwell, July 21, 1936, USDA ASCC Collection, 36,881; *Turlock Journal*, July 24, 1936; "Resolution, Ceres Women's Club, September 10, 1936," Donald Calkins to J. Garst, August 10, 1936, USDA ASCC Collection, 36,881.

57. For Marysville, see below, pp. 252-53. For Sonoma, *San Francisco News*, February 10, 1938. For El Centro, *El Centro Press*, October 22, 1940, El Centro Chamber of Commerce to Garst, May 18, 1936, USDA ASCC Collection, 36,881. For Gridley, "Petition, Property Owners and Residents of Gridley to Jonathan Garst," memorandum, n.d., Williams to Mills, May 3, 1937, USDA ASCC Collection, 36,883. For Windsor, *San Francisco News*, January 5, February 9, 1938.

58. *Bakersfield Californian*, March 2, 1939.

59. Engstrand interview.

60. Charles L. Todd, "Tramping Out the Vintage," *Common Sense* (July 1939): 8.

61. *Pea Picker's Prattle*, December 9, 1939; F. E. McDarter to Hollenberg, March 29, 1938, USDA ASCC Collection, 36,880.

62. "Narrative Report, Region IX, December, 1939," Farm Security Administration Collection, Carton 2.

63. H. L. Tuck to Irving Wood, October 7, 1935, USDA ASCC Collection, 36,880; Winters Camp Reports, February-March 1940, USDA ASCC Collection, 36,889; State Senator B. S. Crittenden to FSA, February 23, 1940, USDA ASCC Collection, 36,887; *Marysville Appeal-Democrat*, July 16, 1936; *San Francisco Chronicle*, March 11, 1937.

64. A. S. Cakebread to Bud Gearhart, March 10, 1939, USDA ASCC Collection, 36,881.

65. *VOTAW*, May 21, 1940; *Marysville Appeal-Democrat*, March 18, 1940; *Bakersfield Californian*, January 11, 1940; "Narrative Report, Region IX, September, 1940," Farm Security Administration Collection, Carton 2.

7

The Migrant Problem
and the Federal Government: II

California reverberated with the migrant problem throughout 1938. By 1939, the state looked increasingly to the nation for aid, but California was in no position to persuade her forty-seven neighbors that she was in trouble. For too many years, boosters had sold the Golden State to the vexation of other Americans. For this reason alone, Californians had difficulty selling the nation the idea that the state deserved sympathy. Nonetheless, there was an additional reason for California's inability to communicate her woes to the rest of the nation. Because her migrant problem was really a unique blend of two problems, her requests for aid seemed nothing more than special pleading.

In their anxiety over the coming of the Okies, Californians focused their attentions upon their own migrant problem only. Although the state insisted that the interstate migration of destitute people was a problem national in its ramifications, her arguments invariably narrowed down to the dislocations wrought by some Okie crop-workers in some California valleys. Other regions were experiencing migrations during the depression: rural southern Negroes were moving to northern cities; Appalachian hill-people were relocating in the Midwest's metropolises; unemployed industrial workers were rest-lessly streaming from city to city in search of work. These movements of people were analogous to California's migrant problem, but Californians showed little interest in them.[1]

Insofar as her migrant problem was an agricultural labor problem, California faced a similar difficulty in communications. Other states such as Michigan and Texas had agricultural labor problems as severe, perhaps even more severe, than California's, but these states did not receive large interstate migrations during the depression. They found it difficult to understand why California saw her own experience as a crisis. In short, California could not make her migrant problem relevant to the other states because she alone was on the receiving end of two major social maladjustments at once: the epic interstate migration of destitute people and the continuing distress of agricultural labor, both of which had coalesced in the Okie crisis.[2]

Nonetheless, California's migration problem spilled into the national arena in 1939. A series of pressures emanating from different groups within California persuaded Congress and the President to look directly at the specific problem of the hundreds of thousands of Great Plains people who had moved to California only to find disaster. These pressures were given additional force in the middle of the year by the publication of John Steinbeck's *The Grapes of Wrath*. After mid-1939, Americans could no longer hear the word "migrant" without thinking of the Joads. The migrant problem was discussed with ferocity at the federal level, but results were limited. Two congressional committees investigated the travails of California's Okies, and one, broadening its goal, moved on to the larger problem of migration growing from the development of the defense industries. In 1941, California's migrant problem died, hastened to its end by the European blitzkrieg.

The peak years of the Okie influx had been characterized by federal indifference to California's plaint that it needed aid in dealing with the "flood of dust bowl refugees." As the migrants poured into the Golden State from 1935 to 1938, individuals and organizations demanded that the federal government admit that interstate migration was a national problem.[3] Pleas for federal aid rested upon the argument that migration had been the result of events outside California's control; depression, dust storms, and farm mechanization were national problems. The federal government should finance California in assimilating her new uninvited citizens by extending grant-aid during the period of non-residence. Moreover, Washington should seek to convince Okies who had not yet migrated to remain in their home states. FSA had absent-mindedly fulfilled the first of these requests in 1938, when it inaugurated the policy of granting relief to unemployed nonresident field workers. The grant-aid program had provoked as many problems as it had solved. Californians, notably those adhering to the California Citizens Association's position, resented FSA's policy. In the absence of federal policy designed to attack the root causes of the migration, these Californians argued, the relief funds simply maintained the Okies for a year, after which they became a burden upon California's harassed taxpayers. Indeed, rather than calming the cries for federal aid, the FSA's grant-aid program had, ironically, redoubled them.

Notwithstanding FSA's flourishing program in California, the federal government took scant notice of California's specific problem until 1939. During the preceding year, neither CCA propaganda nor the incessant discussion of the "migrant menace" during the gubernatorial campaign, evoked response from Washington. This indifference to California's cries was evident in the failure of Jerry Voorhis to prod Congress into action.

Voorhis, a liberal southern California Democrat (San Dimas), was elected to Congress for his first term in the Roosevelt landslide of 1936. Earlier than most Californians, he recognized the severity of the migrant's plight and determined to do something about it. "Of all the jobs I undertook in my first term in Congress," he later recalled, "I believe I worked hardest and worried most about the 'transients.' " Voorhis introduced a number of bills for the interstate migrant and the migratory agricultural laborer, proposing that federal financial aid be distributed to states in direct proportion to the number of migrants they received.[4] In addition, Voorhis asked for uniform residence requirements in all the states, a nationwide employment service for agricultural migrants, and, finally, increased federal aid to the depressed areas that were supplying the nation's migrants. Voorhis spent much of his first term publicizing the migrant problem on the radio and in the press, convinced that his efforts had "something to do with pushing forward the building of migratory labor camps by the Farm Security Administration"; but in Congress his efforts came to nothing.[5] The bills received only mild support and throughout 1937 and 1938 gathered "dust in the files of the House Ways and Means Committee." Indeed, for a brief time in mid-1938, Congress seemed on the verge of restricting federal programs already functioning in California, when a Senate committee favorably reported a recommendation that FSA be required to discontinue the grant-in-aid program. This, too, came to nothing. In the general indifference to the migrant problem, neither positive nor negative action stood much chance of success, unless the Californians in the Congress pursued the problem intensively. This they were not yet prepared to do.[6]

When the first session of the Seventy-sixth Congress convened in early 1939, conditions had changed. CCA's year-long publicity barrage and the gubernatorial election battle had furnished Californians with a new issue. Although deeply divided over what steps to take, the California congressional delegation was now prepared to lay the migrant problem at the door of Congress. Meanwhile, the Roosevelt administration was aware that Democrats, aided by Okies, had finally captured California, and it was ready to consider with Olson a problem it had ignored when Frank Merriam was governor.

This new interest in California's migrant problem did not automatically mean that national solutions would be found, or even tried. The interstate migration of millions of Americans was a complicated affair that defied simple solutions. In any case, migration itself was not the problem. The problem was unguided migration of destitute people from worn-out regions during a period of national economic distress, overlaid by the resentment of residents in regions receiving the migrant stream. Further, California was only one of several states undergoing increased migration, although it was by far the most affected, and the only one complaining so loudly about it.

To attack California's migrant problem effectively, the state's Congressmen would have to attain two objectives: they must unite upon a common program and then persuade an unsympathetic Congress to accept responsibility and to allocate funds. In early 1939, when California's internal politics were tearing the state legislature apart, and not least because of the use of the migrant influx as a propaganda device, the task was herculean. Nor did the future hold promise of better prospects. The European situation was fast deteriorating, and foreign affairs threatened to eclipse internal problems soon.

The migrant problem was uppermost in the minds of California's Congressmen when the Seventy-sixth Congress opened. On January 19, 1939, the state's delegation met in special caucus to attempt to work out a migrant program, selecting Congressman Alfred J. Elliott, conservative Democrat from Tulare County, to lead California's coalition. This united front developed cracks immediately. As the delegation convened, liberal Democrat John H. Tolan (Oakland) introduced a House resolution for the appointment of an extraordinary congressional committee to investigate the migrant problem. Tolan took action without consulting other members of the caucus in a move which brought rumors in the press that the delegation was already split.[7] The rumors were correct; the caucus was divided.

The meeting of January 19 did nothing more than select Congressman Elliott as its leader and adjourn; it had not agreed on a common program. When the focus of the migrant problem shifted to the House floor, spokesmen for the views of both the CCA and the Olson administration publicized their respective positions before Congress. Equally concerned with the problem, both suggested deeply divergent solutions. On January 23, Representative Leland M. Ford of Los Angeles (Republican) delivered an address echoing the CCA petition that had been laid before Congress three weeks before. Ford emphasized the financial dislocations wrought by the influx of indigents. The State Relief Administration had "let down the bars" and migrants had come to California for the bounteous dole. Unless California received relief aid, Ford implied, her taxpayers would go on strike. Ford suggested a relatively easy solution drawn verbatim from the CCA petition: the federal government must force the migrants to remain in their home states, cease distributing FSA grant-aid to nonresidents, and "encourage and aid the return to their homes of the idle thousands."[8]

While Ford presented Congress with simple explanations and solutions, Jerry Voorhis took a broader view of the problem. Voorhis met to work out a deal with members of a southern bloc, which had been formed to eliminate discriminatory freight rates which they alleged were responsible for the South's economic stagnation.[9] Replying to

Ford, Voorhis linked migration with varying rates of regional economic growth: "If conditions were improved in the places these unfortunate people come from, if earning power in the South were improved, fewer of them would come straggling into California."

Scarcely a week after its formation, California's extraordinary committee on migrants was in disarray. Tolan's request for an investigative committee languished; Ford's simple answers comforted the folks back home in the valleys; Voorhis' potential deal with the southern bloc was intriguing but still in the infant stage; Elliott, the delegation's leader, kept silent; and the delegation had not even met for substantive discussions of the migrant problem. Noting the divisions within the delegation, Chairman Elliott announced at the end of January that he would convene a meeting to "frame a policy which the whole delegation can agree to." The caucus assembled on February 2, amid reports that the "hard-boiled school of thought" was dominating the discussions. According to the *San Francisco News*, "treat-em-rough advocates" were determined to "clamp down on the migrants" and push Jerry Voorhis into the background. Voorhis apparently held his ground, and the divided delegation decided upon the only course of action available to it: it would hand the problem to the President. Elliott and Voorhis were delegated to form a subcommittee to collect the facts and submit the problem to FDR.[10]

Elliott and Voorhis represented the opposing points of view of Californians toward the migrants and their problems. Both agreed that the migrants were in dire conditions and, unless given some aid, would deteriorate still more. From that point, however, they diverged. Like Leland Ford, Elliott spoke for groups that the *San Francisco News* had christened the "hard-boiled school of thought": he opposed FSA's expansion in California and disapproved of temporary aid from the federal government, which thrust the migrants onto the California relief rolls after one year. Further, Elliott spoke for California's growers in condemning the size of relief allotments.[11] Elliott insisted that California and the federal government could best aid the Okies by sending them home. Voorhis, on the other hand, believed that migration from one area to another was the inevitable outgrowth of regional economic disparity. The Okies had a right to be in California, and, once there, to be protected from rapacious agricultural employers.[12] Accordingly, he supported FSA's expansion, favored uniform relief laws across the nation in order to ease the relocation of the nonresident unemployed, and supported Governor Olson's desire to achieve equity for California's harvest workers. In Voorhis' view, the best that California and the federal government could do for the Okies was to facilitate their assimilation into their new home state.

This unnatural partnership of dissimilar Democrats presented its report at the White House on February 16. It was a mélange of both points of view. The Voorhis-Elliott brief instructed the President that migration was a national problem, and the federal government could no longer shirk the recognition that Americans who had no state residence were administrative orphans. The brief recommended a variety of proposals for California's Okie problem. Voorhis' sentiments appeared where the brief observed that "in spite of a certain very vocal group of people in California [the delegation] was opposed to 'sending or driving' the destitute unemployed back to their states of origin." Elliott's position prevailed in the affirmation that California would oppose the entry of additional migrants. The report suggested that the federal government take immediate steps to organize a federal farm employment service to provide order for the hitherto unguided migrants, to distribute surplus food to the transients, and to grant funds to the states to defray the costs of aiding the nonresident. The FSA camp system should be extended in other states to attract migrants away from California. Finally, the federal government should finance low-cost housing and public education for migrants in order to ease the California taxpayer's burden.[13]

The Voorhis-Elliott brief made the error of solemnly intoning that migration was a national problem and then presenting solutions for California only. Nevertheless, it received presidential recognition. Although Roosevelt was away on a trip, his secretary, Steven Early, accepted the brief in his name. Early told the delegation that the President was "strongly sympathetic" and had ordered the formation of a special group to "attempt solution of a critical relief problem in California, arising from the migration there of thousands of economically distressed families."[14] Headed by WPA Administrator F. C. Harrington, the group was authorized to call in representatives of federal agencies whose activities were related to the problem.

Roosevelt's positive response met with satisfaction and relief throughout California. The *San Francisco News* best typified the state's reaction. An editorial cartoon depicted a harassed mother (California) stirring a large pot and surrounded by thousands of hungry Okies, outstretched hands carrying empty bowls. A beaming Uncle Sam stood in the kitchen doorway, and the caption exulted, *"AND ARE WE GLAD TO SEE HIM."* Many other newspapers followed the *News'* lead in reporting the formation of the Harrington group as a headline event and praising the President in their editorial pages.[15] Regardless of their position regarding the Okies, Californians could unanimously support the Harrington group—at least until it made specific proposals.

Harrington took action immediately, gathering a study group composed of representatives from other New Deal agencies involved in migrant problems.[16] Following four weeks of consultations and some delays, the Harrington group reported to the President on March 15, 1939. The panel informed the President that interstate migration was indeed a national problem. The result of "extremely complex social and economic factors," the chaotic migration of destitute Americans was not confined to California. Unfortunately, there was precious little that the government could do about it under existing congressional mandates: the federal government could expand a few of its palliative programs; AAA could distribute more surplus food to the hungry migrants; and the United States Employment Service could undertake a "complete and systematic dissemination of information" about agricultural employment opportunities in the several states. Beyond that, however, the executive branch's power was limited. Additional funds were needed from Congress to expand the existing programs of FSA, the Housing Authority, and the Public Health Service, and even these agencies could not solve the problem. What was required, Harrington insisted, was that Congress recognize that "no Federal agency or group of agencies can effectively deal with [interstate migration] in its entirety under their present powers and limitations. If the responsibility of solving the problem of interstate migration is to be accepted by the Federal government, it is my opinion that special legislation to this end would have to be enacted by the Congress." Such legislation, Harrington continued, must provide for "nationwide planning" and might authorize three courses of action:

(a) The resettlement of the migrants who are now in California and other destination States and who can become self-supporting there.

(b) The return of those migrants who are willing to resume residence in their State of origin and giving assistance in establishing them there.

(c) The resettlement of other migrants in those areas where employment suited to their abilities is most likely to be found.[17]

Early transmitted the Harrington report to the California delegation and told Chairman Elliott that the President concurred with its conclusions.[18] The California delegation had thrown the migrant problem to the President six weeks before; now the President had tossed it back. The Okies were once again a problem for the Congress to solve, and the California delegation, which was calling most vociferously for congressional action, would have to supply the initiative.

The delegation reassembled during the first week of April to discuss possible courses of action, and, as usual, found itself split. Representative Ford proposed a state border blockade, Representative Kramer (Democrat, Los Angeles) suggested a bill barring federal aid to any migrant with less than five years' residence in California, and Voorhis insisted that his bills of the previous year be reintroduced. Faced with so disparate a collection of proposals, the delegation agreed only to endorse the already extant Tolan bill for a congressional investigation of the migrant problem.[19] From mid-April to the close of the first session of the Seventy-sixth Congress in August, the California delegation was unable to agree on any substantive measure beyond the Tolan investigation. For the remainder of the session, California congressmen concerned with the migrant problem went their separate ways, each presenting his own panacea. Voorhis was unable to persuade his California colleagues on the Ways and Means Committee to recommend the reconsideration of his bills at hearings on Social Security amendments and the plan died. Meanwhile, Elliott toyed with a plan to bar "diseased indigents" from entering the state. Leland Ford contributed a proposal that would punish the states of origin of the migrants by charging them for relief distributed to their citizens in California. Finally, Tolan produced what may have been the strangest proposal broached during California's five-year migrant crisis. He announced in May that he was "studying the possibilities of settling migrant families of California and the dust bowl in Brazil," explaining that Brazil was eager to open its plateau regions to forty thousand settlers and would find the Okies desirable pioneers.[29]

In early June, Voorhis made a final attempt to force the California delegation into united action. He presented it with a nine-point program, which called, primarily, for additional federal funds to aid in the absorption of the migrants into the state. The delegation, however, was still divided over whether to assimilate, or to exclude, the migrants, and withheld its endorsement, preferring instead to concentrate upon Tolan's investigating committee.[21] In July, Tolan undertook a serious campaign to get his proposed committee before the House Rules Committee, but he had waited to begin action for too long: the Rules Committee was indifferent and would not make room for the resolution.[22] In mid-August, Congress adjourned. The House had taken no action whatever to alleviate California's migrant problem.

The problem of interstate migration did not arise for discussion in the Senate except during early July when Senator Sheridan Downey spoke against an attempted cut in FSA migrant camp funds.[23] The Senate did enter the California migrant problem through the back door of agricultural labor strife. In late 1938, Senator La Follette's Committee to Investigate Violations of Free Speech and the Rights of Labor had quietly slipped into California to expose the activities of the Associated Farmers, in a move undoubtedly linked with the impending gubernatorial election.[24] The committee met deep hostility from conservative and economy-bloc groups: local officials refused to produce subpoenaed records, witnesses called from the Associated Farmer's top echelons disappeared mysteriously when process-servers attempted to track them down, and the farmers' propaganda apparatus attacked the committee violently.[25]

Early in January 1939, the La Follette Committee abruptly ended its California hearings. It had not been broken by its opponents; it had simply depleted its funds and waited for appropriation of more money.[26] Hearings in California were delayed and again delayed, while liberals in the state clamored for money for La Follette's investigators.[27] On April 19, Senators Downey of California and Schwellenbach of Washington introduced a Senate resolution for the appropriation of an additional $100,000 to permit La Follette to investigate labor-busting activities on the West Coast. Despite the objections of

Senator Hiram Johnson, who confessed that he didn't know "half a dozen of the Associated Farmers, and . . . anything about what they are accused of," but who disliked La Follette's liberal "bunk," an amended Schwellenbach resolution finally passed the Senate on August 4.[28] Its funds trimmed to $50,000, the committee reopened its California investigation. It held hearings in late 1939 and early 1940 in Los Angeles and San Francisco, called nearly four hundred witnesses, and published twenty-seven volumes of testimony and exhibits. The La Follette hearings remain today the single most valuable source of material on California labor conflict in the 1930s, but, at the time the hearings were held, their role was less scholarly. Intruding upon a labor system that had gone unpublicized for fifty years, the committee's activities increased tensions between liberals and conservatives within the state and contributed to the growing awareness that the migrant problem was also an agricultural labor problem.

The arrival of La Follette's Committee notwithstanding, California's hopes for federal aid had been dashed, at least until the next session of Congress. The *San Francisco News* and the *Bakersfield Californian* both voiced the state's bitterness at Congress' failure to act.[29] Congressman Tolan's son delivered a perceptive post-mortem on the session. California's delegation, he observed, was neither "querulous nor bashful": when it clamored for aid for the state's fishing, shipping, industrial, and other interests, it got it. If the congressmen were to concentrate their efforts on the "economic maladjustment thrust upon our citizens by the influx of three hundred thousand indigent farm families, they might still sacrifice their energies in futile effort."[30] Tolan's point was that the interstate migrant was an anomaly in federal administrative policy. Until the federal government assumed responsibility for stateless people, there would be no committees competent to discuss the problem nor funds available for migrant programs. Americans did not understand the problem, Tolan continued, and the "emotional wailing of T. W. McManus and the California Citizens Associaiton" did little to enhance their education. This explanation for Congress' failure to act was valid as far as it went: the existing congressional structure *was* unable to accommodate the migrant problem and the anxious complaints of the Californians *did* seem self-seeking, carping, and hypocritical. Nevertheless, it was also the case (although Tolan did not discuss the matter) that the state's delegation had been disunited and had done nothing to make the migrant problem relevant to the other forty-seven states.

If the California delegation had been united, it is still doubtful that it could have brought the migrant problem to the nation's attention. Government reports laden with statistics could not convey any feeling for the condition of the Okies to the Congress. Like Congressman J. F. T. O'Connor, one had to travel to San Joaquin to observe first-hand the meaning of the statistics. A means was needed to force Americans to feel the reality of the migrant problem, and it was the Okies' fortune that they were claimed for literature. When Congress' 1940 session convened, *The Grapes of Wrath* had performed the task that no amount of legislative oratory could achieve. Like *The Jungle* twenty-five years before, the book lodged a severe social problem in the stomachs, not the minds, of Americans.

A California novelist whose love for his native Salinas amounted to a passion, John Steinbeck was no stranger to California agriculture or to its maladjustments. After a false start writing historical romances, Steinbeck turned during the early depression years to the scenarios he knew best.[31] He chronicled the lives of California's Mexican migrants in short stories and wrote two powerful novels set in the state's factories in the field. *In Dubious Battle* (1936) was a brilliant account of an agricultural strike. The book was pilloried as communist propaganda or praised as proletarian literature but was really much more than a one-dimensional piece of uplifting radical prose. The battle Steinbeck narrated was "dubious": the agricultural system brutalized heroes and villains alike. Steinbeck followed *In Dubious Battle* with a perceptive tale of the bindle stiffs. *Of Mice and Men* (1937) used the bunkhouse to tell a universal tale and brought its author national acclaim.

Neither of Steinbeck's novels preceding *The Grapes of Wrath* were political pamphlets. Steinbeck was an artist, and his purposes went far beyond ephemeral social problems. During the mid-depression years, however, he became concerned with the Okies who were pouring into the state and doffed his role as novelist for a brief venture into the field of public-affairs commentary. The result was a powerful documentary first published as a series of newspaper articles, and reissued by the

Simon J. Lubin Society as *Their Blood Is Strong.*[32] In writing this pamphlet, Steinbeck did not create his Okies. Rather, he lived with the real migrants, followed their trek from Oklahoma to California, resided with them on the ditch banks or in the FSA camps, and became friendly with Tom Collins, the FSA's top camp manager.[33] What Steinbeck witnessed in his beloved California valleys affected him deeply. When *Life* offered to pay him for producing an article about Okies for the national publication, he replied: "I'm sorry but I simply can't make money on these people . . . the suffering is too great for me to cash in on it."[34]

Throughout 1937 and 1938, Steinbeck the pamphleteer and Steinbeck the novelist merged in producing the author's masterpiece. *The Grapes of Wrath* was primarily a novel, but more than Steinbeck's other works, it was informed by the hard reality in which Steinbeck had immersed himself. Drawing upon the technique used by Herman Melville a century before, Steinbeck punctuated the tale with interchapters, factual accounts, which supply a splendid introduction to California's migrant crisis. Steinbeck exercised literary license where his novel demanded it: his Joads migrated more than did most Okies once they arrived in California; fewer Okies came to the state in response to grower advertisements than the Joads' story would indicate; and the real Joads did not lose their religion—as Casy symbolically did—on the road west. Nevertheless, the book captured, as no report could, the deprivation and disorientation of the migration, the hostility of the Californians, the heroism and the bigotry of the Okies. Finally, *The Grapes of Wrath* made the dual nature of California's problem crystal clear: the first half of the book told of interstate migrants; the second half of agricultural laborers.

Since its publication, *The Grapes of Wrath* has been the focus of critical controversy. Was Steinbeck attempting social literature or simply producing a work of art? Was he a teleological or a mechanistic philosopher? Is his novel a grand analogy linking man to the organic world or simply a Marxist tract?[35] Whatever the answers to these questions posed by the critics may be, one thing is clear: despite the controversy over whether Steinbeck intended to write another *Uncle Tom's Cabin* or not, the volume had a powerful effect. In terms of its impact, *The Grapes of Wrath* could well have been rechristened "Uncle Tom Moves West."

The Grapes of Wrath was published on March 14, 1939, and was immediately sold out. By the end of April, Viking Press was hard put to keep pace with 2,500 orders a day. In mid-May it was the nation's best seller, and at the end of the year, its sales totaled nearly a half million copies. It was not difficult to account for *The Grapes of Wrath*'s meteoric rise to national popularity. Americans knew little of the Okies, and probably cared less about their deprivations, but they eagerly read a novel that utilized the forbidden Anglo-Saxon lexicon. Steinbeck's Joads spoke a hardy American English, and they wasted little time tempering their anger with gentility. As the book steadily gained acclaim among literary reviewers, few casual readers could avoid the notion that Steinbeck had written a "dirty book."[36]

Steinbeck had produced a sensational book and unintentionally enlisted prurience on the side of the Okies. Every reader drawn to *The Grapes of Wrath* by its reputation as a sexual shocker would find in it a social shocker as well. Rosasharn's shameless maternalism and Casy's womanizing were titillating, but Steinbeck's descriptions of the tactics of the Associated Farmers, the xenophobic hostility of the Californians, and the exploitation and poverty of the Joads were enlightening. In California, discussions of Steinbeck's vocabulary were rapidly displaced by arguments over the validity of his descriptions of the field workers' tribulations. *The Grapes of Wrath* itself became an important event in the history of California's migrant problem.

Steinbeck had wrought a powerful tool for the hands of Californians seeking solutions to the migrant problem. Tom Collins exulted that the novel had shocked the nation and was spurring action from governments. Labor recognized immediately that the book was a weapon in the fight against "exploitation of American labor," and agricultural workers unions were encouraged to greater efforts. Agricultural economists in Oklahoma and California noted that despite Steinbeck's literary license, his exposure of industrial agriculture was "substantially reliable." Upton Sinclair, with singular lack of modesty, considered *The Grapes of Wrath* a likely successor to *The Jungle* and turned to the Bible for analogues. "I remember," Sinclair wrote, "how Elijah put his mantle on the shoulders of Elisha. John Steinbeck can have my old mantle if he has any use for it."[37]

By autumn 1939, literary discourse concerning *The Grapes of Wrath* had all but disappeared in the intense controversy swirling around the book's political implications. Reviewers likened the novel to *Uncle Tom's Cabin* with increasing frequency.[38] Growers could not avoid the logical conclusion: Mrs. Stowe had delivered a powerful blow at the southern slavocracy; Steinbeck was threatening the corporate farms in much the same way. Furthermore, it was becoming increasingly plain that the book was affecting the inland Californians. Whether stung by Steinbeck's unvoiced but powerful appeal to conscience or, perhaps, perversely delighted with the publicity that *The Grapes of Wrath* had brought to their region, residents of the valley towns were flocking to see the film. The Zanuck version of the novel was second only to *Gone With The Wind* in box-office attraction in the San Joaquin Valley in 1939 and 1940.[39] Camp managers reported that *The Grapes of Wrath* was producing a vintage of sympathy for the migrants, and local newspapers echoed that conclusion.[40]

Reacting to *The Grapes of Wrath* with a mixture of fear and outraged self-esteem, growers' groups launched a counterattack. The idea came from Kansas City where, in mid-August, the board of education had been instrumental in banning the book from the public libraries on the grounds of its obscenity. Three days after the Kansas City report had been received in Bakersfield, the Kern County Board of Supervisors banned *The Grapes of Wrath* from all public and school libraries. Unlike Kansas City's authorities, who were protecting public morals, Kern's supervisors were attempting to guard an economic status quo. The supervisors charged that *The Grapes of Wrath* was not so much obscene as it was untrue. The novel was a false accusation against Kern County, and, by implication, all rural California, for "John Steinbeck chose to ignore the education, recreation, hospitalization, welfare and relief services made available by Kern County." Although a good deal of the negative image of the Okie had emanated originally from Bakersfield's leadership and the CCA, the supervisors insisted that their ban was motivated by a desire to protect the Okies from Steinbeck's maligning. Intentionally misreading Steinbeck's purpose, they charged him with "offend[ing] our citizenry by falsely implying that many of our people are a low, ignorant, profane and blasphemous type living in a vicious, filthy manner."[41]

Farmers' groups were deeply involved in the movement to eliminate the novel from public view. The Associated Farmers of Kern County announced that it was "mapping plans for statewide action to follow in Kern County's footsteps." In this they insisted that they were impelled by an unselfish desire to protect the Okies who could not speak for themselves. "We are angry," said President Camp, "not because we were attacked but because we were attacked by a book obscene in the extreme sense . . . our workers with whom we have lived and worked for years are pictured as the lowest type of human life when we know that is not true. . . . You can't argue with a book like that." The statewide campaign to ban the book never materialized, in part because the action of Kern County's supervisors had caused considerable uproar throughout the state, and not the least of it in Bakersfield. At a supervisors' meeting a week after the initial decision, ministers, labor leaders, and citizens' delegations demanded the ban's repeal, and complaints poured in from the American Civil Liberties Union and other organizations.[42] One supervisor reversed his position, but the decision held by a vote of three to two. The ban was not repealed until January 1941. In any case, it had served no purpose. *The Grapes of Wrath* was freely available at the bookstores, and the film drew capacity crowds in Bakersfield. If anything, the ban had intensified local interest in the Okies. The reaction to the ban had been so severe that the Associated Farmers retraced their steps in April 1940 to justify their anti-*Grapes of Wrath* activity as a Machiavellian device to aid Steinbeck. In what may have been the most ironic twist in Associated Farmers' propaganda during the entire migrant crisis, the organization's public-relations director announced that he had deliberately instigated opposition to *The Grapes of Wrath* "to get even more persons to read the book" which, after all, was "desirable in arousing nationwide interest in the migrants."[43]

The ban had failed to elicit a positive response even in other agricultural areas, and farmers' groups adopted a new strategy in their counterattack with a literary onslaught designed to reduce or eliminate the negative image of California agriculture that Steinbeck had implanted in the national consciousness. During early August 1939, newspapers reported that conservative organizations and farmers' groups planned to launch a propaganda campaign to offset the "blighting effects of Steinbeck's popularity."[44] Immediately following Kern's ban, the center of anti-Steinbeck activity shifted to a luncheon at the

Palace Hotel in San Francisco where a coalition of anti-Olson, anti-migrant groups met to plan their strategy. The participants included Thomas McManus of the California Citizens Association, Holmes Bishop, president of the Associated Farmers, Philip Bancroft, Joseph DiGiorgio, Frank Merriam, Harold Pomeroy, and others drawn from business and corporate agriculture. The host was Ruth Comfort Mitchell, a skillful local-color novelist and wife of the conservative Republican state senator, Colonel Sanborn Young (Santa Clara), who had lately gained a notorious statewide reputation as a labor-buster. [45] The assemblage was entertained with addresses proving that John Steinbeck and Carey McWilliams were dangerous foes of the California way of life.

The meeting played more than a symbolic role in the controversy over *The Grapes of Wrath.* In addition to the farmer and business groups, *Readers Digest* and *True Magazine,* two powerful and widely read national magazines, were invited to send representatives to the luncheon. The implication of their presence at the meeting was clear: Steinbeck was to be answered, not ignored, confronted with counter-propaganda, not banned. From the August meeting until the migrant crisis waned, the groups represented at the meeting poured an impressive array of "answers to Steinbeck" into the nationwide debate about the Joads. Scores of articles and book reviews, many of them reprinted at the expense of the Associated Farmers, presented their side of the case. [46] The campaign also trod the literary and cinematic trail of *The Grapes of Wrath:* Kern County's Chamber of Commerce filmed "Plums of Plenty," and Mrs. Mitchell capped the movement with a fluffy, modest, and extremely mild-mannered novel entitled *Of Human Kindness.* [47]

Elsewhere in the nation, the chief criticism of *The Grapes of Wrath* was that it was obscene. But in California, Steinbeck and his novel evoked a multifaceted indictment in which obscenity was only one minor count. The articles, films, and novels hammered at Steinbeck's facts, not his characters' language. Steinbeck was wrong on two counts, his critics charged: he misrepresented the California farmer, and he maligned the true character of the migrant. California was not a state dominated by large farms. Her growers paid the highest agricultural wages in the world, even to the loss of their personal profit. [48] More

than any other group in the state, the farmers looked after the migrants, loved them, tended them, sympathized with them.[49] The mali-
cious volume slandered and maligned the migrants, too, critics of
Steinbeck continued. The "Oakies [*sic*]" are a "kindly people and an
inherently decent American people. Most certainly they are not the
degenerate group that Steinbeck presented in his pleas for sympathy for
them."[50] For Ruth Comfort Mitchell, the typical Okie was the kindly
and fun-loving Lute, a cowboy never seen without his guitar, who
"come because [he] had the itchin in [his] feet" and who, in traditional manner, scratched his itch by marrying the boss's daughter in a
California variant of the American dream.[51]

If all this was so patently clear, if the Okie and the California farmer
so obviously shared a mutually beneficial relationship, how did one
account for John Steinbeck? Ruth Comfort Mitchell explained him
symbolically in her book as "the Black Widow," the beautiful, sensual,
Communist organizer who stole both the love and the wits of a good
rancher's son. "It's the agitators that come in and stir 'em up. I've had
as nice a bunch [of Okies] as you'd wish to see and everything going all
smooth and honky-dorry, and in slides one of these smartaleks and tells
the pickers how abused they are and they walk out on me."[52] In short,
Steinbeck was either a Communist or a communist-dupe. When J. T.
Miron told "The Truth About John Steinbeck and the Migrants" at
Associated Farmers' expense, he set the tone for much of the political
attack upon the novel: "Of all the revolutionary-proletarian fiction, and
I have tried pretty well to cover the ground, I can think of no other
novel which advances the idea of class war and promotes hatred of class
against class, in the most classless society in the world, more than does,
'The Grapes of Wrath.' "[53]

A great deal more could be said of the anti-Steinbeck campaign. Its
history was tortuous and subtle. By the time it ended, the Okie had
become the maligned and heroic American slandered by a pink writer
from the big city. The California grower had been transformed into a
small farmer struggling to keep abreast who, just incidentally, occasionally needed thousands of migrants to harvest his family-sized farm's
crops. The real significance of the campaign was not, however, its
literary or factual merit, but its utter failure. Steinbeck, it was true, had
produced a novel whose content was more real than the facts presented

by his critics. More importantly, however, he had written a novel of great power and quality. Mrs. Mitchell's misfortune was not that Steinbeck knew more than she (which he did) but, rather, that he wrote far better than she, or than any other writer whom the growers were able to enlist. *The Grapes of Wrath* continued to grow in popularity. The anti-Steinbeck campaign had little effect other than to increase the avidity with which the general public sought copies of the book. In 1940 as well as 1939, it was among the nation's best sellers, and early in the latter year, millions of Americans saw the fine film which Zanuck had produced from it.[54]

It is hard to overemphasize the impact of *The Grapes of Wrath* upon California's migrant problem. In a very real sense, the novel created the nationwide interest in the Okies that developed late in 1939. By the turn of 1940, California's migrants—now usually called the Joads—were discussed throughout the nation as a major social dislocation left over from the Great Depression. Prior to the book's publication, articles concerning the problem were rare in the nonscholarly national magazines. In 1940, Americans in New York and Illinois knew as much about Okies as did Californians in San Francisco. *Life* magazine, fully aware of the nation's interest, devoted a center-section spread to photographs of California's migrants: "THESE PICTURES," the journal's staff headlined the article, *"PROVE FACTS IN GRAPES OF WRATH!"*[55] In March, *The New York Times* dispatched one of its best feature writers to the San Joaquin Valley. He returned with a series of articles that were widely reprinted throughout the nation. Radio and cinema did not lag behind newsprint; Americans who did not read the journals saw Okies in the newsreels and heard about them on the national broadcast, "Town Meeting of the Air." The image of the Okie—a being half Andrew Jackson, half degenerate-poor white—was everywhere. There was little exaggeration in the comment of a writer who observed that "whether or not they have read The Grapes of Wrath, most U.S. citizens today have heard of the hordes of migrant farmers who left their worn-out farms to harvest oranges, lettuce and peas up and down California."[56]

In the middle of 1940, Hollywood developed an "Okie boom." The "movie moguls" were "going for Okies in a big way," the *People's World* reported, and a series of second-rate films attempted to capitalize on Zanuck's epic. An Okie heroine followed Route 66 to California in

Gold Rush Maisie. The Dead End Kids went west, were duped into joining a "pink" field workers' union, and roughed-up by Associated Farmers' stooges. In the concluding reel of *You're Not So Tough,* they saved the Okies for democracy and the family-sized farm. Finally, in *Doctors Don't Tell,* Hollywood linked the foreign and domestic problems of the nation in an anxiety-ridden year: German refugees and Okies joined for a jalopy odyssey to Oregon's agricultural valleys.[57]

With the nation following the Okies so avidly, public figures took to the emotional trail that Steinbeck and the Joads had blazed. Franklin Roosevelt led the way. At the annual White House Conference on Children in a Democracy, the President took the opportunity to comment on nationwide radio about a problem that had escaped his administration's interest for three years. The lowest income groups, Roosevelt told the audience, need "dwellings suitable for the raising of children." Many children have no "settled place" at all: they are the children of migrants and migrant workers. New homes would be available for a half million people when the Columbia River Basin project was completed, and, the President mused, why not settle the Joads in them? "I have read a book recently; it is called 'Grapes of Wrath.' There are 500,000 Americans that live in the covers of that book. I would like to see the Columbia Basin devoted to the care of the 500,000 people represented in 'Grapes of Wrath'."[58] As in 1934, when he had set Tugwell to the task of reorganizing the agricultural agencies, Roosevelt's interest in conservation had brought him into the migrant problem, and, once again, he had seen the solution in terms of soil reclamation. Fascinating as was the idea of settling Okies in the Columbia basin, Roosevelt's plan failed to mention how California's crops would get picked. Nonetheless, the idea attracted some interest. Secretary of Interior Ickes proposed that the multimillion dollar Central Valley flood control and irrigation program be utilized as a "permanent solution" for the "thousands of farm families forced out of the Great Plains." Californians turned momentarily to this panacea, and the secretary of the Central Valley Project Association suggested yearly appropriations of $100 million to resettle Okies on new farms produced by the irrigation project.[59] The plan was no immediate palliative, however, and when the projects were completed the Okie problem had ceased to exist.

With the initial impetus supplied by the President, administration emissaries arrived in California to inspect the migrant camps and serve as token reminders of the nation's concern with the condition of the Okies. In February, Frances Perkins toured FSA's installations, visited with the migrants, and joined the women at the camp sewing circles. A month later, Eleanor Roosevelt stormed the state for five days, visiting with the migrants and scolding the Californians for their prejudices. At the ditch-bank settlements, she complained that "such camps were not decent places to live in." She supported Steinbeck; he had told the truth, and she had "never thought the 'Grapes of Wrath' was exaggerated." She had no intention of telling Californians what to do, she told reporters following her tour, but the Okies were "grand people," and it would be "to the state's advantage" to absorb them. Speaking at San Francisco's opulent Opera House, she instructed Californians in the dual nature of their migrant problem: the Okies "aren't migrant farmers, never wanted to be migrant farmers." They were, rather, interstate migrants, and they would have to be resettled on lands reclaimed by irrigation projects.[60] Bakersfield's *Californian* complained that the first lady was unfair in praising Steinbeck but failing to praise Kern County's attempt to aid the migrants.[61] Publisher Harrell must have experienced considerable surprise when ex-President Hoover agreed with Mrs. Roosevelt's description of the situation and her proposed solution.[62]

When Congress returned for its second regular session in the beginning of January, *The Grapes of Wrath* and the controversy surrounding it had produced an entirely different situation from that which had existed during the first session.[63] California's delegation was no more united in 1940 than it had been in 1939, but a national sense of urgency now enveloped its activities. The rest of Congress no longer viewed California's complaints as the special pleading of a state with a reputation as a good-time-Charlie who whined at the first sign of trouble. Even if Congress had desired to ignore the migrant problem, the headlines captured by Roosevelt and by his emissaries to the Okies served as recurring goads to action. The California delegation began the session with the same divisions that had plagued it the year before. As usual, Tolan and Voorhis spoke for the migrants, while Elliott emphasized the need to protect California from the Okies. During the first week of the session, Voorhis reintroduced his plan for grants for migrants under the Social Security Act.[64] Tolan, meanwhile, had apparently reconsidered his vision of Okies farming Brazil's interior plateau. He introduced a plan designed to eliminate the disparate state residence requirements that had been responsible for so many of the migrant's travails. Tolan reasoned that WPA could force each state to adopt a maximum one-year residence requirement by withholding funds from states whose relief rules exceeded that period. He also proposed that states, counties, and cities be reimbursed from WPA funds for their expenses in supporting migrants in a state less than the required year. Anti-migrant groups and journals in California opposed the plan vehemently, contending that it would serve only to encourage additional migrants to seek new homes in the West. They charged the plan was an attempt to make California a "relief heaven." Speaking through Secretary McManus, the CCA expressed its "deep personal alarm" at the Tolan plan and Representative Elliott demonstrated that conflict still tore at the California delegation by wiring home that he would oppose the Tolan proposal.[65]

In February, the initiative shifted to the Elliott wing of the delegation. At a caucus meeting, Elliott vigorously proposed a plan to halt further expansion of the FSA program in California. Representative Jack Anderson (Republican, San Juan Bautista) firmly supported Elliott, contending that the camps were "breeding grounds for agitators."[66] A week later, Anderson clarified his position on FSA before Congress where he attacked the camps as a "powerful magnet on distressed families from the great Southwest."[67] Voorhis and others attacked Elliott with a vehemence equal to that which Elliott had directed at Tolan.

By early March, the crisis atmosphere generated by the Steinbeck novel had pushed the divisions within California's delegation to the brink of violence. With two months of the session already over, and with the delegation unable to agree upon a common program, Elliott once again called the caucus together and invited FSA administrators to attend. Still seeking to end the FSA program in California, Elliott broached the subject to C. B. Baldwin, FSA's assistant administrator. Jonathan Garst, past Region IX administrator, was a communist, Elliott accused, and Baldwin replied with a choice but unspecified epithet.

Elliott removed his coat and offered to fight, but was held down by his colleagues. No sooner was this tiff over than another began when Congressmen Leland Ford (Republican, Santa Monica) and Thomas Ford (Democrat, Los Angeles) squared off over the former's remark that he favored "cutting these people (migrants) right off at the pockets."[68] The meeting ended in total disarray. Elliott took his revenge three days later when he addressed Congress and attacked the FSA. He pointed out gleefully that California had increased its residence requirements two weeks before: FSA would now have to expand its profligate aid to migrants until they had established the lengthier residence. Questioned from the floor, Elliott progressively became angrier. Had he read *The Grapes of Wrath*? He had, and "it is the most damnable book that was ever permitted to be printed." Because of that book, he claimed, California had been maligned and held up for public ridicule. Even Washington, D.C., had slums, Elliott pointed out, but its residents did not get the "fresh air" of California.[69] "Why pick out a State and start dumping [migrants] there, as in California, when the figures I gave . . . show what the American people in that State are doing for these helpless ones?" Elliott concluded with some illogic and a good deal of bluster.

Voorhis replied to Elliott. After *pro forma* courtesies to his colleague, he disagreed point-by-point with Elliott's contentions. The camps did not attract migrants; they helped only a few; and they should be retained, indeed expanded. Nonetheless, FSA could only supply a temporary palliative. A long-range solution to the problem would come only when the nation recognized that "California's hope lies in greater well-being in [the] region from which people migrate." Migration was not the problem; it was a symptom of the deeper malaise of worn-out lands, of a continuing farm problem, of regional disparity in economic affairs. Until these problems were solved, California and the federal government must continue to support the migrants.

Despite these internal conflicts, the Californians did agree on one point: if no specific action could be taken, at least the federal government could take cognizance of the situation and attempt to collect the facts about it. Therefore, the old Tolan resolution, which called for an investigation of the entire problem of interstate migration, should be resurrected. Accordingly, the entire delegation petitioned the House

Rules Committee to hear the resolution and report. Hearings began soon after the Voorhis-Elliott debate, and the Tolan resolution received an immediate boost from the Executive through Secretary of Agriculture Wallace. The Rules Committee heard a good deal of testimony which exhibited "the usual hostility of other states to California." For example, Congressman Michener (Republican, Michigan) suggested that the migrant problem was the result of California crackpot politics, since "incentives like Ham and Eggs . . . have attracted these homeless people into your state." Mississippi Congressman William M. Cosmer asked rhetorically how California would solve the problem "since you have over advertised . . . the virtues" of the state.[70]

Despite these attacks, the Tolan resolution was unanimously endorsed by the House Rules Committee and sent to Congress on April 19.[71] The Tolan resolution came before the House on April 22, and Tolan rose to speak for its adoption. He described the problem of "350,000 homes on the move at this moment—victims of drought, depression, and mechanized farming," and went on to catalog the ills of a state plagued with chaotic and unguided migration: unemployment, friction between the migrant and the community, disarranged human relationships in agriculture that were breeding class warfare. Tolan avoided claiming that migration was peculiarly a California problem. The Golden State had its Okies, but many other states had their equivalents. There were many "trouble spots" in the nation: in the South, where agricultural migrants were even worse off than California's Okies; in Illinois, where industrial workers "meet in search of work, piling up on each other from east and west"; in Virginia, which had become a way station on the Florida-New York migratory route; and these were only a few examples. No single state could solve the interstate migrant problem, Tolan insisted, and the federal government could not even begin the work until it accepted the responsibility and then marshaled its facts: "we know nothing about the cost, the treatment, or any proposed remedies to alleviate the wasteful effects of these trouble spots in interstate migration." "[We] must have the true picture based upon an independent search for facts," Tolan concluded, and the resolution passed without debate.

The formation of the Select Committee to Investigate Interstate Migration of Destitute Citizens (the Tolan Committee) was an important moment in America's slow awakening to the recognition that the simple days of the nineteenth century were gone forever. For two centuries, the destitute had wandered across the continent, filling its emptiness with new communities. This had been the health of the nation, and Frederick Jackson Turner had even seen these movements as the meaning of America. Now, finally, Congress had accepted responsibility at least to investigate the problem and, potentially, to do something about it.

Tolan led his committee skillfully. With his four colleagues, he traveled twenty thousand miles and received testimony from five hundred witnesses.[72] A Californian himself, he did not rest content with studying only the Okies in his own state. He collected detailed information in all the troubled areas and avoided swinging the political axes that congressional committees usually wielded in the depression decade. Where La Follette and Dies had used the investigative function of Congress as a club to bludgeon political opponents, Tolan used his committee simply to collect facts. The facts he collected remain today the most comprehensive body of historical material on migrant problems in the United States.

The great irony of the Tolan Committee was that, for all the sound and fury surrounding its formation, it came too late to help California. Neither the Okies nor the state required an investigation into the migrant problem any longer. Tolan's group did not arrive in California until late 1940, when international events that brought war a year later were already drawing the Okies into the defense industries.[73] There were still Okies in great need in California, but they, too, would soon find an end to their troubles. During the months in which the Tolan Committee held its California investigations, a diminished supply of Okies picked the crops and made sufficient cash to get to the cities. Arvin's camp manager dropped plans to establish a National Youth Administration office at the unit. "I guess there's such a heap of cotton-cash floating round, no room left in anyone's pocket for Government money."[74] But migration to California had not ended. The immense war-industries migration that gave California nearly 2.5 million newcomers was just beginning. But that is another story. The dust-bowl migration, which had brought the Okies to California's inland valleys, which had produced misery and hostility and starvation, which had reached a crescendo in the publication of *The Grapes of Wrath,* and which had finally found its way into the national mind—that migration was over.

The events of 1940 marked a tragic lost opportunity in America's confrontation with rural poverty. The desperate social plight of the nation's migratory agricultural workers had gone unnoticed for decades. California's Okie crisis brought the harvest gypsy to national attention for the first time in the nation's history. *The Grapes of Wrath* evoked a powerful response because a unique collection of coincidences made the victims of corporate, large-scale agriculture apparent. The Okies had not intended to become migratory agricultural workers. They had intended to become farmers. But the only place for them to take in California agriculture was the place of the Mexican and the bindle stiff. If this migration of white Americans had not occurred, Mexicans and tramps would have continued to pick the crops in accustomed poverty and misery. No *Grapes of Wrath* would have been written; no migrant problem would have attracted the nation's gaze; no novel, however brilliant, which chronicled the migratory route of the Pedro Morenos in California's valleys could have become a best seller. The tribulations of the Joads received attention, however, because the nation found intolerable for white Americans conditions it considered normal for California Mexicans or Negroes.

The Tolan Committee's primary goal was to investigate the interstate migration of destitute citizens, but it could not long have studied the Joads in California without being forced to investigate the life of the migratory field worker as well. Indeed, had the war not come in 1941, there still might have been room for hope that Americans would be moved by the spectacular resettlement of the Okies to look into the less spectacular permanent migrations of field workers. But time and Adolf Hitler were not prepared to await this turn of events. The war intervened and split the migrant problem into its component parts. The white interstate migrants moved to the cities, and the Mexicans replaced them in the fields. The nation forgot the Joads, having never seriously confronted the agricultural system that had produced California's migrant problem.

Notes in Text

1. See, for example, Henry Hill Collins, *America's Own Refugees* (Princeton, 1941).

2. See, for example, Carey McWilliams, *Ill Fares the Land* (New York, 1941). It should be kept in mind, however, that California's migrant problem was shared, if to a lesser extent, by the states of the Pacific Northwest and Arizona. Nevertheless, California had by far the greater problem, although this qualification must be recognized.

3. *San Francisco News,* February 13, 1937; January 18, March 15, 1938; *Alameda Times Star,* August 14, 1937; *Farm Labor News,* May 21, 1937; *Bakersfield Californian,* 1937-1938, passim; also "California Conference of Social Work, Committee on Migratory Workers and Transients, 1937," in *Conference Bulletin* 20 (February 1937): 41-44.

4. Jerry Voorhis, *Confessions of a Congressman* (Garden City, 1947), p. 118; *Congressional Record,* 75th Cong., 1st sess., 1937, LXXXI, Part II, 1,900.

5. Voorhis, *Confessions,* pp. 118-119; *Sacramento Bee,* August 6, 1937.

6. *San Francisco News,* May 4, 1938, January 10, March 10, 1939.

7. Ibid., January 20, 1939.

8. *Congressional Record,* 76th Cong., 1st sess., 1939, LXXXIV, Part I, 654-658.

9. *San Francisco News,* January 24, 1939.

10. Ibid., January 30, February 2; *Los Angeles Times,* February 3, 1939.

11. *San Francisco News,* January 30, 1939.

12. Voorhis, *Confessions,* pp. 116-119 passim.

13. *Sacramento Bee,* February 16, 1939.

14. *San Francisco Call-Bulletin,* February 18, 1939; *San Francisco Chronicle,* February 19, 1939.

15. *San Francisco News,* February 21, 1939; *Bakersfield Californian,* February 22, 1939; *San Francisco Chronicle,* February 19, 1939; *Marysville Appeal-Democrat,* February 23, 1939; *San Francisco Call-Bulletin,* February 18, 1939; *Oakland Tribune,* February 20, 1939; *Fresno Bee,* February 23, 1939.

16. In addition to FSA and WPA, Harrington consulted with representatives of the Social Security Board, the Housing Authority, the Surplus Commodities Corporation, the Public Health Service, the Department of Interior's Education Office, and the United States Employment Service. See *Congressional Record,* 76th Cong., 1st sess., Appendix LXXXIV, Part XII, 1,236-1,237; *San Francisco Call-Bulletin,* February 23, 1939.

17. *Congressional Record,* 76th Cong., 1st Sess., Appendix LXXXIV, Part XII, 1,236-1,237.

18. Ibid.

19. *Berkeley Gazette,* April 5, 1939; *San Francisco News,* August 19, 1939; *San Francisco Call-Bulletin,* April 12, 1939.

20. *San Francisco News,* February 25, July 7, May 11, August 7, 1939; *Los Angeles Times,* May 13, 1939.

21. *San Francisco News,* June 6, August 19, 1939.

22. Ibid., July 7, 1939.

23. Ibid., August 19, 1939.

24. Ibid., September 13, October 21, 1938.

25. *Sacramento Bee,* December 13, 31, 1938; *San Francisco Examiner,* November 30, 1938.

26. *Stockton Daily Evening Record,* January 5, 1939.

27. La Follette Committee, *Reports,* 77th Cong., 2d sess., No. 1150, p. 10; *People's World,* January 20, 1939; *San Francisco Call-Bulletin,* February 24, 1939; *San Francisco Chronicle,* March 17, 1939; *Stockton Daily Evening Record,* March 23, 1939.

28. Senate Resolution 126, 76th Cong., 1st sess., April 19, 1939, in La Follette Committee, *Reports,* 77th Cong., 2d sess., No. 1150, pp. 10-11; Hiram Johnson to Doherty, November 9, 21, 23, 1939, Hiram Johnson Papers, Bancroft Library, University of California, Berkeley, Part III, Box 18.

29. *San Francisco News,* August 10, 1939; *Bakersfield Californian,* November 6, 1939.

30. *San Francisco News,* August 24, 1939.

31. Steinbeck has been the subject of scores of volumes of literary criticism. I have found the following especially useful: Joseph Fontenrose, *John Steinbeck, An Introduction and Interpretation* (New York, 1963); Warren French, *John Steinbeck* (New York, 1961); Warren French, *A Companion to The Grapes of Wrath* (New York, 1963); E. W. Tedlock, Jr., and C. V. Wicker, eds., *Steinbeck and His Critics* (Albuquerque, 1957).

32. "The Harvest Gypsies," *San Francisco News,* October 5-12, 1936.

33. Tom Collins to Eric Thomsen, September 19, 1936, U.S. Department of Agriculture, Agricultural Stabilization and Conservation Commission Papers, Federal Records Center, San Francisco, 36,879; Elizabeth R. Otis to author, April 5, 1967, author's personal records; Fontenrose, *John Steinbeck,* pp. 67-68.

34. As reported in Peter Lisca, "John Steinbeck, A Literary Biography," in Tedlock and Wicker, eds., *Steinbeck and His Critics,* p. 13.

35. The wide variety of interpretations of the novel is quite evident in the articles presented in Tedlock and Wicker, eds., *John Steinbeck and His Critics,* passim.

36. See review by Westbrook Pegler, *San Francisco News,* August 11, 1939.

37. *San Francisco Chronicle,* October 14, 1939. For labor: *Kern County Union Labor Journal,* September 1, 1939; *Fresno Bee,* November 10, 1939; UCAPAWA International Executive Board, *Summary Report, October, 1939* (San Francisco, 1939), Carey McWilliams Collection, University of California, Los Angeles. For agricultural economists: Otis Durant Duncan, *The Significance of the Migrations of Oklahoma Farm Population* (Stillwater, Okla., 1939), p. 3; *Kern County Union Labor Journal,* October 13, 1939. See Upton Sinclair, "Sinclair Salutes Steinbeck," *Common Sense* 7 (May 1939): 18-19.

38. John Walton Caughey, "Current Discussion of California's Migratory Labor Problem," *Pacific Historical Review* 8 (September 1939): 353; Malcolm Cowley, "American Tragedy," *New Republic* 98 (May 3, 1939): 382; Lewis Kronenberger, "Hungry Caravan," *Nation* 148 (April 15, 1939), 440; Mike Gold in *People's World,* June 21, 1939.

39. Walter R. Goldschmidt, *As You Sow* (Glencoe, 1947), p. 128.

40. Winters Camp Reports, August, September, December, 1939, USDA

ASCC Papers, 36,889; *Tow Sack Tatler,* October 20, 1939; *Dinuba Sentinel,* April 9, 1940.

41. *Bakersfield Californian,* August 18, 21, 1939.

42. Ibid., August 22, 28, 1939; *Kern County Union Labor Journal,* August 25–September 1, 1939; *National Ham and Eggs,* September 2, 16, 1939; *Sacramento Valley Union Labor Bulletin,* September 8, 1939; "Civic Leaders Protest Ban on Steinbeck's 'Grapes of Wrath'," *Open Forum* 16 (September 2, 1939): 1-2.

43. *Dinuba Sentinel,* April 9, 1940.

44. *San Francisco Chronicle,* August 10, 1939.

45. *Simon J. Lubin Society Confidential News Service,* August 1939; Robert E. Burke, *Olson's New Deal for California* (Berkeley, 1953), p. 31.

46. Philip Bancroft, *Does "Grapes of Wrath" Present a Fair Picture of California Farm-Labor Conditions?* (n.p., n.d.), passim; Virgil E. Combs, *The Joad Family in Kern County* (n.p., 1940), passim; George Thomas Miron, *The Truth About John Steinbeck and the Migrants* (Los Angeles, 1939), passim; John E. Pickett, "Termites Steinbeck and McWilliams," *Pacific Rural Press,* July 29, 1939, p. 74; Lee Alexander Stone, *The Migrant Situation in Kern County* (n.p., February 2, 1940), passim; Frank J. Taylor, "California's Grapes of Wrath," *Forum* 102 (November 8, 1939): 232ff.

47. "Is the Grapes of Wrath Too Hot for Hollywood?" *Look* (October 24, 1939): 12-15; Ruth Comfort Mitchell, *Of Human Kindness* (New York, 1940).

48. Taylor, "California's Grapes of Wrath," 232; Bancroft, *Does "Grapes of Wrath" Present a Fair Picture,* passim.

49. Bancroft, *Does "Grapes of Wrath" Present a Fair Picture?* passim; Combs, *The Joad Family,* 3-7; Pickett, "Termites Steinbeck and McWilliams," 74.

50. *Associated Farmer,* July 15, 1939.

51. Mitchell, *Of Human Kindness,* p. 117.

52. Ibid., pp. 147-150.

53. Miron, "The Truth About John Steinbeck and the Migrants," p. 7; Pickett, "Termites Steinbeck and McWilliams," p. 74.

54. French, *A Companion to the Grapes of Wrath,* p. 106.

55. "These Pictures Prove Facts in Grapes of Wrath," *Life* 8 (February 19, 1940): 10-11.

56. Byron Darnton articles, *New York Times,* March 4-9, 1940; "About Migrants," *Survey Midmonthly* 76 (April 1940): 140; Ray Mork to Fred Soule, September 24, 1939, USDA ASCC Papers, 36,885; *Covered Wagon News,* September 22, 1939; "What Should America Do for the Joads?" *Town Meeting of the Air* 5 (March 11, 1940); "Oases For Health," *Time* 35 (January 15, 1940): 40.

57. *People's World,* May 14, June 22, 1940.

58. Samuel Rosenman, ed., *The Public Papers and Addresses of Franklin D. Roosevelt* (New York, 1941), IX: 57.

59. *Fresno Bee,* January 25, 1940; *Sacramento Bee,* March 15, 1940; *Madera Tribune,* January 23, 1940; *Pacific Rural Press,* March 23, 1940.

60. *San Francisco Chronicle,* April 3, 5, 1940; *San Francisco News,* April 4, 5, 1940.

61. *Bakersfield Californian,* April 5, 1940.

62. *Fresno Bee,* April 5, 1940.

63. The second regular session of the 76th Congress was really the third

session. The second session of the Congress had been the emergency meeting of September 1939 to discuss neutrality legislation. Only the first and third sessions had the opportunity to deal with the migrant problem.

64. *San Francisco News,* January 12, 1940.

65. Ibid., January 8, 13, 1940; *Bakersfield Californian,* January 5, 6, 11, 12, 1940.

66. *Bakersfield Californian,* February 16, 1940.

67. *Congressional Record,* 76th Cong., 3d sess., Appendix, LXXXVI, Part XIII, 958.

68. *San Francisco News,* March 8, 9, 1940; *Santa Barbara News Press,* March 9, 1940.

69. *Congressional Record,* 76th Cong., 3d sess., LXXXVI, Part III, 2,676-2,680. For Voorhis' reply, see pp. 2,680-2,682.

70. *San Francisco News,* March 29, April 2, 1940; *Marysville Appeal-Democrat,* March 29, 1940.

71. *Congressional Record,* 76th Cong., 3d sess., LXXXVI, Part V, pp. 4,800, 4,805. "House Resolution 63. *Resolved,* That the Speaker appoint a select committee of five Members of the House, and that such committee be instructed to inquire into the interstate migration of destitute citizens, to study, survey, and investigate the social and economic needs, and the movement of indigent persons across State lines, obtaining all facts possible in relation thereto which would not only be of public interest but which would aid the House in enacting remedial legislation."

72. John H. Tolan, "Our Migrant Defenders," *Survey Graphic* 30 (November 1941): 615.

73. Tolan Committee, *Hearings,* Part 9, pp. 6,744-6,750.

74. *Tow Sack Tatler,* November 1, 1940.

8

The Founding of UCAPAWA

When they supplanted the Mexicans in California's fields, the Okies intruded upon a labor system that had developed during sixty years in which alien racial groups had picked the crops. The fact that white Anglo-Saxon Americans occupied the roles both of employee and employer in California agriculture during the depression decade presented another facet of the migrant problem. Further, the rise of labor unions attempting to organize the Okies brought additional tension and conflict to rural California, exposing the conditions under which three generations of disorganized and economically impotent laborers had supplied food for America's tables. It is impossible to understand the impact of the Okies without at the same time understanding the labor relations that had become traditional in the agricultural valleys of the state by 1935.

As has been seen, California's growers periodically reaped the harvest of their use of alien field labor in riots and agitation directed against these groups by urban workers. Each time the farming interest protected itself by substituting for the offending minority another against whom hostility had not yet developed. The Japanese replaced the Chinese, who were in turn replaced by Mexicans and Filipinos.

Despite occasional restiveness in the urban areas, growers preferred alien labor to white resident labor. Filipinos and Mexicans provided cheap labor, and they were available when required. Without them, growers feared, profits in farming would disappear.[1] In part to protect this valuable labor supply, there evolved in California agriculture a psychology that equated race with field labor. As in the American South, where labor done by migrants was considered "nigger work," so too in California, growers fostered the dogma that "white labor cannot and will not do our agricultural work for us."[2] Those who utilized alien racial groups frankly stated their preferences for them in terms that bespoke a near-feudal attitude to employer-employee relations.

The assumed inferiority of the migrant laborers left growers free to exploit and to patronize them simultaneously. In the fields, the alien laborer was supplied with the barest necessities. According to the growers, he needed—indeed desired—only his bedroll and a roof under which to lay it; he would neither appreciate nor understand decent accommodations.[3] Furthermore, there was little point in providing better accommodations, since the idyllic life of the field worker left little room for permanent lodging: "Peons? Isn't the word peon a little out of character when applied to a Mexican family which buzzes around in its own battered flivver, going around from crop to crop, seeing Beautiful California, breathing its air, eating its food, and finally doing the homing pigeon stunt back to Mexico with more money than their neighbors dreamed existed?"[4]

Unsurprisingly, a myth grew—nurtured by agricultural journals like the *Pacific Rural Press*—that California was a "patriarchal paradise in which the worker lived under the benevolent wing of the farmer." To the casual observer, the myth could have seemed a fair indication of reality despite occasional outbreaks of rural violence. California's fields had been bloodied when racial riots convulsed the valleys, but the migrants had been victims not perpetrators. The growers argued that they had done their best to protect their defenseless charges. The harvest of 1913 had seen a violent riot and wildcat strike at the Durst Hopfields in Wheatland. In a sense, even the Wheatland riot confirmed rather than denied the myth. The rioters had been white and led by Wobblies, not by the aliens.[5] What usually passed for tranquility in rural California, however, was actually the acquiescence of dissatisfied, but impotent, unorganized alien workers. California's farms were, it was true, factories in the fields, but rural field workers were, for a variety of reasons, unable even to consider organization for collective action. Until the depression of the 1930s, they lagged behind industrial workers in the search for means to achieve a measure of control over the conditions of their own labor.

Growers were accustomed to far more control over their labor supply than most urban employers. California's towns were, essentially, company towns, depending upon the growers, canners, and cotton ginners for their very survival. Growers held the reins of local government, and county officials could be relied upon as allies should any attempt at collective action among the field workers occur.

The legal status of most field workers furnished growers with an additional lever should trouble arise. Most of the Mexicans were aliens, and some had entered the United States illegally. Orientals and Filipinos were denied citizenship in nearly all cases. Consequently, these groups were prey to a form of intimidation not generally available to urban employers: they could be deported, or, as growers euphemistically veiled the threat, repatriated. The polyglot characteristics of the labor force impeded still further the possibility of effective, united action. Linguistic, cultural, and racial differences among California's agricultural workers made even the ethnic composition of the steel industry, for example, seem relatively homogenous. The racial situation was rendered still more complex by the hiring system. Under the "padrone" or contractor system, professional labor shepherds arranged work for gangs of Filipinos, Orientals, Hindus, or Mexicans, herding them to the fields, paying their wages, and preventing contacts with other racial or linguistic groups.

Grower control over alien field workers was reinforced by the invisibility of these racial groups within American politics and culture. Black in the southern states, alien in the West until the coming of the Okies, agricultural workers lacked the vote. Even those with citizenship moved too frequently to establish voter residence. Unrepresented in Congress, unseen by the mass of Americans, they were excluded from state unemployment services or federal labor legislation. Labor unions and the powerful political forces that supported industrial organization gave only lip service to field workers' unions.

Even had labor unions become seriously interested in organizing California's field workers, and even were they sufficiently powerful to overcome the near-total control exercised by employers in the rural areas, they would nonetheless face serious obstacles arising from the condition of labor in agriculture. Migratory agricultural workers were notoriously poor and subject to long periods of unemployment during off-season. Attempts to collect any but minimal dues would be foredoomed. Further, migratory agricultural workers moved frequently. In any agricultural region, the annual labor turnover might be complete. A migrant could, at most times of the year, be anywhere within the state or, worse still for hopeful organizers, picking crops somewhere in Colorado, Arizona, Michigan, Alabama, or even British Columbia. Into what sort of union, AFL leaders might well have asked, should a labor force so migratory be organized? Into geographic locals? By variety of crop? On a national basis? No single traditional organizational pattern seemed to fit the needs of this diverse and nomadic labor force.[6]

This formidable list of difficulties frightened labor unions. A serious defeat in agriculture might weaken the gains achieved so slowly during a half century of conflict in the nations' cities. It was better to let the sleeping dog of agricultural labor lie and hope for better opportunities in the future. Prior to the depression, only the Wobblies had seriously attempted to organize California's agricultural workers, and the IWW's dismal end in the postwar Red Scare returned California's fields to total control by the state's growers.[7] The harvest armies, docile because they were powerless and without allies, kept their silence for sixty years, coming to the fields when needed, packing up their bedrolls and disappearing when the crop was picked.

With the arrival of the Great Depression, California's Filipino and Mexican field workers forswore their accustomed docility for a temporary alliance with communist union organizers. In the massive agricultural strikes of 1933 and 1934 in the San Joaquin and Imperial valleys lay the immediate background for the manner in which California's farmers received the Great Plains migrants. Although few Okies took part in these strikes, challenges and responses that evolved from them would affect the Okies when a second wave of attempted unionization broke over California's industrial farms in 1938 and 1939.[8]

Made restive by wage cuts provoked by the depression, Mexican and

Filipino workers had engaged in 1930 in a number of minor spontaneous uprisings.[9] Ad hoc responses to specific situations, the strikes were sponsored and supported under the aegis of organized labor; two small independent Mexican unions, born in the late 1920s, provided a nominal leadership.[10] The strikes of 1930-1931 involved few workers and were failures. The demands of the Mexicans for better wages and housing went totally unfulfilled. These minor uprisings had, however, caught the eye of the Communist party. The Communists, in the early depression years, adhered to a policy of dual unionism under the banner of their own creation, the Trade Union Unity League (TUUL). In 1931, the TUUL-affiliated Cannery and Agricultural Workers Industrial Union (CAWIU) entered California's agricultural regions. At first, the CAWIU worked with the Mexican unions, then supplanted them as spokesman for California agricultural labor in 1932.[11]

The depression's economic dislocation and the increasingly strident voice of the CAWIU wore thin the alleged docility of the Mexican field worker. In 1933, when their request for higher cotton-picking wages was refused by the San Joaquin Valley's growers and ginning companies, the field workers went on strike, shutting down the valley's cotton industry.[12] Unheralded, indeed ignored, by historians of industrial labor, the San Joaquin Valley cotton strike was a major labor conflict. Between 15,000 and 18,000 workers struck on a 120-mile front for 24 days.[13] The strike ended with outside mediation when a team led by George Creel found an acceptable compromise, and the strikers returned to the fields. Buoyed by their victory, the Communist party's organizers moved south into the Imperial Valley where, the following year, they supplied leadership in a strike of 3,600 Mexican vegetable workers. Alongside the San Joaquin and Imperial outbreaks, a host of smaller strikes dotted California's rural regions in 1933 and 1934. Their combined effects persisted through the decade. Coming when it did, at the moment when radicals seemed intent on shutting down San Francisco's port with a general strike and when Upton Sinclair's EPIC threatened the state's political quietude, the wave of agricultural strikes appeared part of an immense communist conspiracy, and brought a violent response.

The presence of Communist party members among the strike leadership was not a basic cause of the strikes. "The CAWIU was the tail of the dog," one of the San Joaquin Valley organizers recalled thirty years after the cotton strike. Party members were constantly on the move within the strike region, attempting in vain to keep up with spontaneous organizations of cotton workers springing up everywhere in the valley.[14] The Communists had served only as catalysts and supplied organizational and tactical skills. For the growers and local law enforcement agencies, however, they served as convenient scapegoats for strikes whose roots lay deep. The presence of Communists, too, helped to inflame local opinion against the strikers. Tulare's *Advance-Register*, for example, was confident that "the 'strike' would vanish into thin air overnight if the outside agitators were rounded up en masse and escorted out of the Country." In the Imperial Valley as well, Communists were valuable, if unintentional, allies of the larger growers. "After more than two months of observation and investigation," federal conciliator Pelham Glassford was convinced "that a group of growers have exploited a communist hysteria for the advancement of their own interests . . . have welcomed labor agitation, which they could brand as 'Red,' as a means of sustaining supremacy by mob rule, thereby preserving what is so essential to their profits—cheap labor."[15]

Growers relied extensively upon violence, vigilantism, and the criminal-syndicalism laws to subdue the strikers in 1933 and 1934. In the cotton strike, two workers were shot to death at Pixley, another at Arvin by armed men in automobiles, and strikers at Tulare were held incommunicado in stockades set up at the county fairgrounds. In Imperial Valley a year later, mass meetings were tear-gassed, ACLU lawyers kidnapped, and hundreds of strikers jailed. Finally, in late 1934, eighteen of the strike leaders were arrested in Sacramento under the state's criminal-syndicalism law, and eight were convicted and jailed.[16]

California's rural regions were unaccustomed to field labor strikes. Their populations were, moreover, neither large nor diverse enough to supply countervailing or neutral groups to moderate tempers and defuse conflict situations. The pattern of response to agricultural strife, which developed in the farming areas, was characterized by near-unanimity of support for the growers and an easily manipulated willingness to justify the resort to violence. The pattern was evident in valley newspapers. During the San Joaquin strike, for example, the *Visalia Times-Delta* commented favorably on a rumor that the Ku Klux Klan was planning a resurgence in the valley: "it might not be such a bad idea at that. The strikers do not appear to have stood in much awe of the legally constituted authorities who . . . have petted, pampered, and fed the reds and their charges, while harvest moon and torrid sun glowed on cotton fields' thwarted harvest." In the Imperial, the *Brawley News* voiced a similar and typical attitude when some labor organizers were escorted from town by a group of armed farmers: "Not Mob Violence, but Valley Spirit. Mob rule is a thing to be avoided above all others, but it was not mob rule . . . it was a studied, organized movement of citizens seeking the only way out of difficulties threatening the community's peace, when the hands of the law had been tied by the law itself."[17]

After the Imperial Valley strike, relative quiet returned to rural California. Growers, local officials, and their allies were convinced that their toughness had ended the wave of strikes, and thus a habit of stern antistrike and antiunion action fastened upon the growing regions. California's farmers organized quietly in vigilance committees, determined to prevent a recurrence of agricultural strikes. The most important of these to grow out of the strikes of 1933-1934 was the Associated Farmers of California.[18]

With the cessation of labor strife in 1935 there fell upon the agricultural regions a mood of complacency. Confident that quick action had nipped revolution in the bud, growers, now protected by organizations like the Associated Farmers, settled back, expecting rich profit from crops harvested without hindrance from outside agitators. Their misconceived hopes would collapse within three years. The quiescence of 1935 and 1936 was not the result of vigilance, but rather the outward signs of a major reshuffling of California's harvest labor force. The Okies, who had come to the state for the purpose of settling down, were becoming migrant workers in California's fields, replacing the Mexicans who had taken part in the strikes of 1933-1934 and bringing temporary respite from interference with the harvesting of California's crops. Those who utilized large numbers of field laborers were, nonetheless, concerned about the future. Would the peace the Okies had brought with them last? Dr. Clements, in growers' eyes probably the most influential of the state's agricultural labor experts, argued from the beginning of the migration that these newcomers meant potential trouble for the growers:

> This year [1936] 90 per cent of the labor consisted of migratory labor from the South, Midsouth, and Southeast. This labor, mostly white, is supposed to supplant the former Mexican laborers who were what might be termed versatile labor since when the 150 days of agricultural labor were over they could turn their hands to the manual labor of rough industry and public utility and tighten their belts and exist on the minimum of subsistence.[19]

"One Mexican laborer," Clements wrote in another place, "trained in California's requirements from youth, is worth three-to-five out-of-state so called agricultural laborers no matter how honest may be their endeavours to perform."[20] But, Clements continued, displaying the guilt that bothered many of the state's growers, the Okies' "endeavours to perform" could not be honest:

> Another feature in [the Mexican's] favor was that they were adaptable labor. . . .They were impossible of unionizing; they were tractable labor. Can we expect these new white citizens to take their place?
> The white transients are not tractable labor. Being American citizens, they are going to demand the so called American standards of living. In our own estimation, they are going to be the finest pabulum for unionization by either group—the AFL or the subversive elements.[21]

Clements, who showed a deeper solicitude for the Mexican than did his fellow agriculturists, had, nonetheless, identified one of the salient questions, the answers to which would determine agriculture's response to the Okies: would the new migrants be "tractable"? It was the proper question, but for many of the state's growers, Clements, in his zeal for retaining the Mexican, seemed to forget the wave of Mexican-dominated strikes in 1933 and 1934. Frank Taylor, another respected spokesman for the agricultural interests, responded to Clements' rhetorical question by noting in 1936 that the Mexican was becoming class conscious, settling down, accepting relief, and thus striking a blow at California agriculture. Taylor, like Clements, was unsure about the Okie, noting that the newcomers were labor conscious.[22] H. A. Miller, a grower, later told the La Follette Committee that Clements' statements "might" apply in general. Nonetheless, the Okie influx contained a "substantial number" who would not demand "so called American

standards of living."[23] Divided over whether the Mexican or the Okie
was the more malleable laborer, the California growers were uncertain
whether, insofar as the labor union problem was concerned, they
preferred Mexican trouble, of which they knew, or Okie trouble, of
which they were yet ignorant. The answer would be forthcoming in
1937-1938. For Joseph DiGiorgio, one of the state's largest growers,
the Okies, since they had not taken a major part in the San Joaquin
Valley and Imperial Valley strikes, seemed a good bet in 1936.[24] Union
and radical journals during this period consistently accused the Associated Farmers of fighting to halt Mexican immigration and replace it
with southwesterners, the former being too "union-conscious."[25]

Growers, then, accepted the Okies for the temporary relief from
strife they supplied but feared for the future. Others, men who later
aligned themselves with the new migrants when the Okies became a
statewide problem, looked to the future and exulted. They, too, were
Californians and not immune to the strain of racism that had colored
the growers' responses to the migrants. In nearly all the writings of
liberals contemplating the Okies, there was a tacit assumption that they
would solve the state's agricultural problems. With naive optimism, the
San Francisco News, for example, believed that the Okies had ended
the development "fatal to democracy" of a "permanently stratified
society in California." Unlike prior racial groups of field labor, the
journal commented, "these rangy native-born Americans" would
"sooner or later . . . insist on getting their American heritage." With a
romanticism bred of centuries of mythology, the *News* saw the Okies as
"old stock, self-reliant men and women of the breed that came over the
Alleghanies [*sic*] early in the last century to Kentucky and Tennessee
and then moved on. . . . They cannot long be handled as the Japanese,
Mexicans and Filipinos who proceeded them were handled."[26] The
News was not alone in voicing sentiments such as these. John Steinbeck, still a relatively unknown novelist collecting material for a series
of factual articles about the migrants, accepted the notion that something in the Okies' American blood would enable them to succeed
where Mexicans had failed. "Their blood is strong," he announced
when the articles were published under that title:

> One has only to go into the squatter's camps where the families live on
> the ground and have no homes, no beds, and no equipment; and one

has only to look at the strong purposeful faces often filled with pain and more often, when they see the corporation-held idle lands, filled with anger, to know that this new race is here to stay and that heed must be taken of it.

It should be understood that with this race the old methods of repression, of starvation wages, of jailing, beating, and intimidation are not going to work; these are American people.[27]

Steinbeck's implicit assumptions were widespread in California during the 1930s. They would subtly affect labor relations in California's agricultural valleys for the remainder of the decade. Labor unions, as well as growers' organizations, would struggle for control of the Okies, sure in the conviction that, in some almost mystical manner, the migrant's heritage would determine the outcome.

In 1936 and 1937, the focus of California's agricultural strife shifted from the farm to the cannery. Two violent and bloody strikes—in 1936 at Salinas' lettuce packing sheds and in 1937 at Stockton's canneries—captured headlines. These strikes were notable insofar as they involved some Okies fortunate enough to find cannery work, but the majority of strikers were local whites or Mexican and Filipino shed workers.[28]

But in the fields a number of conditions ensured that the strikes of 1933-1934 would not be repeated for some time. From 1935 to 1937, there was little interest in field labor organization either on the part of the traditional trade unions or the workers themselves. It had been the communist-oriented CAWIU, not the AFL, that had taken leadership during the turbulent San Joaquin and Imperial Valley strikes in 1933 and 1934. Immediately afterward, however, the CAWIU collapsed, but not because its leadership was in jail. Rather, it was a casualty of the major shift in communist strategy away from dual unionism. When the TUUL was formally dissolved in March 1935, the CAWIU died with it, leaving a leadership vacuum among the California agricultural workers.[29]

The initial response of AFL unions to the Okie migration varied from indifference and misunderstanding of the condition of the migrants to overt hostility. Craft union journals, in urban centers and even in rural areas less dislocated by the migrants, showed virtually no interest in these less-skilled members of the labor force. Oakland's *East Bay Labor Journal*, for example, did not mention agriculture until

1939, when it began to carry news involving AFL cannery unions. Sacramento's *Valley Union Labor Bulletin,* published a scant sixty miles from the Yuba City-Marysville area, showed little interest in the migrant problem; from 1935 through 1941 it published no editorials on the subject.[30]

Even Kern County's *Union Labor Journal* was slow to respond to the presence of a migrant population camped on Bakersfield's very doorstep. Throughout 1935 and the first half of 1936, the *Journal* was oblivious to California's agricultural situation, although it carried full reports of "wage slavery in the Cotton fields" of Texas and the deep South. Significantly, the *Journal* betrayed its indifference to, and, consequently, its ignorance of, California's agricultural labor problems, when, in June 1936, the state AFL announced that it was considering the possibility of a field workers' union. The paper's headline read: *"MOVEMENT TO ORGANIZE FARM HANDS,"* even though the traditional "farm hand" bore no relation whatsoever to the California agricultural laborer. When the twenty-five members of this short-lived farm-hand union assembled in Bakersfield, the *Journal's* primary concern in the meeting was to affirm that "Lillian Monroe, communist . . . has no connection with the organization."[31]

A year after the AFL had formally endorsed the principle of unions for agricultural workers, Kern's craft unions, as well as some of the skilled orders elsewhere in the state, were uncertain whether to respond to the migrant problem as organized allies of the Okies or as Californians fending off the threat of cheap, imported labor, as their ancestors had done with the Chinese and Japanese in the past. Their reaction to the formation of the California Citizens Association in early 1938 was at first highly favorable. The CCA's petition accused the Okies of "destroying our wage structure . . . periling industry . . . laying a burden of confiscatory taxes upon our property . . . [and] increasing unemployment and distress among our resident population."[32] Echoing CCA arguments, Kern County's organized labor gave sizable support to the petition. The county's Building Trades Council, along with the carpenters, laundry workers, mill men, painters, plasterers, and other smaller crafts, endorsed the petition. To the pleasure of the *Bakersfield Californian,* T. J. Foley, business agent of the Building Trades Council, predicted that most of the city's unions would sign the petition and give it "full endorsement." Were it not for the Okies, Foley insisted, "every man in Bakersfield would be working today." The migrants, he continued, had ruined Kern's reputation as the "white spot" of the nation. Union members circulating the petition among the brother-hoods noted that only 10 percent of those approached had declined to sign.[33] Kern's unions received almost immediately a gentle public admonition from an FSA representative who pointed out that labor should be more careful about its choice of allies in the attack upon migrants.[34] But Bakersfield's unions were only the most united in supporting the move to curtail the Okie influx. The Los Angeles Central Labor Council's 184 locals and 13 others, mostly carpenters, supported the petition elsewhere in the state, and the CCA chairman announced that he had obtained 20,000 signatures at the Labor Day parades of 1938 in Los Angeles and Long Beach.[35]

It was fitting that carpenters' unions were prominent among labor groups allied with the CCA in its antimigrant campaign. It had been "Big Bill" Hutcheson, the Carpenters International president, who had exchanged insults with John L. Lewis at the 1935 AFL convention. When Lewis rocked Hutcheson with a right cross, he served notice that industrial union leaders were determined to smash the AFL's monopoly of organized labor. The schism in labor's ranks extended into California agriculture, and the Okies, like industrial workers elsewhere, became pawns in the rivalry between craft and industrial trade unions.

Just before the AFL convention at Atlantic City in October 1935, ripples of concern about the dissidents in the AFL reached California. The AFL state leadership seriously began to consider organizing the thousands of laborers engaged in field and related agricultural work who could be lost to rival unions. The California State Federation of Labor's 1935 convention resuscitated an earlier, moribund resolution calling for organization of agricultural labor and presented the national AFL with a resolution requesting both increased funds for legal defense and an international charter for a union of agricultural workers. [36] Simultaneously, an organizing committee within the state built support among the craft unions for a statewide conference on problems of organizing agricultural labor, to be held in 1936. The conference met at Stockton in June under the honorary chairmanship of Norman Thomas, and called for the immediate organization of a statewide union of agricultural and related workers.[37] Within a month, the organizational campaign was suspended for lack of funds.

There the matter rested, and would have continued to rest, had not the violent Salinas lettuce packers' strike occurred just when the California Federation of Labor (CFL) held its 1936 annual convention. Noting the seriousness of the problem in California's fields, the convention increased the funds available for agricultural organizational campaigns, in a move which meant, according to the CFL's secretary, "that the responsible labor movement is at last moving into the vast field of workers."[38]

By late 1936, after a series of false starts, California's AFL seemed for the moment prepared to accept into its ranks the mass of Okies, as well as the remaining Mexicans and Filipinos, who, it was assumed, would sooner or later, with or without the support of organized labor, bring labor turbulence to the rural regions. During January and early February 1937, CFL and AFL leaders spoke of organizing one large union of *all* agricultural workers, which, President Green announced, would have a potential membership of 240,000.[39] At a CFL conference on agricultural workers in late February 1937, at San Francisco, delegates voted to organize a new union, the Agricultural Field and Cannery Workers Union of California, with the objective of bringing 200,000 farm workers under one charter, thus producing the largest labor organization in the state. In March, however, the CFL reverted to craft unionism, an untenable principle where field labor was concerned. The state executive committee turned down the conference's request for a single state charter, proposing instead that a charter be granted for crop workers alone. The purpose of this about-face was clarified in April when the executive committee of the CFL claimed that cannery and packing shed workers, in contrast with field workers, were already partially organized into unions. To ask them to ally with the unorganized field workers would be to weaken their existing unions. Although the CFL's convention later that year adopted a resolution requesting that the AFL "bend every effort to the rapid organization of [agricultural field workers] into the American Federation of Labor," the March decision meant, to all intents and purposes, that the AFL would "bend its efforts" not to organizing agricultural migratory workers, but rather to working among the cannery and shed workers.[40] Among these latter groups, the CFL achieved some outstanding successes. Beginning with April 1937, when eighteen organizers were sent among the cannery workers by the CFL, a mass drive signed some 75,000 new members.[41] By late 1938, the CFL claimed thirty-five agricultural locals: among them were three unions of distillery workers, one sheep-shearers local (at San Francisco), sixteen of cannery workers, and eleven of packers and citrus by-product workers. But not one of the new locals involved either field workers or any branch of the cotton industry; not one of the locals was located in the San Joaquin Valley.[42]

The thousands of Okies camped in the valleys had been abandoned by an AFL that remained indifferent to unskilled workers. Organizers who had demanded the formation of one large union to include the Okie pickers, as well as cannery and shed workers, were "undiscouraged by the State Federation Executive Board's sabotage."[43] Forming a rump group, eighteen tiny field workers' locals, some within AFL, and others composed of independent racial groups, convened at Bakersfield in late April 1937 and emerged from their conferences with a State Federation of Agricultural Cannery Unions. In July, these groups threw in their lot with the CIO and met with locals from other states in the first national convention of field workers at Denver, Colorado. Out of this conference came the United Cannery, Agricultural, Packing and Allied Workers of America (UCAPAWA).[44]

The formation of UCAPAWA under the rival CIO banner forced the California Federation of Labor to respond later that year by forming the National Council of Agricultural Workers, which never went beyond the ritual, charter-granting stage. Meanwhile, the CFL lost little time in attacking the CIO's coup. In an open letter to field and cannery workers, CFL Secretary Edward Vandeleur virtually admitted that his federation's abandonment of migratory workers in March had been the signal for the CIO's entry. But, he insisted, that did not matter:

> The Communistic CIO combine is attempting to use farm labor as an instrument for halting the flow of crops to the canneries.
> Having failed miserably in the Cannery sell-out scheme [i.e., the idea of one big union], the red borers are now setting a trap for field workers.[45]

As late as 1939, resolutions calling for organizational efforts among California's field workers were presented at CFL conventions, but

UCAPAWA had arrived first and with greater strength, and the CIO was virtually unhindered by jurisdictional disputes in its attempts to organize field workers. If and when the Okies joined up, it would be under the CIO. During the three years remaining before Pearl Harbor, the CFL and the growers were bound together in mutual hostility to the CIO's attempt to organize the field workers. In private conversation with Philip Bancroft, Ed Vandeleur assured the Associated Farmers president that agricultural workers unions were untenable:

Bancroft: He [Vandeleur] was as good a labor leader . . . as could be . . . I always liked him. We were friends even after he was quite strongly pushed along on the other side. . . . I felt he was very sound. He recognized that farm labor was in a different situation and it was on account of that fact that we couldn't stand a strike at harvest time.

Question: Would you say that as far as you knew Vandeleur was actually against organizing farm labor.

Bancroft: Well, he said he was at that time.[46]

Shortly after the Bakersfield conference that gave birth to UCAPAWA, the Associated Farmers announced that "farmers [would be] willing that their workers should be organized under the AFL banner," but their attitude towards the CIO was uncompromising: "We don't trust Harry Bridges. We won't work with him."[47] As long as AFL field workers' unions existed on paper, the Associated Farmers could choose with whom they would deal. It was not surprising that they were willing to work with Secretary Vandeleur who was as aware of the threat from the "red borers" as anyone else in the state.

Much, if not all, of the Associated Farmers' solicitude for AFL unions was bogus. As the historian of California's farm organizations has shown, the Associated Farmers' union policy actually meant that the "only 'good' union was the distant union."[48] Claiming at first that they opposed only "communist unions," the Associated Farmers, when confronted with noncommunist AFL unions, opposed them too. Relatively safe from AFL entrance into the fields, growers could afford to give vocal comfort to it in order to avoid appearing totally antilabor during these New Deal years. When it became clear that unions would attempt an organizational drive among the Okies with or without AFL aid, the executive secretary of the Associated Farmers hired advertising magnate Clem Whitaker to launch a publicity campaign explaining the growers' attitudes toward farm labor unions. Whitaker was to "get out" a "helpful story" explaining why even AFL unions might be unwelcome. The secretary noted:

> I refer to the one regarding organization of farm laborers by the California Federation of Labor, giving them a hand where they have been fighting the Communists, but pointing out clearly the danger, and our own definite fear that their own previous experiences are true, that unless farm labor organization is dominated and browbeaten by reds it cannot survive, and, of course, even then, not for very long; that in the meantime there will be trouble, and that we do not like to see these unions organized by the Federation, for whom we have great respect in many of their objectives, and then have the Communists step in and take them over.[49]

This unspoken Associated Farmers—AFL alliance was not in itself sufficient ammunition for growers who opposed unionization of their field workers. Even as Whitaker was pointing out that "conservative labor leaders . . . recognize the futility and unsoundness of attempting to organize farm workers," it was obvious that non-AFL unions were following Harry Bridges' advice to launch an "inland march" on the large farms.[50] Growers had little choice but to search out tactics more relevant to this fact. As UCAPAWA developed, grower propaganda changed subtly to accommodate the new conditions, and a two-pronged attack was launched upon the union. On the one hand, UCAPAWA's alleged "Communist Generallisimos" were exposed.[51] On the other hand, a campaign was launched to explain why no union, communist or otherwise, could be tolerated in agriculture.

The experience with communist unions in 1933 and 1934 set the tone for Associated Farmers' attacks on noncommunist unions. The Stockton conference raised old fears that "if past history means anything . . . it is almost a certainty to play into the hands of Communists and radical agitators."[52] So useful was the communist label throughout the period that the Associated Farmers applied it everywhere. When UCAPAWA announced, for example, that it would follow the AFL political policy of rewarding friends and punishing enemies, the *Associated Farmer* commented that the technique was illustrative of the "boring-in tactics so common to the Communists."[53] As UCAPAWA moved from initial formation into organizational activity, the communist issue became still more powerful propaganda. Philip Bancroft called for investigation by the Dies Committee; a private file of "radicals, alien agitators or union organizers" was established and used in attempts to discredit CIO organizers.[54]   Finally, the incessant use of the communist issue enabled the Associated Farmers to present themselves as latter-day minutemen: "The conquest of the coast's radicals over California's soaring migrant population served as a trumpet call for the real 'grass roots' Californians to mobilize in defense."[55]

Anticommunism was not the sole thread in the fabric of responses to UCAPAWA's organization. That there were Communists in UCAPAWA was true; that UCAPAWA was a "communist union" was false. As the red menace theme wore thin, Associated Farmer propaganda demonstrated how far agriculture had lagged behind urban industry. Protected and insulated in rural regions, growers had retained an implacable hostility to labor unions of any kind. In many respects, their responses to unions were reminiscent of the attitudes of the captains of industry during the halcyon days of American industrial development. Even *Fortune* magazine recognized the backwardness of the captains of agriculture when it pointed out that Associated Farmers' tactics in labor disputes were "infinitely less enlightened" than the organization's objectives in less controversial matters, such as housing conditions.[56]

Testifying before the La Follette Committee, for example, "Hank" Strobel, member of the Associated Farmers executive committee and a hero of the "battle of Salinas" during the lettuce packers' strike there when farmers and pickets had battled with tear gas and clubs, affirmed that he had no objection to negotiating with his employees, but he would not countenance outside agitation. How, Senator La Follette asked, could the individual worker negotiate? Strobel replied, as had Thomas Wickes of Pullman to a similar question half a century before, "He could always come and ask for more wages."[57]

When large growers asserted their hostility to *any* organization of their labor, they pinned their arguments firmly upon a mythology of farm life that had nothing to do with the reality of California agriculture. "We farmers," Philip Bancroft asserted, "are much closer to our men than is the average industrial employer. We are their friends and they are ours ... we look out for their interests." The professional unionist, however, "wants to make our men hate us and he wants to make us hate our men."[58]

In short, unions might be acceptable but only in the cities. In another remarkable announcement, Bancroft echoed William Jennings Bryan's "Cross of Gold" speech in explaining why California's farms were different: "The farmers, if necessary, can get along without the cities, but the cities cannot get along without the farmers. . . .The problems of farm labor are so different from those of industry."[59]

Other counts in the indictment of agricultural unions were as disingenuous. Fred Goodcell of the Associated Farmers told readers of the *Pacific Rural Press* that farm workers' unions forced migratory workers to pay *annual* dues in one state although they might be working in that state for only a few months, and such inequity could not be countenanced. In addition, unions meant strikes, and strikes meant pickets. Since the farmers' home was also his place of business, "his wife and children must not be required to pass through a line of hostile pickets." "No man," the Associated Farmers insisted, "should be asked to submit to having his home picketed."[60]

Beneath the wrapping of altruism and mythology, however, grower propaganda retained a hard nub of self-interest. Even a short strike in the fields, farmers argued, could bring disaster; perishables rot quickly, and one or two days' delay in harvesting might wipe out a year's work. Moreover, low agricultural wages kept food prices low; allow unions into the field, and the price of food to the consumer could double. [61] Conversely, if prices did not rise, grower's profits would suffer.

Having established in words their opposition to unions, the large growers, spearheaded by the Associated Farmers, followed through with action designed to withstand UCAPAWA's anticipated onslaught. Their first move involved, paradoxically, toying with the possibility of seducing field workers into an Associated Farmers–sponsored company union. Suggested to Fred Goodcell, executive secretary of the Associated Farmers, by its founders, attorney Alfred Aram and Lillian Monroe, an ex-radical, the proposed union would affiliate with neither CIO nor AFL. It would forego strikes, disavow the closed shop, and affirm that wages in California were low only because an unorganized labor market kept workers from utilizing efficiently the year-round potential for agricultural work. The plan called, further, for an end to the Okie influx, on terms that became the position of the CCA a year later, namely that local workers were being displaced by the new migrants.[62] The idea did not appeal to a number of the Associated Farmers' county units and was officially dropped, but not before UCAPAWA caught wind of the scheme and publicized it in labor journals.[63]

This false start was interesting, but trivial compared to the use by the Associated Farmers of more traditional legal and extralegal methods to oppose potential unions among the migrant workers. Where possible, the Associated Farmers used county government to initiate legal obstacles to organization. From 1935 to 1939, the devices most frequently invoked were the "antipicketing" ordinances in thirty-four of California's fifty-eight counties. Generally justified by the argument that the farm is also a home, these ordinances varied in specifics. Nearly all of them made a misdemeanor of obstructing public passageways, attempting to induce others to quit work or engage in boycotts, or, in nine counties, uttering any noise or gesture during the course of picketing. Potential fines of $500.00 and imprisonment up to six months would face organizers or pickets. In nearly all the counties, arrest meant arraignment before hostile local officials.[64] In addition, the Associated Farmers recognized the continuing value of the state criminal-syndicalism law in preventing organization. Throughout the decade, the group strenuously fought various efforts to repeal the law, itself a memento of the great postwar Red Scare.[65]

The Associated Farmers' extralegal preparations for the CIO "march inland" have been well documented in twenty-seven volumes of La Follette Committee hearings and require little discussion here.[66] They included tactics ranging from the deputizing of hundreds of Associated Farmers members and the organization and training of private armies ("pick handle brigades") to the use of labor spies and the stockpiling of private arsenals. Together, these tactics amounted to what Imperial Valley's Associated Farmers manager aptly called them a month after UCAPAWA's birth: "an excellent formula for getting rid of cockroaches, grasshoppers and CIO organizers."[67]

As the Associated Farmers literally armed for defense against UCAPAWA, the note of vigilantism sounded during the 1933-1934 crisis crept into local statements along with demands for the maintenance of "law and order." By mid-1939, after UCAPAWA had engaged in some small strikes, the president of the Associated Farmers of Mariposa County was exultant: "They call us vigilantes and you know that term has a familiar ring in the ears of the old-timers and we rather like the term, for vigilantes were organized to drive the outlaws out of the state."[68]

Notes in Text

1. California State Relief Administration, "Migratory Labor in California," mimeographed (San Francisco, 1936), p. 30; Stuart M. Jamieson, "The Origins and Present Structure of Labor Unions in Agriculture and Allied Industries of California," La Follette Committee, *Hearings*, Part 62, p. 22,533.

2. California State Relief Administration, "Migratory Labor in California," pp. 159-160; *Los Angeles Times*, May 11, 1930.

3. John Walton Caughey, *California* (New York, 1940), p. 568; Five Collegians in Search of America, "On California Side Roads," *Nation* 149 (November 11, 1939): 536; Roy Pike, letter to Editor, *San Francisco News*, May 23, 1936.

4. *Pacific Rural Press*, quoted in La Follette Committee, *Reports*, 77th Cong., 2d sess., No. 1150, p. 257.

5. The classic study of the Wheatlands riot is Carleton H. Parker, *The Casual Laborer* (New York, 1920).

6. Harry Schwartz, "Organization Problems of Agricultural Unions," *Journal of Farm Economics* 23 (May 1941): 458*ff*.

7. La Follette Committee, *Reports*, 77th Cong., 2d sess., No. 1150, pp. 208-217; Jamieson, "Origins and Present Structure," p. 22,531*ff*.

8. Paul S. Taylor and Clark Kerr, "Uprisings on the Farms," *Survey Graphic* 24 (January 1935): 22.

9. Carey McWilliams, *Factories in the Field* (Boston, 1939), pp. 212-213.

10. Jamieson, "Origins and Present Structure," p. 22,535.

11. Ibid., pp. 22,535-22,537; Porter M. Chaffee, "A History of the Cannery and Agricultural Workers Industrial Union," n.p., typed manuscript, Federal Writers' Project Collection, Bancroft Library, University of California, Berkeley, Carton 35.

12. Agricultural wages in cotton work were generally set in concert by large growers and representatives of the ginning industry. Actually, an interlocking directorate existed in which ginners and growers were often the same man.

13. Jamieson, "Origins and Present Structure," p. 22,536; McWilliams, *Factories in the Field*, p. 220. The best single source on the 1933 strike remains Paul S. Taylor and Clark Kerr, "Documentary History of the Strike of the Cotton Pickers in California, 1933," in La Follette Committee, *Hearings*, Part 54, p. 19,992.

14. Interview with Mrs. Carolyn Decker Gladstein, San Francisco, California, October 5, 1965; see also Taylor and Kerr, "Uprisings on the Farms," 19.

15. *Tulare Advance-Register*, October 16, 1933; Report of Pelham D. Glassford, La Follette Committee, *Hearings*, Part 55, p. 20,304.

16. McWilliams, *Factories in the Field,* p. 228. Mrs. Gladstein (above) was one of the defendants. The sentences were reversed two years later.

17. *Visalia Times-Delta,* October 27, 1933; *Brawley News,* January 26, 1934.

18. The ten largest contributors to the Associated Farmers were: The Industrial Association of San Francisco; the Dried Fruit Association of California; the Canners' League; the Southern Pacific Railroad; Southern Californians, Inc. (an "industrial association" representing antiunion businesses); the Atcheson, Topeka, and Santa Fe Railroad; the Pacific Gas and Electric Company; the San Joaquin Cotton Oil Company; the Holly Sugar Corporation; and the Spreckels Investment Company. Chambers, *California Farm Organizations,* pp. 43-45.

Parts 47 through 75 of La Follette Committee *Hearings* were devoted to the California situation, and the Associated Farmers took up the bulk of the committee's interest. The fact that the Associated Farmers was, in spite of whatever else it might also have been, a powerful "private army" was documented therein virtually beyond dispute.

19. Dr. Clements to Mr. Cecil, memorandum, December 18, 1936, La Follette Committee, *Hearings,* Part 53, p. 19,696.

20. Dr. George P. Clements to Harry Drobisch, February 27, 1936, George P. Clements Papers, Bancroft Library, University of California.

21. Clements to Cecil, December 18, 1936.

22. Frank J. Taylor, "California's Harvest Hand Crisis," *California Journal of Development* 26 (March 1936): 6-7, and his "The Right to Harvest," *Country Gentleman* 107 (October 1937): 8.

23. Testimony of H. A. Miller, La Follette Committee, *Hearings,* Part 53, p. 19,519.

24. Arvin Camp Reports, July 11, 1936, Simon J. Lubin Papers, Bancroft Library, University of California, Berkeley, Carton 13.

25. *Labor Herald,* March 31, 1936; *EPIC News,* July 20, 1936; *Western Worker,* April 18, 1935; see also above, chapter 1, for discussion regarding alleged Associated Farmer conspiracy to advertise for labor in Oklahoma.

26. *San Francisco News,* October 6, 1936, October 8, 1937.

27. John Steinbeck, *Their Blood Is Strong* (San Francisco, 1938), p. 3.

28. La Follette Committee, *Reports,* 78th Cong., 2d sess., No. 398, pp. 1,380-1,384 for Salinas strike, 1,385-1,406 for Stockton Cannery strike. See also Jamieson, "Origins and Present Structure," p. 22,537; McWilliams, *Factories in the Field,* pp. 255-260; *Rural Worker,* September-October 1936.

29. Irving Howe and Lewis Coser, *The American Communist Party* (New York, 1957), p. 271.

30. *East Bay Labor Journal,* 1935-1941; *Sacramento Valley Union Labor Bulletin,* 1935-1941.

31. *Kern County Union Labor Journal,* June 12, August 21, 1936.

32. "Petition by the Citizens of California to Senators Johnson and McAdoo," Lubin Papers, Carton 13.

33. *Bakersfield Californian,* June 18, 1938.

34. *Kern County Union Labor Journal,* June 24, 1938.

35. *Congressional Record,* 76th Cong., 1st sess., 1939, LXXXIV, Part 1, 63; see also *Bakersfield Californian,* June 17, 19, 1938; Thomas McManus, *Report to the California Citizens Association* (Bakersfield, October 1, 1938), p. 29, copy in Bureau of Public Administration Library, University of California, Berkeley.

36. Testimony of Edward Vandeleur, La Follette Committee, *Hearings*, Part 62, p. 22,057.

37. "California Conference of Agricultural Workers, Stockton, June 6-7, 1936," La Follette Committee, *Hearings*, Part 62, pp. 22,678-22,707.

38. Testimony of Vandeleur, p. 22,058.

39. *San Francisco Chronicle*, January 27, 1937; *San Jose Mercury-Herald*, February 19, 1937; *Western Worker*, February 23, 1937.

40. California State Federation of Labor, *Proceedings of the Thirty-eighth Annual Convention, Long Beach, California, September 13-17, 1937*, Proposition No. 48, p. 118.

41. Testimony of Vandeleur, p. 22,058.

42. California State Federation of Labor, *Proceedings of the Thirty-ninth Annual Convention, Santa Barbara, California, September 19-23, 1938*, pp. 41-45.

43. *Western Worker*, April 12, 1937.

44. *Farmer Labor News*, April 30, 1937; *San Francisco News*, July 2, 1937; *San Francisco Chronicle*, April 26, July 12, 1937; *Labor Herald*, July 20, 1937.

45. *East Bay Labor Journal*, August 31, 1937.

46. Philip Bancroft, "Politics, Farming, and the Progressive Party in California" (Oral History Project Interview, Berkeley, 1962), pp. 395-396. See also *Associated Farmer*, April 23, October 17, 1936. In both, the Associated Farmers called the AFL a "good union": "No member of a union affiliated with the AFL has ever been convicted in California of violating the Criminal Syndicalism Law."

47. *San Francisco Call-Bulletin*, May 20, 1937.

48. Chambers, *California Farm Organizations*, chaps. 8-9 passim, especially p. 62.

49. "Executive Secretary, Associated Farmers" to Clem Whitaker, September 17, 1936, La Follette Committee, *Hearings* Part 68, p. 24,914.

50. Whitaker to Executive Secretary Ralph H. Taylor, October 10, 1936, La Follette Committee, *Hearings*, Part 68, p. 24,915.

51. *San Francisco Examiner*, February 27, 1939.

52. Ralph H. Taylor in *San Jose Mercury-Herald*, October 4, 1936; *American Citizen*, June 30, 1936.

53. *Associated Farmer*, November 17, 1937.

54. "Minutes of the Associated Farmers Executive Committee, March 31, 1939," La Follette Committee, *Hearings*, Part 67, pp. 24,685-24,686; Testimony of Stuart Strathman, Associated Farmers Field Secretary, La Follette Committee, *Hearings*, Part 56, pp. 20,392-20,394; "Meeting, Board of Directors, Imperial County Associated Farmers, April 20, 1937," La Follette Committee, *Hearings*, Part 55, p. 20,344.

55. *San Francisco Examiner*, March 2, 1939.

56. "Migratory Labor: A Social Problem," *Fortune* 19 (April 1939): 116.

57. Frank J. Taylor, "The Right to Harvest," *Country Gentleman* (October 1937): 7-9: See also testimony of Joseph DiGiorgio, La Follette Committee, *Hearings*, Part 48, pp. 17,657-17,658; Testimony of H. M. Strobel, La Follette Committee, *Hearings*, Part 53, p. 19,482.

58. Philip Bancroft, *Protecting Your Food Supply* (1938), p. 3.

59. *Oakland Tribune*, December 8, 1937.

60. *Pacific Rural Press*, June 19, 1937; *Associated Farmer*, January 30, 1937; Miller Testimony, p. 19,436; *Stockton Record*, April 5, 1937.

61. Professor Paul Taylor, an ardent foe of the large growers, admitted that this fear on the growers' part was real. But, he pointed out with much logic, newspapers, railways, and many other industries sell perishable products; yet they accept collective bargaining and unions in order to *avoid* strikes. Paul S. Taylor, *Adrift on the Land* (New York, 1940), p. 18. Bancroft, *Protecting Your Food Supply,* passim.

62. Goodcell reports of conferences with Alfred Aram, La Follette Committee, *Hearings,* Part 68, pp. 25,264-25,269.

63. *Agricultural and Cannery Union News,* August 17, 1937.

64. Bancroft, "Politics, Farming and the Progressive Party," p. 360; Testimony of Henry Fowler, La Follette Committee, *Hearings,* Part 47, p. 17,213; Katherine Douglas, "West Coast Inquiry," *Survey Graphic* 29 (April 1940): 228; Chambers, *California Farm Organizations,* pp. 108-109.

65. *Associated Farmer,* April 23, 1936; *People's World,* April 7, 1939; Chambers, *California Farm Organization,* pp. 108-109; Robert E. Burke, *Olson's New Deal for California* (Berkeley, 1953), pp. 130-131.

66. La Follette Committee, *Hearings,* Parts 47-75.

67. H. T. Osborne to Arthur Arnoll, July 16, 1937, La Follette Committee, *Hearings,* Part 55, p. 20,347.

68. *Los Angeles Times,* July 16, 1939.

9

The Failure to Organize the Okies

By June 1937, rural Californians had chosen sides, with memories of the conflicts of 1933 and 1934 still sharp. In the midst of the Okie migration, a determined union and an equally determined organization representing heavy users of agricultural labor were prepared to struggle for control of the new arrivals. The result of the struggle would depend upon two things: the allies UCAPAWA could muster and, more importantly, the success of the new union in gaining the allegiance of the Okies.

UCAPAWA's goal of organizing the field workers was an exceedingly difficult one to achieve. The fledgling union had to cope with all the obstacles that had prevented earlier efforts from succeeding. In addition, powerful opposition could be expected from the growers and the AFL. On the other hand, UCAPAWA had advantages and allies that no agricultural union in California's previous history could muster. By 1938 and 1939, it appeared that the union might succeed where earlier unions had been destroyed. UCAPAWA's advantages lay in three areas. First, private organizations and other unions were in a position to give support. Second, the federal government's relief and rehabilitation policies promised unexpected benefits to organizers. Finally, perhaps the greatest advantage available to the union lay in the attitudes of

Culbert Olson. With his election in 1938, California had a governor
determined to enhance the bargaining power of the migrants.

The most important of the private organizations, the Simon J. Lubin
Society, had been founded in 1936. Its namesake, the first commissioner of the Division of Immigration and Housing, had struggled until his
death in the mid-1930s to alert Californians to the character of corporate agriculture. From its offices in San Francisco, the Lubin Society
poured into the state a steady stream of information and propaganda
usually directed against the Associated Farmers. Working closely with
members of the California offices of FSA, the society served as a
coordinating agency for agricultural unions, providing them "with facts
and figures . . . when they enter[ed] wage negotiations with farmers
and canners."[1]

Itself a miniscule organization—until 1938 it had no paid staff—the
Lubin Society had become a powerful propaganda force when it seized
the opportunity to coordinate private relief activities during the San
Joaquin Valley floods. Thereafter, its pamphlets and speakers were in
considerable demand. The Lubin Society's secretary noted that its
successes were far larger than its formal membership. It had been
particularly important in helping Olson to win in at least four counties
in the 1938 election, sabotaged an Associated Farmers attempt to
extend its activities into other states by preceding it with a successful
propaganda campaign wherever its speakers went, and performed a
major role in persuading the La Follette Committee to come to California. Perhaps most significant of its activities was its function as a
clearinghouse for union information. Local, national, and district chapters of the UCAPAWA were constantly in need of data. They relied for
it upon the Lubin Society which, after 1938, had the time to provide
it.[2] As the Lubin Society gained strength, its activities expanded to
include the problem of Okies as well as the problems of agricultural
labor. It reprinted Steinbeck's articles in a pamphlet entitled "Their
Blood Is Strong," thereby publicizing the "racial" change that had
overtaken California's harvest armies.

By October 1938, the Lubin Society had been joined by another
private organization with similar goals. The John Steinbeck Committee
to Aid Agricultural Organization had a stronger racial bias than the
Lubin Society in that it concentrated on the Okies as Okies rather than

upon the problems of all agricultural workers, although the first chairman, Carey McWilliams, did not see any difference between Okies and Mexicans insofar as the agricultural labor problem was concerned. But Helen Gahagan Douglas, who became chairwoman when Olson called McWilliams into his administration, was oriented more closely than McWilliams had been to the charity aspect of the migrant problem.[3] The Steinbeck Committee was, in short, more paternalistic than its ally the Lubin Society. Nonetheless, it reorganized itself in 1939, changed its name to The Committee to Aid Agricultural Organization during the controversy of 1939 over *The Grapes of Wrath,* and supplied some financial support to UCAPAWA.[4]

Compared with the Associated Farmers, the Lubin Society and the Steinbeck Committee were weak. They were pamphleteers and functioned well in that role, but they lacked power. A more powerful ally of UCAPAWA was another union, the Workers Alliance, which claimed in 1939 a total membership of 42,000, 12,000 of them paid up, organized into 186 locals. Led by radicals, some of them Communists from the dual-unionism period, the Workers Alliance was primarily a pressure group designed to protect unemployment relief scales against the onslaughts of economy-minded legislatures. Because the interests of those on relief and the agricultural migrant coincided frequently, UCAPAWA and the Workers Alliance were natural allies.[5]

During labor disputes or periods of labor undersupply, agricultural workers on relief were extremely vulnerable. Unless they were carefully watched, administrators friendly to the growers could restrict relief payments, thereby forcing the striking or unemployed migrants to go to the fields. Throughout the depression years, the Workers Alliance vigorously played a watchdog role. In addition, when UCAPAWA became involved in a strike, the alliance bent its effort to prevent its members from accepting work as strikebreakers.[6]

In the balance of power between agricultural unions and growers' organizations, the state government played a larger role than the private organizations. Depending upon the direction in which it chose to throw its support, the state government could foster or hinder the development of unions among the migrant workers. The Republican administration of Governor Frank Merriam had impeded labor organization in the fields, and the governor's public statements on unions generally accorded with those of the Associated Farmers. "Every major strike in California in the past four years" he announced in 1938, "was led by Communists." He had, he continued, "found no fault with AFL leaders."[7]

With regard to agricultural labor organization specifically, Merriam also acceded to the Associated Farmers. In mid-1937, with UCAPAWA in its initial stages of organization, groups representing California growers presented for public view an eleven-point "farm labor policy." Point five in the program demanded special status for agriculture: "Because of the perishable nature of agricultural products and because of the many uncontrollable factors and elements in producing and marketing such products which might cause ruinous losses to producers, farm laborers, and consumers, agriculture, while not opposed to collective bargaining, must be kept free from the effects of the imposition of the 'hiring hall' and the 'closed shop.' " In action, such a policy meant total grower control over hiring, and, considering the oversupply of agricultural labor in 1937, would have been a powerful antiunion device. Governor Merriam expressed "complete approval" of the program and promised to cooperate fully with it.[8]

It was not Merriam's union policy alone, but also the state's relief policies, that impeded agricultural organization until January 1939. Once again, lessons learned by the growers during the 1933-1934 strike wave affected labor policy during the period of the Okie migration. From 1933 to 1935, state relief agencies were given federal monies through FERA only on condition that they follow the policies laid down by Harry Hopkins.[9] One of Hopkins' policies was that relief funds were to be distributed solely on the basis of need. If a client was in need of relief because he was on strike, that was none of the relief agency's concern. During the 1933 San Joaquin Valley cotton strike, the California Emergency Relief Administration, operating under federal advice, "rendered material assistance to the strikers in their dual [other] role as needy unemployed," and, by giving food to hungry strikers, "established a precedent of importance."[10]

The implications of Hopkins' policy were lost neither upon the growers nor the Republican administration. When control over relief reverted to the state in late 1935, the Pomeroy policy plugged the loophole that had protected striking workers. The Hopkins policy was retained, but with a twist. The presence of a strike in progress remained none of the relief agency's business but with far different result. If agricultural work were being offered, the reliefer was required to accept it or be thrown from the relief rolls. Strike or no strike, the policy remained: "No Work—No Eat." Pomeroy's successor in the State Relief Administration, Dewey Anderson, reversed the earlier Merriam strike policy. Hitherto, reliefers had been forced from the rolls in order to draw the prevailing wage. Now, only a fair wage, determined by liberal Olson appointees, would justify wholesale evictions of reliefers.[11] As it turned out, during labor conflicts the fair wage set by the SRA generally approximated the strikers' wage demands.

In addition to its friendly position on relief, the Olson administration gave positive support to UCAPAWA. The coming of the Okies, Olson told Senator La Follette, had injected additional difficulty into the problems of California agriculture, and brought new urgency to the need for unions. There was, he pointed out, a "constant influx of new workers unfamiliar with local conditions. . . . As long as workers are not organized in California agriculture, they are likely to be subjected to discriminatory treatment of one kind or another."[12] Commenting in another place upon Steinbeck's novel, Olson linked the Okies to the problem of agricultural labor even more intimately: "Migrants glut our labor market, and some industrialists have shown a willingness to exploit them. Repeated attempts to set a minimum wage of twenty-seven and a half cents for agricultural laborers [UCAPAWA's demand in the 1939 strike] have failed, although most small farmers admit this is rock bottom for a decent existence."[13] McWilliams, as was his habit, expressed the same sentiment more brusquely: "I think the 'Joads' should organize and that we should make it possible for them to organize. . . . Organization is particularly necessary in California where the big farmers are organized for the express purpose of keeping wage rates as low as possible."[14]

Olson's and McWilliams' statements in support of UCAPAWA reaffirmed and strengthened the hostility directed at them by growers' groups. The attack levied upon the Olson administration through the CCA, the Associated Farmers, and the Farm Bureau rested in part upon the government's intervention in labor disputes. Philip Bancroft, for example, expressed a sentiment common to large growers at a meeting of the executive committee of the Associated Farmers. "Governor Olson," Bancroft asserted, "was so surrounded with men of strong radical leanings that he cannot learn the truth about labor and migrant problems in the agricultural areas or get the facts about particular disturbances."[15]

If the transfer of state power from Merriam to Olson seemed auspicious for labor union organization among the Okies, so too did the continuing presence of New Deal agencies and attitudes within the state. The Roosevelt administration did little actively to foster union-ization among the Okies, and it acquiesced in their exemption, as agricultural workers, from the Social Security, NLRA, and Wages and Hours legislation. Nonetheless, the New Deal did nothing to prevent agricultural labor organization and its Farm Security and Work Projects Administrations in California enhanced UCAPAWA's opportunities among the Okies. As was the case with the Olson administration, it was in the areas of housing and relief policy that the New Deal served as an unspoken ally for agricultural labor unions.

During the Merriam years, the state offices of WPA had been accused of complicity in maintaining low agricultural wages. Few critics, save the Communist party after its breach with Roosevelt in the latter days of the New Deal, could find similar fault with the FSA's California office. Although this federal agency's primary purpose had little rela-tion to the problem of labor conflict in agriculture, FSA frequently played an unintended role in the drive to organize the Okies. In order to understand FSA's involvement in labor disputes, one must be aware of the intimate connection between agricultural labor housing and unions.

An agricultural economy utilizing migratory labor inevitably requires temporary housing accommodation for the field workers, and the state's larger growers provided camps at which migrants could pitch their tents or lay their blanket rolls. But by the late 1930s many of the state's growers who hitherto had accepted these often squalid camps on their ranches were developing a more paternalistic attitude towards the housing of their workers.[16] In part, this was the result of Carey McWilliams' constant muckraking about intolerable housing conditions in rural California. In addition, the San Joaquin Valley floods had raised public clamor for alleviating these conditions, and even the Associated Farmers, for all their violent hostility to unions, were aware of the need for meliorating the housing problem.[17] As early as 1934, Madera County had built its own public camp for housing migrants under the leadership of health director Lee Stone.

The FSA migrant labor camps merely supplied with federal funds what growers would otherwise have had to build at their own expense.[18] By the late 1930s, only a few growers objected to the camps on the grounds that they were "too good for the workers." The powerful grower lobby that opposed the FSA camp program did so because labor organizers at these federal islands were not subject to the same recruiting problems as their counterparts in private camps or rural shacktowns.[19]

The logistical situation facing agricultural labor organizers was exceedingly complex and not heartening. The potential union members moved about with ease, but when settled, they could be located in any one of three types of dwellings. Their residence might, for the moment, be within a private, grower-owned, or ditch-bank camp; they might have taken temporary lodging at one of the FSA camps; or they could be migrants in the state long enough to have established a permanent home at one of the little Oklahomas. Each of these types of settlement posed a different problem for the organizers.

From the beginning of its organizational campaign, UCAPAWA had to write off the private camps and ditch-bank settlements as inhospitable ground. The ditch-bank settlements generally contained the newest, poorest, and least employed of the migrants. Filthy and disease-ridden, such housing lacked meeting areas and offices for unions and survived by the sufferance of local health officers. Moreover, the camps, "invariably located upon the premises of the employer [exercised] a somewhat coercive influence upon employees."[20] When labor disputes occurred, growers in concert with local officials evicted strikers from the camps. The strikers, in turn, sought temporary shelter on ditch banks from which they were subsequently expelled by local health officials, who noted their real or alleged hazard to public health. Private licensed camps, maintained either by growers or local businessmen, were as unfertile a soil for unions as the ditch banks. Also, union organization could be prevented simply by barring the organizer's entrance to the camps. Should a union take root among the residents, those who were suspected of being members were weeded out and replaced by other migrants who were as yet unorganized.

Life in the Little Oklahomas imposed different, but nonetheless severe, restrictions. In the Okies' shacks, organizers and migrants were safe from coercion by growers. It was difficult, however, to find locations for mass meetings except in the larger towns like Bakersfield, Marysville, and Fresno, where labor temples were available if local organized labor was willing to supply facilities for the CIO. Years of close relations between the growers and the townspeople boded ill for union drives in these towns. Antiunion sentiment was strongest in regions dominated by large ranches, and these were precisely the areas where the bulk of Okies settled.[21]

These difficulties were surmountable. Even were organizers to eschew drives in the towns or private camps, the expanding FSA program provided a base for union activity. In late 1935, even before the opening of the first two federal migratory labor camps, and well before UCAPAWA's birth, advisers to the Resettlement Administration were concerned about the implications of the program for labor policy. A statement prepared for Walter Packard, RA's regional director, pointed out that "the very existence of federally controlled camps may tend to attract labor organizers, because of the confidence that on government property they will be protected in the exercise of their lawful activities and constitutional rights. The possible implications of this situation, for the conduct of public camps, should be fairly faced." After some hesitation, Packard did face these implications. He notified his superior in Washington that he was "thoroughly convinced that the program of establishing labor camps should be pushed as fast as possible" despite the problem of labor organizers.[22]

Many of RA's employees were in total sympathy with agricultural labor unions, but recognized in them an Achilles heel for the federal agency. "Personally," one noted, "I welcome the desire . . . to organize for purposes of collective bargaining. . . . I firmly believe that not until they organize is there any real hope of their being able to improve their social and economic condition." But, he continued, "reactionary interests" suspect that the federal government sympathizes with this desire, and "will be quite ruthless" in attempting a showdown on the issue.

Rather than publicly support agricultural unions in the camps, the RA should adopt the neutral position that agricultural workers are "entitled to their constitutional rights," which include the right of lawful assembly.[23]

This argument gradually became RA's informal policy. Addressing the Stockton Conference of June 1936, Jonathan Garst, new regional director of the RA, spoke of the camp program to the delegates seeking to organize California's field workers. In response to questioning from the floor, he held to the neutral policy: "Anyone in the camps is entitled to his full constitutional rights. . . . We do not propose to say who shall visit the workers in their homes. . . . As far as the right of free speech in these camps is concerned, this certainly will not be curtailed whatsoever by the RA." Thus, unions could enter the camps on organizational drives. Were a strike to develop, no notice would be taken. "Many people have stayed . . . without working when they couldn't get jobs. If they are out on strike it is the same to us as if they were out of jobs."[24] And, it followed logically that the federal government would be "bound to protect [strikers] from any interference or harassing techniques" should a labor controversy erupt.[25]

Finally, as the camp program moved into full swing, formal policy made in Washington, D.C., replaced ad hoc decisions on labor relations. Regional advisers were informed by directive that FSA policies did not include participation in negotiations involving agricultural workers and employers. This policy, however, was not to be construed to "impair the right of the camp population to join or to refrain from joining a union for collective bargaining or to engage in any other legal activity."[26]

Such, then, was RA-FSA policy regarding unions of California agricultural workers. It was not the kind of positive support that allowed industrial union organizers to announce, "President Roosevelt wants you to join a union!" But, as Woodrow Wilson discovered, even neutrality can favor one side in a conflict. In the context of labor relations in rural California, neutrality appeared courage to liberal Congressman Jerry Voorhis.[27] UCAPAWA made no attempt to establish local union headquarters on the ditch banks, and evidence of any union activity in the private camps is rare. More frequently, organizers established local headquarters in a federal camp and then launched a "sweep" operation in the surrounding countryside, returning when necessary to the FSA sanctuary.[28] The success or failure of any organization drive, then, hinged upon the Okies in the less temporary Little Oklahomas and the federal camps.

As the growers had feared, it was in the government camps that UCAPAWA mounted its most serious organizational campaigns. CIO organizational drives took place at one time or another in at least eight of the camps: Winters, Westley, Gridley, Arvin, Shafter, Indio, Visalia, and Marysville. At least five of them—Visalia, Arvin, Shafter, Marysville, and Gridley—had functioning Workers Alliance and/or UCAPAWA locals. Support of labor organizations by local camp managers, who were given virtual autonomy regarding labor union activity in their camps, proved to be an important factor in unionizing in the camps. At the Indio unit, the manager and the local UCAPAWA agreed, in light of local hostility to the union, that organizational activities should take place outside the camp. But at most of the other camps for which records exist, it is clear that the managers and UCAPAWA representatives worked together in attempts to foster union consciousness among the Okies. At the Marysville camp, where the presence of a socialist, Milan Dempster, as manager, had led to powerful grower opposition and boycott, Dempster's replacement invited CIO officials to speak at camp meetings. Campers noted that the CIO "was working with the FSA" to "work out . . . something constructive" for the residents' benefit. The Shafter manager allowed UCAPAWA organizer Bud Fisher to write a weekly column for the camp newspaper until pressure from the *Bakersfield Californian* forced the column out of existence, although other union activities at the camp continued. Organizational activity at the Arvin camp went unhampered by the unit's manager, and the *Tow Sack Tatler's* editor was a UCAPAWA organizer, Samuel Birkheimer. At Visalia, Gridley, and even Indio, before that camp's manager had persuaded UCAPAWA to go elsewhere, CIO locals operated openly. At the Visalia camp, UCAPAWA's members met every week, Thursday evening. At the Indio camp, Okies in another local read each week a union column asking "which class for me" during early 1939.[29]

In mid-1939, Jonathan Garst resigned. FSA employees worried that his replacement, Lawrence I. Hewes, would take a harder line on the issue of labor relations. "We must not be biased," he affirmed, but he also cautioned that he "would not allow a definite organizing campaign in the camps before picking time, or mass meetings of unions in the camps."[30] Nonetheless, neutrality remained Hewes' rule. Unions no longer could establish headquarters in the camps, but there was no objection to their acquiring or recruiting members on federal property.[31] Since most camp managers were friendly to organizational campaigns, the change in policy meant little change on the local level.

During its early years, the FSA camp program was subjected to hostility from a wide variety of sources, and for many reasons. Community criticisms of the camps sat well with growers, whose objections were directed specifically at their independence from local control and their potential use as sanctuaries for those they considered to be agitators. Had it not been for the unionization drive of the 1930s, one student of Sonoma County agriculture concluded, growers' attitudes toward the government camp there would have been more positive. Such was the case in all the counties in which federal camps were established. The decision to build a camp invariably brought opposition from growers who feared the camp would become a center of agitation.[32] In Marysville, where one of the first camps was established, June 1936 was filled with rumors of a plot to "burn 'em out." To the south, the erection of a unit at Arvin brought from Roy Pike a plan to build a competitive string of grower-owned camps in the San Joaquin Valley.[33] In the Imperial, plans to build at Brawley elicited public petitions and private pressures upon FSA from the area's state senator.[34] So powerful was this reaction during the early years of the program that FSA, which had hoped to work with the support of the growers, found its momentum temporarily slowed.[35] The program continued, nonetheless. Unable to stop the program, growers were forced to oppose camps already in existence.

Despite FSA's occasional panic that vigilantes would attack the camps, not even the Associated Farmers ever seriously considered such action.[36] There was a major difference between embattled farmers attacking CIO recruiters and night riders taking on the federal government. From 1935 through 1941, not one overtly violent act against the FSA took place. Instead, farmers and their organizations launched a propaganda barrage through their journals and refused to hire migrants from a number of the camps. The purpose behind this concerted attack was to coerce FSA to reexamine its policy regarding unions among the campers.

In the view of the president of Imperial Valley's Associated Farmers, the migratory camp proposed for Brawley was "a present from Mr. Wirin [of the ACLU] and General Glassford who did not appreciate the Valley hospitality during their Communistic efforts at the time when they attempted to organize the Valley." This attitude conformed with most public statements in farm journals and rural dailies. The *Pacific Rural Press*, for example, continuously editorialized against the camp program. The RA, the journal insisted, neither "resettles" nor "administers"; it simply "participat[es] in labor uproar, working with agitator radicals." FSA camps, the *Press* charged, attracted Okies to California, where "Leaders of the Communist Workers Alliance act as greeters to the migrants." Finally, the newspaper explained, farmers "feel that these camps might become centers of radicalism."[37] Other farm groups echoed the *Pacific Rural Press* and the Associated Farmers. J. J. Deuel of the California Farm Bureau Federation announced that "the Resettlement People are a bunch of agitators. . . . What they're at Arvin [FSA camp] for is to agitate among working people. Maybe it isn't communism, but it's the personal liberty idea. . . . Camps should be controlled by the farmers themselves."[38]

In some locales, public disapproval of the camps because they were "breeding grounds for radicalism" was accompanied by a farmer boycott of the campers for the same alleged reason. The Indio camp, for example, received such a boycott, as well as a request from the Riverside County Board of Supervisors that it close. The camp's manager noted that the supervisors liked the camp "as a housing project"; but, he added, indelicately, "the nigger in the woodpile behind the attack is of course the 'Workers Alliance' " which was threatening to take control of the camp. At the Winters camp, a boycott of labor was broken only by a bumper apricot crop which "*forced* the growers to rely upon the Camp." At the Marysville camp, where two years after its completion an originally hostile local population had come to accept and even welcome its presence, Associated Farmers units launched a campaign charging that manager Milan Dempster, socialist candidate for governor in 1934, was controlled by agitators. Frightened by the Associated Farmers campaign, residents of the camp who had voted, a week before, not to allow labor organizers on the site, asked that their names be published and made available to grateful farmers.[39]

The most significant grower attack upon FSA camps took place at the Shafter unit, just north of Bakersfield in the cotton growing region of the San Joaquin Valley. There, in mid-1938, just as the state was awakening to the Okie surplus camped in the San Joaquin Valley, sixty "leading cotton growers" formed a committee with the "general understanding that they will not have much to do with the Shafter camp while it remains under the present [government] management."[40] At precisely the same time, Thomas W. McManus, a Bakersfield insurance executive, Alfred Harrell, publisher of the *Bakersfield Californian,* and Arthur S. Crites of the Kern County Building and Loan Association joined with a number of Bakersfield business and farming executives to found the Committee of Sixty, out of which grew the California Citizens Association. McManus, chairman of the association, was also a powerful voice in the movement opposing the camp program, and charged that the Communists "infest the migratory labor camps of the Farm Security Administration."[41]

The threat of unionization in California agriculture brought reaction from the larger growers directed not solely at the unions, but also at state and federal agencies whose policies might ally them with agricultural unions, notably UCAPAWA. A good deal of the motivation underlying the alliance of the growers with the CCA and the anti-Olson, anti-New Deal coalition lay in matters not related to politics. The CIO's initiative in organizing agricultural labor thus produced a backlash that lent still further power to the movement that brought frustration to Olson's New Deal.

UCAPAWA moved into the fields in early 1938, seeking to organize the Okies and the remaining Mexicans and Filipinos into the "one big agricultural" union that the AFL's leaders had considered a pipe dream. Provided with federal sanctuaries, buttressed after January 1939 with the aid and comfort of the Olson administration, working among potential unionists who, the mythology argued, would not tolerate what Mexicans had accepted as normal, UCAPAWA seemed to hold the

key to California's migratory agricultural labor problem. Throughout
1938 and 1939 UCAPAWA labored—and brought forth a mouse.

This is not intended to imply that California's fields had suddenly
become in actuality the idyllic paradise invented by agricultural publicists. The years 1937 through 1939 witnessed a number of serious,
often violent, agricultural labor conflicts. This fact, however, requires
qualification. Many of the labor disturbances of this three-year period
were wildcat outbreaks unrelated to the CIO's attempts at unionization.
One contemporary noted in 1940 that Okie strikes were unique in that
they were spontaneous outbreaks arising out of specific conditions and
not union-sponsored movements. In 1937 and 1939 such spontaneous
work stoppages occurred in most of California's major growing areas.
The Sacramento Valley saw Okies strike at Marysville and Winters in
the fruit orchards. At Westley in the San Joaquin, migrant pea-pickers
walked off the job in 1939. At Nipomo, in the huge truck-farming
region near Pismo Beach, southwesterners, awaiting in misery a pea
crop delayed by late frost, struck spontaneously for double the going
wage.[42]

More often than not, labor unions became involved in such disputes
as these by default, rushing to the area after the initial outburst, hoping
to lend organizational ability and gain new members from the spontaneous strike. During the Winters apricot strike in 1937, for example,
the pre-UCAPAWA Agricultural Workers Union "anticipated trouble"
and hastened to "invade the district." UCAPAWA took a similar role
during the Marysville fruit pickers' strike in 1939. A spontaneous
walkout in May gave the union courage to call a formal strike in
August.[43] UCAPAWA actually organized and led the Okies in one
major strike only: the San Joaquin Valley cotton strike of October
1939, which was the union's last and best effort. Its failure in this strike
was magnified by the fact that, despite the aid and comfort of all
UCAPAWA's private and public allies, the union achieved no gains.

In 1938, Kern County's cotton harvest, halved by the Agricultural
Adjustment Act, had not gone undisturbed. UCAPAWA had called a
strike for piece rates of $1.00 for each hundred pounds of cotton
picked, in opposition to the growers' offer of 75 cents. The growers
refused to deal with the union, and the Merriam administration enforc-
ed the Pomeroy policy, dropping from the relief rolls able-bodied men

refusing to work for the prevailing 75 cents wage. UCAPAWA organized pickets and strike committees, but picking proceeded apace, never seriously disrupted by the dispute. Indeed, the major union-grower controversy during the strike revolved about the question whether, in light of the fact that picking had not been slowed, it could be called a strike at all.[44]

The Kern incident of 1938 paved the way for the Madera-centered cotton strike one year later. This was a set-piece battle demonstrating all the advantages and liabilities inherent in UCAPAWA's situation. Immediately upon the inauguration of the Olson administration, Commissioner of Immigration and Housing Carey McWilliams, recalling the dispute of late 1938, established a fair wage of 27½ cents per hour or $1.25 per hundred weight for picking the 1939 harvest. Men refusing to work for less would not be evicted from the State Relief Administration's rolls.[45] When the growers announced through the Agricultural Labor Bureau of San Joaquin Valley that the cotton wage for 1939 would be 80 cents per hundred weight, or 20 cents per hour, the Workers Alliance bent its efforts to prevent workers on relief from accepting the proffered wage. In October, UCAPAWA entered the dispute, calling a strike for the wages set by the SRA.

The conflict that arose quickly became the largest agricultural workers' strike in California since the cotton strike of 1933. Picketing began on October 12, 1939. Caravans of Okie jalopies patrolled rural roads as flying squadrons of farmers intimidated the strikers. The strike held for two weeks. Picking virtually ceased, and growers, bewildered by this abnormally effective walkout, called out the Associated Farmers. The years of preparation for potential labor conflict bore fruit. Minor attacks on picket lines culminated at Madera on Saturday, October 21, when three hundred Associated Farmers' deputies under command of the local sheriff attacked a strikers' rally with bludgeons, fan belts, tire chains, and pickhandles. The Highway Patrol, called in hurriedly by Governor Olson, ended the battle with tear gas.

The events at Madera touched off spontaneous cotton stoppages in the upper valley. At Corcoran, Pixley, Arvin, and many other cotton centers, the Okies walked out while UCAPAWA organizers rushed south to organize them. Meanwhile, the Olson administration announced that the wage set earlier that year by the State Relief Administration was equitable. During the strike, the FSA camps served as unofficial head-quarters for the unions, especially at Shafter, Arvin, and Visalia. In addition, UCAPAWA gained unexpected support from the small-scale growers of some localities, who were receiving less benefit from AAA than their larger counterparts and were angered that they had little control over wages set by the ginning companies and large growers.[46]

Despite these allies, UCAPAWA's cotton strike collapsed. Within two weeks of the strike call, gins in Madera were operating at 50 to 100 percent output and a week later cotton picking was reported normal throughout the length and breadth of the valley. Most important, the strikers had returned to the cotton fields, in nearly all cases, at the growers' original wage offer.[47]

All in all, UCAPAWA had accomplished little during its two-year experiment in agricultural labor unions. Compared with the 1933-1934 organizational and strike activity of the Trade Union Unity League among the Mexicans, CIO's failure was even more noteworthy. In 1933-1934, for example, the CAWIU had led twenty-three strikes involving 42,000 field workers.[48] On the other hand, in 1937, as the total number of field workers' strikes in the nation rose, California saw only 4,000 workers involved in sixteen strikes. In 1938, the tale was much the same: 4,800 workers involved in twelve strikes, while once again the national total rose. The first six months of 1939 saw only 4,000 California workers in a total of six strikes. Only the San Joaquin Valley cotton strike of late 1939 approached the magnitude of those of the early 1930s, and this was primarily due to the violence used by the Associated Farmers in breaking the strike. In 1940, UCAPAWA changed directions, left the fields, and followed the AFL into the canneries, where it achieved enormous gains. At its 1939 convention, it had been able to report a total paid-up membership approaching only 3,000 out of a labor force of agricultural workers that fluctuated from just under 50,000 during slack periods to 150,000 at peak picking time in September.[49]

For four years, the AFL and CIO had argued over the questions of who should organize the Okies and into what type of unions. The Associated Farmers had built powerful organizations in agricultural counties to fend off UCAPAWA's anticipated attacks. Meanwhile, state and federal organizations had prepared policies to use when the clash between the Okies and the farmers came. But the crisis that was so fearfully awaited for so long never materialized.

Contemporary critics of the Associated Farmers and of California's industrialized agriculture—Senator La Follette, Carey McWilliams, John Steinbeck, and others—frequently laid the blame for the failure of agricultural unions on "farm fascism." In all their writings, there was the implication that Associated Farmers' violations of civil liberties and the rights of labor had broken unions that would otherwise have succeeded. It was, of course, true that the state's large growers, in concert with finance and business leaders, had built an extremely powerful labor-busting organization, and Senator La Follette was unquestionably correct in his many comments to that effect. Of the Madera strike, for example, his conclusion was a powerful indictment of the Associated Farmers, and deserves quotation at some length:

> . . . betrayal of duty by the constituted authorities of Madera are not, it seems clear, to be charged to them alone. Behind and above these officials stand those organizations which, in intimate co-ordination, loosed and directed forces to beget official and private lawlessness in Madera. The Agricultural Labor Bureau of the San Joaquin Valley and its strong right arm, the Associated Farmers, together fixed and enforced the wage rate which the strikers protested. In the course of their enforcement campaign, the Associated Farmers carried with them, through sheer domination of the local scene, the officials who ought to have administered constitutional laws with equal justice. In short, the Madera strike of 1939 shows that labor relations in that county were lawlessly controlled by a private group strong enough to command the suspension of those laws which they violated and the perversion of other laws to obtain their ends. . . .Whatever the motives of its sponsors and leaders, the fruit of the movement at Madera is unacceptable to men of good will.[50]

Writ large, La Follette's conclusions applied to all agricultural counties in California that were dominated by large ranches and heavy use of migratory laborers. If La Follette's appraisals and those of Steinbeck, McWilliams, Paul Taylor, and a host of others were not "dispassionate," as the Senator claimed, they were, nevertheless, accurate. At the same time, they were somewhat irrelevant.

Indictments of the Associated Farmers must be understood in the light of the attitudes and ideologies of the depression decade. This was a time of dualistic interpretations during which all conflict was economic conflict. A secular Manichaenism subsumed all struggle under a "good-guys"–"bad-guys" hypothesis. Rampaging plutocracy, tasting control by the people for the first time since Woodrow Wilson's era, was fighting the efforts of the good guys (labor unions, Democrats, liberals) to bring sorely needed social justice. In the light of such events as the Republic Steel massacre, the Scottsboro affair, the formation of the American Liberty League, such a view of reality was seductive and persuasive.

There was, nonetheless, a blind spot in the depression view of reality. It is no patronization of the critics of the Associated Farmers to point out that in an atmosphere charged with Steinbeck's magnificent portrayal of the Joads, and colored by the failure of Culbert Olson's attempt to wrest control of California from the hands of its rural and urban plutocracy, it was difficult to recognize that the Okies were unprepared for, in most cases indifferent and frequently hostile to, the attempt to organize them. The Associated Farmers *did* repress the occasional efforts of the fledgling UCAPAWA. That this repression proved crucial was due to the disinclination of the Okies to support the union.

Despite the charges of communism leveled at UCAPAWA, the union's policies conformed with traditions developed over the previous sixty years by Samuel Gompers and his successors. Its politics, for example, were those of "rewarding friends and punishing enemies." More important, its vision of the union's role in social and economic affairs was strictly voluntaristic. UCAPAWA's enabling resolution called for a labor front to achieve the inclusion of agricultural workers in federal and state labor legislation, but its deeper attitude toward government's role was expressed to Senator La Follette by one of its district organizers:

> . . . since I take it this committee may make recommendations on the basis of its findings, I should like to state for the record that in the experience of the entire labor movement it is the process of collective bargaining which produces the fundamental social readjustments. Favorable laws help, but there has never been a law that couldn't be interpreted two ways and there has certainly never been a law affecting the conditions of labor which took any effect until backed by the organizational strength of labor itself.[51]

UCAPAWA's voluntarism was a trap, which led it to attempt to organize the Okies under virtually impossible circumstances. UCAPAWA's ally, the Committee to Aid Agricultural Organization, assumed, for example, that unions could solve California's agricultural and migrant problem where all else seemed destined to fail. Begging the question, it announced that "through organization, the agricultural workers can achieve a decent life. . . . Even the problem which has baffled all government agencies, the flow or westward migration of dispossessed farm families, can be met by a union." Recognizing the critical problem of the labor surplus augmented by the Okies, the committee continued: "At present the incoming families drive down the wages of the whole industry. A union could prevent desperate competition for jobs."[52]

Of course a union could solve the problem, provided it organized the great majority of the available or potential Okie labor supply. And, since it had accepted, without reservation, the voluntaristic principle, UCAPAWA spent its two-and-a-half years of life in full awareness of the power over its survival it had given to the new migrants. Each year the new union called with increasing stridency, and some anxiety, for redoubled efforts among the migrants. "Organized labor is forced to take a stand on the question of what to do with the dust bowl and other transients who are here and competing for all jobs," the union announced shortly after its birth. A month later, it distributed among its members a resolution that "wherever migratory workers gather our members will make every effort to fraternize with them; take them into our unions." With the launching of its mass organizational drive among the dust-bowl people in the San Joaquin Valley in April 1938, the Kern County chairman of UCAPAWA announced that, unorganized, the Okies were "a menace to all labor."[53]

The April drive failed. The following June, UCAPAWA exhorted its members to practice the "slogan *AN INJURY TO ONE IS AN INJURY TO ALL*. Immediate steps must be taken to win the confidence of these [Okies] workers and to make special efforts to organize them, so that they will not serve the purpose of the Associated Farmers." By February 1939, UCAPAWA had taken to the radio, pleading with its listeners: "Please—and I emphasize the word 'Please'— write or wire your congressmen and Senators" to urge the extension of the FSA camps. In the meantime, the announcer went on, the "dust bowl refugees" will be organized, "as rapidly as we can. . . . But that isn't easy. . . . It takes brave men and hard workers to tackle that job. I assure you labor has such brave men and will accomplish the task as soon as humanly possible."[54]

Unfortunately for UCAPAWA, the task required more than bravery. In order to organize the migrants effectively, UCAPAWA would find it necessary to induce three men to join up for each one job available in the fields, since that was the magnitude of the Okie oversupply. Further, it would have to organize them in hostile areas. Finally, and most important, it would have to overcome the Okies' resistance to unions. UCAPAWA's organizational drives did not fail for lack of effort, nor for lack of beachheads from which to launch unionization campaigns. They failed, primarily, because the attempt to convince the Okies that the solution to their wretched conditions lay in unions was quixotic.

During the early stages of the dust-bowl migration, the Okies were in no emotional condition to be unionized. Later, after UCAPAWA's formation, traditional ideologies, reinforced by local California attitudes hostile to unions, asserted themselves among the Okie population. An examination in depth of the various conditions and attitudes that prevailed among them from 1935 to 1941 is necessary in order to understand why the concept of collective action failed to take root.

Had the CAWIU survived, or had UCAPAWA been born from 1935 through 1937, it is doubtful that serious organizational efforts could have met with success among the newcomers. This was not simply because the Okies were too numerous, but rather, because in the early stages of the migration, they were too demoralized, too defenseless, too disoriented to overcome the built-in hindrances to agricultural labor's organization even had they desired to form unions. Any attempt at unity in collective action was doomed by the oft-noted phenomenon that people have neither the energy nor the desire for social action when caught in the depth of economic dislocation. Only when slight improvements broaden future horizons do demands arise for reform. The Okies conformed to this pattern. It took far too much effort to survive, even to consider the possibility of improvement.

Observers of the Okies were nearly unanimous, from 1935 through 1937, in noting among the migrants a sense of despair, perhaps of anomie, induced by the repeated shocks they had sustained. "They sense demoralization," Paul Taylor wrote in 1935. Aimless wandering had confused and disappointed these migrants, he continued. One had told him: "I'm not smart enough to know what ought to be done; it sure doesn't suit me."[55]

Even if farm wages were higher in California, the repeated jolts of migration followed by job-seeking wore the Okies down. "In all," one FSA camp manager in the San Joaquin Valley wrote, "it has been a very discouraging week for the campers. Men, accustomed to hard work willing to work have been thrown out of employment. . . . The very thought of relief bows down the head of the biggest and the strongest. Evenings, as they gather round for counsel with the camp management, they discuss this problem. On their way to bed they are determined to go to town and make relief application. [But] the morning finds them undecided and they burn the now precious gasoline supply and roam the country in search of work at any price." Six months later, his colleague in the Sacramento Valley noted: "There is absolutely no organized labor movement among the farm laborers in this district . . . our campers . . . seem to shy away from the idea. . . . Those who have seen first hand the workings of a strike, etc., are too close to the years of starvation and privation to be actively interested. Particularly is this true of refugees from the draught [sic] areas." And, to the south, in the rich Imperial, migrants underwent "a general descent into apathy." This demoralization made of the Okies an extremely pliable labor force and enhanced the satisfaction of the state's growers with them. When migrants seeking work showed up at a San Joaquin Valley grower's door, a *Business Week* reporter noted, "they are usually welcome. . . . Experience has shown that most of the newcomers won't have anything to do with farm labor organizers *for a time, at least,* and this condition may tend to relieve the pressure."[56]

During their first years in California, then, and regardless of what their ideological position on unions might be, circumstances had made of the Okies exceedingly poor material out of which to build labor unions. In California's fields, where the bulk of migrants sought work, the psychological condition of the Okies, their oversupply, the vehement opposition of the Associated Farmers, and the lingering memory that Communists had been involved but a few years ago—all these had combined with the traditional attitudes of the trades unions to prevent or retard renewed attempts at organization until 1937.

When UCAPAWA's organizational campaign began in early 1938, however, conditions were more propitious for a concerted effort among the Okies. The migration from the dust bowl had slackened appreciably since the peak years of 1935 through 1937, and by harvest time in the fall of 1938, well over 200,000 of the Okies had been in California for two years or more. They had settled into the routine of life in California, and despite their still desperate condition, they no longer suffered the uncertainty of the initial days of transplantation. Many were now legal residents entitled to relief; others were virtually permanent settlers at the expanding federal camps. UCAPAWA's failure to enlist more than a trivial amount of these migrants cannot be explained solely by recourse to the initial disorientation of migration.

As the Okies settled into their new lives in California, what observers had called their tradition of rugged individualism reasserted itself after the disorientation had passed. The greatest irony of the migration lay in the assumption by Steinbeck and others that, because the Okies were white Americans they would respond to California agriculture in a manner different from the Mexicans. They were totally correct, but their interpretation of that fact stood its implications upside down. Precisely because the Okies were rural Americans with that streak of individualism, they were less malleable material for union organizers than were the Mexicans. Rugged individualism and collective action do not mix well. This social equation escaped those who sought to enlist the Okies as unionists.

There is no need here to recall in any detail Richard Hofstadter's recognition, against a backdrop of years of one-eyed and uncritical applications of Parringtonian and Beardian maxims, that the American farmer accepted for years a self-image that made permanent organization for economic action impossible. Hofstadter argues with great force that the twentieth century witnessed the development of a "hard side" of agrarian discontent: farmers recognized their role as businessmen and joined for cooperative action. In a sense, the Associated Farmers represented this hard side of American agriculture gone sour. These were farmers organized powerfully for defense, and, indeed, offense.

Even California growers not organized into the Associated Farmers were nonetheless members of powerful marketing cooperatives, Sun-Kist, the Fruit Growers Exchange, and others.

The Okies were, conversely, losers in the agrarian shift from "pathos to parity." Their fathers, and the Okies themselves fortunate enough once to have owned a spread of their own, were "the characteristic products of American rural society," the "harassed little country businessman who worked very hard, moved all too often, gambled with his land, and made his way alone"—and, one might add—"and lost." [57] They had not made the Associated Farmers' shift from pathos to parity.

These Okies could not have been transformed overnight into men with firm urban orientations. Unions were not within their ken. In despair over their children's next meal, they might indulge a momentary flirtation with collective action, but they would not remain constant for a period longer than the crisis.

Reminiscing about his days with the Farm Security Administration, Paul Taylor recalled a conversation he had with an Okie near the Casa Grande cooperative farm in Arizona. This man had been farming upon a small spread bordering the project and he expressed great admiration for its well-tended fields and mechanized crops. "But," he told Taylor as the two observed the collectively owned chicken coop nearby, "I can't figure how each one of them tells *his* chickens from the others." [58] Casa Grande itself bore out the inability to understand the collective principle inherent in this man's comment about the chickens. An experiment in cooperative agriculture undertaken by FSA, the fertile, large acreage ranch brought considerable profit to its carefully chosen members, most of them erstwhile southern Great Plains farmers. The profits were, however, insufficient to allay the sense of failure they experienced at being part of a cooperative project. Preferring instead to seek status and power on his own farm, each of the cooperators took his profits, and the experiment was disbanded in 1943. [59]

Casa Grande was located in Arizona. Had the farm been on the other side of the California border, the results would have been no different. California's Okies viewed themselves as farmers—albeit down on their luck, broke and busted and dusted—and not as laborers. One federal official told an interviewer: "These are men who got a shotgun and guarded a stalk of cotton that was hanging over the fence so that the farmer on the other side of the fence wouldn't pick it. They're the greatest individuals on earth. They'd die," he added, forgetting the hivelike character of California agriculture, "in a factory."[60]

This is not to say that once they had adjusted to the conditions of life in rural California all the migrants accepted passively the repeated indignities and economic deprivations to which they were subjected. They did react at times, and violently. Farmers and tenants of the Great Plains, from the Populists to the Farm Holiday Association, had reacted violently since the 1890s, and Oklahoma had played an especially significant role in agrarian protest.[61] No less than three farmers' unions had arisen among Oklahoma's tenants *after* Bryan's 1896 defeat, and the violent Greencorn rebellion of 1917 had taken place in eastern Oklahoma, the portion of the state from which most of California's Okies had migrated.

These uprisings had been typical agrarian movements. Quick to action, farmers on the lowest rungs of the Southwest's economic ladder had engaged in momentary, convulsive spasms of frustration. None of these movements, however, had persisted. In many respects, much of California's agricultural labor conflict from 1937 to 1939 shared the characteristics of Oklahoma's earlier agrarian radicalism. It has been noted above, for example, that an outstanding peculiarity of strikes by southwestern whites was their spontaneity and the absence of organization by formal labor unions.

Various studies of the Okies found that only small minorities of them had ever had contact with formal labor unions. Only 4 of 126 Okies on WPA in Santa Clara had any previous affiliation, and only 1 was an active member.[62] In Modesto's Little Oklahoma, by 1938 a well-settled, stable Okie town, 30 percent of the migrants in the state for some time had belonged, either in the past, or at the time of the interview, to a union. The Okies, in short, had had little prior experience with unions. One sociologist noted with some exasperation that few "even partially understood the purpose of unionization," a conclusion supported by the wife of an FSA camp manager who observed that incoming Okies "had little sense of union organization."[63]

Nor did the organizational propaganda of either the Workers Alliance or UCAPAWA, tailored as it was by urban, union-oriented Californians for urban labor, conform with the psychology of the migrants. Its tone was strident, class-conscious, and ideologically alien. It was not designed to meet the migrants' prior rural, midwestern background. The following, reproduced at length in order to demonstrate the tone of such propaganda, was more strident than many such articles, but not atypical:

> The establishment of a facist dictatorship in U. S. A. would undoubtedly assure a retrogression from which civilization might not recover for ages and from which it would certainly not recover for many years. I know of only one means of insuring our safety—the workers of America must find self-expression in economic, in social, and in political matters. Labor to us extends from the unskilled industrial and agricultural workers throughout the so-called white-collar groups, including technicians, teachers, professional groups, newspaper employees, and others. If the fate of Germany is to be averted from this Nation, we must and we shal secure a strong, well organized disciplined and articulate movement.
>
> Fascism comes to power as a party of attack on the revolutionary movement of the proletriat on the masses of the people who are in a state of unrest; yet it stages it accession to power as a "revolutionary movement against the people on behalf of the "whole Nation" and for the "salvation of the Nation. Facism is a most ferocious attack by capital on the toiling masses. Folks wake up. Don't stand and let these parisites destroy our rights to live as human being and not like dogs. Think! don't be fools, help us and help yourself."[64]

At other times the Okies were exhorted to support the International Labor Defense as an arm in "the struggle against imperialism." Unfamiliar slogans were hurled at them: "Unity of all crafts and all works!", "Solidarity of all workers and crafts," and "strength rests in unity." An attempt to persuade the Okie wives to support the union was headed "An Appeal to Women of Our Class." In other camps, migrants were cajoled against becoming "Mr. Blocks" (from an old Wobbly song) and told to ask themselves "which class for me?"[65] In only one camp did organizers depart from conventional union sloganeering. At Arvin, the resident organizer, fully aware of the Okies' ignorance of unions, promised to "try to explain what organized labor is and how it works."[66] This realistic approach was rare in UCAPAWA ranks and, in any case, there is no evidence that it had any more effect than the more typical appeals.

A thorough reading of the camp newspapers strengthens the impression that the majority of the Okies passively ignored these appeals.

Some resented the insistent and aggressive union columns and organizers. The Arvin camp's council, for example, voted in favor of a motion "that all Unions keep literature off the bulletin board, and not to have any Public Union Meetings in the Camp, or on the Camp Property."[67] Other camps, like the units at Marysville and Indio, frequently reverberated with disputes among the campers themselves over the propriety or "Americanism" of allowing the CIO's "outside agitators" into the camp.[68]

Americanism was inextricable from the issue of unionism in the Okies' view. The Okies were individualistic; they were also, in the manner of Midwest farmers, patriotic; and patriotic, in the familiar American syllogism, meant anticommunistic. Migrants rejected unions if they perceived them as radical, and the equation between the CIO and the Communists was common among them. Many migrants objected to the Reds with a vehemence only slightly outmatched by the Associated Farmers. As the Marysville camp philosopher put it, unions "won't do us a bit of good unless its' one hundred percent, and unless all the radicals are killed off."[69]

The more radical labor organizers were well aware that they would have to conceal their ideological positions if they were to have any hope of success among the migrants. Carolyn Decker recalled that the "superpatriotic Okies" who found unions alien could be unionized only by men who "were 210 per cent Americans and spoke the language of the Okies." Miss Decker was "acutely aware of their limitations . . . if the usual 'wild-eyed Communists' had come into contact with them, the Okies would have thrown them out." Richard Neuberger found in the Okies as much suspicion of Harry Bridges and NLRB "as in any conservative Eastern businessman." Little Oklahoma's residents despised "agitators," "blindly" believing that strikes were fomented for the purpose of overthrowing the government.[70]

The Okies' rejection of radicals of any stripe accounts for still another peculiarity of the spontaneous strikes in which they did engage. Unprepared for leadership by California's radicals, they could easily be moved to action by their religion. Even during the early stages of the migration, what the Communists considered the "Holy Roller aspect of Okie psychology" had instinctively led them to seek out preachers as potential strike leaders.[71] Throughout the 1930s, a number of Okie strikes conformed with this pattern. Preaching a strange mixture of religion and strike propaganda, evangelists, Baptist and Pentecostal preachers played major roles in some labor conflicts involving the migrants.

The Okies' abiding indifference to collective action and hostility to radicalism might have crumbled or become diluted in an urban environment. In the many rural towns and cities of California, however, these attitudes were one of the migrants' few advantages. In effect, antiradicalism was one key to the acceptance of the migrant by the local resident, and this surely strengthened the Okies' prior convictions regarding alien ideology and unions. Such cities as Modesto, Fresno, Marysville, and Bakersfield, and the countless smaller valley towns, were intensely antiunion. Their total reliance upon a single industry—agriculture—had fostered in residents a tendency to take on the ideological characteristics of the growers, and a good deal of Associated Farmers publicity reinforced these attitudes among the townspeople. Despite communist and liberal protestations to the contrary, most townspeople supported the Associated Farmers' strikebreaking activities for the quite sensible reason that they feared agricultural strikes would harm them economically.[72] Local business and trades people were easily deputized by the Associated Farmers for use in "beef squads."[73] In this atmosphere, the Okies' resistance to unions stood them in good stead, easing their absorption into the community. Sociologists observed that by adopting local antiunion attitudes the Okies avoided becoming identified as a community of potentially dangerous laborers. Instead, they were able to achieve acceptance as individuals from the local population.[74]

Another facet of the migrants' background lent additional complexity to any attempt at unionizing them as part of a drive to sign all California farm labor up. Should the organizer allay fears of radicalism and implant a consciousness of the value of collective action, he still had to deal with the obvious and intense racism that the migrants brought with them from the Southwest. Few migrants recognized the irony in their situation. Many had fled from home for fear that to remain meant to be forced into "nigger work." Their flight, however, had thrust them directly into "nigger work" in California. There were, in fact, few Negroes in California agricultural labor during the 1930s, although there were Mexicans and Filipinos in profusion. And, to increase the irony, the Okies were undercutting the wages of these racial groups. One migrant, for example, told a reporter in the aftermath of the 1939 cotton debacle that the Filipinos received the good work in grapes because, unlike the whites, they were organized.[75]

Some of California's agricultural strife during the latter 1930s was a direct result of the racial tensions loosed by the coming of the Okies.[76] In some places, growers set wage rates on a racial basis, reflecting the greater speed and efficiency of Mexicans and Orientals. During the 1937 harvest at Yuba City, for example, Mexicans, hired through labor padrones, received 35 cents per hour; Americans, on the other hand, were paid only 30 cents, a "result of the dust bowl labor surplus." At the massive DiGiorgio farms, "workers were broken down into castes." The few skilled Orientals received good wages and "nice houses." Next in line were the Mexicans. The "bottom of the heap workers" were "the poor whites living in tents."[77]

Even where wage rates were equal, the other racial groups resented the new migrants for their effect upon wages, and the Okies resented the racial groups for traditional psychological reasons. A few strikes occurred as a direct result of the Okies' displacement of the Mexicans and Filipinos, the latter groups demanding a cessation of unfair competition from the whites.[78] Where open conflict did not occur, tension between the groups was fed by rumor and mutual fear. Organized Filipinos and Mexicans frequently refused to join multiracial unions unless organizers gave evidence that the Okies would also join. Conversely, an early organizational attempt at the Arvin camp was delayed because the organized Mexicans, already unionized, were absent picking crops and "without their assurance and backing" nothing further could be done.[79]

Growers consciously utilized these racial tensions as a union-delaying device.[80] Such tactics as wage-determination by race and the use of one nationality to break the strike of another kept racial tension alive. Nonetheless, the Okies themselves contributed to the interracial tension through their own racism. "You guys are OK," Okies frequently told Carolyn Decker "if only you weren't such Nigger-lovers." Many of the Okies had a "vitriolic dislike of Filipinos," while others complained that Californians were unconscious "nigger-lovers": "I have not noticed," one Okie wrote, "California critics condemning the Filipinos, Japanese, or any other foreigners. But when United States born citizens want to come here, they say we cut wages and lower their standard of living. I do not believe in cutting wages either, but I will do so before I will steal or go on relief." The problems inherent in the attempt to unify the disparate groups were best expressed when one of Wasco's Okies refused to join a multiracial union because "You can't equalize me wi' no nigger."[81]

In the federal camps, along the ditch banks, at the Little Oklahomas, up and down California's immense growing region, the Okies refused to conform to a self-induced deception sincerely believed by those who saw in them a class-conscious rural proletariat ripe for collective action. Communist newspapers, refusing to give up orthodoxy in light of the facts, continued to present a classical proletarian vision of the migrant: "We'll have to fight," the union organizer announced, in a news release reminiscent of *Waiting for Lefty*, and "scores of stern American faces nodded assent."[82] As the Associated Farmers suffered "setback" after "setback", the Okies and Arkies and Texans gathered without the slightest sign of discrimination, organized strikes and "by gosh . . . they won."[83] Never able to command or control a sufficient number of the migrants, however, more practical union organizers left the fields in desperation as they gradually realized that the Okies were not their allies but their potential enemies. Publicly announcing that Okies were pouring into unions, organizers admitted privately that the Okies' "general conservatism plus their lack of training in coopera-tion . . . make them poor material for organization."[84] Meanwhile, reports from FSA camp managers told of the migrants' low interest in organizational drives.[85]

The Okies were not, for the moment at least, organizable. They could at times be persuaded to leave work, however, and this accounted for the success of UCAPAWA in stopping cotton picking for two weeks in the autumn of 1939. But the ultimate collapse of the San Joaquin Valley strike and of UCAPAWA's other efforts indicated an even more disturbing aspect of the Okie migration. During many strikes, the Okies furnished the growers with a steady stream of workers.

Okies labored in the fields during the course of every agricultural labor conflict researched in this study. During the bloody Salinas

lettuce strike of September and October 1936, for example, the city's
Little Oklahoma fell prey to a rash of violent episodes as night riders
from strikers' camps hurled sticks and stones, as well as names, at
nonunion workers in the shacktown.[86] At the Stockton cannery strike
the next year, Okies were again prominent as strikebreakers, and the
local union's secretary-treasurer was disturbed about the prospect that
Filipino strikers would "use other methods of dealing" with the imported white men.[87]

In the field even more than in the shed and cannery, destitute Okies
helped harvest crops under strike conditions. At both the Shafter and
Arvin camps, Okies worked during the stillborn 1938 cotton strike. An
Arvin farmer complained to the Washington office of FSA that her
cotton pickers were finding threats of violence pinned to their doors
each morning at the FSA camp.[88] When fruit pickers at Marysville
struck in May, and later July 1939, resident FSA campers and imported
strikebreakers with cars bearing Oklahoma licenses aided the Earl and
Dantoni fruit ranches in harvesting the crops. They were, they told the
disillusioned camp manager, satisfied with wages and working conditions.[89]

During the massive 1939 strike, Okies played a larger role as
strikebreakers than as pickets. This strike was UCAPAWA's last chance,
and the frustration of some strikers at their neighbors' refusal to follow
them out of the fields bred tension at the Shafter and Arvin camps. The
units' newspapers harangued the working Okies with poems and
threats:

> You Okies and Arkies get off the row
> You know you can't beat the CIO
> Get out of your white trailers if you want a raise
> We're not fooling around many more days.[90]

and:

> Scabers, Scabers, Scabing on the Union. We
>   Hope you Scabbers starve,
> You'd better come down and join the Union.[91]

These threats frightened some of the "scabers." Rufus Hughes, a
Missouri Okie, was "afraid someone would beat me up, so I laid off. . . .

Now that some of the other guys are going back to work and the farmers say we'll be protected, I'm going back to work, too." Sixty percent of the campers worked through the strike. Finally, crowning all the contradictions in its proletarian vision of the Okies, UCAPAWA threw picket lines around the FSA camps to prevent the Okies going to the fields. Most ignored the picket; the fainthearted "went out the back way, to work." Meanwhile, fearful rumors spread that "a new stampede" was developing in Texas and Oklahoma. Reports of the strike had produced "caravans of cars moving westward" headed for Madera County. Their occupants hoped to "take the place of cotton pickers then on strike."[92]

That the Okie was likely to be a strikebreaker was a fact not lost upon the local growers in regions where the migrants congregated.[93] By 1940 and 1941, after UCAPAWA had all but surrendered its hope of unionizing field workers, growers were developing the habit of looking for Okies and Arkies when a strike seemed imminent. In one case, labor disturbances had "scared" the local migrants and "they were streaming south on U.S. 99." The grower who had been searching for them did what he considered the next best thing—going to the Sacramento and Stockton red light district and rounding up forty bums.[94] And, of course, Okie strikebreaking further enhanced their assimilation in the antiunion towns. As the mayor of Winters told campers, the FSA unit was now most welcome in the Sacramento Valley, especially since "Okies don't strike."[95]

The coming of the Okies to replace the Mexicans had, at first, brought fear from those who believed that the safety of the near-feudal social structure of California agriculture lay in the exploitation of foreign laborers. In typically American fashion, growers feared, and liberals exulted, that because the Okies were white American Anglo-Saxon Protestants, their very presence would rebuild rural California into a democratic society.

Nothing could have been further from the truth. The impact of the Okies' coming was to impede unionization and lower the already intolerable standards of living of agricultural labor. These dispossessed, worn-out victims of the agricultural revolution were not soldiers in the army of social equality. Because of their background and their misery, they were pliable, exploitable, too desperate even to attempt what the

Mexicans had accomplished in 1933 and 1934. And, rural Americans that they were, their ideologies conformed, not conflicted, with the ideologies of their exploiters.

Only by late 1940 did some of California's liberals become aware that the theories of the depression decade did not apply to the Okies, even though they may have applied to urban labor. The Olson administration seemed to be on the verge of recognizing that the Okies' background, conditions, and lack of roots in the community, required not the "sturdy self-help tradition" of organized labor, but governmental interference to protect the migrants.[96]

By then, however, it was too late. Europe was at war, and the United States was girding for what nearly all Americans knew to be inevitable entry into the conflict. The defense boom and Pearl Harbor forestalled reconsideration of the techniques for protecting the labor force in the factories in the field. The Okies moved to the cities, and California's farmers, saved once again by events cataclysmic and tragic for everybody else, found a new, malleable, and alien labor supply in the Mexican *bracero*.

Notes in Text

1. *Rural Worker*, April 1937; "Lubin Society-History," n.d., Simon J. Lubin Papers, Bancroft Library, University of California, Berkeley, Carton 4.

2. "Lubin Society-History."

3. *San Francisco News*, October 28, 1838; John Steinbeck Committee, *What Is the John Steinbeck Committee to Aid Agricultural Organization?* (n.p., 1938), passim.

4. Committee to Aid Agricultural Organization, *Program on Organization, Housing, Health, and Relief for Agricultural Workers* (n.d., n.p.), p. 6.

5. Stuart M. Jamieson, "The Origins and Present Structure of Labor Unions in Agricultural and Allied Industries of California," La Follette Committee, *Hearings*, Part 62, p. 22,540; see also the feature article, Anna Louis Strong, "The Story of Kern County's Workers Alliance," *People's World*, June 16, 1939.

6. Jamieson, "Origins and Present Structure," p. 22,540.

7. *Fresno Bee*, April 25, 1938.

8. *Oakland Tribune*, July 9, 1937; *Pacific Rural Press*, July 17, 1937.

9. See Clarke A. Chambers, *California Farm Organizations* (Berkeley, 1952), pp. 82-97, for an extensive discussion of the interrelation between labor and relief policy.

10. Paul S. Taylor and Clark Kerr, "Documentary History of the Strike of the Cotton Pickers in California, 1933," La Follette Committee, *Hearings*, Part 54, p. 19, 993.

11. Chambers, *California Farm Organizations*, p. 85; *People's World*, January 22, 1938; Robert E. Burke, *Olson's New Deal for California* (Berkeley, 1953), p. 87.

12. Culbert Olson, "Governor Culbert L. Olson's Statement Before Senate Committee on Education and Labor," San Francisco, December 6, 1939, pp. 3-4.

13. *Bakersfield Californian*, August 15, 1939.

14. "What Should America Do for the Joads?" *Town Meeting* 5 (March 11, 1940): 15.

15. "Minutes of the Associated Farmers Executive Committee," La Follette Committee, *Hearings*, Part 67, p. 24,723.

16. *San Francisco Chronicle*, March 18, 1937.

17. "Chet" to Fred Goodcell, February 9, 1937, La Follette Committee, *Hearings*, Part 70, p. 26,105.

18. Cora S. Keagle, "A Model Migratory Camp," *California Cultivator* (February 12, 1938): 120.

19. John Beecher,"The Migratory Labor Program in California," report, n.d., p. 11, Farm Security Administration Papers, Bancroft Library, University of California, Berkeley, Carton 9; Emily Huntington, *Doors to Jobs* (Berkeley, 1942), pp. 204-205; *People's World*, March 14, 1938.

20. Testimony of Carey McWilliams, La Follette Committee, *Hearings*, Part 59, p. 21,889.

21. The argument that California's rural towns were, in reality, company towns controlled by the farming industry and ideologically conditioned by that control is presented in the following: Walter R. Goldschmidt, *As You Sow* (Glencoe, 1947); Lillian Creisler, "Little Oklahoma, or, the Airport Community" (Master's thesis, University of California, Berkeley, 1939).

22. "Statement Prepared for Walter Packard to Be Forwarded to Washington, August 3, 1935," Harry E. Drobisch Papers, Bancroft Library, University of California, Berkeley; Walter Packard to W. W. Alexander, n.d., Paul S. Taylor Collection, Bancroft Library, University of California, Berkeley, Carton 3.

23. Eric Thomsen to Jonathan Garst, August 3, 1936, U.S. Department of Agriculture, Agricultural Stabilization and Conservation Commission Papers, Federal Records Center, San Francisco, 36,879.

24. "Jonathan Garst Address at Stockton Conference," manuscript, n.d., Farm Security Administration Collection, Carton 9.

25. Frederick Soule to Tom Collins, April 20, 1937, USDA ASCC Collection, 36,881.

26. W. W. Alexander to All Division Directors, April 18, 1938, La Follette Committee, *Hearings*, Part 59, p. 21,936.

27. Jerry Voorhis to Jonathan Garst, November 2, 1938, USDA ASCC Collection, 36,880.

28. *UCAPAWA News*, September 1939.

29. Evald Swanson to H. M. Coverly, May 5, 1941, USDA ASCC Collection, 36,884; *Voice of the Agricultural Worker*, April 23, 1940; *Covered Wagon News*, February-March, 1939; *Bakersfield Californian*, March 24, 28, 1939; *Tow Sack Tatler*, September-October, 1939; *The Hub*, April 11, 1941. For Visalia, *The Hub*, passim; for Indio, *Happy Valley Weekly*, 1939 passim; for Gridley, *Tent City News*, 1939 passim.

30. "Hewes and FSA Policy," memorandum, n.d., Lubin Papers, Carton 6.

276   Dust Bowl Migration

31. *Fresno Bee*, June 11, 1941; *People's World*, June 23, 1941.

32. Frank Anthony Speth, "A History of Agricultural Labor in Sonoma County, California" (Master's thesis, University of California, Berkeley, 1938), p. 79. The histories of the construction of each of the California camps comprise a major portion of the USDA ASCC Collection. See also "Review of Steps Taken in Development of the Program for Farm Laborers," Drobisch Papers; La Follette Committee, *Reports*, 78th Cong., 2d sess., No. 398, pp. 1,223-1,225.

33. *Marysville Appeal-Democrat*, June 1935 passim; *Yuba City Herald*, July 9, 1936; *Western Worker*, May 1936.

34. John Phillips to Jonathan Garst, February 19, 1937, Lubin Papers, Carton 13; "Resolution, Imperial County Farm Labor Council, May 12, 1936," USDA ASCC Collection, 36,881; see also La Follette Committee, *Hearings*, Part 68, pp. 11,583-11,596.

35. Statement of Jonathan Garst, *Labor Herald*, September 1, 1938.

36. "Garst Address at Stockton Conference."

37. Chet to Fred Goodcell, February 9, 1937; *Pacific Rural Press*, June 13, 1936, May 29, 1937, September 17, 1938.

38. *San Francisco Chronicle*, March 13, 1937; *Bakersfield Californian*, August 5, 1940.

39. Ray Mork to John Henderson, May 6, 1939, USDA ASCC Collection, 36,884; Winters Camp Reports, June, 1939, USDA ASCC Collection, 36,889; *Marysville Appeal-Democrat*, June 14, 22, 1938; *Sacramento Bee*, June 22, 1938.

40. Arthur Siemers to Ed Rowell, July 9, 1938, USDA ASCC Collection, 36,886.

41. Thomas W. McManus, *Report to the California Citizens Association* (Bakersfield, October 1, 1938), p. 2.

42. Norman Lowenstein, "Strikes and Strike Tactics in California Agriculture" (Master's thesis, University of California, Berkeley, 1940), pp. 36-38; Carey McWilliams, "California Pastoral," *Antioch Review* 2 (March 1942): 104-106.

43. McWilliams, "California Pastoral," 104-106; *UCAPAWA News*, August 1939.

44. A good resume of the 1938 strike appears in La Follette Committee, *Reports*, 78th Cong., 2d sess., No. 398, pp. 1,492-1,527.

45. Chambers, *California Farm Organizations*, p. 89.

46. Testimony of T. R. Rasmussen, La Follette Committee, *Hearings*, Part 62, p. 22,066; *Tow Sack Tatler*, October 1939 passim; *Visalia Times-Delta*, October 23, 1940; La Follette Committee, *Hearings*, Part 47, p. 17,463.

47. *Madera News*, quoted in La Follette Committee, *Hearings*, Part 51, p. 18,926; *San Francisco Chronicle*, October 27, 1939.

48. La Follette Committee, *Hearings*, Part 47, p. 17,382.

49. Katherine Douglas, "West Coast Inquiry," *Survey Graphic* 29 (April 1940): 228; Harry Schwartz, *Seasonal Farm Labor in the United States* (New York, 1945), p. 99; Jamieson, "Origins and Present Structure," p. 22,540.

50. La Follette Committee, *Reports*, 78th Cong., 2d sess., No. 398, pp. 1,526-1,527.

51. La Follette Committee, *Hearings*, Part 62, p. 22,713; long quotation from Rasmussen testimony, p. 22,067.

52. Committee to Aid Agricultural Organization, *Program on Organization*, p. 6.

53. *Agricultural and Cannery Union News (UCAPAWA News)*, August 17, 1937; UCAPAWA, *Resolution on Migratory Labor*, September 4, 1937, Lubin Papers, Carton 12; *People's World*, April 26, 1938; *Sacramento Bee*, April 26, 1938.

54. *Labor Herald*, June 2, 1938; "Labor on the Air," CIO broadcast, February 4, 1938, Lubin Papers, Carton 14.

55. Paul Taylor, "Again the Covered Wagon," *Survey Graphic* 24 (July 1935): 351.

56. Arvin Camp Reports, February 22, 1936, Marysville Camp Reports, August 29, 1936, Lubin Papers, Carton 13; Interview with Mrs. Eleanor Engstrand, Berkeley, California, September 7, 1965; "Flee Dust Bowl for California," *Business Week* (July 3, 1937): 36 [italics mine.]

57. Richard Hofstadter, *The Age of Reform* (New York, 1955), p. 46.

58. Conversations with author, September 1965.

59. Edward C. Banfield, *Government Project* (Glencoe, 1951), pp. 107, 231-260, and conclusion.

60. *New York Times*, March 6, 1940.

61. Work Projects Administration, Federal Writers' Project, *Labor History of Oklahoma* (Oklahoma City, 1939), pp. 33-42.

62. "Migrant Families Assigned to WPA in Santa Clara County," memorandum, n.d., Lubin Papers, Carton 10.

63. Creisler, "Little Oklahoma," p. 41; Engstrand interview.

64. *Covered Wagon News*, February 16, 1939.

65. *The Hub*, March 8, 1940; *Covered Wagon News*, March 9, 17, 1939; *Happy Valley Weekly*, January 14, February 4, 1939; *Tow Sack Tatler*, October 28, 1939.

66. *Tow Sack Tatler*, September 29, 1939.

67. Ibid., April 21, 1939. The following year the camp witnessed a similar incident. The camp council's chairman wrote to the FSA's Washington, D.C., office complaining that "the camp has been practically run" by the CIO in collaboration with the manager. J. H. Ward to Earl R. Bechner, n.d., USDA ASCC Collection, 36,880.

68. *VOTAW*, April-May 1940, passim. *Happy Valley Weekly*, December 17, 1938. In June 1938, the Marysville campers voted on the issue of allowing union speakers into the camp. Of the 403 ballots cast, 154 opposed the unions. Many who voted with the majority did so on the grounds of "free speech" rather than positive feeling towards unions. See *Sacramento Bee*, June 10, 1938.

69. *San Francisco Chronicle*, March 10, 1937.

70. Gladstein interview; Richard L. Neuberger, "Refugees from the Dust Bowl," *Current History* 50 (April 1939): 35; Creisler, "Little Oklahoma," p. 75.

71. Gladstein interview.

72. McWilliams, "California Pastoral," 111.

73. La Follette Committee, *Reports*, 78th Cong., 2d sess., No. 398, passim.

74. Goldschmidt, *As You Sow*, p. 172; Creisler, "Little Oklahoma," p. 74; Winters Camp Reports, January 1941, USDA ASCC Collection, 36,890.

75. *Christian Science Monitor*, December 11, 1939.

76. Testimony of McWilliams, 21,776; Mrs. Robert McWilliams to Hiram Johnson, February 11, 1935, Federal Writers Project Collection, Carton 10.

77. *Agricultural and Cannery Union News*, August 17, 1937; Helen Hosmer to

Arthur Lundin, n.d., Lubin Papers, Carton 14; *Kern County Union Labor Journal*, August 6, 1937

78. *Monrovia News Post*, March 11, 1940; *Oakland Tribune*, September 17, 1936.

79. *News Notes of the Simon J. Lubin Society*, December 22, 1937, copy in Carey McWilliams Collection, University of California, Los Angeles; testimony of McWilliams, 21,776; Arvin Camp Reports, July 4, 1936, Lubin Papers, Carton 13.

80. *Kern County Union Labor Journal*, August 6, 1937; ——— to A. L. Schafer, n.d., Federal Writers Project Collection, Folder 709; *Oakland Tribune*, September 17, 1939.

81. Gladstein interview; Marysville Camp Reports, September 7, 1935, Drobisch Papers; *Sacramento Bee*, March 23, 1938; Goldschmidt, *As You Sow*, p. 78.

82. *People's World*, June 16, 1939.

83. Ibid., November 17, 1938, June 16, 1939, January 23, 1940; *Daily Worker*, November 9, 1939.

84. *Farmer Labor News*, April 23, May 21, 1937; *New York Times*, March 4, March 6, 1940; *Kern County Union Labor Journal*, February 7, 1941; Douglas, "West Coast Inquiry," 227; J. J. Murray Jr., "Arabs of the Asphalt," *Catholic World* 153 (May 1941): 140-149; Ben Hibbs, "Footloose Army," *Country Gentlemen* 110 (February 1940): 42.

85. Yuba Camp Reports, July 1941, USDA ASCC Collection, 36,892; Arvin Camp Reports, July 4, August 15, 1936 USDA ASCC Collection, 36,879; *Tent City News*, August 5, 1939.

86. *San Francisco Examiner*, October 8, 1936.

87. Robert Meegan to Helen Horn, November 26, 1936, Lubin Papers, Carton 12; *Marysville Appeal-Democrat* July 15, 1937.

88. Charles Barry (manager, Shafter camp) to E. J. Rowell, September 14, 1938, USDA ASCC Collection, 36,885. See also letter from "BMR" to Mr. Hollenberg, October 28, 1938, in same place.

89. *Marysville Appeal-Democrat*, July 10, 18, 26, 1939; *Tent City News*, May 13, 1939.

90. *Covered Wagon News*, October 21, 1939.

91. *Tow Sack Tatler*, October 28, 1939.

92. *San Francisco News*, October 25, 1939; Shafter Camp Reports, October 1939, USDA ASCC Collection, 36,885, 36,886; *Bakersfield Californian*, October 28, 1939; *Carpinteria Herald*, January 5, 1940.

93. Gladstein interview.

94. *New York Times*, March 9, 1940.

95. Winters Camp Reports, January 1941, USDA ASCC Collection, 36,890.

96. Testimony of George Kidwell, La Follette Committee, *Hearings*, Part 50, pp. 18,221–18,227.

10

Epilogue

Pearl Harbor was only the symbolic end of California's Okie problem. World War II really came to California's inland valleys a year earlier, when the defense boom pulled the Okies into the urban areas where they took jobs in the shipyards and the munitions plants and began their slow process of assimilation into the state. In late 1940, the radical press noted a decline of interest in the Joads and, all its exhortations to the contrary, it could not renew the excitement which *The Grapes of Wrath* had generated a year before.[1] Ernie Pyle, astute as always, observed that the Okies had "left the headlines and people sort of forgot them." Now the focus of attention shifted to an anticipated "defense migration" before which the movement of the Joads would pale.[2] Congressman John Tolan understood well the effects of the impending war. In April 1941, he persuaded Congress to change his committee's name and mission:

> The situation had shifted as we watched it; the problem of destitute migration, born out of the unemployment of the thirties, was in process of dissolution, and was rapidly being transformed into job migration. If an adequate defense labor supply was to be recruited, millions of Americans had to move to fill the defense demand for workers in factories, fields, mines and offices. . . .

In April, Congress by unanimous resolution reconstituted us as the
select committee investigating national defense migration. . . .[3]

In the spring of 1941, fearful reports of an impending farm labor
shortage spread from the San Joaquin Valley. A serious undersupply
materialized in neighboring Oregon, and that state's growers scrambled
to persuade California's once-maligned Okies to move north.[4] By the
middle of the year, agricultural economists were uncertain just what lay
in store for California's growers. Some argued that California's harvest
labor supply remained adequate; others, including Carey McWilliams,
admitted that a severe labor shortage could develop in 1942.[5] Migrants
no longer stopped first in the agricultural valleys before moving on to
the cities: they went directly to the war industries centers.[6] In October
1941, the *San Francisco News,* one-time scourge of the farmers, reported that the once-plentiful supply of labor had disappeared overnight
and that farmers "had to scout the highways for workers to pick their
cotton and grapes." And, finally, two weeks after Pearl Harbor, the
Okies remaining in the valleys committed themselves to the war effort:
"We, the residents of this community [the FSA camp at Firebaugh],
have inherited the tasks passed on to us by the generations gone before.
We must take the place of the men and women who planted and hoed
and harvested the crops during the growth of this nation. We have
another war and again the soldiers must be fed and clothed. And—We
will do our part."[7]

By the spring of 1942, the Okie who had kept to the field was no
longer the pariah he had been two years before. As the labor scarcity
grew, he had become the unsung hero of inland California. In Tulare
County, the Okie was welcomed by the residents, and he became
accustomed to high earnings and a new sense of pride.[8] During 1943,
the *Fresno Bee* carried only one article about migrants and none in
1944 and 1945. From Watsonville and Palo Verde, however, came
reports that suggested that California agriculture had come once again
full circle: in November 1942 and again in March 1943 the FSA
imported Okies from Missouri and Arkansas to harvest California's
crops. Growers met the arrivals with fanfare and jubilation.[9]

In fact, the Okies were too welcome—and too expensive. California
agriculturalists began once again to cast about for substitutes for the
Okies who were now able to compete in the urban labor market.

Prisoners of war, criminals, children, wives and mothers—all were draft-
ed into an army of patriots whose national duty became the harvesting
of California's lush crops. None proved satisfactory. California growers
began to remember wistfully their flirtation with the Mexicans. In
August 1942, after a year of negotiations, Washington and Mexico
arranged an international agreement for the importation of *braceros.* [10]
The *braceros* crossed the border by the tens of thousands, and the FSA
camps, once the focus of a depression experiment in social planning,
became a housing agency for them. The camps changed their names,
too; they were no longer "farm worker's communities" but, rather,
"farm labor supply centers."

During the depression, the interstate migration of destitute white
Americans and the problem of farm labor had coalesced in the Okies.
When World War II ended, California's unique migrant problem was
gone, split into its component parts. By and large, the Okies were in the
cities. They had become one more of the many ex-migrant groups that
composed the nation's fastest-growing state. War, not congressional
legislation, had solved their problem. For them, in the thunder of guns
had been as well the jingle of cash. Absorbed into the working class in
the cities, they were assimilated by California as well. Like other old
Californians, they now complained of the influx of new migrants—
many of them black—who were ruining property values and destroying
the character of the state. [11]

In California's valleys, the problem of migrant labor remained. As it
had in the 1920s, an invisible army of *braceros,* augmented by illegal
wetbacks, moved across the state picking the crops. In the years of
retrenchment following the war, the FSA program was liquidated by an
economy-minded Congress, and in California "squatting returned, with
typhoid and dysentery." [12] In 1948 and 1949, Californians fought
again over the problems of migrant labor when the question arose of
disposing of the FSA camps. Still the debris of California society,
migrants pick the crops today and the casual traveler, journeying north
from Los Angeles to San Francisco on Highway *99*, looks down from
the ridge of the Tehachapi upon the magnificent factories in the fields
below.

Notes in Text

1. *People's World,* January 27, 1941; *CAAW News,* November, 1940.

2. *San Francisco News,* December 7, 1940; April 3, May 13, 1941.

3. John H. Tolan, "Our Migrant Defenders," *Survey Graphic* 30 (November 1941): 615.

4. *San Francisco News,* March 21, May 9, 1941.

5. "The War and California Agriculture," *Transactions of the Commonwealth Club of California* 36 (June 15, 1942): 207*ff.*

6. Carey McWilliams, "They Still Keep Coming," *New Masses* (March 31, 1942): 10; California Department of Employment, *Defense Labor Migration in California* (1941), pp. 3-4.

7. *San Francisco News,* October 28, 1941; *Camp Herald,* December 19, 1941.

8. U.S., Department of Agriculture, Bureau of Agricultural Economics, *Current and Anticipated Rural Migration Problems, Tulare County, California* (Berkeley, 1945), passim.

9. Joel Warkentin, "A Decade of Migratory Labor in the San Joaquin Valley, 1940-1950" (Master's thesis, University of California, Berkely, 1952), p. 18; *Watsonville Register,* March 3, 1943; *Palo Verde Valley Times,* November 19, 1942.

10. The history of the *bracero* program is told in Otey M. Scruggs, "The Evolution of the Mexican Farm Labor Agreement of 1942," *Agricultural History* 34 (July 1960): 140-149.

11. Catherine Archibald, *Wartime Shipyard* (Berkeley, 1947) pp. 40-57.

12. Paul S. Taylor to John ———, May 25, 1949, Paul S. Taylor Collection, Bancroft Library, University of California, Berkeley, Carton 3.

BIBLIOGRAPHICAL ESSAY

An extensive bibliography for this study is included in my doctoral dissertation of the same title, University of California, Berkeley, 1969 (available from University Microfilms, Ann Arbor, Michigan). No general discussion of literature concerning California's dust-bowl problem exists elsewhere, however, and it is the purpose of this bibliography to apprise readers of sources useful to an understanding of the topics covered in this volume.

Manuscript Collections

Several large manuscript collections provide opportunities for intensive research in nearly all areas significant to this volume. By far the largest is the Work Projects Administration, Federal Writers' Project, Oakland, Collection, Bancroft Library, University of California, Berkeley. In addition to clippings and transcriptions of journal and newspaper materials, the collection includes many unpublished manuscripts documenting California's migrant problem from several different perspectives. Of equal value, if smaller in size, is the Paul S. Taylor Collection, Bancroft Library, University of California, Berkeley. Professor Taylor played a significant role in aiding California's absorption of the migrants, and his papers include a wide variety of source materials relating to the subject. Finally, the Carey McWilliams Collection, Institute of Government and Public Affairs Reading Room, University of California, Los Angeles, supplied materials unavailable elsewhere. Mr. McWilliams' position as head of the State Division of Immigration and Housing placed him at a unique vantage point, which is reflected in the collection.

Manuscript sources dealing with California's farmers and their responses to the migrants are relatively sparse, with the exception of the George P. Clements Collections, one located at the Bancroft Library, University of California, Berkeley, the other at the Special Collections Library, University of California, Los Angeles. The Simon J. Lubin Papers, Bancroft Library, University of California, Berkeley, contain some of Mr. Lubin's private papers, as well as records of the Simon J. Lubin Society. These latter contain materials relating to California farm organizations, but the society's antagonism to the state's larger farmers makes it necessary that this collection be approached with some caution. Finally, a wide variety of material relevant to labor conflict in California agriculture may be found in the Paul S. Taylor Collection of Materials Relating to Agricultural Strikes in California, Bancroft Library, University of California, Berkeley.

Several collections focus upon the California state government and its involvement with the migrants. The Culbert Olson Papers, Bancroft Library, University of California, Berkeley, are disappointing but contain some significant letters, draft addresses, and interoffice memoranda. The Harry E. Drobisch Papers, Bancroft Library, University of California, Berkeley, contain large amounts of materials relating to the genesis of the state's migrant camp program as well as items of great value for the period following the camp program's transfer to the federal government. The Carey McWilliams Papers, mentioned above, fill in many gaps left open in the Olson and Drobisch collections. Finally, although Hiram Johnson was in Washington D.C., during the period covered, his papers at Bancroft Library, University of California, Berkeley, contain several important letters bearing upon Republican anxiety over the Olson-Okie political alliance.

There is no scarcity of manuscript materials regarding the federal government's role in migrant programs in California. A small but highly useful collection, located at the Bancroft Library, University of California, Berkeley, is the United States Department of Agriculture, Farm Security Administration, Region IX, Papers. Of far greater significance, however, are the United States Department of Agriculture, Agricultural Stabilization and Conservation Commission Papers, Record Group 145, Federal Records Center, San Francisco. Within this immense collection are housed records of the construction, administration of, and the reports of each of the migrant camps in California. In addition, the collection contains materials covering the relations between the camps and nearby communities, as well as incomplete sets of the mimeographed newspapers published by the migrants at each of the units. Sources involving the impact of the migrants upon federal agricultural programs may be found in the United States Department of Agriculture, Bureau of Agricultural Economics Papers, Record Group 83, also at the Federal Records Center, San Francisco.

In addition to the manuscript collections cited above, the Gianninni Foundation Library, University of California, Berkeley, contains many unpublished mimeographed or typescript items, separately cataloged and unavailable elsewhere, that bear upon all phases of California's migrant and agricultural problems.

Documents

Published documents, state and federal, are a rich source for studying California's migrant problem. California's State Relief Administration published several dozen monographs concerning the migrants and their future within the state. The most outstanding are M. H. Lewis, *Migratory Labor in California* (San Francisco, 1936) and *Transients in California* (San Francisco, 1936).

Federal documents include many important monographs. The Bureau of Agricultural Economics deserves mention for the following: Marshall Harris, *Magnitude and Distribution of Landless Farm People* (Washington, 1941); Tyr V. Johnson and Frederick Arpke, *Migration and Settlement on the Pacific Coast* (n.p., 1941); and *Migration to California, 1930-1940* (Washington, 1940). The Farm Security Administration's publications included several noteworthy items, whose titles make their value to this study clear: Alma Holszchuh, *A Study of 6,655 Migrant Households in California* (San Francisco, 1939); Carl C. Taylor et al; *Disadvantaged Classes in American Agriculture,* Social Research Report No. VIII (Washington, 1938); and *Community Activities and Education Among Migrant Farm Workers* (San Francisco, 1941). The WPA's monographs and research bulletins provide demographic analyses as well as economics-based studies of the movements and settlement of Americans during the depression years. Some exemplary items are: C. E. Lively and Conrad Taeuber, *Rural Migration in the United States,* Social Research Monograph No. XIX (Washington, 1939); John N. Webb, *The Migratory-Casual Worker,* Social Research Monograph No. VII (Washington, 1937); John N. Webb and Malcolm Brown, *Migrant Families* (Washington, 1938); and Malcolm Brown and Orin Cassmore, *Migratory Cotton Pickers in Arizona* (Washington, 1939).

The *Congressional Record* and *Appendix,* 1935-1941, are fruitful sources for material on California's pleas for federal aid, but far more useful are several major congressional committee hearings and reports. This study has relied very heavily upon the La Follette Committee's Hearings and Reports, officially titled: *United States Senate, Subcommittee of the Committee on Education and Labor, 74th Congress, Pursuant to Senate Resolution 266, A Resolution to Investigate Violations of the Right of Free Speech and Assembly and Interference with the Right of Labor to Organize and Bargain Collectively.* Parts 46 through 75 of the hearings deal with California, and, while the committee's antifarmer bias is evident throughout, the volumes nonetheless constitute a splendid collection of testimony and records. Nearly the entire official records of the Associated Farmers, subpoenaed by the committee, are reprinted here, as well as many detailed studies of the agricultural labor situation in the state.

The Tolan Committee's Hearings are nearly as valuable as the La Follette Committee's, although less biased in presentation and broader in scope. Where the La Follette Committee was concerned with the Okies as migratory laborers, the Tolan Committee devoted its hearings to the problem of interstate migration, before and during World War II. Throughout, the hearings provide extensive sociological and economic data on population movements in the United States and the dislocations attendant upon them. The committee's official title was: *U.S.*

Congress, House of Representatives, Select Committee to Investigate the Interstate Migration of Destitute Citizens, Pursuant to House Resolution 63 and House Resolution 491, 76th Congress. Under the 77th Congress, the committee was retitled *The Select Committee to Investigate National Defense Migration.*

Finally, much of value for a study of the Farm Security Administration's activities may be found in the Hearings of the Cooley Committee, despite the obvious hostility of its members to the FSA. They may be found under the title: *U.S. Congress, House of Representatives, Committee on Agriculture, Hearings on House Resolution 1388 to Provide for Continuance of the Farm Labor Supply Program up to and Including June 30, 1948, 80th Congress.*

Newspapers and Periodicals

Nearly forty of California's daily and weekly general-interest newspapers were utilized during the course of this study. Of these, several were researched intensively. The only California newspaper to take a consistently promigrant position during the entire period was the Scripps-Howard *San Francisco News,* which also provided the most comprehensive reporting of the California migrant situation. *The San Francisco Examiner,* the *Bakersfield Californian,* and the *Marysville Appeal-Democrat,* on the other hand, took negative positions on the Okie influx throughout the period, and represent, respectively, the San Francisco Bay Area, the San Joaquin Valley, and the Sacramento Valley. The *Brawley News* and *Orange News* are valuable for local attitudes in the Imperial Valley, while the *Los Angeles Times* represents the state's southern metropolis.

Special-interest newspapers also played a major role in the research for this study. Labor journals, especially the *East Bay Labor Journal* (Oakland), *The Farmer-Labor News* (Modesto), the *Kern County Union Labor Journal* (Bakersfield), and the *Sacramento Valley Union Labor Bulletin* (Sacramento), provide insight into the attitudes of established labor organizations toward nonunion migrant farm laborers. Organizations intent upon unionizing the migrants published several journals, including the *Committee to Aid Agricultural Workers News,* the *Rural Observer* (journal of the Simon J. Lubin Society), the *UCAPAWA News*

(Philadelphia), and the short-lived *Worker* (Berkeley, California Conference of Agricultural Workers).

The attitude of third parties and pressure groups toward the migrants, as well as material implicit to a study of the relationship
between the Okies and radical movements, may be found in: *EPIC
News* (Oakland), *Ham and Eggs for California* (Los Angeles), the
American Civil Liberties Union News, Open Forum (Northern California ACLU), and *People's World* (San Francisco, Communist Party).

The official newspaper of the Associated Farmers, *The Associated
Farmer—From Apathy to Action,* was published sporadically beginning
in late 1936, and presents the public face of that organization. More
useful, if less voluminous, was the irregularly published *American
Citizen,* produced by Colonel Henry Sanborn, who achieved considerable notoriety for his antilabor activities during the Salinas lettuce
strike.

No study of the Okies themselves would have been possible without
the migrant camp newspaper. Here only did the migrants speak for
themselves, despite the attempt of various camp managers to make the
papers "socially conscious." Nearly every camp published its own
mimeographed newspaper, usually on a weekly basis, although publication schedules were not always met. The papers are not readily available
and I have found no complete sets. However, the Agricultural Stabilization and Conservation Commission Papers, San Francisco; the Farm
Security Administration Collection, Bancroft Library, Berkeley; and,
finally, the University of California, Berkeley, general library, together
provide nearly complete runs of the more significant migrant camp
newspapers. These are: *Camp Herald* (Firebaugh); *Covered Wagon News*
(Shafter); *Happy Valley Weekly* (Indio); *The Hub* (Visalia); *New Hope
News* (Thornton); *Pea-Pickers Prattle* (Brawley); *Tent City News*
(Gridley); *Tow Sack Tatler* (Arvin); and Voice of the Agricultural
Worker (Marysville).

Many periodicals and journals studied California's migrant problem
in depth. *Rural Sociology, Land Policy Review,* and *Monthly Labor
Review* provide useful statistical and demographic articles covering
migration on the national, as well as the California, level. Other journals, notably *Survey Graphic, Survey, Survey Mid-Monthly, Social*

Forces, Transactions of the Commonwealth Club of California, Pacific Historical Review, and *Agricultural History,* focus more directly on California.

Less scholarly, more partisan, periodicals fall into several broad categories. *Nation, New Republic,* and *New Masses,* tended throughout the period to stress the conflicts between Californians—notably farmers—and the migrants. Their positive bias lies, of course, with the migrants. Also oriented towards the conflict between migrant and resident were several journals which tended, consistently, to view the coming of the Okies with alarm. Most representative of this group are *Country Gentlemen, Pacific Rural Press,* and *California.* Those interested in the activities of private charitable groups will find useful articles in *Missionary Review of the World.*

Books and Pamphlets

Agricultural conditions during the late depression years generated several studies of especial significance to an understanding of the movement of the Okies to California. James Agee and Walker Evans, *Let Us Now Praise Famous Men* (Boston, 1941), is a brilliantly evocative account of the travails of rural people in the South. While the volume does not deal directly with the Okies, its mood nonetheless provides deep insight into the problems of southern rural people, including California's migrants. Other books useful to an understanding of conditions in the four Okie states during the depression are: Carleton Beals, *American Earth* (Philadelphia, 1939); Carl F. Kraenzel, *The Great Plains in Transition* (Norman, Okla., 1955); Carey McWilliams, *Ill Fares the Land* (Barnes and Noble, 1967); and Dwight Sanderson, *Research Memorandum on Rural Life in the Depression* (New York, 1937).

A large number of works deal with the causes of rural migration during the depression. Many of these volumes reflect the emotionally charged atmosphere of the era, and view the migrations as tragic consequences of land misuse and poorly conceived legislation. Among the more useful of such works are: Nels Anderson, *Men on the Move* (Chicago, 1940); John Blanchard, *Caravans to the Northwest* (Boston, 1940), which treats Washington and Oregon rather than California;

Henry Hill Collins, Jr., *America's Own Refugees* (Princeton, 1941); John Steinbeck, *Their Blood is Strong* (San Francisco, 1938); and Paul Taylor, *An American Exodus* (New York, 1939).

In addition to the narrative and relatively subjective works cited above, several valuable demographic studies supply raw data as well as theoretical models for rural-urban, and rural-rural, interstate migration during the 1930's. Those with a national perspective include two immense compilations supervised by Donald J. Bogue, and published by the Scripps Foundation Studies in Population Redistribution: Bogue et al, *Subregional Migration in the United States, 1935-1940,* Vol. I: *Streams of Migration Between Regions* (Miami, Ohio, 1957), and Bogue et al, *Subregional Migration in the United States, 1935-1940,* Vol. II: *Differential Migration in the Corn and Cotton Belts* (Miami, Ohio, 1953). Also useful are: Carter Goodrich et al, *Migration and Planes of Living, 1920-1934* (Philadelphia, 1935); Philip E. Ryan, *Migration and Social Welfare* (New York, 1940); and Warren S. Thompson, *Research Memorandum on Internal Migration in the Depression* (New York, 1937). Other volumes that focus more closely on the Oklahoma-California migration include: E. J. R. Booth, *Agricultural Adjustment and Farm Labor Underemployment in Eastern Oklahoma, 1910-1950* (Stillwater, Okla., 1961); California State Chamber of Commerce, *Migrants, A National Problem* (San Francisco, 1940), whose title is misleading, for its subject is California; William T. Cross and Dorothy E. Cross, *Newcomers and Nomads in California* (Palo Alto, California, 1937); Otis Durant Duncan, *The Significance of the Migration of Oklahoma Farm Population* (Stillwater, Oklahoma, 1939); J. T. Sanders, *The Economic and Social Aspects of Mobility of Oklahoma Farmers* (Stillwater, Oklahoma, 1929); and Warren S. Thompson, *Growth and Changes in California's Population* (Los Angeles, 1955).

For my general understanding of intragroup conflict among farmers and between large farm operators and their tenants or laborers, I owe a special debt to Richard Hofstadter, *The Age of Reform* (New York, 1963). The move from "pathos or parity," as Hofstadter describes it, is also clearly evident, but from a slightly different perspective, in Grant McConnell, *The Decline of Agrarian Democracy* (Berkeley, 1953). There is a surprising dearth of published sources related specifically to California's farmers and their organizations during the period under study here. Those volumes that do exist, however, are uniformly valuable. Clarke Chambers, *California Farm Organizations* (Berkeley, 1952), focuses upon the Associated Farmers during the 1930s and will remain the standard for similar studies in the future. Carey McWilliams' studies of California agriculture, *Factories in the Field* (Boston, 1939), and *California: The Great Exception* (New York, 1949) are extremely useful, despite their clear hostility to California's agribusinessmen. Portions of Oliver Carlson, *A Mirror for Californians* (Indianapolis, 1941), treat the problem in a vein similar to that of McWilliams.

Ever since Henry George's *Progress and Poverty,* migratory farm labor in the United States has been subjected to intensive study. Carleton Parker, *The Casual Laborer* (New York, 1920), is the classic on the subject. Edith Lowry, *They Starve That We May Eat* (New York, 1938), reflects in its title the conditions of farm labor. Harry Schwartz, *Seasonal Farm Labor in the United States* (New York, 1945) is the most scholarly treatment of the subject. Carey McWilliams' books, mentioned above, treat migratory labor in California in as much detail as they describe the development of California's agricultural system. Statistical works covering the extent and composition of California's agricultural labor force include Lloyd Fisher, *The Harvest Labor Market in California* (Cambridge, 1953) and Davis McEntire, *The Labor Force in California* (Berkeley, 1952).

My model in analyzing the impact of the migrants upon California's rural communities draws upon the insight of Mary Margaret Wood, whose *The Stranger—A Study in Social Relationships* (New York, 1934) remains valuable, despite its date of publication. I have also been greatly aided by Walter Goldschmidt, *As You Sow* (Glencoe, Ill., 1947), an outstanding anthropological treatment of the interrelationships between farmers, farm workers, and rural communities in the San Joaquin Valley.

Robert E. Burke, *Olson's New Deal for California* (Berkeley, 1953) provides an exhaustive history of Olson's administration, although Burke has, I believe, underemphasized the role of the Okies in providing Olson's enemies with a powerful political weapon. Federal activities surrounding California's migrants tend to be ignored even in studies of the Farm Security Administration. Sidney Baldwin, *Poverty and Politics* (Chapel Hill, 1968) contains this weakness, but is invaluable in documenting the conflicts and cross-pressures under which FSA was forced to operate at the national level. Bernard Sternsher's massive *Rexford Tugwell and the New Deal* (New Brunswick, 1964) supplies several important clues for understanding the FSA program in California, while David E. Conrad, *The Forgotten Farmers* (Urbana, 1965) is disappointing in its treatment of farm labor on the Pacific Coast. An outstanding case study of the collapse of one FSA project in the west (Casa Grande Farms, Inc.) is Edward C. Banfield, *Government Project* (Glencoe, Ill., 1951).

Finally, the dust-bowl migration produced several significant works of art. John Steinbeck, *In Dubious Battle* (New York, 1936) and *The Grapes of Wrath* (New York, 1939), must be treated as literature, not journalism. They are, nonetheless, remarkably insightful and useful for all aspects of this study. Woody Guthrie's folk-poetry in "Talking Dustbowl," *Folkways Records, FA-2011* (New York, 1950) tells the tale from one "Okie's" point of view. Ruth Comfort Mitchell, *Of Human Kindness* (New York, 1940), fails dismally as art and as an answer to Steinbeck from the farmer's point of view.

Theses and Dissertations

Several significant unpublished Master's and Ph.D. dissertations touch various aspects of California's migrant problems. For California agriculture and migratory labor, the following are especially useful: Levi Varden Fuller, "The Supply of Agricultural Labor as a Factor in the Evolution of Farm Organization in California" (Ph.D. dissertation, University of California, Berkeley, 1940); Laurence I. Hewes, "Some Migratory Labor Problems in California's Industrialized Agriculture" (Ph.D. dissertation, George Washington University, 1945); Norman Lowenstein, "Strikes and Strike Tactics in California Agriculture" (Master's thesis, University of California, Berkeley, 1940). Studies dealing with the Okies as interstate migrants, and their impact upon the state, include: Lillian Creisler, "Little Oklahoma, or, the Airport Community" (Master's thesis, University of California, Berkeley, 1939); Walter Evans Hoadley, "A Study of One Hundred Seventy Self-Resettled Agricultural Families, Monterey County, California, 1939" (Master's thesis, University of California, Berkeley, 1938); Mary Helen Williamson, "Unemployment Relief Administration in Kern County, 1935-1940" (Master's thesis, University of California, Berkeley, 1941); and Ruth Molander, "A Study of 101 Migrant Families Receiving Assistance Under the Regulations of the California 'Aid to Needy Children' Law in Kern County, in June, 1940" (Master's thesis, University of California, Berkeley, 1943). Finally, a study which places into perspective the role of migrants in producing political change in California during the depression years is Royce Deems Delmatier "The Rebirth of the Democratic Party in California, 1928-1938" (Ph.D. dissertation, University of California, Berkeley, 1955).

Index